HEALTHCARE LAW AND ETHICS AND THE CHALLENGES OF PUBLIC POLICY MAKING

Drawing on Sir Ian Kennedy's extensive experience in healthcare law, ethics and public policy-making, this book explores vital issues in the law surrounding healthcare and regulation. The book contains a range of published and unpublished essays and speeches with the addition of notes and commentaries by the author that bring the pieces up to the present day.

Those who want to understand developments, from transplants to confidentiality, from COVID-19 to public inquiries to regulation will find a rich seam of rigorous, informed analysis. The author's unique range of experience allows him to share insights on a variety of issues; from the conduct of the disgraced breast surgeon, Ian Paterson, to research at Porton Down, to the economics of innovation in drug development at NICE. His abiding interest in the welfare of children informs his trenchant forensic examination of how children fare in the NHS.

Those involved in or with an interest in law, moral philosophy, and public policy will find much food for thought.

Healthcare Law and Ethics and the Challenges of Public Policy Making

Selected Essays

Ian Kennedy

•HART•
OXFORD • LONDON • NEW YORK • NEW DELHI • SYDNEY

HART PUBLISHING

Bloomsbury Publishing Plc

Kemp House, Chawley Park, Cumnor Hill, Oxford, OX2 9PH, UK

1385 Broadway, New York, NY 10018, USA

29 Earlsfort Terrace, Dublin 2, Ireland

HART PUBLISHING, the Hart/Stag logo, BLOOMSBURY and the Diana logo are trademarks of Bloomsbury Publishing Plc

First published in Great Britain 2021

A catalogue record for this book is available from the British Library.

Library of Congress Cataloging-in-Publication data

Names: Kennedy, Ian, 1941- author.

Title: Healthcare law and ethics and the challenges of public policy making : selected essays / Ian Kennedy.

Description: Oxford ; New York : Hart, 2021. | Includes bibliographical references and index.

Identifiers: LCCN 2021017100 (print) | LCCN 2021017101 (ebook) | ISBN 9781509950447 (hardback) | ISBN 9781509950485 (paperback) | ISBN 9781509950461 (pdf) | ISBN 9781509950454 (Epub)

Subjects: LCSH: Medical care—Law and legislation—Great Britain. | Medical policy—Great Britain/ | Medical ethics—Great Britain/

Classification: LCC KD3395 . K454 2021 (print) | LCC KD3395 (ebook) | DDC 344.4103/21—dc23

LC record available at https://lccn.loc.gov/2021017100

LC ebook record available at https://lccn.loc.gov/2021017101

ISBN: HB: 978-1-50995-044-7
ePDF: 978-1-50995-046-1
ePub: 978-1-50995-045-4

Typeset by Compuscript Ltd, Shannon

'How far that little candle throws its beams!
So shines a good deed in a naughty world'.
Portia, *The Merchant of Venice*, Act V, Scene I

For Jack, Tom and Emma who taught me about love

ACKNOWLEDGEMENTS

My sincerest thanks to Roberta Bassi at Hart Publishers, whose support and enthusiasm (and love of the ballet) made putting this book together possible and fun.

CONTENTS

Introduction

What's this book about? Well, it's an eclectic selection of my writing, some previously published, some in the public domain but only obscurely so (eg a Review for the National Institute for Health and Clinical Excellence – NICE), and some hitherto unpublished. The pieces show me wrestling with challenges in the world of health law, ethics and policy, which has been the world I've inhabited for most of my professional life. Others take you behind the scenes in a public inquiry. Others examine what regulation is all about and what it can offer. Given my six years sorting out the mess after the MPs' Expenses Scandal, there are pieces which touch on that experience. And, as someone who began life as an academic and slowly backed into the limelight, I offer my experience and thoughts on dealing with the media.[1]

As I say, an eclectic mix but that has been a feature of my professional life. Some academics spend their lives in teaching and scholarship. I wanted to do more. I wanted to take what I was involved in to a wider audience, hence my involvement in broadcasting on radio and television.[2] I also wanted to 'do' things as well as talk and write about them, hence my willingness to chair reviews and try to shape the development of public policy, whether it was about the licensing of medicines, the use of foetal tissue for research, the control of rabies, or the transplanting of pigs' hearts into humans.

It will be clear from the book that I have a longstanding interest in and concern for the health and welfare of children and young people. My mother was a school teacher and I'm sure I inherited from her the teaching bug and the conviction that education of young people was very, very important. The circumstances of my early life underlined this. My parents were not well off. My father was an electrician who worked shifts for 20-odd years to bring in a bit of extra money for my two older brothers and me. The effects and after-effects of the Second World War stamped themselves on my growing up, a time of just getting by. The welfare state and the fact that I passed the 11-plus exam which took me to an excellent grammar school meant that the world opened up for me. But life in the school holidays was still spent with friends who had not had my luck. I saw how they continued to live in the shadow of a collapsing local economy and narrowing opportunities. I promised myself, as I went off to school and then university, that I would not forget what I knew of that world; that I would try to make it better for children in the future.

[1] For my biography, see p 343.

[2] From talks on the old BBC Third Programme during the interval of a performance of a Symphony on such matters as mental health, to hosting *After Dark* on television's Channel 4, to my BBC television series of '*Doctors' Dilemmas*'.

Another theme that you will see rehearsed is regulation. I've been involved in regulation in the public sector for a long time, ever since I was appointed as a 'lay member' (ie not a doctor) of the General Medical Council. Regulation is a regular whipping boy of business people, entrepreneurs and those who want to get on with things without too much of what they see as interference. Of course, one person's interference is another's protection. If you work at height on a construction site, wearing a hard hat is common sense, as are a variety of other measures. If you are doing the construction, you may feel they are an added and unnecessary expense or simply that they are interference from a 'do goody' state, though why seeking to do good should be a term of abuse has always mystified me. Without effective regulation, corners may be cut. It may not always end up like Grenfell Tower where so many people perished in a fire that should have never happened but the risk is always there. That's what regulation is about – risk management. In my work in the public sector I have tried to explain how regulation can be a force for good. It's an uphill battle, as professionals resent what they see as interference and, to some, an undermining of their professional raison d'etre. As I explain, regulation needn't be oppressive, needn't work against the grain. But it has to be understood, by the regulator as much as the regulated.

As I mentioned, one of my forays into public life was the almost seven years (with no time off for good behaviour) that I spent regulating the financial affairs of MPs after the great Expenses Scandal of 2008. One of the great challenges, as you will see, was to get MPs, journalists and the wider public to understand what the job involved.

Although, as I said earlier, what follows is an eclectic mix, is there any overarching theme for you to take away? Yes. I would hope that you would recognise the value of reasoned argument and persuasion as ways of serving the common good and, where appropriate, pointing to change. The arguments may not prevail. But prevail or not, they reflect a commitment to a discourse based on reason. In a world in which reliance on 'alternative facts' can serve as an argument and in which tweets on Twitter have become for some the preferred mode of communication in the public arena, the hope is that you will see that there are other (and dare I say) better ways of shaping the future.

Postscript

As I was preparing the book, the world was overrun with the Covid-19 pandemic. One of the pieces offers a view which reinforces my call for a discourse based on evidence and reasoned argument in the face of ideology masquerading as considered public policy and conspiracies masquerading as fact. The values of collective solidarity in the face of an existential threat to public health have battled the rise of individualism and selfishness, in which rules to safeguard us all only apply to others. Public health refers to the health of the public. We are all affected by each other's actions. But when the government panders to this sense of individualism it is no surprise that England (in particular) has among the worst toll of deaths and illness in Europe. Controls have not been strict enough or have been too late. The classic public health approach of test, trace, isolate has been ignored. An ignorant and ill-equipped private sector has gorged on the riches thrown away by government as the established public health systems (particularly regarding contact tracing) were sidelined.

Should there ever be a public inquiry, it will be too late for the tens of thousands whose illness and death could have been avoided. It will be too late for the tens of thousands unable as a consequence of the extent of the pandemic to get care for non-Covid illnesses. It will be too late for the millions damaged by the unnecessary depth of the economic recession brought on by failing policies. It was no joke to respond to one of the ill-conceived relaxations of restrictions with the comment – 'hug your granny in November – bury your granny in December'.

PART I

Children

I have never got used to the way in which, as a nation, we treat our children. I have never ceased to be both amazed and depressed. A rich country with a health service which, on its face, is there to take care of us all, where children are concerned simply lets down far too many. Clichés abound – children are our tomorrow and so on. Yet go to the inner city housing estates or the rural towns and you'll see the pinched faces of poverty and hardship. Tomorrow for them is where the next meal is coming from, where they can be safe when the next outbreak of fighting erupts, where they can get proper schooling, where the jobs will be.

For too many children and young people the story of the National Health Service is one of neglect. An NHS which should be concerned with promoting good health and preventing ill-health, particularly as regards children in their early years, concerns itself instead principally with responding to ill-health. It's an illness service rather than a health service. If that were not bad enough, the NHS is regarded by those who operate it as if it were an island. It's not an island. It's part of a fabric of public services including social care and education which should be seamlessly conjoined to promote children's welfare. In the case of those children who most need these services, so far from being seamless, the fabric is full of holes. Children routinely fall through the holes. They suffer as a consequence and our clichés betray us.

In what follows you will see the evidence and the arguments which support my anger. Yes, there are lots of children and young people who are well and well-looked after. But societies should be judged by their failures rather than just their successes. And in too many cases the NHS and the wider society fails too many children.

1

Caring about Children – Who Cares?[1]

I spent my first four years sleeping in a hammock, slung between girders in the cellar of the house my parents rented, as the bombs fell. We were poor, not privileged. Life was tough, financially and emotionally. The constant fear of the bombs and for my father's safety took its toll on everyone, especially my mother. But, growing up, I was lucky on two counts. I was clever, and the UK had just created its welfare state. I floated on the opportunities it gave me: all the way to university in London in the swinging 60s – the decade of sex, drugs and rock and roll; something, sadly, that no-one told me about at the time!

I was a serious young man. I had promised myself while still at school, that if I ever escaped the industrial wasteland of my childhood, I would not forget those who remained behind. If you have been poor, you never forget. It's what you make of those memories that matters. That's what I'm going to talk about. It's for you to judge whether what I have to say helps you. And, I suppose that's a clue. Wanting to help and a sense of duty were my parents' gift (or curse) to me.

But, you might say, I'm a lawyer and I specialise in policy. So, how can I help? You might think, I'm about as much help as … (I'll let you finish the sentence).

Well, stay a while ….

I trained as a lawyer, largely because I was no good at anything else. I soon became fascinated by the moral and legal challenges which run through health and healthcare. There was no subject called Medical or Health Law. I and a couple of others started it in the UK.

My background as a beneficiary of the UK's welfare state caused me to focus on the public sector and the patient/citizen – not the private sector and the professional. My concern was with those who have been called the 'descamisados': those without a shirt on their backs.

And, it didn't take long before I was drawn to the way my society and particularly the NHS dealt with children and young people. The 'vulnerable' they are called, although, of course, it is we who make them so. They are not necessarily vulnerable, if cared for and about. I saw it as a life's work, a noble work, to draw on my own past, concentrate on the less well-off, and ask how we can do better for children.

When I gave BBC Radio's Reith Lectures in 1980, entitled Unmasking Medicine, I dedicated one of the six lectures to the care and welfare of children. I called it 'Suffer the Children …'. It seemed to me that we had got so much wrong in caring for children.

[1] Unpublished paper written in February 2013 reflecting my continuing interest in the welfare of children.

Those from comfortable middle-class homes didn't know about, nor care much about the welfare of the less well off, save when it came to buying their Christmas cards from a fashionable children's charity, or talking of feral gangs loitering outside their favourite bistro. We had the highest child pedestrian accident rate in Europe because children had to play in the streets and cross busy roads to school – no nanny and no SUV for them. We had a food industry dedicated to ensuring that children became addicted to sugar. And the tobacco industry lurked to entrap the 12 and 13 year-old.

Not much has changed in the years since those lectures. The nannies are now Polish rather than French and the SUVs have better sound systems. But, for most children, their health and welfare and their access to healthcare in the UK is not much better.

Coca Cola and McDonalds turn our children into obese sugar junkies. The fashion industry peddles anorexia and cosmetic surgery. Alienation, poverty and cultural isolation breed anger, envy, and crime. Two nations of children exist occupying their separate worlds, barely intersecting: one nation fearing, the other resenting, what they see of the other. And the divide grows, whether it's child mortality, exploitation by criminal gangs, teenage pregnancy, care of those with long-term needs, the disabled, or those with mental health problems.[2]

The proposed solutions to this state of affairs are as many as the explanations. To most, we are dealing with a wicked problem beyond real solution. Hasn't the world always been this way? Children have always been on the losing side.

This is too pessimistic. Realising that there is no particular solution, or raft of solutions – that the magic wand school of policy never existed – doesn't mean that there aren't ways of improving things. I'm interested in government and public policy as one route to effecting change: in a welfare state (just about!) the role of the state is still important. It's also important, of course, by default, by not acting, in those states where government chooses not to be engaged.

My starting position is that the state, my state, has failed many of our children, the descamisados, for many years, despite the aspirations of the welfare state and the good intentions of many. The rhetoric has often been heady. The reality has fallen significantly short. To the question – who cares, the answer would have to be, too few.

What to Do?

If I had my day and my way, I would focus my efforts on the culture in which we care for and about children. By culture, I mean what people and organisations believe and how they behave. The culture has to change to put the welfare of children at centre stage.

[2] At the time of writing, the footballer Marcus Rashford's campaign to ensure that children who need them should have access to free meals during school holidays was initially rejected by the government. Feeding children is parents' responsibility, not the state's, the Conservative government responded, overlooking inconvenient truths about poverty and unemployment. In the face of public uproar, the government backtracked. Rashford then pushed again. Again he was rebuffed. Again there was uproar. Again the government gave in. Rashford is a hero but his actions are no substitute for considered public policy, though they may be all there is in the present political context.

The following is my manifesto, based on my experience in the UK. It is for others to decide if anything I say strikes a chord for them in their various worlds.

Integrated Services for Children

- money – the money for the health and welfare of children, in all its forms, must be consolidated in one fund, not separated into silos marked education, health, social care, criminal justice and the like;
- responsibility – the responsibility for the money and how it should be allocated must rest with a Cabinet-rank Minister, as regards macro-allocation, and suitably qualified elected officials at a local level as regards local priorities and allocation;
- the hitherto competing claims of various sectors, or silos, of government must be recalibrated as complementary rather than competing. Children and their needs must be understood and responded to holistically. For example, schools must have the health and resilience of children as one of their objectives, just as social services must be engaged in education and mental health.

The Health, Welfare, and Healthcare of Children

- just as the various services provided by the state must be integrated to serve children effectively, so health services themselves must be integrated. The approach must be holistic. A parent should not have to traipse from pillar to post, trying to crack the system which is supposed to be caring for her child, telling the same story again and again to different professionals. This isn't modern healthcare; it's medieval. It happens every day!
- there must be agreed standards of performance in the care of children, developed by healthcare professionals in consultation with families and children;
- healthcare for children is Byzantine in its complexity. The parent or young person sees so many doors: go through the wrong one and you are lost;
- there must be networks of services, designed for children and beginning with a single point of contact, someone who can navigate a way for the parent or child to get what is needed, whether community care for the long-term disabled, maternity care, mental health care or whatever;
- there must be a significant focus on the early years of children from disadvantaged and poorer backgrounds: 'disadvantage begins at birth and accumulates throughout life'.[3] Apart from its being just and right to do so, the social benefit in the form of the integration of parents and children into society and the economic and social benefits that accrue is very considerable, as is the saving otherwise dissipated in social care and (often) the criminal justice system.

[3] M Marmot, *The Social Determinants of Health*, 2nd edn (Oxford: Oxford University Press, 2006).

The Organisation of Services

- the financial incentives and rewards in the system for providing health and healthcare must be aligned with the holistic, integrated approach to services: perverse incentives must be driven out. Equally, the regulation of services and professionals must also reflect this approach;
- data about compliance with standards of performance and outcomes is at the heart of modern health and healthcare. It must be collected, analysed and routinely published as a mechanism for accountability and as a tool for improvement.

Professionals

- training in the care of children must be a prominent part of the training of health-care professionals rather than, as now, a declining interest;
- training in collaborative working, working in teams, must be part of the training of all those who care for children: teachers should train with healthcare professionals, social workers, the police, and others, according to a common curriculum, to understand each other's roles and responsibilities and to enable them to work together in the interest of children. Such training must also be designed to break down the tribal isolationism of healthcare professionals, as regards some other healthcare professionals and all non-healthcare professionals.

And, Three Final Things

- government and those designing services must reconnect with professionals of all stripes and types. Their commitment is too often taken for granted and their alienation can corrode the care that children receive;
- every aspect of services for children (and that's every aspect) must be designed with the interest of child and parent in mind. 'I exist to provide for you' must replace the too common 'I'm a professional: this is what I do';
- leadership, leadership, leadership is at the heart of any regeneration of a system. It has never been more needed (and more lacking) in the NHS and more widely in government in my country. Without it, nothing is possible. With it, if not everything, lots is possible.

So, this is what I would do if I ever got my hands on the levers of power.

2

Getting it Right for Children and Young People

Overcoming Cultural Barriers in the NHS So as to Meet Their Needs[1]

Foreword

I began this review of children's services in the NHS in the autumn of 2009. The sense was that the NHS was not performing as well as it could: that children and young people (and the reference to young people is very important) were not getting the best deal. Pockets of excellent practice exist, but they are just that. The sense is that they are islands in a sea of mediocrity, or worse.

I was asked to see if I could get to the bottom of why this might be the case. There was, for me, a certain poignancy in the request. For as long as I can remember, services for children have been described both as an important priority for the NHS and in the next breath as a 'Cinderella' service, save that this Cinderella has never got near to the ball. Nearly 30 years ago, I called one of my Reith Lectures[2] 'Suffer the children', in which I lamented the state of health and healthcare of children. Report after report over the decades have echoed the same message. In the public inquiry into paediatric cardiac surgery at Bristol Royal Infirmary,[3] my colleagues and I urged improvements in children's care. Now, 10 years later, I am returning again to the theme. Robert the Bruce and spiders come to mind.

In carrying out this review, I have travelled around England and spoken to a great many people. Wherever I've been, I've seen enthusiasm, commitment, and a real sense of caring and duty. I pay tribute here to the dedication of a wide range of professionals. They leave home in the morning wanting to do their best for the children and young people whom they look after. It is this knowledge which makes it that much more tragic,

[1] This Review was commissioned by the then Chief Executive of the NHS in 2009 and published by the Department of Health in September 2010.

[2] I Kennedy, *The Unmasking of Medicine* (1981) (London: George Allen & Unwin), based on The Reith Lectures: Unmasking Medicine The Listener Nov–Dec 1980.

[3] *Learning from Bristol: The Report of the Public Inquiry into children's heart surgery at the Bristol Royal Infirmary 1984–1995* (London: The Stationery Office, 2001).

for children and for those caring for them, if, for whatever reason, the services provided don't on occasions pass muster. It is this knowledge that makes it all the more important for us to figure out why the system isn't working and set it on the road to recovery. This review is my contribution to the process.

Postscript

I should add that just as I was completing the final draft of the review, a new government came into power. Much of what I had concluded about the mechanisms for change, not least the role of respective departments of state and of local organisations such as Children's Trusts, has had to be revisited. This is because the landscape of policy is changing. That being the case, any proposals for change that I make, if they are to have any prospect of being translated into policy, must take account of these changes and work with the warp of current government policy. The difficulty that I encounter, however, is that the Government's policy is not yet firmly set out. The result is that the section in which I propose the way in which policy can be got right and put into operation is more general than originally drafted. I have concentrated on setting out the principles, leaving the precise mechanisms for giving effect to them to be worked out as the Government's policy develops.

Post-Postscript

This review, at the time of writing, is over 10 years old. Sadly little has changed in terms of the failings and weaknesses I set out. The names of Departments of State have changed, as they regularly do. The names of Ministers have changed, as they regularly do. Some of the institutional architecture has changed – a wrecking ball here, a faux architrave there. But, little has changed for children and young people. If anything, the circumstances of those at the wrong end of the arc of affluence have got worse. 10 years of governments committed to a policy of 'austerity' has meant a hollowing out of the public sector. The NHS and other elements of the welfare state have been brought to their knees. Inequality in access to and provision of public services has become a national scandal, though you wouldn't know if you just paid attention to the complacent and often dishonest rhetoric of those who should care. And, if further proof were needed, the government's response to the pandemic of Covid-19 which is ravaging the country as I write, plus the tragic fairy-tale world conjured up as we leave the EU, should suffice.

1. Introduction

1.1 I was asked to carry out this review amid widespread concern about the services provided by the NHS to children and young people. This concern relates in part to a number of tragic and high-profile cases, for example the death of Peter Connelly in

Haringey in 2007 and the investigations and reports that followed.[4] But concern goes much deeper and wider. Many people who work in and use the NHS would agree that the services provided do not measure up to the needs of children and young people. They are not good enough in a number of ways.

1.2 Of course – and I need to emphasise this in case what follows is seen by some as too critical – there are examples of excellent care throughout the NHS and I shall refer to some of them. Equally, there is no doubting the commitment of all those working in the NHS to provide the best possible care and service. Yet the concern remains that there are things about how the NHS works which prevent it from achieving the sustained and significant improvements in care that children and young people have a right to expect.

1.3 My brief was to identify any shortcomings in the services provided by the NHS to children and young people, and seek to discover what lies behind them. I was asked to focus on the culture of the NHS: to identify the cultural barriers that lie in the way of change. I was asked to make recommendations to support sustained improvement (and sustainability is critical) over the medium and longer term in outcomes for children receiving services. Of course, there are also structural problems or barriers that contribute to the overall picture. I also examine these as they interact with the cultural forces.[5]

1.4 Sadly, this is by no means the first review of services provided for children and young people. There have been many.[6] Much of what I say, therefore, is not new. What is new, however, is a renewed determination in the NHS and government to do something to make the services better.

1.5 The review was carried out over eight months, from October 2009 to May 2010. During this time I met a wide range of individuals and groups, including NHS clinicians and managers, policy-makers, agencies working with the NHS, voluntary (third sector) organisations, and children and young people, their parents and carers. I visited a range of services, from children's centres to specialist acute and mental health services. I also received over 100 written submissions from individuals and organisations, including many from parents/carers and young people chronicling their own experiences and making suggestions for improvement. I am very grateful to them all.[7]

[4] These include: Care Quality Commission, *Review of the involvement and action taken by health bodies in relation to the case of Baby P* (London, Care Quality Commission, 2009); and Ofsted, Healthcare Commission and HM Inspectorate of Constabulary, *Joint Area Review: Haringey Children's Services Authority Area* (London: Ofsted, HCC and HMIC, 2009).

[5] The terms of reference are set out at Annex A.

[6] As well as the Bristol Royal Infirmary Inquiry cited in note 3 above (which includes a summary of previous reports on pages 416–17), these include: Ministry of Health, Central Health Services Council, *The welfare of children in hospital* (the Platt Report) (London: HMSO, 1959); Committee on Child Health Services, *Fit for the Future: The Report of the Committee on Child Health Services*, Volume One (the Court Report) (London: HMSO, 1976); Audit Commission, *Children First: A study of hospital services* (London: HMSO, 1993); House of Commons Health Select Committee, *Hospital Services for Children and Young People, Session 1996–7, Fifth report* (London: HMSO, 1997); Lord Laming, *The Victoria Climbié Inquiry* (London: HMSO, 2003); Healthcare Commission, *Investigation into 10 maternal deaths at, or following delivery at, Northwick Park Hospital, North West London Hospitals NHS Trust, between April 2002 and April 2005* (London: Commission for Healthcare Audit and Inspection, 2006); and Lord Laming, *The Protection of Children in England: A progress report* (London: The Stationery Office, 2009).

[7] Full lists of engagements and the written submissions I received are set out in separate Annexes B, C and D (not reproduced).

1.6 My review concentrates on understanding the role of culture in the NHS. It focuses necessarily on those areas where there are cultural barriers to change and improvement. It talks largely about how services in the NHS are planned, commissioned, organised and provided, and how they interact with one another and with other public services. The more that I sought to analyse what the NHS was doing, the more it became clear that I had to focus not just on the NHS but on the NHS's interactions with other organisations and services. The culture in and of the NHS deeply affects how it sees itself and others and is seen by others. It became clear that examining the NHS's position in a wider system of care and support is a crucial element in understanding and improving the NHS's provision of services to children and young people. Thus, while I focus on the NHS, I point out that the NHS must be understood as operating in a much broader environment if change is to be achieved.

1.7 My review covers the range of care provided by the NHS for children and young people.[8] I do not go into detail about specific services, except when this allows me to illustrate a larger point. That said, submissions to the review did highlight a number of areas that are frequently overlooked and call for particular attention. They include: services for disabled children and young people; mental health; speech and language therapy; play therapy; and health visiting. I was greatly assisted by these submissions. I believe that the analysis that I offer, and the recommendations which flow from it, should provide a framework for change in these particular areas as well as many others.

1.8 In my approach to the health and welfare of children and young people, I adopt the perspective of the United Nations Convention of the Rights of the Child[9] and of the World Health Organization.[10] I am not concerned only with the presence or absence of disease; I am concerned to emphasise the role of the NHS, with others, in promoting the well-being of children and young people and in keeping them healthy and resilient for the future, as well as treating illness and injury from time to time.

1.9 I recognise the various initiatives taken by government and the NHS over the past decade. There has undoubtedly been a concerted effort, at least at the level of policy, to raise the profile of services for children and young people, and to give them a higher priority.[11] Indeed, the range of policies that has been developed is recognised as among the best in the world. The *National Service Framework for Children, Young People and Maternity Services* (2004), published by the Department of Health (DH) and the Department for Education and Skills, was a significant watershed.[12] It set out the

[8] I refer from time to time also to maternity services.

[9] The Convention states that the state shall 'ensure the child such protection and care as is necessary for his or her well-being [...] and, to this end, shall take all appropriate legislative and administrative measures' (Article 3). In relation to involving children in their care, it states that 'States Parties shall assure to the child who is capable of forming his or her own views the right to express those views freely in all matters affecting the child, the views of the child being given due weight in accordance with the age and maturity of the child' (Article 12).

[10] 'Health is a state of complete physical, mental and social well-being and not merely the absence of disease or infirmity' (Preamble to the Constitution of the World Health Organization).

[11] One senior official commented to me that there has been more done at the level of policy for children in the last 10 years than in the previous 50.

[12] DCSF has, since the general election of May 2010, become the Department for Education (DfE). See later for the implications of this change for my analysis and recommendations.

standards that services for children and young people were to meet. *Every Child Matters: Change for Children* (2004), published by HM Government, set children's health and well-being in the context of the Government's commitment to their welfare. Last year saw the publication by DH of the three-part *Healthy Child Programme* (2009), which sets out an 'early intervention, clinical and prevention public health programme', running from birth to the age of 19. The strategy for children and young people's health *Healthy Lives, Brighter Futures*, published jointly by DH and the Department for Children, Schools and Families (DCSF) in 2009, set out simultaneously a comprehensive vision for child health and well-being, child health services, and how these should interact with other agencies. These overarching policies are supported by a range of more specific guidance on such matters as mental health, maternity services and safeguarding. Guides to commissioning services for children and young people have also been produced, and guidelines on clinical services for them have been developed by the National Institute for Health and Clinical Excellence (NICE).

1.10 I also recognise the increasing extent of the collaboration between DH, DCSF (now the Department for Education, DfE) and others on a number of projects designed to improve the health and well-being of children and young people, such as the development of Children's Trusts. Specific initiatives, such as the joint funding by DH and DCSF of short breaks for those caring for disabled children, also need to be recognised.

1.11 Such policies and projects sit within a determination across the whole of government to give greater priority to children and young people, as illustrated by the previous Government's cross-departmental Public Service Agreements (PSAs). PSA 12 called for the improvement of 'the health and well-being of children and young people'.[13] Another two PSAs addressed the same aim, by calling for the need to keep children safe (PSA 13),[14] and a focus on young people's health (PSA 14).[15]

1.12 All of that said, the premise of the invitation to conduct this review is that the ambition represented by these developments has not always been matched by results. I will be asking in what follows whether, and if so why, this is so. The analysis and recommendations that I offer are based on the evidence provided to me. The scale of the review, both in terms of staff and its relatively short timescale, meant that I could not commission specific pieces of research or analysis. My recommendations are therefore largely at a strategic level. I do not set out detailed proposals to put into practice what I recommend. Should what I recommend be accepted, translating it into practice will be the next vital step in bringing about the much-needed changes that I recommend.

1.13 In the next section, I set out the current picture of the NHS's services for children and young people. It serves as the basis for a critical examination of the premise behind the review: that there exists a gap between the rhetoric of the NHS and its reality,

[13] HM Government, *PSA Delivery Agreement 12: Improve the health and well-being of children and young people* (London: HM Treasury, 2007).

[14] HM Government, *PSA Delivery Agreement 13: Improve children and young people's safety* (London: HM Treasury, 2009).

[15] HM Government, *PSA Delivery Agreement 14: Increase the number of children and young people on the path to success* (London: HM Treasury, 2007).

between how the NHS talks about services for children and young people and the priority awarded them, and what in fact it delivers. I conclude that the premise is largely valid. I then analyse the cultural factors responsible. Finally, I make recommendations about the way forward.

2. Services for Children and Young People – An Overview

Services Provided by the NHS

2.1 The NHS is traditionally divided into a number of sectors.[16] The divisions reflect historical choices, such as the separation between primary and secondary care, which itself reflects a political compromise forged at the birth of the NHS. Such separations have, over the years, developed a life of their own and, far from being a convenient way of organising the service, have deeply affected the way in which the whole of the NHS has come to serve the population. Separations have become entrenched. Territories have been established. Careers have come to be mapped against them; bureaucracies have defended them; they were not designed with patients in mind; and patients have had to cope with them. In the case of children and young people, this has meant that pregnant women, parents/carers with their children, and the developing young person have had to negotiate the system. Moreover, it is a system which over the years has become increasingly complex, something that I will reflect on more fully in due course.

2.2 Reflecting the traditional divisions of the NHS, the services provided are broadly those in primary care, secondary care (mainly in the hospital) and in the community, and mental health care (child and adolescent mental health services – CAMHS). They also extend to schools through the school health team.

2.3 However, this description tells us very little. It is more instructive to look at the landscape of services from the perspective of the children and young people and their parents/carers.

Making Contact with Services

Services in the Community – GPs, Health Visiting and Children's Centres

2.4 Most children and young people will make contact with the NHS through their GP. Typically, a pre-school child will visit the GP around six times per year.[17] Much of this contact has to do with early development and public health measures, such as immunisation or self-limiting illnesses. A school-age child will see their GP on average

[16] For a general introduction to the NHS, see R Klein, *The New Politics of the NHS: From creation to reinvention* (Oxford: Radcliffe Publishing, 2006).

[17] Department of Health, *Making It Better: For children and young people* (London: DH, 2007) p 2.

between two and three times per year.[18] Even though children account for around 40% of the workload of a typical GP,[19] the majority of the population, and therefore also the majority of the average GP's patients, are adults. Most of the additional contractual (financial) incentives for GPs (as set out in the Quality and Outcomes Framework[20]) relate to the care of adults.

2.5 Babies in the first months of life receive care and support from health visiting services, including referral to more specialist care if needed. This support is important at what is a time of significant change for families, and where the amount of information and advice about babies, families and parenting can be daunting. Many health visiting teams are now based in children's centres. For parents and carers, this means that their health visitor has ready links to a wide range of services provided at the centres, and can provide advice and information about them. Available services might include those provided by the NHS, such as speech and language therapy, as well as other relevant services such as playgroups, or classes in parenting skills or in healthy cooking.[21]

Accident and Emergency Departments in Hospital (A&E)

2.6 Children, young people and their parents or carers are often either unwilling or unable to gain access to the care of a GP or health visiting services. They choose to go instead to the A&E department of a hospital. Around half of infants (under 12 months) and a quarter of older children will attend A&E in a typical year. Around 26% of all those attending A&E are children.[22] Nearly one-third of calls to NHS Direct concern children.

2.7 Children and young people therefore attend A&E not only in emergencies, but also in cases that could be addressed outside hospital. Such use of A&E is unnecessary and inappropriate, given that A&E is designed and intended for accidents and emergencies. This recourse to A&E departments is because they are an accessible and high-profile service and provide guaranteed care around the clock. When combined with a parent's or carer's concern about a child, uncertainty about their condition and desire for problems to be addressed quickly, A&E is the default option. Direct access to A&E is particularly attractive to those who live on the margins of society, who are not registered with a GP, or who are unaware of the range of services that the NHS provides. Also, of course, A&E is used in evenings and at weekends when the great majority of GPs' practices are closed.

[18] ibid.

[19] Children represent 19% of the population (Office for National Statistics), but account for up to 40% of a typical GP workload (RCPCH response to *Our NHS, Our Future*).

[20] Only four of 128 Quality and Outcomes Framework indicators relate specifically to children. These include one relating to maternity services.

[21] I saw such services available on my visits to children's centres.

[22] There were around 3.6 million attendances at A&E by children aged 0–18 in 2008/09. This does not include attendance at minor injury units and walk-in centres (NHS Information Centre statistics).

Figure 2.1 Attendance by children at A&E by time of day, June 2009

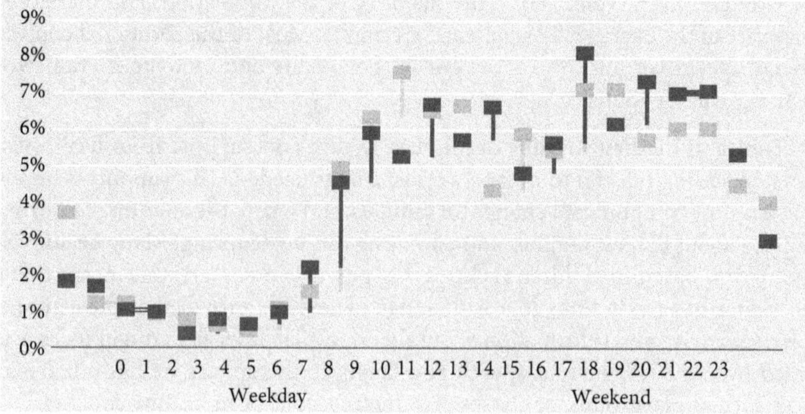

Figure 2.2 Attendance by children at A&E by time of day, November 2009

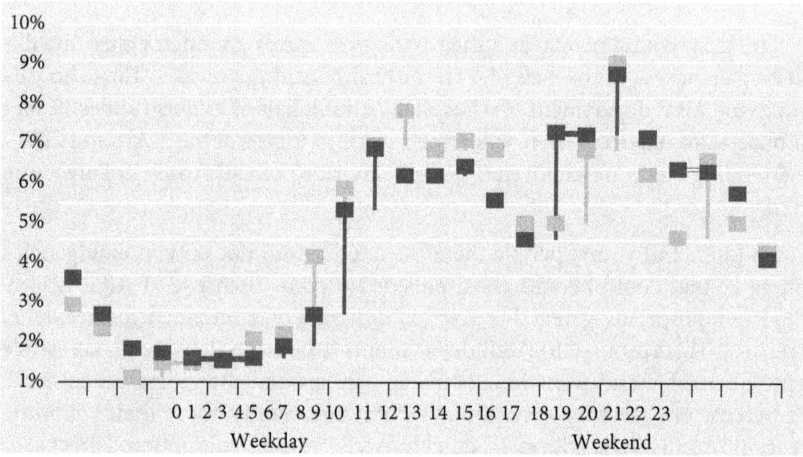

This analysis[23] shows that attendance differs slightly between winter and summer months, but an overall pattern of high usage in the evenings (up to around midnight) is clear.

Specialist Care

2.8 GPs and A&E are the two most common routes through which children and young people are referred to specialist NHS services. Such services range from care in hospital to community children's nursing and paediatrics, CAMHS, and

[23] This analysis has been helpfully provided to me by Ian Machonochie from Imperial College London.

therapy services such as physiotherapy, speech and language therapy, and occupational therapy.

Specialist Care in Hospitals

2.9 Every year around one in 11 children receives specialist outpatient care in hospital, and around one in 10 to 15 is admitted for inpatient care.[24] Specialist hospital care for children and young people often consists of complex, highly technical procedures carried out by highly trained specialist staff. In environments that are dedicated to the care of children and young people, staff are aware of what is required to provide the best possible experience for their sick patients. Specific efforts are made to make the environment welcoming to children, and staff are aware of their needs, desires, anxieties and frustrations. Additional specialist services, such as play therapy or distraction services to manage pain, improve children's experiences of treatment as well as helping to manage parents' and carers' anxieties. Increasingly, youth workers are available as part of young people's teams, They were described to me by the Young People's Health Special Interest Group as 'important players' in designing services for young people, given the fact that they work closely with them and discuss, and sometimes address, health problems.

Mental Health Services

2.10 Children and young people with mental health problems may be referred to CAMHS. These services are mostly based in the community, but there is also a small number of inpatient and secure beds for those with serious conditions. For the most part, children and young people get access to these services through referral, but some services, mainly for young people, are also available through self-referral. On occasions, services are located away from dedicated health premises, for example in schools, youth centres or sports centres.

Specialist Community Services

2.11 Children with complex needs or long-term conditions, such as asthma, epilepsy, diabetes or palliative care, may receive specialist community nursing care. The focus is on helping children to lead a normal life to the greatest extent possible. Nurses co-ordinate clinical care, as well as supporting others, including professionals from outside the health services such as teachers, parents and carers, in providing care for the child. Children who would previously have been cared for either in hospital or full time at home are supported to stay in school and play a full part in school life. They are therefore given the opportunity to achieve their potential alongside their peers and are given the best chance of becoming independent as adults.

[24] Department of Health, *Making It Better: For children and young people* (London: DH, 2007). This publication also notes that the profile of specialist care is changing – 'Over the past 30 years or so the number of children admitted to hospital has more than doubled, but the average length of stay has reduced from 8 to 2 days'.

Therapy Services

2.12 These services include speech and language therapy, physiotherapy and occupational therapy, dietetics and others. They are provided by a range of professionals, usually as part of a multi-disciplinary team. They may be offered or available in hospitals, general practices or settings in the community such as children's centres.

Keeping Children Safe

2.13 The NHS has an obligation to make various provisions to ensure that children are safe. Of particular importance are duties relating to 'safeguarding'.[25] This duty has greatest significance in the context of abuse of children and young people. It extends not merely to taking action when there is suspicion that a child or young person is being abused, but also to providing care and support for the victims of abuse. Partly as a result of high-profile cases, professionals in the NHS are expected to be more aware than ever before of the importance of safeguarding and of taking appropriate action to ensure that children and young people are safe.[26]

The NHS Working in a Co-ordinated Manner

2.14 Children and young people, like any other patients, move through the NHS from one service to another, for example from the GP to the hospital to the community children's nurse. Networks have been developed formally for cancer and care of the newborn. They are increasingly being used for palliative care, children's surgery, child protection and other areas of children's medicine such as gastroenterology and respiratory, cardiac and renal services. The service is only as good as the efficiency of the organisation of these pathways of care.

The NHS's Interaction with Other Services

2.15 Just as there are divisions between elements of the health services provided by the NHS, so there are between the NHS and other public services. Again, the divisions are historical in origin and bureaucratic in nature.

[25] These duties arise from various sections of the Children Act 1989 and the Children Act 2004, as amended. Duties vary by type of organisation, with primary care trusts (PCTs) and strategic health authorities (SHAs) being subject to more provisions than NHS providers or special health authorities. More information on the legislation most relevant to safeguarding is available in HM Government, *Statutory guidance on making arrangements to safeguard and promote the welfare of children under section 11 of the Children Act 2004* (London: Department for Education and Skills, 2007) and HM Government, *Working Together to Safeguard Children: A guide to inter-agency working to safeguard and promote the welfare of children* (London: DCSF, 2010) p 336 f.

[26] See, for a review of progress, Care Quality Commission, *Safeguarding Children: A review of arrangements in the NHS for safeguarding children* (London: Care Quality Commission, 2009).

Social Services

2.16 Children and young people who need both health and social care include those with a disability or long-term condition, those who are looked after, and those who are potential or actual victims of physical, mental or sexual abuse or neglect. The links between the NHS and social services need to be suitably robust and aligned if the child or young person's health and well-being are to be maximised. A particular feature of these links is the importance of sharing information between professionals.

Education

2.17 Children and young people with health problems often require help to enable them to start or continue with their education, something that is vital if they are to fulfil their potential and live as independently as possible as adults.

2.18 Children and young people with long-term conditions or complex needs can be supported in school through specialist equipment and treatment, often supported by community children's nursing teams or school health teams. Teachers or other staff can be trained in the procedures necessary to support a child or young person, including how to operate special equipment. NHS staff can assist in raising awareness of ill-health and disability and in training staff in schools, supported by PCTs and Local Authorities. Acutely ill children can continue their schooling in hospital. Teachers in hospital work with a child's regular teacher to develop work programmes and monitor progress during the time in hospital.[27] This might include taking exams. All of this collaborative effort requires close co-operation between the NHS and schools, with professionals from health and education co-operating in understanding a child's overall needs and their role in meeting them, within a system organised to achieve this end.[28]

2.19 Education also contributes to the health and well-being of children more widely. DfE's SEAL (Social and Emotional Aspects of Learning) programme encourages children in primary school to think about their emotions and their reactions to them, including seeking help and support when needed.[29] A pilot programme, Targeted Mental Health in Schools (TaMHS), aims to support a variety of mental health services delivered in schools.[30] Both of these programmes provide children and young people with ways of addressing actual or potential problems related to mental health and emotional well-being at school, with the aim of preventing the development of more serious mental health problems and the distress and disruption they cause.

[27] I saw a very good example of this at University College Hospital, London.

[28] I was impressed by the work of Newcastle's Children's Acute Nursing Initiative team.

[29] DCSF described SEAL as 'a comprehensive approach to promoting the social and emotional skills that underpin effective learning, positive behaviour, regular attendance, staff effectiveness and the emotional health and well-being of all who learn and work in schools'.

[30] DCSF described TaMHS as 'a three-year pathfinder programme aimed at supporting the development of innovative models of therapeutic and holistic mental health support in schools for children and young people aged five to 13 at risk of, and/or experiencing, mental health problems; and their families'.

Police and Criminal Justice

2.20 The NHS works with the police in relation to safeguarding and caring for vulnerable children and young people, including those who offend against the criminal law as well as those who are victims of abuse. A large proportion of young people in the criminal justice system have a significant need for healthcare, especially in relation to mental health.[31]

Working Together and Sharing Information

2.21 Sharing information is a prime example of collaborative working between organisations. It requires them to have the technical capability to share information appropriately, for example compatible IT systems. It also requires organisations, and professionals within them, to trust one another and to be aware of the benefits that sharing information will have for the child or young person, and to have ways of working that enable this to happen.

2.22 Clearly, if organisations are to work together effectively, they must agree on what information to share and how to do so. The NHS is no exception. How this works in practice is a major theme throughout this review.[32]

3. Is the NHS Meeting the Needs of Children and Young People?

3.1 My terms of reference[33] proceed from the premise that, while some NHS services for children and young people are very good, others are poor. The assertion is that although these services have been represented as a priority in the NHS for decades, the reality has fallen short of the rhetoric. The premise is also that the services have the potential to be better were it not for 'cultural factors' inhibiting their improvement. I now need to determine how valid the premise is.

General

3.2 The quality of services for children and young people varies across the country. A recent assessment by the Healthcare Commission showed not only that a large number of services are in need of significant improvement, but also, importantly, that there are some excellent services from which others might learn.

[31] See paragraphs 3.51–3.52 for more information on mental health and the youth justice system.

[32] For a recent evaluation of how well healthcare organisations manage information, see Care Quality Commission (2009), *The Right Information, in the Right Place, at the Right Time: A study of how healthcare organisations manage personal data* (London: Care Quality Commission). This report also touches briefly on information-sharing between the NHS and social care organisations.

[33] The terms of reference state that 'successive HCC and CQC reports and other evidence indicate that good practice is not always embedded effectively. While the NHS responds positively to specific initiatives and reports, short-term improvements tend not to be sustained'. The full terms of reference are included at Annex A.

Figure 3.1 Overall Healthcare Commission scores for children's hospital services (across six services)

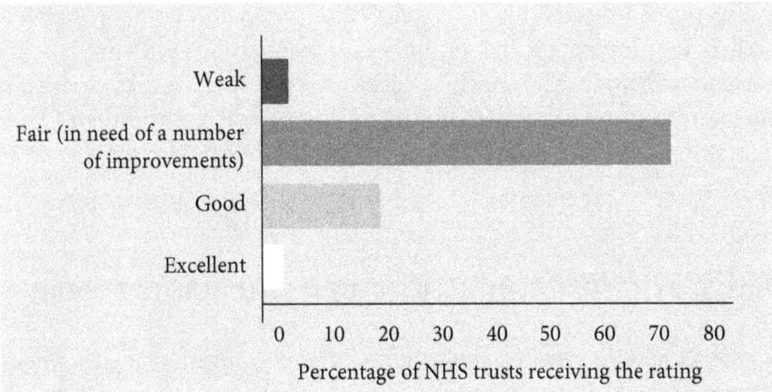

3.3 Further evidence comes from international comparisons of outcomes.[34] Child mortality rates continue to fall and are now at a historic low. However, rates have fallen less quickly than in other EU countries and are now lagging behind. Infant mortality is influenced by a wide range of health and social circumstances, and is therefore an important proxy indicator of health and the performance and contribution of both the NHS and other public services. The UK also has some of the highest rates of teenage pregnancy[35] and low-birth weight babies in Europe.[36] Again, these are indicative of broader shortcomings in services.

Figure 3.2 Infant deaths in the UK and EU, 1992–2006

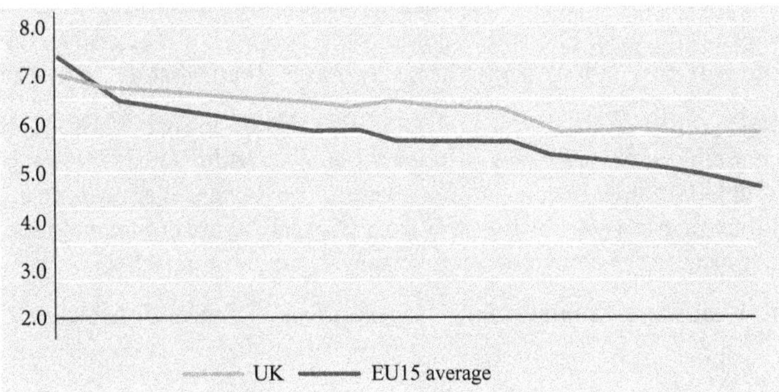

[34] For a brief discussion of international comparisons in health outcomes for children, see A Kraft 'Are health services in England failing our children?' (2007) 335 *British Medical Journal* 268–69.

[35] A teenage mother under the age of 18 presents a particular challenge to the NHS, in that she is both technically a child or young person and also a mother. The lines of demarcation between various services make it hard for the NHS to see her as both.

[36] Royal College of Paediatrics and Child Health, *Modelling the Future: A consultation paper on the future of children's health services* (London: RCPCH, 2007).

3.4 A recent study for UNICEF[37] ranked the UK bottom out of 25 industrialised countries for well-being enjoyed by children, based on a range of measures. Importantly, this study also ranked the UK lowest as regards children and young people's subjective sense of well-being, showing a lack of optimism from children themselves about their own health and well-being.[38] If nothing else, such international comparisons suggest that we can learn from other countries in providing a good environment for children to grow up in, taking account of the role of health and other public services in contributing to this.

The Relative Priority Given to Children and Young People

3.5 There is a real sense among professionals and organisations that services for children and young people in the NHS have a low priority. It is important, however, to understand what this might mean. Certainly, on one level, it is entirely proper that these services attract less attention than those for adults, for the quite simple reasons that adults make up 80% of the population and that, as adults grow older, their needs for care get greater. So, if the assertion is to mean anything, it must be rephrased to state that children and young people receive a disproportionately lower priority. Measures of this would include the extent to which the care of children and young people figures in the imperatives of management and delivery, in the relative funding allocated, and in the realisation that investment in the care of children and young people will reduce the cost of care later in life. On each of these criteria, children and young people do clearly attract a lower than appropriate level of support within the NHS.

3.6 I will refer later to the NHS's Operating Framework, the basis for action by managers up and down the land. The care of children and young people gets no mention, apart from warm words, when it comes to the hard choices about what has to be delivered.[39]

3.7 The President of the Royal College of Paediatrics and Child Health (RCPCH) told me that children's health is 'a 'Cinderella' subject within medicine' and that 'The NHS is designed by older people for older people'. The Royal College of Nursing told me that 'Children are not a priority for NHS trusts. Specialists are enthusiastic about working together around the child, but senior managers are not interested'.

3.8 The Healthcare Commission, in its report on the state of healthcare in 2008, wrote:

> 'While many NHS trusts and PCTs have worked hard to raise the profile of children's services, concerns remain about the priority given to children's issues by some NHS trust and PCT boards and by independent healthcare providers'.

3.9 I heard the same message from many who wrote to me about their children. One area of particular concern is the care of children and young people with disabilities.

[37] UNICEF (2007) *An overview of child well-being in rich countries*, Innocenti Report Card 7.
[38] Ibid, p 34.
[39] See paragraphs 4.112–4.124.

As I will point out several times, many parents and carers were frustrated by the difficulties in negotiating their way through an often hostile environment to secure help for a disabled child. Moreover, there appears to be only limited recognition that one of the consequences of extraordinary advances in care is the growing number of disabled children and young people who have very complex needs. There are, for example, over 6,000 technology-dependent children and young people. Their needs must be factored into the calculation of priorities, as must the fact that they will now progress to adulthood.

3.10 Perhaps the most obvious, although somewhat crude, measure of the priority given to children and young people by the NHS is the amount of funding allocated to their care as a proportion of the total funds of the NHS. The total allocation to the NHS is around £110 billion. The overall amount spent on children and young people is not clear (which may itself say something), but DH estimates that the figure is around £6.7 billion. The RCPCH offers the estimate of £3.1 billion (2007). The Healthcare Commission put the figure at £3.2 billion (2008). The differences may lie in the extent that a service can be disaggregated and that the element wholly dedicated to children and young people can be identified. The spending on CAMHS is said by DH to be £523 million. Another way of assessing the balance of spending is to compare what is spent on the NHS for the care of children and young people with that spent by other services. The social care budget is £4 billion. The budget for education is £35.4 billion. The spending on children and young people (including those up to age 25) by the criminal justice system is said to be £7 billion. How much of this last amount could be saved through a strategic shift of policy and resource by the NHS to preventative measures, and early intervention to support children and families at risk, is a theme that I shall pursue.

Particular Services

3.11 I set out above the general landscape of services. I now ask how the various areas of service that I have previously identified measure up: whether the premise that reality falls short of the rhetoric is true here as it is in general terms. My aim is to describe what I perceive to be the current state of affairs. Once I have done so, I will be able to analyse why this has come about (the 'cultural barriers'). Then I can offer proposals for change.

Services in the Community – GPs and Children's Centres

3.12 Despite the high number of children coming into their surgeries, many GPs have little or no experience of paediatrics as part of their professional training.[40] This means that, technical competence notwithstanding, many GPs lack the confidence to assess and treat children effectively, something that comes from specialist training and experience. The practical consequence of this is that they will often refer children to

[40] In many parts of the country, 40–50% of GPs will have had no formal paediatric/child health training. This is despite the fact that 25% of their patients are children, and up to 40% of consultations are with children and families (RCPCH response to *Our NHS, Our Future*).

specialist care when better trained and more experienced practitioners would regard this as unnecessary. Examples include children with a fever, or asthma, or common ailments such as constipation and straightforward problems of behaviour. For children and parents/carers, this causes not only the disruption of additional appointments and consultations, but also worry and frustration, as problems may remain undiagnosed or untreated. And, of course, from the point of view of the NHS, it is extremely inefficient and wasteful of resources. Furthermore, the fact that GPs' surgeries are closed at those times when parents/carers and young people often need access to a GP produces dissatisfaction with the service and resort to the local hospital's A&E department.[41]

3.13 Given that the majority of their patients are adults, caring for children and young people is low on most GPs' priorities. One senior manager commented to me that the biggest single problem is getting GPs to be interested. One illustration of this is that they frequently fail to attend meetings called about safeguarding.[42] This, in turn, is a problem that reflects poor working relationships between GPs and other services, as in part it results from meetings often being arranged or rescheduled at short notice, which means that GPs are unable to attend due to clinical commitments.

3.14 As regards the services provided by children's centres, it is obvious that parents and carers clearly value them, including the ease of accessibility that comes from providing them on a single site close to where they live. Many parents/carers would like them to provide yet more services, including primary medical care (which is now beginning to be available in some areas). However, many parents/carers do not associate children's centres with health services, possibly due to poor communication and consequent lack of awareness of what is on offer.[43] Take-up of health services is, therefore, comparatively low, especially compared with childcare and nursery education.[44]

A&E

3.15 The NHS has consistently attempted to educate people about the range of services available from the NHS for parents and carers with sick children, so that the services of A&E departments will only be used when appropriate – and, it must be stressed, sometimes it is appropriate. Equally, there are occasions when it is not. But A&E is always there and always open, when other services are not; and it is far from obvious to a parent/carer which services are available, and to which people, at which times. Navigating through the complexity of NHS services, finding the system's

[41] 'Changes to general practitioner out-of-hours care have resulted in increasing attendances to emergency departments' (*Modelling the Future*, RCPCH 2007 – see note 42). Also, see the graphs on p 18 on attendance at A&E. Changes to out-of-hours arrangements also mean that GPs have fewer opportunities to develop experience in seeing and treating children.

[42] A senior police officer commented that 'if any of five people from the NHS might turn up at a meeting, then you just have to hope you get someone good'.

[43] 'Our focus group participants used children's centres largely for childcare services, and for involvement in social groups but did not associate them with health services' (Audit Commission, *Giving Children a Healthy Start* (London: Audit Commission, 2010)).

[44] Audit Commission, *Giving Children a Healthy Start* (2010).

preferred point of access for each child, can be difficult for even the most articulate and well informed. A&E becomes the default option. The NHS and those who use its services suffer as a consequence.

3.16 Children and young people's experience of A&E will vary by age, location and time of day. Children's hospitals and larger general acute hospitals often have either a dedicated paediatric A&E department or a separate section of A&E for children. Staffed by clinicians with specialist training, these departments are aware of and able to address the different clinical needs of children and young people, as well as their anxieties and those of their parents or carers. For children entering adult A&E departments the experience can be quite different. An intimidating setting is often exacerbated by the presence of injured, drunken or violent adults. This is a problem encountered especially at night, when dedicated paediatric A&E services are more likely to be closed.[45]

3.17 Lack of training in treating children and young people may lead staff to treat them inappropriately, however unintentionally. This includes not recognising children's different clinical needs, or not engaging with them in an age-appropriate way or, for younger children, not engaging with their parent or carer appropriately.[46]

Specialist Care

In Hospital

3.18 Children and families may have to travel some distance to receive specialist care. In successful networks of care built around specialist children's hospitals, or large teaching hospitals with specialist children's facilities that also involve larger district general hospitals, children will receive the best possible quality of care as close to where they live as possible.[47] Without successful networks, children may receive inappropriate or poorer-quality treatment locally, or else may be required to travel long distances unnecessarily, receiving treatment in specialist centres that could just as easily take place in their local hospital. Such experiences cause unnecessary inconvenience and frustration. They also mean that care may be of poor quality or even dangerous.

[45] 16–18% of hospitals provide insufficient cover for paediatric emergencies at night (Healthcare Commission, *Improving Services for Children in Hospital* (London: Healthcare Commission, 2007)).

[46] The benefits of specific training, including formal training in communication with children and young people, as well as evidence of young people's desire for greater involvement in decision-making about their care, are explored in more detail in *Improving Services for Children in Hospital*. These are vital issues, to which I will return.

[47] For example, in the case of paediatric surgery, the percentage of operations carried out in district general hospitals has been falling over the last 10 years, reflecting a trend to increased specialisation that has improved outcomes (Department of Health, 2007). However, the Chair of the Children's Surgical Forum of the Royal College of Surgeons of England was of the view that 'while there are some examples of a network operating effectively, the key barrier to transforming the delivery of surgical services for children is the current inability of the NHS to develop and support clinical networks in practice' (Royal College of Surgeons of England's submission to the review).

3.19 Smaller centres that lack dedicated specialist facilities also lack the range of supplementary services which can make such a difference to a child's experience of hospital, often due to lack of funding rather than lack of recognition of their value. For example, the management of pain is often poor,[48] and I was told of at least two hospitals where play therapy services, so important as regards the experience children have of treatment, have recently been withdrawn for financial reasons.[49]

3.20 The smaller number of children using these smaller centres may also mean that staff lack sufficient experience in caring for them, sufficient specialist training, or both, especially if the child or young person has rare, specialist or complex needs. Indeed, a number of hospitals and their specialists see too few cases for the facilities and skills to be kept up to date.[50]

3.21 For parents/carers and children, the variation in the level of service is confusing and frustrating and seen as unfair.

> 'We've never really had any bad experiences at [Great Ormond Street Hospital]; however, smaller, more local hospitals are more daunting, where staff have little specialist knowledge and do not embrace disability or difference'. *Parent of disabled child*

Mental Health Services

3.22 Young people using CAMHS have, in most cases, already overcome significant anxiety and risk of stigma to gain access to services. Often the need to be referred for such services is a potent factor in their not being used.[51] But self-referral, although attractive to some young people, is relatively uncommon.[52]

3.23 Young people are often further distressed by inappropriate environments, including being treated on adult wards.[53] I also heard from young people how, on occasions, the attitudes and behaviour of staff can be insensitive to their specific needs and concerns.

3.24 CAMHS also care for victims of assault and abuse, and are increasingly involved in safeguarding. Using these services in this context can cause anger and frustration for the children and young people being cared for.[54] They feel that they are being labelled by the service as suffering from a mental health problem which they do not have.

[48] Healthcare Commission, *State of Healthcare 2008* (London: The Stationery Office, 2008). This was also mentioned during review meetings.

[49] The services were mentioned independently in two communications to the review.

[50] In 2007 the Healthcare Commission found that, in 8% of trusts, surgeons carrying out elective surgery did not carry out a sufficient number of operations to maintain their skills to work with very young children, and that 16% of paediatric inpatient units were carrying out less than the professionally recommended minimum level of interventions (Healthcare Commission, *Improving Services for Children in Hospital* (London: HCC, 2007)) I recognise that special arrangements may be needed for remote areas.

[51] The Mental Health Foundation noted that both children and young people and their parents/carers are more comfortable with mental health services provided in generic, non-stigmatising settings, including non-health settings such as schools or youth centres (Summary of evidence for the Good Childhood Inquiry).

[52] One outstanding example of a service based on self-referral that I visited is the Brandon Centre in Camden, north west London.

[53] Healthcare Commission, *State of Healthcare 2008* (London: The Stationery Office, 2008).

[54] View submitted at a meeting with independent experts.

Specialist Community Services

3.25 Despite major successes in some areas,[55] availability of these services is still a problem. Specialists are confined to a small number of conditions and there are fewer of them than are needed. This means that many children are unable to benefit from these services.

Therapy Services

3.26 Many parents and carers are frustrated at the lack of availability of specialist therapy services, including speech and language therapy, physiotherapy and occupational therapy, which are often dwarfed by services for adults. Finding that their child is entitled to services does not mean that such services are available in their local area. Parents/carers report that services are overloaded, or that they have to travel long distances to receive them.

3.27 Parents/carers of disabled children in particular often feel that getting access to suitable health services is dependent on a 'constant battle of resources', as investment in high-tech interventions to keep severely disabled children alive has not been matched by investment in services to support them in leading their lives (including in the transition to adulthood):[56]

> 'The paed[iatrician] will refer us for other services if I push and push but they are not offered. I'm tired of fighting – it's exhausting!' *Parent of child with Down's syndrome*

3.28 The impression is gained that such services, and therefore both the people who need them and those who provide them, are a low priority for the NHS. Even where services are available there is often a recurring problem about sharing information. Failure to share information between therapists and others looking after the child or young person, such as medical or nursing teams, is a common frustration.

> 'We see so many different specialists at so many different times and there is no working together and little contact and information-sharing'. *Parent of disabled child*

This is something that I will return to later.

Keeping Children Safe

3.29 Despite the increased awareness in the NHS of the need to safeguard children and young people, it is acknowledged that, on occasions, the NHS fails to provide a safe and supportive environment. For example, young people are reluctant to tell health professionals about abuse, for fear that they will not be believed or that no action will be taken.[57]

[55] For example, hospital admissions for childhood asthma fell 40% during the 1990s, despite an increase in diagnoses (Department of Health, *Making It Better: For children and young people.* London: DH, 2007)).

[56] This was mentioned in meetings with both senior officials and third sector organisations. One senior manager commented that people get 'operations five times faster than wheelchairs'.

[57] T Palmer and C Raby, *Taskforce on the Health Aspects of Sexual Violence Against Women and Children: Consultation with Children* (2010).

3.30 Evidence from the Care Quality Commission shows that many NHS trusts need to do more in relation to their duties regarding safeguarding children. They need to ensure that clinical staff are trained to the necessary level and that they keep this training up to date, that strategies for safeguarding are in place and that their effectiveness is audited, and that trust boards and senior management ensure that they keep safeguarding under regular review, rather than merely respond to serious incidents.[58] Worryingly, the Commission noted that the need for action in some of these areas had been given priority in previous reviews, but that action had still not been taken.

3.31 There is also other evidence that lessons have not been learned from previous tragedies. Lord Laming's recent report on safeguarding children[59] indicates that recommended guidance and other actions are not being implemented. This shows clearly that services which need to make improvements are, for whatever reason, not making them.

3.32 The Government's definition of safeguarding includes 'ensuring that children [grow] up in circumstances consistent with the provision of safe and effective care' and 'enabl[ing] children to have optimum life chances and enter adulthood successfully'.[60] I have heard how recent tragedies have led social services and others, including the NHS, to focus attention and resources overwhelmingly on protecting children from abuse, to the exclusion of the broader obligation to safeguard their well-being and resilience. This means that outside the formal child protection system a wider, often unrecognised group of children continue to lead constrained and unfulfilling lives, at risk from a wide range of problems and poor outcomes and prevented from achieving their full potential.[61]

> 'There has been a negative change [in safeguarding in the past year] – more work and more pressure on staff plus more difficulty engaging other agencies because of the stress they are experiencing'. *Designated doctor for safeguarding*

Access to NHS Services

3.33 Access is a key dimension of the provision of services. The services offered by the NHS fail those for whom they are intended if, as is too often the case, children and young people are unable to gain access to them, or if difficulties in doing so are put in their way. This is particularly important for children and young people with complex needs, who require many services to work together around them.

[58] Care Quality Commission, *Safeguarding Children: A review of arrangements in the NHS for safeguarding children* (London: Care Quality Commission, 2009).

[59] Laming, Lord, *The Protection of Children in England: A progress report* (London: The Stationery Office, 2009). The report also highlights other problems, including training and support from practitioners and the sharing of information between organisations.

[60] HM Government, *Working Together to Safeguard Children: A guide to inter-agency working to safeguard and promote the welfare of children* (London: DCSF, 2010) p 34.

[61] Royal College of Paediatrics and Child Health, *Modelling the Future III* (London: RCPCH, 2009) p 8.

The NHS Working in a Co-ordinated Manner

3.34 A number of parents and carers wrote to me expressing their frustration at the lack of co-ordination between the many services that their children required. Appointments are scheduled on consecutive days and at multiple locations, when arranging them in the same place on the same day would save a long journey and time off work. Support groups for parents/carers routinely meet during office hours, meaning that working parents/carers are unable to receive the vital support that they provide.

> 'Over the last 18 years I have never been able to see two consultants on the same visit. This has cost me a fortune in transport costs and time. My child is profoundly disabled, and has been under orthopaedic, neurological, spinal, and general paediatrics … all at the same time. Yet we have never had a combined appointment'. *Parent*

3.35 Parents and carers expressed their frustration that diagnoses, advice and other information from one episode of care are not passed to the team conducting the next. In some cases, parents/carers felt forced to take on the role of co-ordinating their child's care themselves.

> *Question: In your experience, how well do the different services contributing to your child's care work together to meet your child's needs?*
>
> 'They don't! I'm the hub of everything! I have to tell the paediatrician for example what services my son is using so that he can mark it down on a bit of paper'. *Parent*
>
> 'The biggest problem is lack of communication between health professionals … It should not be up to parents to copy clinic letters and relate details to other professionals'. *Parent*

3.36 Both young people and the parents/carers of younger children are frustrated at having to re-explain their or their child's condition to a number of different services because of a lack of effective information-sharing. In some cases, this frustration is compounded by a high turnover of staff, meaning that patients must explain their story not only many times to different services, but many times to the same service, as staff change.

3.37 When information is communicated to children and young people or parents/carers, it is often in a form that is barely understandable to the people it relates to. Professionals in the NHS lapse all too frequently into jargon, which is baffling and intimidating to parents/carers and children. This includes organisational as well as clinical jargon.

> 'It's a whole new world and new language for parents to learn if they have never had any experience of special needs before. A better explanation of what each service is, why your child might need it, less jargon and how to access it should be made available'. *Parent*

3.38 Such problems are not inevitable, even in cases where complex care is required. I have seen examples of services that are careful to use accessible language and have developed devices for doing so, for example writing care plans in the first person and ensuring that they are then understandable to the person for whom they have been written.

3.39 Problems of co-ordination reflect the sheer complexity of the services that some children and young people need: a complex range of clinical services supported by complex organisational arrangements. As more services come to interact and work around the needs of a particular child or family, this complexity multiplies. The danger is real that services lose focus on whom they are there to serve, as each service or clinical team provides the best it can without sufficient regard to how children and families view the 'whole picture' of the care that they are receiving. Public perception of the NHS is that it is a single, universal system providing co-ordinated programmes of care. There is little recognition or understanding of the complex array and interplay of organisations, units and teams of which it actually consists.[62]

3.40 Lack of co-ordination of services is particularly evident for young people whose care is passed from children's to adult services. The transition of a person's care between clinical teams is a phenomenon created by the system. It views care from the perspective of organisations providing services, rather than the children and young people being cared for. The 'problem of transition' arises from the administrative divisions between different NHS services. A young person's needs, and the care that they require to meet them, evolve, yet the experience is that services change abruptly when they reach an arbitrary point (usually either their 16th or 18th birthday). 'Transition', in reality, often amounts to no more than 'transfer'. For many young people, transition is experienced as a disruptive discontinuity in their care, as they move suddenly from child services, with a specific child focus and (often) trained staff, to adult services with different staff, different settings, different attitudes to patients and no training in the care of children and young people or in dealing with parents/carers.[63]

> 'Upon turning 18 a person's needs do not change, but the range of services available to them becomes radically different!' *Young person*
>
> 'We have started asking all consultants that we see regularly at children's hospitals where we will be referred to next year when she reaches 16, but nobody has yet been able to answer my questions as they do not know'. *Parent of disabled child*

3.41 In some cases, the thresholds for receiving care are different. Children and young people with mental health problems may stop receiving CAMHS at the age of 16, but the threshold for receiving mental health services as an adult is different. The consequence may be that, at 16, a young person's problems may abruptly be considered to be below the threshold that will qualify them to receive adult mental health services. The absurd consequence is that their condition may well deteriorate before they can get help.

[62] In a recent publication, the RCPCH draws attention to the official government position that 'The NHS is not a collection of separate and autonomous units of varying degrees of independence, responding to the invisible hand of the market and incentives and reforms. It is, in fact, a healthcare system. The different parts, whether GPs or consultant nurses working in primary care or acute care, are all working for the benefit of patients, whose pathway of care often crosses the boundaries of professions and organisations. This system requires active management by both PCTs and SHAs as local system managers', noting that this is the stated intention for the future rather than a description of the present (RCPCH, *The Comprehensive Spending Review, Public Service Agreements and the NHS Operating Framework*, RCPCH Policy Briefing, 2009)).

[63] More information on transition, including young people's views about their care and good practice examples, is included in Department of Health, *Transition: Getting it right for young people – Improving the transition of young people with long term conditions from children's to adult health services* (London: DH, 2006).

3.42 The shortcomings in care arising from transition add weight to a wider feeling that young people, or adolescents, are a 'forgotten group', caught between child and adult and therefore also between bureaucratic barriers and professional spheres of influence.

> 'One of the main cultural obstacles … for young people is the lack of recognition of them as distinctly different to children as well as adults … Many young people are at risk of falling out of view of children's services and either get lost as a minority group in adult services or are lost in the transition between them'. *Young People's Health Special Interest Group*

> 'Usually professionals are competitive and try to take one another's work, but not the 16–19 age groups, probably reflecting a lack of knowledge, skills and facilities'. *Consultant paediatrician*

3.43 Two other factors worth mentioning in any consideration of the NHS working in a co-ordinated manner are the extent of the involvement of parents or carers in the care of children and young people, and the involvement of children and young people themselves. As regards parents/carers, I was told on a number of occasions how they felt that they were not properly involved in what was going on.

> 'I found out later that an assessment had been carried out … I had no prior knowledge [and was not] invited to attend. A 'report' was sent directly to the school and I did not receive this until last day of term … Again due to the timing, this left me no opportunity to discuss this with anyone … These services send letters without being clearly titled and without clear explanations of clinical terms … no proper examples of how conclusions are being made and no input or consideration of parents and their expertise and knowledge of their child'. *Parent*

3.44 As regards children and young people, not only was I told of occasions when they felt that they were not really involved in their care, but there is also another deeper cultural point. DH and the NHS are anxious to suggest that the NHS's services respond to the needs expressed by the public. The only catch is that the only members of the public who are routinely surveyed are in fact adults. There is no regular survey of children and young people. Not asking means not knowing.

NHS Interaction with Other Services

Social Services

3.45 Children, young people and their parents/carers are often frustrated that the health and social care services do not have a 'joined-up' approach to the services that they provide. Simple needs for care may go unmet as NHS and social care organisations dispute which is responsible for funding a particular need. Such disputes can be very disruptive for the child. They may, on occasions, result in a child's condition deteriorating, resulting in pain and distress as well as additional costs. For example, I heard of one case in which a child discharged from hospital required a plastic feeding tube, which cost around £2.50. The responsibility for funding this tube was disputed by health and social care organisations. By the time the case was finally settled out of court, it had cost around £20,000.

3.46 Of particular importance and concern are failures of health and social care to work together in the context of safeguarding. In 2008, the Healthcare Commission stated that 'Our recent work in Haringey looking at arrangements for the protection of children found that systems were not adequate to enable agencies to work together effectively on behalf of children'.[64]

Education

3.47 Despite the obvious need for close collaboration between professionals in health and education to ensure that children with long-term or serious health needs do not lose out in education, and the enthusiasm of most head teachers for school health services and recognition of the benefits they provide,[65] some head teachers and schools are reluctant to make the necessary commitment. They are concerned about the implications for the safety of the child and the risk to which they might be exposed to by assisting with healthcare for which they believe they are insufficiently qualified.[66] That said, with sufficient support, most are happy to contribute to care that clearly is in the best interests of the child.

3.48 If children do not receive appropriate support from the school, at worst those with severe health problems receive a 'double whammy' as their ill-health damages their education by disrupting their schooling, either through being forced to stay at home or by long stays in hospital. Children with severe or long-term conditions receive enormous benefit from continuing their education during their treatment. And there are social as well as educational benefits. Continuing in education is a signal, to the child himself, the parents/carers and the peer group, that a child with a severe or complex health condition continues to belong to the 'community of children' and does not become defined by their condition.

3.49 A particular area of concern is mental health. Young people with mental health problems told me that, although support from school was good once their diagnosis was made and treatment begun, they were frustrated that schools did not provide them with more help during the early stages of their illness prior to formal diagnosis.

3.50 These young people considered that schools could do a lot more to identify and help pupils who were showing signs of mental illness. This view is supported by the Mental Health Foundation, in their submission to the Good Childhood Inquiry, which argues that 'Schools need to be able to identify emotional problems in children early on and seek timely help and support to deal with them'.[67]

Police and the Criminal Justice System

3.51 Strong links between the police and the NHS are often lacking, with NHS organisations described by one senior officer as some of the police's 'weakest' partners. This means that investigation and intervention in cases of suspected abuse are not as

[64] Healthcare Commission, *State of Healthcare 2008* (London: The Stationery Office, 2008).
[65] View submitted at a meeting with a professional body.
[66] View submitted at a meeting with third sector organisations.
[67] Summary of evidence for the Good Childhood Inquiry.

co-ordinated as they should be. Police forces often find it difficult to engage with health services, as the complexity of the NHS's internal organisation, matched with a high turnover of staff and frequent structural reorganisations, means that they do not know which organisation or whom within the organisation they should talk to.[68]

3.52 Over 200,000 children and young people come into contact with the criminal justice system each year. Over 2,000 find themselves in some form of institutional setting. They are acknowledged to have multiple health problems, including problems with mental health (as high as 90%), learning disabilities, speech and communication, and sexual health. Many have not been immunised. Over half have been 'looked after' in homes. At least 60% have problems with substance abuse. They frequently come from a chaotic family environment. Early intervention to break the cycle of deprivation and decline into anti-social behaviour is crucial.[69] But, although the criminal justice system seeks to do its part, once the children and young people leave the system, there is no effective continuity of care. The criminal justice system operates in a silo. There is no effective partnership with the other services for children and young people. The child or young person just gets back onto the conveyor belt of social exclusion.

Working Together and Sharing Information

3.53 Children, young people and parents/carers are often frustrated that organisations fail to share relevant information appropriately.[70] This mirrors the frustrations and problems already referred to in the case of poor sharing of information between NHS organisations.

3.54 Failure to share information, for whatever reason, can mean that organisations do not know of relevant information about children and young people's problems or their care. Social workers may be unaware that NHS services have a suspicion that a child is being abused. This is damaging in two ways. Not only will social services be unable to take action that the information would have prompted had it been shared with them, but they might also hold information which, when combined with that held elsewhere, gives a more complete picture which can better inform the actions of all agencies.

Missed Opportunities

3.55 In addition to the NHS's failing to meet its potential in providing for children and young people, decisions about how to configure services and where to place more or less emphasis have led to its delivering less than optimal outcomes. And, of course, missed opportunities during childhood and adolescence mean increased problems for the NHS later in life.

[68] This was mentioned by senior police officers on more than one occasion.
[69] See paragraphs 3.59–3.61.
[70] This point was emphasised in a number of submissions to the review. For example, parents' and carers' frustrations about the lack of information-sharing between the clinical teams caring for their child are explored above.

The Early Years

3.56 The importance of investing in, and concentrating services on, the first years of life cannot be overstated. As highlighted in Professor Michael Marmot's review of health inequalities,[71] and elsewhere,[72] the determinants of health and well-being, whether good or bad, start before birth and accumulate over a lifetime, with a particular importance attached to the very early years. As a result, giving every child the best start in life is widely recognised as crucial in improving the health and well-being of the population as a whole, as well as being the most important step required to tackle health inequalities[73] and to contain long-term demand on the NHS.[74]

3.57 In the light of this somewhat self-evident proposition, I was unpleasantly surprised to discover that evidence submitted to the review shows that investment in services for children and young people is lowest in the very early years, which are the most crucial in the development of the brain, and increases only at the point when development slows.

Figure 3.3 Public spending and brain research: the disconnect

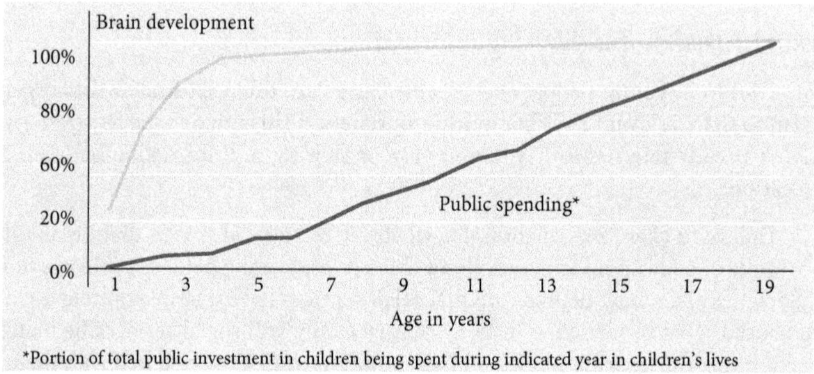

3.58 If services are to influence how children grow up and prosper, much more investment and effort are essential in this crucial early period.

Promoting Positive Health and Well-being

3.59 In addition to other measures, a more general focus on promoting health and preventing ill-health, together with early intervention services for mental health

[71] The Marmot Review, *Fair Society, Healthy Lives: Strategic review of health inequalities in England post-2010* (London: The Marmot Review, 2010).

[72] 'The single most effective method to improve the long-term health of the whole population is to invest in the health of children and families' (RCPCH, *Modelling the Future III* (London: RCPCH, 2009) p 15).

[73] The Marmot Review, *Fair Society, Healthy Lives: Strategic review of health inequalities in England post-2010* (2010) Executive summary.

[74] Royal College of Paediatrics and Child Health, *Modelling the Future: A consultation paper on the future of children's health services* (London: RCPCH, 2007).

problems, is of critical importance.[75] Failure to provide such services for children and young people before they reach adulthood, bearing in mind that mental health problems in adulthood begin in childhood, leads to the situation in which, as the previous Government noted, 'Mental illness accounted for more disability adjusted life years lost per year than any other health condition in the UK', including cardiovascular disease and cancer.[76] The total cost of mental illness, including treatment, formal and informal care, lost employment, premature mortality and reduced quality of life, was calculated at more than £77 billion for 2002/03.[77]

3.60 These costs, including opportunity costs and their effects on family, employers and the individual as well as on the state and its agencies, can be no more than speculative. They do, however, serve to demonstrate not just the importance of mental health and health services, particularly for children and young people, but also the interdependence and overlap of different public services' priorities and objectives. Investment in early intervention, and particularly early intervention for young people with mental health problems, can potentially save millions of pounds for the NHS and for the education system. Further savings will be made in reducing the costs of unemployment, social care and benefits, and costs to the criminal justice system.[78]

3.61 While I emphasise the financial cost, what is also at stake in calls to improve the services provided by the NHS for children and young people is a fundamental issue of social justice. Providing care for those who need it, especially those who are vulnerable or unable to care for themselves, is a matter of fairness. It is not just about economics, but also the kind of society in which we want to live. Preventing a mental health problem becoming a crisis, or providing support and intervention to give a baby the best possible start in life (rather than waiting for problems to develop in childhood or adolescence) serve both a moral and an economic purpose.

Conclusion

3.62 This brief overview clearly shows that the premise of the review, that services are not as good as they could be, is broadly valid. International evidence shows that better outcomes are possible, and recent developments and examples of excellent practice show that positive change is possible in the NHS.[79]

[75] About 75% of adults with mental health problems first experienced mental health problems in childhood (J Kim-Cohen, A Caspi, TE Moffitt et al, 'Prior juvenile diagnoses in adults with mental disorder' (2003) 60 *Archives of General Psychiatry* 709–17.

[76] HM Government, *New Horizons: A shared vision for mental health* (London: DH, 2009).

[77] Sainsbury Centre for Mental Health, *The economic and social costs of mental illness* (2003) Policy Paper 3.

[78] For example, I was advised that in year one of the Family Nurse Partnership (FNP) programme in Tower Hamlets, an assessment was made of how many children had not been placed in care as a result of the FNP programme. The estimate was six children. Given that it costs £2,500 per week to keep a child in residential care, and assuming an average of three years in care for each of the six children, the saving just in this particular area would be £3 million per year, less the cost of the programme of £250,000 per year.

[79] I was very impressed with the services I saw at St Stephen's Children's Centre in Newham, east London, where a range of services, including NHS services, were offered in an integrated manner. I shall refer to other examples in the next chapter.

3.63 However, there is also considerable evidence that changes to improve services are not being made; that planners, professionals, parents/carers and children and young people themselves remain unhappy with aspects of current services; and that opportunities to invest in services that will bring significant long-term benefits are being missed. In the next chapter, I analyse in more detail the reasons for these problems, including the factors currently preventing services from changing for the better. I do so from the perspective of the culture of the NHS.

4. Cultural Barriers and How to Address Them

4.1 The preceding chapter leaves no doubt that change is needed. The child and the young person must be at the centre of the services provided by the NHS and other agencies. They must be involved in the shaping and delivery of those services. The services must be organised around the children and young people: they should not have to work out which door to go through to get what they need. The services must be responsive to their needs, not organised around buildings or the preferences of staff.[80] The services must meet the expectations of good practice that we are entitled to call for. Those providing the services must regularly monitor and review their performance by reference to whether they are meeting the needs of those they exist to serve. The services must be delivered efficiently on behalf of the taxpayer. And, above all else, it is as they start out in life that children must be given the greatest possible assistance in making a start which will equip them with the well-being and resilience to become the successful citizens of the future.

4.2 Very little that I propose here is new. It has been said countless times.[81] What perhaps is new is the concentration on the cultural roadblocks and the role that they have in causing the NHS to sell children short. What is also new, and welcome, is the growing awareness in many parts of the NHS and government of the need for the sort of changes that I am proposing. I will, therefore, be working with the warp of policy as it currently stands, not against it.

4.3 In this section, I set out a way forward for services for children and young people. I do so by identifying cultural barriers or roadblocks in the way of change[82] and proposing ways whereby they can be removed or avoided. My proposals for change are couched in general terms: there will be many details to fill in. And, of course, change will be slow, as is always the case when habits and assumptions of long standing have to be modified or abandoned.

4.4 It can and probably will be objected that the changes that I propose will cost too much, given that we are entering a period of constraint in terms of the money available for our public services. My response is that the shortage of money can always be used,

[80] One young person explained the current system by saying that 'they expect your illness to adjust around what they can offer'.

[81] Chapter 1 gives some examples.

[82] See the helpful analysis offered in the report by Barnardo's policy research unit (February 2010).

and often has been in the case of children's services, as the reason to justify the status quo or to do nothing. Moreover, to the person who says 'Do you know how much it will cost the nation to do what you recommend?', my answer is a simple one: 'Do you know how much it will cost the nation if you don't take action, and take action now?' Secondly, the fact is that the best services are usually the cheapest, since they are, by definition, more efficiently organised and more effectively delivered. Thirdly, my proposals, for example, for integrating services would, simply through the process of integration alone, save money by eliminating duplication and delay. Fourthly, investment in early intervention and the prevention of ill-health saves money 'downstream'. It is so blindingly obvious that it needs to be said again and again: today's children and young people are tomorrow's adults. Unless the NHS wants to go on responding to the never-ending and growing numbers of adults presenting themselves for care, it needs to direct an increasing element of its energies to cutting down those numbers by intervening earlier. Fifthly, while the economic case is strong, fundamentally caring properly for and about children and young people is a question of social justice. They deserve better of us.

The Approach

4.5 My review has uncovered many cultural barriers standing in the way of improving the services of the NHS for children and young people. These barriers were created, and operate, at a number of levels, from Whitehall, through regional and local organisations, to contacts between individual professionals, and with children, young people and those looking after them.

4.6 The most important barriers can be grouped under five headings, as I set out below. In practice, of course, they cannot be so discretely categorised. They run together and overlap, and reinforce each other. They appear in a number of forms. For example, breaking down services into an ever-increasing number of sub-specialisms (atomising them), and defining children by their condition, as opposed to taking a more holistic view, cause problems not only between the NHS and other organisations, but also between different parts of the NHS, between different professional groups, and between the professional and the child or young person.

4.7 Before embarking on my analysis, I must make one point very clear. Concentrating on barriers to improvement does not present the whole picture of the state of children's services. We must not forget that very many children are well looked after and receive a range of services not dreamed of only a few decades ago. Moreover, I do not suggest that the problems that I identify are to be found throughout all parts of services for children and young people, or that all members of a professional group will think and act in the way in which the behaviour of some is described. I have visited and heard about a large number of excellent services where many, if not all, of the barriers to change and improvement have been met and overcome.

4.8 The approach that I adopt is as follows:

- getting policy right;
- the vehicle for change;

- changing the NHS;
- the NHS working with others; and
- changing/challenging how people work.

4.9 Why have I chosen this approach, beginning with policy rather than practice? It might be objected that it is looking at the problem through the wrong end of the telescope. If I am concerned with culture, surely, it is said, the real focus should be on what is happening 'at the frontline', not in the corridors of power where policy is made. Moreover, the objection continues, action and change take place locally. So, that is where my review should begin. Failure to change is because of local inaction. It is easy to point the finger at government and policy-makers, but it misses the target. The argument reaches its peak by asserting that, in fact, those actually in 'the frontline' pay little attention to policy and government. They merely work in their time-honoured and unchanging way, and it is their failure to change that is at the root of any problems that I may identify. The role of government is at best limited.

4.10 I reject this view. I do not reject the central importance of what has come to be called localism, of focusing on what is happening at the point where services are delivered. It informs much of what I will say. But I insist that, in the case of the health and well-being of children and young people, policy and government is the right place to start. The reason is that services are delivered according to certain centrally ordained imperatives and funds follow these. The Operating Framework and performance frameworks set the context. They shape the culture in which the NHS delivers its services. And children and young people do not get much of a look-in, as has been seen, when it comes to these twin drivers of action. So, it does matter what government does, what policy it sets. It matters because those 'at the frontline' are either at the front of the queue or at the back, when decisions are made about what to concentrate on and what to do. Those caring for children and young people are at the back, because that is where policy puts them. They may try their hardest to push their way forward, but the imperatives cascading down from government keep them in their place. That is the culture of the NHS.

4.11 And there is a further reason to begin at the top. It is born of the need to change the culture and behaviour of over a million people who work in the NHS. Such a change is not achieved by telling them to change, or by blaming them for the state we are in. It is achieved by leadership: leadership at all levels of the NHS and beyond. Government and the NHS must set the pace through the development of a national vision and through policies to realise it. Professionals also must show leadership through rediscovering themselves, what they stand for and their sense of purpose. But the professionals are the orchestra. Government is the conductor and calls the tune.

Getting Policy Right

4.12 Cultural tensions begin in Whitehall. Until this review was in its final draft form, there were two principal departments of state responsible for children's health and well-being: the Department of Health (DH), and the Department for Children, Schools and Families (DCSF). They had very different approaches (almost philosophies) in relation to children and young people's well-being.[83] Following the change of government, DCSF has been renamed the Department for Education (DfE). The implications of this change of name, including what it might mean for departmental structures and responsibilities, are not yet clear. However, it is obvious that a change of name alone means very little in terms of culture. The continuation of staff and responsibility for policy at DfE, for the moment at least, will mean that its underlying philosophy remains.

4.13 DfE is dedicated entirely to, and therefore entirely focused on, children and young people. It is responsible not only for their health and well-being, but also their welfare more broadly (including, of course, their education). It takes a 'holistic' view of children, setting their health and well-being in a broad social context. By contrast, for DH, children are one group of the population among many, and a relatively small group at that, who do not make a major claim on the resources of the NHS. Within DH, children and young people must compete for priority and attention against powerful other interests and needs, not least of older people, who have significant political clout. DfE does not have to consider the relative merits of attending to children rather than any other group. Children and young people are their exclusive concern.

4.14 The two departments also have contrasting perspectives on the relationship between services and those who use them. DH and the NHS take an 'intervention-based' view of their role. By and large, they organise and deliver interventions to make sick people better. By contrast, DfE focuses on the broader notion of well-being.

4.15 Fundamental differences in departmental philosophy manifest themselves as tensions, as policy is translated into practice, from national, to regional, to local level. As one senior official, speaking before the change of government, put it to me:

> 'You might think that DCSF and [DH] don't work for the same Government'.

4.16 The evidence presented to me was that DH and DCSF took very different approaches to effecting change within the services for which they were responsible. DCSF relied heavily on prescribed action from the centre. By contrast, in recent years DH has, at least on the surface, become less prescriptive, with local autonomy and decision-making being given greater prominence in the NHS's operating model. Whatever the reasons for this difference at national level, locally it means that NHS bodies may have a degree of freedom of action which the children's services departments of Local Authorities have lacked.[84]

[83] In their submission to me, the NHS Confederation advised that, when members were asked to name the top barrier they were experiencing in the development of services for children and their families, they highlighted the lack of national strategic clarity, as between DCSF and DH.

[84] One example of this was the preparedness of DCSF to ring-fence funding for a particular purpose, while allocations by DH to primary care trusts are not ring-fenced. This can cause significant tension and, ultimately, frustrate the objectives of the policy, where organisations are required to work together. A well-known example was the announcement of funding for palliative care and short breaks for the carers of disabled children in 2008, together with equipment such as wheelchairs. DCSF's contribution was ring-fenced. By contrast, DH's contribution was provided as part of a general allocation and, as a result, only some of it was used for the purpose intended.

4.17 This may all be about to change. The new Government has a clearly articulated aim of ensuring greater local accountability and freedom, and reduced prescription, control and performance management from the centre of government, across all public services. Recently announced plans to remove the NHS from day-to-day political control by the creation of an autonomous NHS Board charged with commissioning services are a clear example of this. Similar structural changes are anticipated in relation to other public services. Such changes, if suitably co-ordinated and successfully implemented, may have the effect of more closely aligning the 'philosophies' of government departments and thereby alleviating the frustrations of the public services which, at local level, must collaborate and work together to ensure that government policy is effectively joined up. For the moment, however, it is clear that the various differences in philosophy between government departments which I have alluded to will continue to cause confusion and frustration at local level.

4.18 Apart from tensions in Whitehall, it is important here to notice one other factor that is crucial in getting policy right: the place of children in DH and the NHS. Within the NHS as a whole, children have a low profile. The inevitable consequence is that their needs also are given a low priority. In some ways this is unsurprising. They form only a small proportion of the population (around 19% of the population is under 16) and are thought to be broadly healthy. Moreover, and this is a point stressed by many of the professionals whom I met, children and young people do not have a vote. It is well recognised that the votes particularly of older people (the so-called 'grey' vote) are important in ensuring that their needs are addressed by the NHS. Having disparate needs, children also lack an organised lobby of the type which has developed on behalf of older people in recent years.

4.19 The challenge for the NHS as a whole is seen almost exclusively as being how to deal with demographic changes and the ageing population. The scenario is one in which demand for services will rise and changes in services will be needed. Against this background, the profile and priority which the NHS assigns to children are likely to get even less, unless something is done.

4.20 The low profile enjoyed (if that is the word) by children also affects, as I have pointed out,[85] many individual NHS services. Outside specialist paediatric services and settings, NHS professionals often have little training in caring for children, and little awareness of how their needs differ from those of adults. As children are only one small section of their patients, staff such as GPs or clinicians in A&E departments have little time to devote to children and young people's needs outside the clinic or the surgery. This leads, for example, to poor engagement by healthcare professionals with colleagues from other services and with meetings of Local Safeguarding Children Boards, and a failure to ensure that their practices are 'young people friendly'.

4.21 It is therefore clear that the isolation of policy for children and young people's health and healthcare within DH, separate from wider policy relating to children and young people, which is currently the responsibility of DfE, has two detrimental effects.

[85] See paragraphs 3.11–3.32 for more information on this.

It forces care for children and young people into an unwinnable battle with adult care for influence on policy, and, because policy on children emanates from more than one government department, it frustrates local co-operation as differences in departmental philosophy and priorities are played out in practice.

4.22 The radical yet necessary conclusion must be that responsibility for policy relating to children's healthcare and wider well-being must be brought together. My reason for adopting this approach is that the needs and interests of children and young people as regards health and healthcare are more likely to be advanced effectively if they are seen as part of a holistic approach to their overall welfare.

4.23 The aim of this shift in responsibility is to achieve three principal objectives. The holistic approach to the provision of public services to children will inform the way in which the NHS delivers health services for children, irrespective of the particular department of government which sets the policy. Secondly, providing a single departmental home for policy relating to children's well-being will mean the end of interdepartmental tensions and contradictions which have previously caused so much frustration for those planning and delivering services for children and young people at local level. Thirdly, children and young people will have the undivided attention of one single, powerful policy grouping within a single department of state, a necessary if not sufficient condition for ensuring that their interests receive appropriate attention, or, at the very least, a more joined- up form of attention across health and social care and wider well-being than previously.

4.24 The precise architecture of government is not for me to determine. Moreover, it changes over time. What is important for me is that policy aimed at improving the lives of children and young people is properly co-ordinated by government, such that their needs, including their needs for health and healthcare, are addressed holistically. This is far more important than precisely where in Whitehall this policy is to be made. There are a number of options. It could be made in DfE, DH or elsewhere. Although DfE currently retains responsibility for policy relating to education and children's services, proposed changes to DH may provide an opportunity for responsibility for these policies to lie within a newly conceived Department of Public Health (DPH).[86] As I shall argue below, the importance of positive health, including mental health and well-being for children and young people, would fit in well with such a change. The well-being of children and young people could be at the heart of DPH's role. It would be able to take on responsibility for a large element of the holistic approach to well-being that I advocate, including mental health (child and adolescent mental health services – CAMHS), disability and the care of those with long-term conditions as well as more typical 'public health' services.

4.25 What matters is not the precise location of responsibility for policy, but that this responsibility is brought together under one administrative and governmental roof, so that there is both the holistic view of the welfare of children and young people necessary to co-ordinate services and the clout within Whitehall to require them to be delivered.

[86] The argument for this will be all the stronger if DfE reverts to a narrower focus on education, as its change of name seems to suggest.

Recommendation 1: Responsibility for policy relating to the health and well-being of children and young people should be brought together in a single government department. In addition to health and healthcare, this responsibility should extend to include as many other aspects of public services used by children and young people as possible.

4.26 Before going further, I also need to recognise and respond to those who might ask why children and young people, and not those with dementia, or some other large sub-group of the population, should receive such very special attention. The answers are both socio-moral and economic. Children and young people have, as the premise of this review assumes, been comparatively neglected as a group by the NHS for a very long time. This is not fair to them and reflects badly on us. We are charged with their welfare until they may take responsibility for themselves. We fail in that charge if we do not do our best to provide them with the best possible opportunity by way of health and healthcare and other services to grow into adulthood able to flourish and fulfil themselves. They are, therefore, special. And, of course, to neglect their needs is merely to guarantee that the burden on the NHS will continue to grow as they take the problems of childhood and adolescence into adulthood. It makes good economic sense to invest in the welfare of children and young people.

4.27 And, I stress, what is needed is action. There is no shortage of policies, frameworks, guidance and other similar documents which have appeared regularly from DH and other departments. Taken together, I have no doubt that England has some of the best and most detailed policy and guidance in relation to children and young people in the developed world. The only difficulty has been translating it into action! Indeed, it is clear that having so many players in the formation and dissemination of policy, from departments of state to a complex web of local organisations, works against the aim of delivering effective services to children and young people. In fact, it virtually ensures that the services will not be efficient or effective.

4.28 It would be my fervent hope, therefore, that the new Government could curb the temptation to continue this never-ending treadmill of policies. Time and effort would be better spent over the next five years in establishing a clear direction for change, preferably reflecting the approach that I am taking here, and then ensuring that it is actually implemented, ie that rhetoric becomes reality.

4.29 There are two major challenges that flow from the approach that I am proposing. Firstly, the boundary between the responsibilities for the care of children and young people, and the care of adults, must be very carefully mapped out. This must be an early task for government. This mapping of responsibilities has a virtue. It will mean that the problem of transition, from young person to adult, long the cause of complaint and unhappiness, will now be exposed as a critical area.[87] It will receive the attention it needs, across the spectrum of public services as, for example, adult health and social

[87] See paragraphs 3.40–3.42 for a discussion of 'transition'.

care align themselves with children's health and social care as regards the respective responsibilities that they have and how they will work together.

Recommendation 2: Relevant elements of government and national organisations must clearly establish, and agree on, their respective responsibilities in relation to the care of children, young people and adults, how these responsibilities interact, and how services for them can be appropriately aligned.

4.30 Secondly, funding for the health and healthcare of children will have to be identified and separated out from the totality of funds currently allocated to the NHS. These funds would then be allocated, by the responsible department of state, to those bodies and organisations responsible for the delivery of services for children and young people at local level. Just as in the discussions above relating to responsibility for making policy, there is more than one possible model for how services could be delivered locally. What is important is that they perform certain functions and take on certain duties, not that they have any particular form or structure. This is a vital issue to which I return below.

Recommendation 3: Funding for the health and healthcare of children and young people and for 'transition' to adulthood must be identified, separated from the funding dedicated to the care of adults, and transferred to the responsible government department for further distribution to organisations at local level.

4.31 I take this view on separating out funding because I believe that a radical change from the past is the only way in which the culture of the NHS will shift away from its unbalanced focus on services for adults and on the acute sector. And, in the light of what I have said about transition to adulthood, a further sum should be identified specifically to manage that transition.

4.32 What is important here is, firstly, that the sum to be spent on children and young people is *separated out* from that spent on adults. Only then will it be possible to achieve the necessary *transparency* in relation to how much is spent on children and young people's care. Secondly, this money must then be *separately allocated* to the organisations responsible for managing care at local level (which, depending on the model chosen, may or may not also have other responsibilities – and other budgets). Only then will the system achieve the necessary accountability for how this money is spent. Being clear about what we are spending on children and young people's care, and on how we are spending it, is vital in ensuring that they get the deal to which they are entitled.

4.33 To those who say that such calculations will be difficult, the answer must be that if a coherent policy is to be adopted regarding services for children and young people, the sums must be done. Furthermore, DH is already committed to identifying and separating out budgets for the NHS (which will be allocated to the NHS Board) from those for public health (which will be allocated by the Department of Public Health to local organisations which, at the time of writing, are yet to be finalised). Separate allocations in other areas may follow. If it can be done in these areas, it can be done for children and young people and for transition.

4.34 If a major cultural barrier to serving the interests of children and young people, as reflected in the tensions and inefficiencies within government, involves a transfer of responsibility within government, what flows from this in terms of the NHS and its services? The first step lies in identifying how the necessary changes are to be achieved.

The Vehicle for Change – Local Partnership

4.35 It is clear from what has gone before that services for children and young people must have certain features if they are properly to meet their needs. In essence, they must be organised in a way whereby all the relevant agencies and professionals in a given area, with the active participation of children and young people, agree a common vision for the healthcare, health and well-being of children and young people, and collaborate in achieving it.

4.36 There are a number of ways in which this could be achieved. Under the previous Government, local organisations providing services to children and young people were brought together under the overall co-ordination of Children's Trusts. It is not currently clear whether the new Government will seek to use and develop Children's Trusts in the way set out by the previous Government. If it does, they will be ideal vehicles for the type of change I propose. If it does not, in essence, this does not matter. What matters is not what the organisation is called, or its specific structure, but that there is, *for every area (perhaps coterminous with that of the Local Authority), an organisation dedicated wholly to meeting the needs of children and young people, and which exists to bring local public services together in order to do this.*

4.37 Given the many options for the exact configuration of such an organisation, for the moment, and given the current uncertainty as to the precise direction to be taken by the new Government, I shall call it simply the Local Partnership.

Recommendation 4: There should be a dedicated Local Partnership in every Local Authority or similar area which is responsible for the planning and delivery of children and young people's health and healthcare at the local level and for integrating these services into all of the services provided.

4.38 From the analysis so far it will be clear that one fundamental question that I am seeking to address is: what is for the state or the centre and what should be left to local delivery? The history has been one of centrism, of tinkering with structures, and of tight financial and managerial control through the Operating Framework and performance frameworks. What I am proposing here is clear responsibility for all aspects of policy relating to children and young people at the centre, and local, really local, delivery through the Local Partnership.

The Role of the Local Partnership

4.39 The Local Partnership must bring together agencies concerned with the welfare and care of children and young people in a particular locality so as to agree how the respective services that they provide should be delivered. The aim here is to ensure that the activities of local organisations providing public services, including the NHS, are co-ordinated in the best interests of children and young people.

4.40 Once an agenda (currently in the form of the Children and Young People's Plan) has been agreed, the Local Partnership must have the tools at its disposal to ensure that it is delivered. This is not the place to attempt to establish organisational arrangements for the Local Partnerships, except to remark that the challenge is to avoid unnecessary bureaucracy while creating an entity that can function independently of the various agencies of which it is constituted. A lean organisation is called for which does not duplicate what already exists in the constituent agencies. At the same time, the Local Partnership as an organisation must have the responsibility for agreeing the agenda or plan between its constituent bodies and have the power to require it to be delivered. As it was put to me (referring to Children's Trusts), 'There is a need to turn a good, soft partnership-working model into a decision-making body, driving the integration agenda and setting priorities for spending to meet local needs'.[88] Equally, this is not the place to speculate in detail about how Local Partnerships should be managed and held to account. However, it is obvious that the Local Partnership must have clear arrangements for governance and accountability, and that these must be worked out to fit in with national structures and approaches to accountability as they develop (for example, those relating to the NHS Commissioning Board, the public health service, and the relationship between national and local government), including proper financial accountability for funds provided to Local Partnerships by national government.

4.41 Importantly, Local Partnerships must also incorporate suitable arrangements to ensure that there is local accountability to the public. This may be through links to the democratic accountability of Local Authorities, the proposed introduction of democratic accountability in the NHS, or another mechanism. The key point is that the Partnership must ensure that there is some way in which it is accountable to the people it is there to serve.

Recommendation 5: The Local Partnership must establish mechanisms to ensure that there is local accountability to the public.

Recommendation 6: The Local Partnership must have the power to require that a Children and Young People's Plan is drawn up and implemented.

[88] View submitted at a meeting with senior officials in Hammersmith and Fulham Council.

4.42 As regards health and healthcare, the Local Partnership should undertake a systematic examination of the needs of the population falling within its responsibility. This must be done using appropriate analytical tools, not least by segmenting or profiling the population in terms of their respective needs, particularly identifying those most in need. Then there must be an analysis of how resources should be allocated to reflect the picture identified. This will inevitably involve examining how resources are currently spent, so as to make necessary adjustments. Such adjustments will make the health service itself and its interaction with other services more efficient. Throughout these processes, the views of local healthcare professionals are of the greatest importance and must be heard. Not only are they experts in what may be needed and how it can best be delivered, but they must see the Local Partnership as an arrangement that they can buy into, in that it shares their concerns for the welfare of children and young people. The local healthcare professionals must be engaged in all matters, policy, governance and the commissioning of services, and at all levels. Only if they are will the integration of the NHS's services into a wider set of services be possible. And this integration is essential if all services are to be aligned to meet the common goal of securing the welfare of children and young people.

Recommendation 7: The Local Partnership's plan must set out the agenda for children and young people's health and healthcare.

Recommendation 8: The Local Partnership's plan must integrate the agenda for children and young people's health and healthcare into the overall plan for all the services that the Local Partnership is responsible for providing, so as to ensure that a holistic approach to the care and welfare of children and young people is adopted.

4.43 Given the intrinsic limits on resources and the constrained fiscal times ahead, local organisations will have to take a number of tough decisions with regard to priorities in investment and spending. A Local Partnership bringing together all local public services is an ideal vehicle for making these decisions for at least two reasons. By being wholly focused on the concerns of children and young people, the Partnership can ensure that their voices are heard as priorities are determined. Indeed, it would be an advantage to take a further step by seeking to ensure that there is some mechanism to enable the Local Partnership, in its structure, to be broadly representative of the community served, so that there will be a degree of local democratic legitimacy in decisions, something which may be said to be lacking currently, as regards primary care trusts (PCTs). In particular, the Local Partnership should be required to devise and operate mechanisms through which children and young people's voices can be heard and appropriately acted upon.

Recommendation 9: The Local Partnership must create structures whereby the views of children and young people can be sought and taken account of in the planning and delivery of health and healthcare services.

4.44 Secondly, by being an organisation bringing together all relevant public services, the holistic approach to the welfare and well-being of children and young people, seen as so important by so many, will be the prevailing cultural approach. Then, once the needs of the children and young people for whom it is responsible are identified, the Local Partnership must ensure that they are provided for in an efficient and effective manner. To do so, the Partnership must have the requisite information. I shall explore these and other points in what follows.

4.45 I recognise that the localism represented by this approach invites the danger of structural atomisation: too many small organisations literally cluttering up the landscape. For reasons of size and because of the fact that networks and pathways of care will often transcend boundaries of a Local Partnership, it will be imperative that the Partnerships develop ways of co-operating in groups, whether on a permanent or an ad hoc basis. Such groupings, and the need for and nature of collaborative action, must be reflected in Local Partnerships' thinking about the services they themselves are organising, including the commissioning of services across a number of Partnerships where this is appropriate. Localism will, on this basis, be achieved, but not at the expense of atomising services. Moreover, localism in this form will provide the necessary space for local action and initiative which Government historically has been reluctant to grant.[89]

How Local Partnerships Can Take the Agenda Forward

4.46 The fundamental benefit of using Local Partnerships as the vehicle for change lies in the fact that Partnerships would exist to put the interests of children and young people first. The Partnership would be the one organisation to bring together and co-ordinate all the public services that exist in the locality to provide for children and young people. These include the NHS, social services, education, police and, often overlooked but crucial, housing. Given that the problems that children and young people encounter are more often than not the product of the interaction of a variety of social forces, the response has to be equally multi-faceted.[90] For example, the family living in crowded, unsafe accommodation, in which no one has had gainful employment for several generations, and where a parent or carer is an alcoholic and the children are the

[89] It was put to me by one senior official that the further one gets from central control, the fewer the levers available to government, so the ones available become very critical – enter the Operating Framework.

[90] The young women who were the clients of the Family Nurse Partnership (FNP) programme in Tower Hamlets encountered significant problems with housing, education and employment and in claiming benefits. The FNP programme works with a range of hostels for the homeless, bed and breakfast accommodation, hotels and agencies such as Street Matters, an agency that safeguards young women at risk of sexual exploitation.

victims of violence and neglect, is a family whose needs have to be addressed. They are the ones who appear in A&E departments, who become teenage parents, who suffer from a variety of mental health problems, who are excluded from schools, who are most frequently mugged or stabbed. If their needs are not addressed, another generation will emerge to repeat the cycle, at huge cost to them and to society.

4.47 Responsibility and accountability for implementing the Local Partnership's plan should lie with the Partnership itself, rather than with its constituent organisations. The Partnership will then assign to the various services their objectives. These will be managed by the particular service but in a collaborative way. The services will report to and be held responsible by the Partnership. Not only will this ensure that each service knows and understands what the others are doing, but it will also require services to co-operate with each other in the achievement of the overall aims as established by the Partnership. Indeed, this is one aspect of the overall leadership provided by the Partnership that is particularly worth mentioning here: that the cultural barriers which have been described as existing between those providing various services will have to break down. The leaders of the various services will regularly come together around the same table. They will have to do business with each other.[91] Moreover, and critically important in terms of the culture of the services provided, the complexity of the services and their interaction will have to be addressed. The particular complexity of the NHS must be an early focus of attention. Its habitual organisation around buildings and the working practices of professionals, particularly doctors, will have to be replaced by a real commitment to designing and delivering services around the needs of children and young people. No longer will their care, health and welfare depend on their choosing the right door to gain access to an otherwise impenetrable service.

4.48 An extension of this comprehensive overall leadership is the benefit of co-location. This was cited on numerous occasions as a critical step in breaking down the cultural barriers that get in the way of services working together. The benefits include allowing discussions to be organised more easily, and hence decisions to be taken more quickly. Co-location also helps organisations to build trust through increased contact with each other.[92] Thus, both managerially and in terms of the design and delivery of services, to the extent that it can be achieved, services, or elements of them, should be co-located. It should be one of the Local Partnership's most important goals that wherever co-location would deliver better services it should become a reality, given the benefits that flow from it.[93]

[91] One model worth considering is as follows. The leaders of the relevant services should serve as members of the Local Partnership, and thus be involved in the determination of the plan. They should then meet regularly themselves as leaders to co-ordinate the actions required to implement the plan. These actions will then be taken by the various organisations.

[92] I saw evidence of this in action in Hammersmith and Fulham and in Croydon, and was told of plans in a number of other places to adopt it as a policy.

[93] Co-location is identified as 'a major factor' in promoting integrated working in the report of Barnardo's policy research unit (February 2010). The unit also identifies as 'factors that promote integrated working', 'understanding the role of other professionals … regular contact/communication … compatible information-sharing systems …' and 'strong commitment to change'. I gratefully draw on these in what follows.

4.49 Given the fact that the new Government has yet to publish its White Paper on health and healthcare, it is not yet clear what form Local Partnerships could take at local level, nor how the local NHS which they will have to interact with will be organised. Whatever final organisational landscape emerges, it is vital that Local Partnerships play the role that I have outlined, and that they operate under the principles that I have set out here: a holistic focus on children and young people and their needs; a duty to ensure that local organisations work together; accountability to the public; an emphasis on efficiency; and the active involvement of children and young people. These must be the basic principles by reference to which services for children and young people are organised. They are a necessary, if not sufficient, condition of making services better for children and young people.

Recommendation 10: The Local Partnership must operate according to the following principles:

- **There should be a holistic focus on children and young people.**
- **There should be a duty to ensure that local organisations work together.**
- **There should be appropriate ways of ensuring accountability to the public.**
- **There should be an emphasis on efficiency in the provision of services.**
- **Children and young people should be actively engaged and involved.**

Local Partnerships and Funding

4.50 I have proposed earlier that the funds for the health and healthcare of children and young people should be separated from those funds spent on adults (with proper attention to the period of transition). I now propose that these funds should be made available to Local Partnerships to be spent in accordance with their local agenda and plans.

Recommendation 11: The funding of health and healthcare services, and all other services for children and young people, must reflect and give effect to the Local Partnership's agenda and plan.

4.51 Two important consequences flow from this. Firstly, it means that each service must manage its funds to achieve the goals set for it. And since some of those goals will be specifically designated as goals shared with other particular services or with all of them, the funds must to that extent be shared with or incorporated into the funds of these other services. One device for achieving this is to pool budgets. This may not be necessary (or even desirable sometimes).[94] What is necessary is the need to embrace a

[94] Audit Commission, *Means to an End: Joint financing across health and social care* (London: Audit Commission, 2009).

cultural approach to funding which says that the purpose of the service's funding is to achieve the best possible result for the children and young people served. It is not any service's private cash, to protect and guard against what are seen as the predations of others. It must serve the holistic goal which is the basis of the new culture being put forward.

4.52 This objective will be that much easier to achieve if the policies that guide decisions emanate from only one department of state rather than, until recently, two which do not always see eye to eye. I recognise that, currently, decisions of particular organisations reflect, to an extent, the regime of performance management and regulation that they exist under. If they are required by a regulator to do something, they will tend to do that something. In the future, therefore, performance management and regulation must also be aligned towards facilitating collaboration.

4.53 The second important consequence is that this approach will produce savings. Indeed, as I have indicated, the pursuit of efficiencies must be a major objective of every Local Partnership.

4.54 The savings will take a number of forms. Duplication of action, whereby different services involve themselves with children and young people in different ways at different times in an unco-ordinated and unsystematic way to address aspects of the same issue, will be eliminated. Priorities will be agreed across services so that funds spent by one will not be wasted because of the lack of support by another. Efficiency will be improved through greater clarity over what is to be done and who is to do it. And, as I will set out in more detail later, the Local Partnership's focus on well-being will enable concerted action by all services in the promotion of well-being, the prevention of ill-health and social harm, and the early intervention of services to build the capacity of children to be healthy and resilient. This focus will pay dividends, among them financial dividends, in future years. The financial burden borne by the state in addressing the demands placed on the NHS, the benefits system and the criminal justice system because of the failure to take early action will be reduced.[95] And, make no mistake, this financial burden dwarfs, and has dwarfed for decades, the cost of investing in the health and well-being of children and young people. A further benefit arising from using a Local Partnership as the agency to orchestrate the delivery of services lies in its role in commissioning (purchasing) and providing services. I will set out the details later, but it is important to make some general points here.

4.55 One of the most important advantages of the Local Partnership, as detailed above, is that it has the ability to bring together staff from different public service organisations, to co-ordinate their actions and focus them around the needs of children and young people. Once these organisations have come together to plan what is needed, they should continue to work together in commissioning the services. This will ensure that the benefits of joint commissioning, including not only the reduction of duplication and inefficiency as services overlap but also the co-ordination of services for mutual benefit, are spread across the full range of services, for the maximum benefit of children and young people.

[95] See paragraphs 3.52 and 3.59 for estimates of this burden in the context of mental health.

4.56 The commissioners within the Local Partnership will not just be concerned with healthcare. The team will also consist of those responsible for commissioning the various other services provided locally for children and young people. There will, therefore, be a single, integrated team of commissioners. This is the point of breakthrough for the new holistic approach, and a radical departure for the NHS. There will be a single team of commissioners for all services for children and young people, with a single person responsible for delivering the common agreed agenda as regards those services.[96]

Recommendation 12: The Local Partnership should have a dedicated team drawn from NHS commissioning organisations, Local Authorities and elsewhere, which is responsible for commissioning all services, including health and healthcare services, for children and young people.

4.57 Whatever configuration Local Partnerships take, one of their most important objectives must be that, in relation to health and healthcare, the needs of children and young people must no longer be swamped by the claims made on NHS commissioners (whatever form they end up taking) for services for adults. And, as I have already said, healthcare professionals from across the range of NHS services, particularly general practice, but also the acute sector and community services, must engage and be engaged in the commissioning of services. In this way, commissioning by reference to the pathways of care taken by children and young people, so crucial if services are to be well delivered, can be properly reflected and orchestrated. Furthermore, the historic weakness in the commissioning of NHS services for children and young people will be remedied by the active engagement of healthcare professionals, working alongside other professionals.

4.58 The commissioning of services from the NHS will sit alongside (literally and figuratively) the commissioning of all the other services for children and young people. The connections and interactions of the various services can be choreographed so as to make them truly complementary. Savings in terms of greater efficiency, early intervention and the avoidance of duplication will be immediately realised.

Recommendation 13: The commissioning of all services, including those of the NHS, called for by the Local Partnership's agenda and plan must be carried out in such a way as to ensure that the services are complementary and efficiently delivered.

4.59 Turning now to the provision of services, how is this to be organised? Given the need to envisage services holistically, it is important to avoid compartmentalising the services provided by the NHS in the way that they are currently conceived of, divided

[96] I was told by senior officials in Hammersmith and Fulham Council that this bringing together of all commissioning of local services under a single director has 'for the first time, vitalised the joint agenda in a way that nothing else has so far achieved'.

between tertiary, secondary, primary and community care. And the interaction between the NHS's services and those of other public sector agencies must equally be organised to maximise their integration and co-operation, rather than, as now, the opposite. What this means in essence is that the providers of services should respond to the needs of those commissioning them.[97] Providers must, therefore, ensure that children and young people are looked after by the right people in the right place at the right time. I will spell out what this means in more detail in what follows. In general terms, it means that the services provided by hospitals must be inextricably linked to and integrated with those provided through community services and then also with general practice and with those provided by other public services.

Changing the NHS

The Low Profile of Children

4.60 One of the immediate effects of vesting policy in the hands of a single department or branch of government is that the profile of children and young people will rise. No longer will they be left to compete on unequal terms for attention with adults on whom the large majority of the present DH's funding is currently spent. Rather, they, their interests and needs will be the sole and specific concern of an influential group of policy-makers. All those fighting a difficult and currently unsuccessful war on behalf of children will be brought together. They will find themselves alongside colleagues with the same interests working to the same goal. They will thereby increase both the co-ordination between themselves and their overall influence in the making of policy, for instance as the NHS Board and its role in commissioning services develops.

The Complexity of the NHS as a Provider of Services and its 'Atomisation'

4.61 Caring for children is often complex, requiring the involvement of a number of organisations and professional groups. For example, children with long-term conditions such as asthma, epilepsy, or diabetes may have their care managed by a children's community nurse specialist, with contributions and support from paediatricians, the school health team and their GP. In many cases, those providing NHS services must also work with other organisations, for example schools, social services or the police, as I will explore in greater detail later. Treating children and young people can be more complex, and therefore more expensive, than providing equivalent care for adults. For example, children undergoing painful procedures may require play or distraction therapy in addition to their clinical care. They may require specialist equipment, or staff with specialist training, as will young people with long-term conditions.

4.62 Services often fail to take sufficient account of this complexity. The services for children and young people suffer because proper account is not taken of the difficulty

[97] The experience of the NHS organisations I talked to in Newcastle was that organisations providing services arrange what they do and their priorities around the needs and priorities of the Children's Trust. They recognised that it was in their organisational interest to do so.

of planning and commissioning them, as provision must often be co-ordinated along pathways that cross a number of services and settings. The following map of the 'delivery chain' for services aimed at reducing obesity in children and young people is illuminating.

Figure 4.1 Organisational relationships and funding flows for tackling childhood obesity – a complex picture

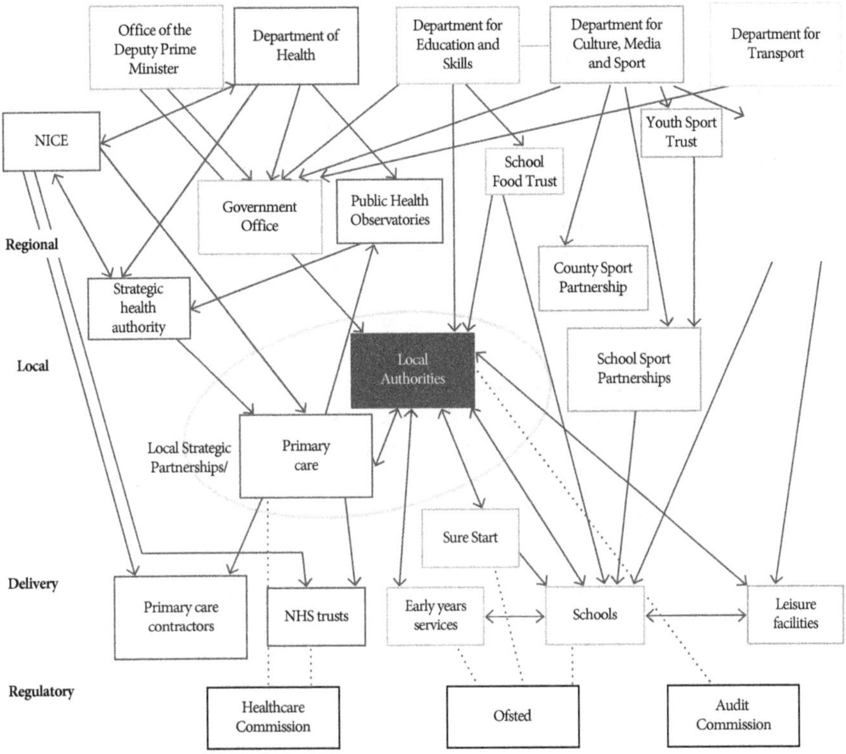

4.63 This complexity also causes problems financially, as additional services, necessary for high-quality care, add further costs. Services such as those provided by play therapists or youth workers are therefore at constant risk of cost-cutting. They are not seen as contributing to clinical outcomes, but this is to fail to appreciate that the child's overall experience of care and treatment is a very important outcome of care.[98]

4.64 The complexity of the NHS, therefore, as seen both from the inside and the outside, is a major barrier to offering the services that children and young people need and deserve. From the inside it is justified, or at least explained, on the basis that medical care is complex, as are patients. Professionals learn their way around it and become like guerrilla fighters, beating the system on behalf of their patients. From the outside, it is seen as representing a challenge which frequently frustrates the efforts

[98] Lord Darzi, in his report *High Quality Care for All*, identified the experience that patients have of their care as being of central importance in measuring the quality of care provided.

of other professionals.[99] The premise for the future must be that the NHS is there for children and young people, rather than that the child or young person is there for the service. This means that the complexity must be addressed and managed. It means that current ways of working must change both from the inside and the outside.

4.65 The starting point must be a network of arrangements. Ordinarily, there should be one point of contact at the centre of the network. The obvious candidate is the general practice. This would have a number of consequences, all of which reflect cultural habits of the past that must be left behind. First, the practice must be accessible. This means that a service must be available around the clock which meets the needs of children and young people. This cannot, of course, mean that each general practice must be open. That would be too expensive and totally inefficient. But we cannot continue to tolerate the existing arrangements whereby, in the absence of real alternatives, children, young people and their parents and carers opt for the A&E department. This is equally too expensive and inefficient. What is needed, therefore, is a better, more efficient system than that which currently exists. And, in discussing what it might be, it is important to draw attention to a cultural barrier which has recently emerged to bedevil efforts to provide services for children and young people. I refer to the concept of 'out-of-hours' services, an expression that owes its origins to an agreement reached between GPs and DH. Leaving aside criticisms of the services that are provided, the concept is bewildering. It is so utterly focused on the world, the needs and concerns of the professional. Children, young people and their parents/carers do not understand the notion of being ill or needing help 'out of hours'. They recognise the idea of the routine and the unusual. And the unusual happens when it happens. And help is needed when it happens.

4.66 So, something needs to be done as regards services currently described as 'out of hours'. I recognise that change will not be easy. But the need is pressing and a solution is needed, even if the mechanism for reaching that solution is not clear. Access to the services provided by general practice (or some form of polysystem[100]) must be available at all times. And since such access must form part of the agenda and plans drawn up by a Local Partnership, the Partnerships themselves must have a role in making it happen in the case of children and young people. Whether this is achieved through a grouping or a federation of general practices, through greater use of NHS Direct, or through some other means must be resolved as a matter of urgency. I am aware that discussions are currently taking place to introduce arrangements whereby GPs' practices will commission services that will provide necessary services at all hours for seven days a week, perhaps, where necessary, through groups or a federation of practices. Whatever the approach adopted, change is long overdue and essential if children and young people and their parents and carers are to get access to care and advice when they need it.

4.67 Being accessible also refers to the physical location of the general practice. General practices have been established in schools and children's centres. They could be

[99] See paragraph 3.51 for evidence of the difficulty which the complexity of the NHS causes for the police.

[100] Polysystems are described by Hammersmith and Fulham Council as 'a network of primary and community clinicians providing an extended range of care; including many treatments currently carried out in hospitals. They are supported by a hub, the polyclinic or general practice, and provide services from GPs' surgeries, health centres, pharmacies and patients' homes [and from] schools, children's centres and leisure centres'. They are described as being 'at the heart of the transformation of health services' in the area.

'branch offices' of a larger practice co-located in such a way as to offer services without exposing other children and young people in the school or children's centre to infection. Such developments are essential. Of course I recognise that, in rural areas, the principle holds good, but more creative ways will have to be employed to deliver it efficiently. But such developments reflect what I see as a central cultural shift: that the service comes to the user, rather than the other way around.

4.68 What is contemplated is a single point of access, open at all times, at which the child or young person, with a parent or carer or alone, is assessed and routed to the most appropriate professional, whether nurse, counsellor or doctor, for the most appropriate treatment, wherever it is best provided.

Recommendation 14: There should be a single point of access to the NHS's services for children and young people. This should be through general practice or the hub of some form of polysystem.

4.69 Secondly, the general practice must be at the hub of the network of services that the Local Partnership, taking account of the views of all those organisations providing services in the area, has determined are necessary. Thus, for example, the various services provided by secondary care must be accessible to the general practice. There must be a point of contact so that the general practice and the child or young person can negotiate their way through the hospital element of the network. The general practice will take on a more positive role: not so much the 'gatekeeper' of the past, more the 'navigator' of the future. The same requirement of a point of contact must exist as regards other parts of the network, whether it is maternity services, health visiting, the school health team, the care of those with long-term conditions or of the disabled, or the care of those with mental health problems. The general practice has a particularly important role, as the hub of a network of services, to ensure that the services are sustainable over time. I was advised of the need for a critical mass of services and professionals, particularly in any network of hospital services. It is therefore essential that, when considering networks of care, Local Partnerships take into consideration the different geographical areas and distribution of populations so as to ensure that various networks are organised effectively and efficiently, and that services are commissioned and co-ordinated accordingly.

Recommendation 15: The services provided by general practice or a polyclinic should be accessible, available at all times, and at the centre of a network of NHS services for children and young people.

4.70 A critical feature of being the hub, whether it is the traditional general practice or some other mechanism within a polysystem, is the control of information. As has been seen, the weakness in sharing information among those coming into contact with the child or young person is one of the most serious shortcomings in the NHS's care of children and young people. The solution lies in ensuring that information is received at one central point and is then available to those whose work brings them into contact with the child or young person.

Recommendation 16: Information about the care of children and young people must be collected and consolidated at the central point of access, the general practice or the hub of some form of polysystem, and be available to all who provide services for children and young people.

4.71 There will be all sorts of objections raised, including the perennial concerns over confidentiality and cost. I will return to these later, but make the following observations here. I have seen a system in place in Croydon's Family Justice Centre in which a room full of paper records, supplemented by electronic equivalents, is open to all professionals working in the particular unit (concerned with domestic violence and safeguarding children). The professionals included doctors, social workers, lawyers and the police. What made the system work was trust between the professionals and leadership. Confidentiality was a given, but so was the recognition of the need to share information in the interests of those being served.

4.72 As regards cost, again the observation can be made that the cost of not collecting information and sharing it according to strict protocols is the mess that currently afflicts how we respond to the needs of children and young people. This mess is far more costly than investing in collecting information, both in human and financial terms. It did not need the most recent horror story of Peter Connelly[101] to tell us this. We already knew. But cultural proclivities to defend professional territories and see information as power have meant that doing the obvious has been defeated by doing the obdurate. This cannot go on.

4.73 Of course, some general practices are already far advanced in their systems for sharing information with hospitals and others. Their experience will serve as the basis for building an approach across the whole of the country. Such an approach needs action. And clearly there will be a cost to the general practice in having the responsibility of collecting and sharing information. I propose that there should be a dedicated information officer in every general practice or group of practices, or at the hub of a polysystem.

Recommendation 17: There should be a dedicated information officer in general practices or at the hub of polysystems responsible for the collection, co-ordination and dissemination of information about the care and welfare of children and young people in the relevant area to those providing services and who need to know. This information should ordinarily be made available to children and young people, and their parents and carers. The information officer should also be responsible for managing communication with children and young people and their parents and carers.

[101] Also known as Baby Peter.

4.74 The benefits in terms of efficiencies that would flow from having an information officer significantly outweigh the costs. Moreover, I propose that the information should ordinarily also be made available to the children and young people, and their parents and carers. To take just one simple example, as I have already said, I heard frequent stories from parents/carers and young people of being asked to go to this and then that place for this or that appointment or test. Oftentimes, they found themselves in the same place on a number of separate occasions. Sometimes, they arrived only to be told that they were not expected or that relevant documentation was missing. On other occasions, they missed appointments because of poor communication, and found themselves criticised for doing so. This is not a service fit for the 21st century. It is a form of bureaucratic purgatory, which professionals lament but preside over. They do not wish it to happen. So, let them work together to stop it. The information officer is an important step and the cost would be readily recouped.

4.75 The third point to make is that those in the general practice must have the necessary training and skills to carry out the role that I envisage.[102] This means that all GPs and practice nurses in particular, but also all those other professionals attached to general practice or who form part of the polysystem, must be enabled to make up the gaps in training which I have already referred to. Both initial training and revalidation should include the comprehensive care of children and young people, as should the Quality and Outcomes Framework. Moreover, a general practice should seek to ensure that one GP in the practice has specialised knowledge in this area of care. Such care should, in other words, be a recognised professional pathway, leading, perhaps, to joint appointments between the general practice or polysystem and the hospital. Given that training takes time, in the short term paediatricians from the hospital sector and community paediatricians should be available to general practices or polysystems to provide the necessary service, delivering more care closer to home.

Recommendation 18: All GPs, practice nurses and other professionals attached to general practice or who form part of a polysystem should, as a matter of urgency, receive training in the comprehensive care of children and young people.

Recommendation 19: The initial training for GPs, the Quality and Outcomes Framework and the system of revalidation should all incorporate the need for training in the comprehensive care of children and young people.

Recommendation 20: General practices and those at the hub of polysystems should seek to ensure that there is at least one professional who has specialised knowledge in the comprehensive care of children and young people.

[102] One challenge for general practice is to recognise that the inclination to care for children and young people as a member of the family must not prevent the identification of dysfunctional families in which the parent/carer constitutes a risk to the welfare of the child because of alcohol or substance abuse or violence.

4.76 The purpose of the hub is to ensure that the complexity of the NHS confronted by the child, young person or parent/carer is diminished. But complexity takes many forms and it will require concerted effort to eliminate it. One form is the extraordinarily complex systems for organising care, particularly within the hospital sector, but also as between hospitals and other parts of the NHS. Departments of this and that exist. Sub-departments or new departments spring up. The language to describe departments is technical and obscure and excludes people, e.g. cardiac rather than heart, renal rather than kidney. The patient confronts a maze, which sometimes even someone in the hospital may not know how to negotiate. Equally, organisations on the outside, trying to advance the interests of children and young people, complain that it is difficult to get to grips with the system so as to know whom to talk to.[103]

4.77 One particular feature of the complexity of the NHS is its organisation of services according to the conditions that they treat or the interventions that they provide. As conditions and services are categorised, and thereby differentiated, they become atomised, separated from one another. This process of categorisation or atomisation is then extended to and imposed on patients. They are labelled according to their condition, becoming the 'responsibility' of a particular specialism. A major reason for this is the continuing 'institution-based' view of the NHS, which, as I have already said, defines services around buildings, particular procedures, or professional groups, rather than around the people who use them. And the view is often reinforced by public and political rhetoric: 'hospitals' are the symbol of, and the synonym for, health services more widely.

4.78 This imposition of bureaucratic organisation on services has the obvious consequence of imposing an anti-holistic categorisation on the children and young people who use them. Young people told me how they felt dehumanised and 'defined by their condition', and that this categorisation by condition led to pressure to 'live up to their diagnosis' by conforming to received medical opinion of how those with a particular condition should behave.

4.79 This can be particularly damaging when a child or young person has multiple needs. The fact that many disabled children often receive very poor service from GPs can be seen as partly resulting from their being perceived as 'belonging' to the specialty that deals with their disability and therefore outside the concern of other clinical groups. As The Newcastle upon Tyne Hospitals NHS Foundation Trust put it:[104]

> '[P]atients know that when they seek help … they are using the national health service. What they are often unaware of is that it is made up of separate elements which have differing policies and practice and hence can communicate ineffectively with each other, duplicate work and in certain respects compete'.

4.80 This need not be. As I have suggested, there must be a system of points of contact that can guide the general practice, the polysystem, the child or young person, and the outside organisation to what is needed. That is what service is about. Children

[103] See paragraph 3.51.
[104] Newcastle upon Tyne Hospitals NHS Foundation Trust, *Better together* (2010).

and young people need to be under one umbrella with fewer points of access. The many departments and other accretions of hospital life need to be addressed and simplified. The key to this simplification is to identify the pathway of care that children and young people should (rather than currently do) follow, both in and out of the hospital.

4.81 This process of rethinking how services are organised and delivered will not be easy for organisations or professionals.[105] Both tend to prefer the familiar and respond to the exercise of local muscle. But it is essential if children and young people's needs are to be met. And it can be done. Clear pathways of care for children are essential to avoid the risks of fragmentation of services. There is a need for networks to ensure that, where possible and appropriate, care is delivered close to home, including in primary and community care settings, but delivered in highly specialist centres if clinically necessary. The networks are more effective if formalised and managed. Examples can be found in areas such as newborn care, palliative care and children's surgery but there is a need to focus on wider aspects of children's care too including urgent care. Manchester Children's Hospital is developing these networks alongside their redevelopment proposals as is Newcastle[106] and there are examples to be found in most regions. However, a more comprehensive approach needs to be taken.

4.82 I have left till last two further aspects of complexity which should not be overlooked. First, there is in my view a barely detected epidemic of mental health problems in young people.[107] For a variety of reasons, an important one being the fear of stigma, these young people may not be prepared to see general practice as the natural place to go to seek advice and help. Services should ensure that the young person has another door into the system. One such door is through the school health team. It was put to me strongly that children's nurses with particular skills in mental health care, in the prevention of problems and in early intervention could make a significant contribution to addressing the hidden epidemic. Working alongside teachers, and beginning in primary schools, they could reduce the numbers of those subsequently needing CAMHS. Another door is through self-referral. The young person must be made aware and be confident that self-referral to appropriate providers of services, which may include suitably configured general practice, is possible. Self-referral also has implications for those

[105] More information on pathways and networks for the care of children and young people, including an analysis of the challenges to changing services successfully, is available in Royal College of Paediatrics and Child Health, *A guide to understanding pathways and implementing networks* (London: RCPCH, 2006).

[106] In *Better together*, Newcastle upon Tyne Hospitals NHS Foundation Trust writes: 'We seek to once and for all bring about a cohesive pathway of care for patients [all patients including children and young people] from home to hospital and home again. The decision as to how and where to treat patients will be based on their needs and preferences … to ensure that they are seen by the right person, with the right information, the right training, the right equipment, in the right place at the right time.'

[107] See, for example, the report of Barnardo's policy and research unit (February 2010). The report draws attention to groups of children and young people at particular risk: 'Looked-after children are around five times more likely to have a psychiatric disorder than the general population … At least 95% of young offenders … in one survey showed evidence of one or more of the main types of disorder, many facing multiple disorders.' The Royal College of Nursing described mental health as the biggest health priority for children and young people, with 1 in 4 showing some emotional and behavioural problems by the age of 8. I was told by a senior paediatrician that paediatricians need more training and experience in mental health. He described it as 'one of the biggest gaps in their current training.' Minor emotional problems were being left unaddressed and were having major effects later.

commissioning and providing services. They must ensure that the services are appropriately designed to meet the challenges of self-referral, not least as regards sharing information. The young person then needs help about where to go and how to do it. The voluntary sector has much to offer here.

Recommendation 21: Urgent action is called for to respond to the mental health needs of children and young people. Mental health services must be available and accessible, including through self-referral, and be integrated with other services, particularly through schools.

4.83 Secondly, there are those children and young people whom the system does not currently come into contact with, save in some emergency. They may be those living in areas of deprivation, or in some other way on the margins of society. Here, the critical importance of interaction between all the agencies that exist to meet the needs of children and young people so as to work together is most plain to see. Whatever the way in which the child or young person comes onto the radar of a public service and whatever the particular service may be, the information needs to be fed into the central hub, so that an assessment can be made as to whether the intervention of NHS services is required. Of particular significance here are programmes for early intervention which I shall discuss at length in due course. Of equal importance are those children and young people who come into contact with the criminal justice system. If ever there was a need for services to come together and work in an integrated fashion, it is here. The child or young person needs education and healthcare and has a range of other needs. If these are provided, there is the prospect of a better future. If not, the cycle of deprivation and damage goes on.

Commissioning

4.84 The approach that I have adopted places responsibility for commissioning services on the Local Partnership. In this way, children and young people are given the profile that they have historically lacked, since caring for them is the only responsibility that the Local Partnership has. Commissioning will reflect the Local Partnership's planning, and will therefore ensure that children and young people's health needs are integrated into and seen as part of their needs more broadly. No longer will we have the situation in which the PCT left it to juniors to look after commissioning for children and young people while their seniors wrestle with the important job of meeting the needs of adults. Nor will it be 'the loneliest job in the world'[108] as felt by one person responsible for commissioning services for children and young people. Instead, commissioners of healthcare services, with their colleagues from other services, will be able to concentrate on and specialise in services for children and young people. Admittedly, there will still be priorities to be argued out, but the argument will only be about what is most needed for children and young people and what best serves their needs. It will not be an

[108] Quoted in a meeting with senior officials.

argument, in the case of health and healthcare, about the respective needs of children, young people and adults, in which children and young people always come off worse.

4.85 Secondly, commissioning can adopt and drive forward a holistic approach to the needs of children and young people.[109] Currently, the lack of experience and expertise in commissioning in health and healthcare for children and young people stifles the integration of services. Lacking both the capability and the authority to bring together and shape services across pathways, commissioners are forced to purchase discrete packages of care from individual providers, resulting in a fragmented service. By buying services in this way, commissioners adopt and reinforce an anti-holistic language and outlook.

4.86 Moreover, commissioners currently often lack sufficient knowledge of the services that they are commissioning, and so are unable to challenge providers about the quality of the services, or about the integration of one service with others. Quality, therefore, becomes something determined by the local provider's offer rather than the commissioner's insistence. Nowhere is this more problematic than in relation to CAMHS, where both clinicians and managers with experience of providing care expressed concern about commissioners' knowledge, especially of specialist services.[110] For the future, as I have emphasised, local healthcare professionals in all sectors of the NHS will be intimately involved in commissioning services from the NHS.[111] Their understanding of what is needed and how it should be organised will be crucial. The consequence will be that the commissioning of various public services on the basis that they are integrated will, in turn, require that the services work in an integrated manner.

4.87 Thirdly, those charged with commissioning care should ensure that, through their contractual relationship and the volumes of funds at their disposal, they require of the various parts of the NHS that they work in the manner already described: designing services around children and young people, establishing a single portal of access, through the general practice or polysystem, identifying the normal pathways of care and requiring the collection, analysis and dissemination of information. This is what commissioning is about: buying only those services that serve the needs of the community for which the commissioner is responsible and ensuring that the services are both effective (they produce the right outcomes) and efficient (they provide value for money).

Recommendation 22: Those commissioning health services for children and young people should use their influence through commissioning, contracting and funding to require providers to design services around the needs of children or young people, establish a single portal of access, ensure that care is delivered in line with the normal pathway of care, and require the collection, analysis and dissemination of information.

[109] See RCPCH response to *Our NHS, Our Future*.

[110] One professional body commented that, in relation to CAMHS, 'Commissioners are usually inexperienced, junior, or lack clout'.

[111] Clinicians across primary, secondary and tertiary care should decide how to allocate a shared budget, working in close partnership with patients, managers and local politicians (RCPCH response to *Our NHS, Our Future*).

Leadership

4.88 Children need champions: strong leaders who will advance their interests at all levels in the NHS. I met many inspirational leaders, at all levels. However, within the NHS as a whole, leadership in the cause of children and young people is lacking. Senior staff are focused elsewhere, often on meeting the current priorities for performance management, which largely exclude children and young people. Clinicians who are advocates for children and young people often lack influence. Their lobbying for increasing the priority of care for children and young people has, to date, been broadly unsuccessful. Those caring for children 'are not the biggest players in the clinical system'[112] and are not well placed within professional hierarchies. They often lose out to other, more powerful, professional and patients' groups in the contest for resources and the attention of senior management. Designated members of trusts' boards, or champions on the board for children, are 'tokenistic, if they exist at all'.[113]

4.89 It should not be a surprise, therefore, that a recurring theme in the submissions made to me and in the meetings and conversations I have had is the need for effective leadership on behalf of children and young people. It is important to understand what is being said. It is not that there is a shortage of extremely dedicated and thoughtful advocates of the interests of children and young people, from Whitehall to local communities. Rather, it is to observe that, while they make telling arguments (and have been doing so for decades!), they get only limited attention. They are treated as some form of background noise: tolerated and occasionally thrown something, but not regarded as being where the action is in the NHS. As has been seen, a good illustration at the top of the system is the Operating Framework emanating from DH, which sets the direction of the NHS. The needs of children and young people have largely been ignored over the years. They barely feature in what is the managers' bible. Recently, some progress has been made but it is limited and largely rhetorical, its importance being stressed in narrative but without a link to specific actions or performance measures.[114] It does not go to the heart of what the NHS should be doing for children and young people. There seems to be a blithe unawareness or lack of interest in the fact that failure to attend to children and young people's needs just means another generation of adult patients bringing their problems, many of which could have been resolved or mitigated if addressed earlier on. Sisyphus continues, with increasing difficulty, to roll the stone up the hill.

4.90 A further illustration is provided by the establishment in 2009 by DH of the National Quality Board, to direct the production of standards relating to quality which are to be observed by the NHS. The first thing that the Board did was to set criteria which would guide the areas or conditions to be given priority in the production of standards. One of the two overarching criteria was identified as being the 'burden on the NHS' represented by any condition. Such a criterion immediately prevents the needs of children and young people from ever being given priority. They represent just less

[112] View submitted by an NHS senior manager.
[113] View submitted at a meeting with a professional body.
[114] See paragraphs 4.111–4.116 for an analysis of the current Operating Framework in relation to services for children and young people.

than 20% of the population, so the burden of the other 80% is clearly greater. That the burden on this 80% could be reduced by redirecting some attention here and now to children and young people did not register. The approach was centred on adults and the acute sector. Condition-spotting-and-swatting was again at centre stage. As policy is developed by government over the next months, it will be important to reflect on how efforts to establish priorities for the NHS as a whole risk discriminating against children and young people: another reason for separating them off, and the funding that relates to them. Leadership comes in many forms at all levels. For the purpose of this review, I detect the need for leadership in the cause of children and young people, meaning making something happen rather than saying something should happen, from the top to the bottom of the NHS. I have seen what inspired leadership can do, bringing professionals together, getting leaders of services round the same table, negotiating protocols with previously warring professional tribes, having the vision that a local school could become the focal point for a range of services for the health and welfare of a whole community struggling with disadvantage and deprivation.[115] Such charismatic leadership is inspiring but ultimately over-dependent on the energy and vision of one person or a small group. Leadership has to be sustained and sustainable.

4.91 It should be a duty of the Local Partnership, and one of its most important tasks, to create the environment in which leaders can flourish, realise their vision and bed in progress for the benefit of those who will inherit the vision. They have to be trusted and allowed to innovate (or even fail, if in the failure lessons are learned and acted upon). It is only through such innovation and experiment that the most important improvements in service for the future will be identified and implemented.

Recommendation 23: Local Partnerships should identify and foster leaders across the range of NHS services and give them the opportunity to flourish.

4.92 Such an approach to leadership seems strangely distant from the style of management in the NHS that was frequently described to me. It was put to me that managers, as leaders, 'managed up', meaning that they looked towards the centre of the system to be told what to do or to check that what was envisaged was alright, rather than feeling free to act for themselves, within acknowledged boundaries.[116] This was not peculiar to the NHS and, by association, DH. Those who worked within the ambit of DCSF/DfE looked with the same keen eye as to what was expected of them.

4.93 This looking to the centre produced at least two unfortunate consequences. First, having two departments of state with different agendas resulted in two sets of

[115] On my visit to St Stephen's Children's Centre in Newham (east London) I was shown a wide range of services, including therapy services (such as speech and language therapy), CAMHS, maternity services, family support services, childcare and parenting classes. The centre recognises its role as the hub of a local community in a deprived area where there are many people who would not normally have access to, or use, services. For this reason, they stress openness, approachability and friendliness.

[116] Paragraphs 4.111–4.124 (Priorities and management) explore this issue in more detail.

professionals sitting down to collaborate and finding that they are being asked to march together but to different tunes. Secondly, it produced an attitude of aversion to risk, to the use of judgement and to innovation. Nowhere is this clearer than in the case of safeguarding children and child protection. A system has been built based on what are called processes and on compliance with procedures. Leadership in the form of bringing teams together and placing the child at the centre of everyone's concerns struggles to prevail. Instead, there is a retreat behind compartmentalised professional walls, with everyone concerned to show that what is asked for by way of process and procedure has been done. It will surprise no one that the object of the exercise, the actual welfare of the child who may be at risk, may be overlooked from time to time.

4.94 Perhaps I should mention in passing two further unfortunate consequences. Firstly, it has been a feature of the NHS that it is constantly subject to reshaping and reorganising from the centre. As it was put to me on a number of occasions, continuity of relationships between professionals is vital in building good services for children and young people. Continuity allows trust between professionals to develop, a feature of which can be a healthy 'culture of challenge', as I saw in Sheffield and Leicester.[117] Reorganisations force new relationships on professionals, meaning that trust must be built anew. Good services can deteriorate very quickly when good people move on. Secondly, centrism, represented by the Operating Framework, national targets and the like, sits awkwardly with the call issued by Lord Darzi in his review of the NHS.[118] He called for innovation to be given its head at a local level. He was right, but tell that to the local manager or professional. The temptation to try something has to be resisted in the face of the imperative to produce a particular result in a particular timescale. The sound of cultures clashing rings out.[119]

4.95 Again, this must change. In the case of safeguarding and child protection, for example, there needs to be a rediscovery of the importance of content over form. Outcomes for children are the only things that matter. The Local Partnership has a central role in ensuring that those who lead those local agencies that could have a role in safeguarding work together and to a common vision. Most important, the Local Partnership and those organisations that make it up must realise that having a plan, or creating a partnership (so-called 'partnership-working'), are not ends in themselves, warranting congratulation and relaxation once created. They are mechanisms to do a job. Whether the job is done is the only measure of success. As it was put to me, in conversations with the police, the first responsibility of all partners is not to the partnership, but to the children and young people. Agencies and organisations must feel able to challenge each other. They must not resile from their duty out of concern to avoid straining relations in the partnership. Professionals are there for the children and young people, not the partnership.

[117] On a visit to Glenfield Hospital in Leicester, it was clear that the sense of support and understanding felt by the parents/carers of very sick babies was due in part to the fact that nurses and staff had worked together for a long time (over 20 years in one case) and trusted each other.

[118] Darzi, Lord, *High Quality Care for All: NHS Next Stage Review Final Report* (London: DH, 2008).

[119] I heard a counterview from a senior official in DH that localism was fine, but only if the right people were in place. Currently, it was said, the biggest risk is not that innovation will be squashed, but that poor practice would remain unchallenged. This ambivalence in policy and practice contributes to the malaise I am referring to.

4.96 More generally, as I will explore in the section on professionals working together, leadership rests on an understanding of how professionals of various stripes think and perceive the world; how they work together and why they do not. This argues for greater engagement of professionals as leaders. Too often they cast themselves, or are cast, as outsiders, put upon by 'the system'. This is an easy position to adopt, if the concern is one of tribal standing and purity. It fails children and young people, however. Professionals of all types need to re-engage with the mission that they chose: to serve children and young people. The system must allow them to do so.

Promoting Positive Health

4.97 The importance of preventing or mitigating ill-health and promoting good health is so obviously central to the NHS, if it is to be a 'health' rather than an 'illness' service.

4.98 In the case of children and young people, some success has been achieved in securing attention. 'Public health' is the one area in which the Operating Framework stresses the needs of children and young people. Obesity, teenage pregnancy and substance abuse are identified as areas for action by the NHS.[120] But there are significant gaps where the cultural bias of the NHS towards identifying itself with the diagnosis and treatment of disease induces a kind of myopia. Against this background, the new Government's intention to create an autonomous public health service provides both a significant opportunity and a challenge. The opportunity is to ensure that positive health has the focus and funding that I believe it requires. I set out my reasoning for this below. It is to be hoped that it can be achieved.

4.99 The challenge is that the creation of a public health service could see the NHS withdrawing further from the field of positive health and well-being. This must not be allowed to happen. One of the habitual features of the culture of the NHS until now has been to label the prevention of disease and promotion of health as 'public health' as a means of pushing it to the edges of the 'real' work of the NHS. There has been little or no tradition of adopting a model of positive health in which it is the job of the NHS to keep people, especially children and young people, out of hospital and surgeries as much as possible.[121] The savings in funds, in productivity gained, in benefits not needed have been calculated an incalculable number of times.[122] But the culture of the NHS just does not shift. Part of the answer lies in the attitudes of healthcare professionals, defining what people need as being what they provide: ever more technical skills. These skills are, of course, needed and have worked wonders. But, in the greater scheme of things, even greater wonders would be worked by emphasising the pursuit of positive health.

[120] There are Tier 2 Vital Signs in all of these areas. The obesity measure relates specifically to school-age children.

[121] *Our health, our care, our say* (2006) represented a step in the right direction in terms of policy from DH, albeit that little change in terms of results from the NHS followed.

[122] For example, see D Wanless, *Securing our Future Health: Taking a long-term view* (London: DH, 2002). See paragraph 3.59 for an estimate of the burden in the context of mental health.

4.100 Perhaps one explanation of why the NHS has never committed itself entirely to this cause is because it is clear that the NHS can do only a limited amount about what causes ill-health and what can prevent it. Housing, education, employment, social cohesion, even genes are some of the important ingredient factors. So, the NHS retreats into affecting what it can affect; responding to illness rather than seeking to prevent it, wherever and whenever possible.

4.101 It is for this reason that I propose that change at local level must be driven by a Local Partnership with representation from across the full range of relevant public services. The Partnership can call on the NHS, but can look beyond it. It can co-ordinate action by all agencies, including education, social services, housing and youth justice as well as the NHS. Currently, as I shall set out in more detail later,[123] not only is the NHS very limited in terms of what it can do, but it also has little incentive to work with others to provide the integrated services required. Firstly, the benefits of early intervention, for example, usually accrue some years in the future. This means that they are irrelevant to the in-year assessments of organisational performance that feature so significantly in the NHS. Secondly, many of the most significant interventions will primarily benefit organisations other than the NHS. For example, early intervention to tackle behavioural disorders is likely to produce significant long-term benefits in terms of savings in social care and the criminal justice system, but less obvious returns for the NHS.

4.102 The result is that the NHS adopts a range of unhelpful, inward-looking perspectives, focusing only on its particular place in the broader scheme of things. Such an approach would fall away if the services provided by the NHS for children and young people fell within the remit of a Local Partnership, as I have described it. It would be for the Partnership, rather than its individual constituent organisations, to assess overall benefit, and do so by reference to the collective agendas and funding of all the respective agencies. Moreover, ensuring that the views of children and young people themselves are heard, as I have set out earlier, together with appropriate mechanisms for accountability to the local community, will make a further contribution to this overall assessment of benefits. Individual organisations, as a consequence, will be drawn yet further from their narrow, institutional focus which has caused so many of the problems that I have described here.

4.103 As part of the Local Partnership's approach to securing the well-being of children and young people in their community, I would draw attention particularly to the areas of mental health and care in a child's early years. Mental health is significant here, because most adult mental health problems begin in childhood. Doing nothing to combat mental health problems in children and young people is not, therefore, the cheapest option. It is the most expensive option.

4.104 I also mention care in the early years because perhaps the single most important cultural shift that is needed from the NHS is to invest in the development of children in their early years (from minus 9 months to 2 or 3 years old). These early years are absolutely central to the developmental fate of a child. Yet until recently they have

[123] See paragraphs 4.114–4.115.

received virtually no attention. A huge cultural shift must take place. Resources must be invested in the early years of children, concentrating on those most at risk, whose parents/carers are least able to provide what the child needs.[124] To those who recoil at the possible cost, there is already evidence of the benefits in financial, let alone human terms.[125] And by investing significantly in early intervention, the cultural context of the discussion of children and young people moves from response to illness to the pursuit of well-being and resilience.

Recommendation 24: A significant shift in the allocation of resources must take place, whereby there must be much greater investment by the NHS, and other agencies, in services for children and young people in their early years, concentrating on those most at risk of not having the opportunity to flourish. Such investment should be a very important consideration for all Local Partnerships as they set their priorities.

4.105 Of particular interest in this context is the development of the Family Nurse Partnership (FNP) programme. In my visit to Tower Hamlets in east London, I was impressed by the energy and enthusiasm of those involved in developing one of the pilots. It is clear that FNPs are labour-intensive and would appear, on the surface, to be expensive. But if the results reflect those obtained in the United States, and there is already evidence to that effect,[126] the savings, as I have said, will be very significant indeed. In my view the introduction of FNP and other such schemes aimed at early intervention should be a priority for incorporation into Local Partnerships' planning. Equally, I was impressed by the thinking behind 'Total Place'.[127] While in its infancy, this initiative, by bringing together agencies across the locality, precisely reflects the position

[124] 'Disadvantage starts before birth and accumulates throughout life' and disadvantage leads to significant inequalities in health. The Marmot Review, *Fair Society, Healthy Lives: Strategic review of health inequalities in England post-2010* (2010) Executive summary, p 20.

[125] A range of evidence for early intervention is brought together in: DCSF, *Early Intervention: Securing good outcomes for all children and young people* (London: DCSF, 2010). See especially chapter 3.

[126] I have already mentioned the estimated benefits in relation to social care from the FNP programme in Tower Hamlets. In addition, the evaluation of the first year of FNP in the UK is promising, showing some positive evidence in areas such as smoking cessation, alcohol consumption, breastfeeding and healthy eating. It also showed that family nurses thought that the programme helped their clients to cope better with pregnancy, labour and becoming a parent (J Barnes, M Ball, P Meadows, J McLeish, J Belsky and the FNP Implementation Research Team, *Nurse-Family Partnership: First year pilot sites implementation in England. Pregnancy and the post-partum period* (2008)). Further research is currently being undertaken. The experience of Sheffield's Multi-Agency Prevention and Intervention Services also offers early evidence of savings, through, for example, reductions in teenage pregnancies and in substance abuse (correspondence with Children and Families Service). Evidence gained from operating programmes in the United States suggests that there are a number of positive effects on outcomes, including better maternal health, reduced numbers of accidents, increased readiness of children for school and increased employment. Individual studies also show significant benefits in relation to safeguarding and criminal justice.

[127] It is important to note that the policy behind the Total Place approach contemplates significant interaction between central government and local communities. As I remarked earlier (paragraphs 4.9–4.11), policy from central government sets the framework within which local action can take place, and to a degree, for example through the use of financial incentives, seeks to steer what that action may be.

that I am taking here, namely that the focus of services must be on children and young people in a particular area rather than on organisations or institutions. Intrinsic in the concept is that agencies come together to both plan and deliver services in an integrated manner.

4.106 At the same time, by concentrating on early intervention and its preventative effects, Local Partnerships will be able to avoid an overemphasis, in terms of the allocation of resources, on child protection, which, because of recent events and the risk-averse mentality produced, has tended to take an increasing slice of available funding. As one professional put it, current decisions about funding are not focused on early intervention: rather, 'the money follows the murders'.

4.107 Perhaps the strongest argument in favour of co-ordinating services through Local Partnerships is that early intervention can be made central to the overall vision of those commissioning and providing local services. The Local Partnership's sole mandate will be to care for the needs and interests of children and young people. The need to persuade managers in the NHS of the importance of early intervention falls away. In the prevailing culture in the NHS, preventative strategies and health promotion are at best poor relations; early intervention is barely on the radar of NHS managers (it was variously described as a 'luxury' and a 'hobby'). By contrast, Local Partnerships can place it at centre stage. And, given that early intervention is best delivered through the integrated efforts of schools, children's centres and community care, they will be able to focus on the prevention of illness through the variety of services that they offer to parents/carers and young children. I was greatly impressed by my visit to the children's centre in Croydon where I saw social workers working alongside a general practice and community nurses, with educational facilities available for both young children and their parents/carers. And the focus was not just on children. There was, in addition, a youth club catering to the needs of young people.

4.108 It is instructive to note the call issued by the former Children's Commissioner for England. Adopting the same approach that I set out here, he called for an 'ecological' approach to child maltreatment. He urged that focusing 'only on preventing maltreatment is less effective than a positive approach of building child-care skills, self-esteem and financial independence'. He went on: 'Many of the children at high risk of maltreatment grow up with multiple disadvantages: lack of vital preschool learning opportunities, behavioural problems, harsh inconsistent parenting, poor schools, food insecurity, unhealthy diet causing under-nutrition or obesity and dental disease, and an increased risk of illness and death from sudden infant death syndrome, infections, substance abuse, suicide and violent crime'.[128]

4.109 Perhaps the fact that is most overlooked regarding strategies about early intervention is the use they make of 'social capital'. Parents, grandparents, siblings and carers are drawn into the strategies and become active participants and agents for involving others, thereby, in turn, creating additional social capital. Properly understood and mobilised, this use of social capital not only saves money but also lays the foundation for

[128] A Aynsley-Green and D Hall, 'Safeguarding children: a call to action' (2008) 373(9660) Lancet 280–81.

a movement towards a healthier environment in which children and young people can grow up. Parents/carers talk to other parents/carers and a wider community of engagement develops. I saw, for instance, a simple example of exposing children and their parents/carers to a healthier diet in the children's centre in Croydon by recruiting mothers to make smoothies for their children using a variety of fruits. What appeared to be play was in fact an introduction to healthy eating. Using social capital produces social capital. Mobilising and drawing on the resources of families and the wider community in promoting the health and well-being of children and young people achieves results, and is extremely cost-effective.

4.110 This same thinking applies to schools. Properly understood, a school, particularly a primary school, is not an island. It is a community and part of a larger community. Schools can be used and at the same time reach out themselves to play a part in social affairs, from children's centres to criminal justice.

Recommendation 25: Local Partnerships should recognise the value of, and consider ways to promote, 'social capital', including involving families and the wider community in promoting health and well-being for children and young people.

Priorities and Management

4.111 Children and young people are identified as a priority for management in the NHS.[129] Yet the practice of performance measurement and management has not reflected this rhetoric, and it is to these practices that managers respond.[130] The NHS's key performance indicators, the Vital Signs, include (in 2010/11) seven (from a total of 63) which relate specifically to children and young people (including maternity care). However, none of them is in the most important 'tier one', to which the vast majority of management's attention and resources are devoted. Furthermore, five of the seven are 'public health' measures and therefore outside the mainstream of the NHS's attention.[131]

[129] DH/NHS, *The Operating Framework for the NHS in England 2010/11* (London: DH, 2009) pp 16–18.

[130] Senior NHS managers explained to me that they interpreted the Operating Framework in conjunction with performance management information and priorities (from strategic health authorities), and that from this a 'folklore' emerged about the NHS's 'real priorities'. One manager also quoted a Local Authority Chief Executive's view that the NHS's response to nationally-imposed priorities was 'awesome'. In a separate meeting, one senior NHS manager said that managers viewed the Operating Framework as their 'job description' and that they 'want[ed] to be told what to do'. Moreover, a senior official in Whitehall offered the view that managers follow the Operating Framework 'so slavishly' that there is no flexibility to respond to the needs or demands of any other organisation or group.

[131] The measures relating to children are: percentage of women who have seen a midwife or a maternity healthcare professional, for assessment of health and social care needs, risks and choices, by 12 completed weeks of pregnancy; under-18 conception rate per 1,000 females aged 15–17; obesity among primary school-age children; proportion of children who complete immunisation by recommended ages; percentage of infants breastfed at 6–8 weeks; effectiveness of CAMHS (percentage of PCTs and Local Authorities that are providing a comprehensive CAMHS); and parents' experience of services for disabled children. The last of these is a tier 3 indicator; all the others are tier 2.

4.112 The current approach represents a clear expectation, expressed through the chain of performance management, that fulfilling the priorities set out in the Vital Signs should take precedence over all other activity. The Operating Framework itself states that:

> '[O]rganisations need to be entirely driven by existing commitments and the NHS Vital Signs tiers 1 and 2'.[132]

4.113 Such a clear indication of priorities means that currently only the most accomplished managers will be able to devote any significant time to other commitments, including the broad range of services not mentioned in the Vital Signs that are needed to care for children and young people. The system is ripe for change. The new Government has this top-heavy centrism in its sights.

4.114 The conflict between rhetoric and reality, in terms of performance management, also applies to the NHS's collaboration with other agencies. It is a feature of the current approach to management and performance in the NHS that the Operating Framework treats the NHS, and encourages those in the NHS to regard themselves, as an island. The need for increased collaboration between the NHS and other services is stated explicitly in the Operating Framework and elsewhere. Indeed, in some cases this requirement to co-operate is enshrined in statute. Yet the performance measures against which PCTs are currently judged give little incentive to take this co-operation seriously.

4.115 Successful collaboration, when translated into effective, integrated services, can be expected to contribute towards the successful achievement of a number of important measures of performance. However, such collaboration does not make a direct and explicit contribution to the most important priorities of performance management. There has remained, therefore, an incentive for the NHS to neglect collaboration in favour of other priorities, which have been designated by the NHS as more important, and which are more wholly within the NHS's control. Funding spent on helping other agencies to achieve desired outcomes is money not spent on achieving outcomes for the NHS. And if money allocated to the NHS is not delivering for the NHS, in the island world of the NHS, this constitutes failure. And failure is to be avoided at all costs (of course, other public agencies fall victim to the same tendency). Performance management (and regulatory) systems, therefore, have reinforced the institution-based view of public services and discouraged collaboration and joint working. As I have said, for a variety of reasons this is particularly likely to disadvantage children and young people.

4.116 When children and young people are mentioned in the Operating Framework, it is in the context of reducing their admission to hospital.[133] This illustrates the narrow focus of the NHS's concern. It addresses the internal needs of the NHS as a system seeking to manage resources. It does not address what the NHS should do for children and young people so as to ensure that they are not admitted to hospital. The consequence is, as I have explained, that those who commission services for PCTs do not give great precedence to the needs of children and young people, driven as they are by the Operating Framework. This again must change.

[132] DH/NHS, *The Operating Framework for the NHS in England 2010/11* (London: DH, 2009) p 46.
[133] DH/NHS, *The Operating Framework for the NHS in England 2010/11* (London: DH, 2009) p 16, para 2.18.

Recommendation 26: The new Government, when considering changes to the performance management of the NHS, and in designing the mechanisms by which it should in future be held accountable, must ensure that the various organisations providing services at a local level are given incentives to work together, and that the performance management of individual public service organisations calls for and takes into account actions that produce positive outcomes for children and young people, the effect of which may be reflected as the achievements of other public services.

4.117 The principal mechanism for indicating what is expected of GPs, the Quality and Outcomes Framework, equally provides little incentive to GPs to give priority to the needs of children and young people. Of 128 indicators of quality, four refer specifically to children (one of which actually refers to antenatal care). There are 1,000 points in all that can be gained by the practice. These points translate into awards of money. Nineteen points relate to children and young people (six of which refer to antenatal care).

Recommendation 27: The Quality and Outcomes Framework should be reviewed so as to include a broad range of measures concerning the health, healthcare and welfare of children and young people.

4.118 The Local Partnership must use its commitment to integrated working in the interests of children and young people, whereby all organisations and agencies have to collaborate in achieving the Partnership's agenda and plan, so as to break the mould of the NHS's insularity. The approach to management and performance will reflect the plans agreed by all the agencies and managed by the Local Partnership. Children and young people will be the sole concern. They will not be an add-on extra or overlooked group.

4.119 Let me now touch on two matters of very great importance for the future management of performance. The first relates to data. Data in many areas of health and healthcare for children and young people is poor or non-existent. This must change. Data is necessary for effective management. It is also crucial for self-critical professional practice and for efficient commissioning. Data sets are currently being developed, that is, bodies of data that tell the story of performance and allow for setting benchmarks for the future. They have been extremely slow in coming, reflecting the low visibility of children's services. It has to be recognised that no self-respecting health service should find itself in the position of being unable in a number of areas of its activity to discover whether its performance is good, bad or indifferent when judged against national or international norms of performance. Data relating to maternity, care of the newborn, and of children and young people, including health promotion, safeguarding, acute care, longer-term conditions, disability and CAMHS, must be generated, used for analysis and published.

Recommendation 28: Data sets must be agreed as a matter of urgency by the NHS and government covering the range of services provided to children and young people by the NHS and data must be collected, analysed and disseminated to those who need it within the Local Partnership. The data must allow services to be held accountable for the quality of the outcomes achieved.

4.120 Secondly, data is only worth collecting and analysing if it is about what you want to know. What we need to know is whether the services provided for children and young people are of the appropriate quality. The indicators of successful performance are crucial. Historically, they have been expressed as targets or standards and there have been a large number. I propose that we depart radically from this past.

4.121 I propose that there should be only one indicator or criterion of successful performance: satisfaction with the service. The police have recently adopted a similar approach whereby, for the purpose of performance management, the culture of targets has been replaced by one single strategic objective: public confidence.[134] I substitute the notion of satisfaction for the notion of confidence, but they are broadly the same thing. The point is to focus the minds of those providing the service on meeting the legitimate expectations of those whom they are serving. There are at least two profound arguments in favour of adopting this single criterion of satisfaction. The first is that, although superficially it appears to limit the range of inquiry by being only a single criterion, in fact it achieves the opposite. This is because the concept of satisfaction effectively captures the whole range of factors that children and young people may bring to bear in assessing the quality of the outcome for them. This, in turn, will provoke an iterative process of research and discovery as to what it is that children and young people do in fact value in all of the environments in which they are cared for. Secondly, given this process of research and discovery, professionals will be drawn to, and wish to, meet the elements of satisfaction that are of importance to children and young people.

4.122 In the context of healthcare, however, satisfaction needs to be deconstructed. It is crucial to be clear about what is being measured. Children and young people as patients and members of the public are expert in certain areas of care: their needs and desires (whether convenience, or communication, or respect, or privacy); and the longer-term outcomes, such as whether they can walk without a stick, or do without medication. But they are not experts on the technical aspects of their care. There is therefore no point in asking children and young people, as patients or users of services, whether they are satisfied with the technical elements of their care. They cannot take a view because they do not know enough.

4.123 So, as regards the technical features of care, the same criterion, satisfaction, should be used, but it should be differently defined. It should be satisfaction by reference to whether the outcomes achieved meet or satisfy the benchmarks of performance

[134] For a more detailed explanation of this work, including further analysis of the advantages of using satisfaction as an indicator of organisational performance, see D Halpern, *The Hidden Wealth of Nations* (Cambridge: Polity, 2010) pp 42–43 and 208–10.

developed by professionals (in conjunction with children and young people). This element of satisfaction can be both subjective (was the professional satisfied with the outcome?) and objective (did the outcome meet current benchmarks of performance?). The subjective captures the ambition and commitment of the professional. The objective takes us into the world of data, analysis, norms of performance and benchmarks, and asks, should the professional be satisfied. So, standards will not have suddenly disappeared. The huge emphasis currently being placed on such benchmarking across the clinical professions must continue, not least the work of the National Institute for Health and Clinical Excellence (NICE) in developing a range of standards. It must, however, ultimately be focused on one single objective: the satisfaction of the children and young people and the satisfactory nature of the outcome reached.

4.124 Outcomes for children and young people will occupy centre stage. Satisfaction will be the sole measure: satisfaction from two perspectives, that of the child or young person and that of the professional (in conjunction with the child or young person). The system of performance management within the NHS must reflect this approach, as must the external regulatory system of the Care Quality Commission.

Recommendation 29: There should be a single criterion for measuring the quality of the NHS's services for children and young people – satisfaction. There should be two elements to satisfaction: whether children and young people are satisfied with the outcome achieved, by reference to what they are able to judge; and whether the professional should be satisfied, by reference to the current appropriate benchmarks of performance. The internal performance management and external regulation of the NHS must reflect this approach.

Addressing Tensions within the NHS

4.125 One of the sharpest tensions in the NHS as regards the care and well-being of children and young people lies in the contrast between various features of the architecture of the NHS, such as competition, choice and payment by results on the one hand, and, on the other, the view of all those involved with children and young people that continuity of care, as regards both people and institutions, is what matters most.

4.126 The answer must lie in effective commissioning. Commissioners must seek to ensure that the healthcare that they commission is appropriately organised to provide continuity as the child grows and develops. This is particularly important in the case of children who are disabled or have long-term or complex needs.

4.127 Moreover, young people do not engage with services as do adults. Traditional models of providing services may not, therefore, be appropriate. Young people do not respond well to letters. The text message and the internet are their ways of being in touch, Moreover, children and young people, branching out on their own, need guidance as to where to go for services and what may be available. The NHS has not been particularly active or successful in responding to this need. Nor has it felt the pressure to do so, given that children and young people do not represent sufficiently large a group to cause the system to respond to them. Again, it will be the task of commissioners, orchestrated through the Local Partnerships, to ensure that the needs of children and young people are addressed, and in addressing them, that young people in particular are heard and listened to. The importance placed by the new Government on 'patient choice', both as a good in itself and as a tool for improving services, makes it all the more essential that mechanisms exist to allow children and young people to be heard and for their needs, including particularly continuity of care, to be heard.

Recommendation 30: When designing and implementing mechanisms to give effect to choice within the NHS, due regard must be given to the needs of children and young people, both to be supported in making choices and to receive continuity of care over time.

NHS Working with Others

4.128 As I have pointed out, providing high-quality services for children and young people requires the NHS to work collaboratively with many other public sector agencies.[135] These include primarily social care services, education and (in relation to safeguarding, adolescent mental health and substance misuse) the police and youth justice systems. They may also include others such as housing, planning, benefits services and Jobcentre Plus.

4.129 Each of the institutional differences between these bodies forms a barrier to successful collaboration. Each has a different management structure, framework for performance management and form of regulation. Each has its own budget that may be constrained or ring-fenced in various ways, and for which each alone is accountable. Each answers to different ministers, deals with different stakeholders, and addresses different areas of public concern.

4.130 These formal barriers both delineate and exacerbate differences in organisational perspective or 'world view'. Such views are grounded in the varying professional perspectives of each organisation's staff. Agencies have different views of their relationship with the child or the family, and different 'rules of engagement' with both clients and other agencies. These differences in approach make inter-professional tensions inevitable. For example, some NHS staff expressed frustration that they were unable to discuss cases informally with social workers, because no formal referral had been made. One clinician expressed frustration that 'they [social services] are always asking "is this a referral"?'[136] From the perspective of the child or family using services, such tensions appear not only unnecessary, but also frustrating and confusing. While they remain the same people with the same set of needs, they are viewed, and therefore treated, differently as they fall for examination through different professional lenses.

[135] See, for example, principle 5 of the NHS Constitution.
[136] View submitted at a meeting with NHS managerial and professional staff involved in safeguarding children.

4.131 An additional factor affecting the NHS's current capacity to work effectively with others is that, as I have pointed out, the sheer size and complexity of the NHS cause problems for other organisations seeking to engage with it.[137] This is not helped by the internal structure of the NHS, which often means that responsibility for children and young people within any particular organisation is spread across a number of staff. For example, commissioning children's services and safeguarding children might be the responsibility of different directorates in a PCT. This causes confusion for Local Authorities, where responsibility for children is contained in a single management structure and hierarchy. Organisations are also unclear about whom to engage with in the NHS, whether commissioners or providers, or both, about any particular issue. Difficulty in engagement, therefore, makes both the organisation and the practice of working with others more difficult, and less effective, than it should be.

4.132 For the future, the first step that the NHS needs to take in working with other agencies is to understand them and how they perceive children and young people and their role in relation to them.[138] Even within the NHS, healthcare professionals take differing views of their responsibilities. The GP may see the child or young person as part of a family and seek to care for the family. Other healthcare professionals may adopt a different stance. These differences of view also exist between healthcare professionals and others, whether social workers, educationalists, housing officials or police, and need to be understood. Social workers, for example, may be neither suitably trained nor sufficiently supported to take action to resolve difficult cases, as they see it as their role to manage cases rather than to seek to improve the circumstances of the children and young people or to solve problems.[139] This is in contrast to the interventionist approach of both the healthcare professional and the police. These differences of approach reflect differences in policy at governmental level and differences in training and ethos.

4.133 Against such a background, it is clear that merely agreeing to work in partnership, or making a commitment to do that which is in the best interests of the child, will not take us very far. While all can sign up to it, it will mean different things to different people and the seeds of disagreement and disharmony will be sown. What is needed is a common vision that is strong enough to bind all the agencies together while taking account of different perspectives and different points of departure. This will enable a 'rich discussion within a culture of inter-professional respect' which was recognised as a vital prerequisite of effective joint working in this area.[140] It will require significant leadership from the Local Partnership, supported by an acknowledgement by the leaders of its constituent organisations that such a common vision is essential and must take precedence over any individual organisation's concerns. Where apparently irreconcilable differences remain in any particular case, the course of action must be to refer back

[137] The call is regularly heard for the NHS to make itself more manageable, consolidating its activities under just a few general headings, eg health promotion, accidents, chronic illness and acute illness.

[138] One senior manager commented that NHS communications on safeguarding were 'completely silo'd'. Effective safeguarding will require joint working at local level, but organisations outside the NHS are not involved in formulating national communications.

[139] View submitted at a meeting with independent experts.

[140] View submitted at a meeting with NHS managerial and professional staff involved in safeguarding children, Sandwell.

to the common values of the various organisations and to identify how each can add value to the overall welfare of the child or young person. In this way, differences can be characterised as operational rather than as matters of principle. With a commitment to work together, disagreements will be about a particular approach to a particular case. Progress can then be made.

Recommendation 31: Local public services, led by the Local Partnership, must develop a common vision for all services for children and young people, so as to enable the services to work together.

4.134 One illustration of this problem and its possible solution may help. It is clear that healthcare professionals and social workers approach the challenge of child protection from different perspectives. The social worker has a procedure to follow and is disinclined to resort to pragmatism or act on their own discretion. One of the procedures to be followed is that the circumstances of the child about whom concerns are raised must meet a particular threshold. The healthcare professional (and the police) may be more used to the exercise of discretion and consequently more prepared to step in earlier than the social worker.[141] Moreover, the threshold for action that they apply is lower. The risk of arguing about the way forward and overlooking the immediate needs of the children and young people in these circumstances is very real. The aim must be to arrive at an understanding of common responsibility whereby a decision is made that all can accept. The risk taken by one organisation is offset by the responsibility it shares with all the others.[142]

4.135 Of course, collaboration requires participation. A major complaint raised against the NHS is its poor performance as a partner in joint activities with other agencies.[143] This is so even when its participation is required by law. PCTs are currently described as the local bodies least engaged with Children's Trusts and safeguarding boards. The police have described the NHS as its weakest partner. Others have described the isolation of the NHS in terms of 'Fortress Health'.

4.136 It is true that partnerships have begun to develop at the senior levels of various organisations. Top managers may work well together once they take the plunge. But problems exist lower down in the organisations where staff bring their particular professional/managerial outlooks to their work and are constantly looking over their shoulders at what is expected of them in the form of national targets

[141] View submitted at a meeting with senior police officers.

[142] Shared responsibility means that all partners are responsible for an agreed course of action, not simply that they agree how responsibility will be passed between them as cases progress (view submitted at a meeting with NHS professionals involved in safeguarding).

[143] It was put to me by a senior official that 'health was a poor partner – the most likely organisation not to be at the table'. This was compared with the performance of the police service, which in recent years had refocused its activities from policing to 'community citizenship'. See my reference to the police and measures of performance at paragraph 4.121.

and performance indicators.[144] Moreover, as funding becomes tighter, the desire or tendency of each organisation to hoard its own money and not to spend it towards a common aim is in danger of becoming entrenched.

4.137 With all the agencies responsible for the welfare of children and young people under the overall direction of the Local Partnership and with an obligation individually and collectively to implement the Partnership's agenda and plans, this isolation by and of the NHS should cease. There will still be the challenge of motivating professionals who are actually delivering services to accept a new collaborative way of working, but at least they will all see that they have the opportunity for the first time of being part of a larger organisation dedicated solely to the interests of children and young people. I will consider in due course how this motivation may be inspired.

Changing/Challenging How People Work

Children and Young People

4.138 It is axiomatic that, as young people grow and mature, so they must be increasingly engaged in their health and healthcare. I have already stated that the arrangements for the governance of Local Partnerships must include a place for the voices of young people to be heard and listened to. They must have a place in the design and appraisal of the services offered.[145]

4.139 One of the most important tasks for Local Partnerships will be to grasp the nettle of arbitrary boundaries placed around services, based on birthdays. Historically, the line between young person and adult has reflected their legal categorisation. This distinction has been translated into the division of funding as between services for adults and those for young people. Clearly, there has grown up a determination that the budget for adults is protected from the depredations of those responsible for children, and vice versa. Such bureaucratic wranglings may be necessitated by the way in which the system is designed, but they immediately lose sight of the purpose for which the funds exist: to care for the interests of young people as they move into adulthood. And, of course, this is a process that varies from individual to individual. While it may be bureaucratically convenient to draw a clear line between the two streams of funding, it makes no sense at all to the young person. Future arrangements (whether related to organisational structure, funding streams or performance management) must ensure that there is a greater flexibility, allowing for greater continuity of care even into early adulthood. This is a great prize to be won in terms of the future welfare of adults. It is something that must be settled initially by government: what I have previously described as the challenge of transition.

[144] The NHS Confederation explained how contrasting regulatory and performance management demands, as discussed above, made it difficult for managers appointed jointly (for example a PCT and Local Authority) to give consistent messages to staff working for more than one organisation. It is for this reason that they argue that joint appointments at senior level must be mirrored lower down organisational hierarchies.

[145] I was impressed by the initiative in NHS Central Lancashire where 'Young Advisers' have been appointed. This is part of a larger strategic vision about children, young people and maternal health developed by the Strategic Health Authority in the North West.

Recommendation 32: Arrangements must be agreed, regarding funding and other matters, to address the changing needs of children and young people as they mature, including greater continuity of care into adulthood. Ensuring a smooth transition between children's and adults' services should be a priority for local commissioners.

4.140 Children and young people are entitled to age-sensitive care. Largely, this is a matter of professional expertise and I will address it in due course when I talk about the role of professionals. Here it may be helpful to raise a number of points that have to do with how the NHS deals with children and young people and how children and young people feel that they are dealt with.

4.141 It seems an obvious point that services for children should be designed and delivered with the perspective of the child in mind. Where this happens, as in, for example, Sheffield or Manchester Children's Hospitals, the effects are remarkable both as regards the child or young person and their parents or carers, and as regards the staff, who feel that they can provide the service they were trained for and go to work for. Lessons need to be learned. Where it does not happen, the picture is one of children, young people and parents/carers trying to negotiate a maze of services.

4.142 It does not take a great deal of insight to realise, for example, that support groups planned for parents/carers which are laid on in the middle of the day will necessarily exclude parents/carers who are at work. Equally, it is just plain common sense that staff in the NHS and indeed in other services should relate to children, young people and parents and carers using language which can be understood and avoid patronising attitudes. Children and young people complain that they are not regarded as active agents in their healthcare but rather as passive recipients. I was told by young people that many professionals currently lack either sufficient expertise, or a suitable professional attitude, to deliver age-appropriate care.[146] As a result, they feel that professionals lack respect for them and their problems. They feel that they are either treated like children and so feel patronised (one 14-year-old told of how she was asked to colour in pictures to show her feelings), or else treated like adults and, as a consequence, insufficiently supported.[147]

1.143 Engagement with parents and carers is often inconsistent and inappropriate. This was made clear again and again in submissions and meetings. For some older children, parents/carers may be asked their views as proxies for a child or young person who is quite able to express their own view. For example, a parent or carer may be asked for consent, or involved in a child's treatment, when such engagement should be with the child directly.[148] Parents and carers of younger children often feel insufficiently involved and informed about their child's care, or suspect that professionals do not talk to each other. Many

[146] View submitted at a meeting with third sector organisations.

[147] I welcome the recent effort to change traditional ways through the publication by DH of standards designed to make services more 'young people friendly' under the heading of *You're Welcome*.

[148] It was put to me forcibly by young people that their parents or carers were asked for contact details but nobody asked them for their details.

parents and carers of disabled children in particular feel responsible for 'co-ordinating' their child's care between a number of professionals, including ensuring that information is shared between them.[149] At the same time, I also came across many examples where parents and carers had not been kept informed about their child's treatment.[150] This must change. The NHS should be required actively to conduct research on a regular basis to determine what children and young people expect and want from it. It is already clear that young people have two fundamental priorities in their dealings with the NHS: that the staff be friendly and that confidentiality be observed.[151]

Recommendation 33: NHS services for children and young people should be designed, organised and delivered from the perspective of the child, young person and parent or carer. Relevant NHS services should regularly assess the expectations and views of children and young people using the services, and should take action in the light of the findings, which should be made public.

Professionals

4.144 I have shown already that the way in which professionals within the NHS interact with each other and with professionals in other organisations does not always best serve the interests and needs of children and young people. I heard frequently of professional groups' limited acceptance of the need to work together. Everyone to whom I spoke agreed with the need for more inter-professional working, yet almost all also had examples of where this was lacking. Paralleling the development of specialities within professions, each profession defines itself not only by its own role, but also in opposition to the roles of others. Professional identities are created around a unique domain of knowledge and skills and sphere of influence.

4.145 Defined in opposition to one another, professions become 'tribes' which both jealously guard the tasks and the information within their unique domain and, simultaneously, reject involvement with other tasks which are seen as not for them. For example, I was told that teachers can be unwilling to assist pupils with long-term conditions with the medical care that they require in order to stay in school, or that concerns about safeguarding from hospitals may not be passed on to social workers because healthcare professionals think that they can sort out the concerns for themselves. As I have said, these problems stem to some extent from professions' differing 'world views', which determine not only how they approach their daily work, but also their attitude to the children and families they serve and to other professionals.

4.146 Children and young people are pupils, patients, social problems, homeless and sometimes also parents or carers. They are victims or potential victims of crime, or potential or actual perpetrators of crime. They need support within their family, or

[149] See paragraphs 3.34–3.35.
[150] See paragraph 3.43.
[151] View submitted at a meeting with health professionals specialising in the care of young people.

protection from them. All professionals can agree that 'the child' is at the centre of their work, yet each views 'the child' through a different lens.

4.147 It goes without saying that there is a clear need for the various areas of expertise that have grown up in healthcare in recent years. But this has led professionals, largely in hospitals, to become more and more specialised. The care and treatment of children have become increasingly atomised. GPs, outside hospitals and with limited training in paediatrics as a consequence of this growing atomisation of care, have tended to refer children and young people to hospital rather than address problems themselves. Clearly, the child or young person who needs long-term care will benefit from such referral. The need will be identified and the care organised so as to ensure that the child or young person is cared for in the most appropriate place, whether at home or elsewhere. But, often, referral is unnecessary. The cost to the system is considerable.

4.148 What changes are needed? The future should be designed on the basis of what the child or young person needs from time to time from the services provided by the National Health Service, alone or in conjunction with other agencies. The future must be one of a holistic approach to the child or young person. The future as I have proposed lies in making the general practice or the polysystem the initial point of contact. There, a cadre of frontline staff will assess the child or young person. They will be generalists, but have the necessary training in paediatrics and child health, including mental health, to determine when to care for the child or young person themselves, when to refer them elsewhere and, in keeping with the holistic approach, when to engage other agencies. The savings in efficiency as well as the avoidance of unnecessary anxiety or upset to the child or young person will be considerable.

4.149 Of course, the holistic approach should not be limited merely to general practice and the first point of contact. It should pervade the approach taken by all professionals, even the most specialised. I saw a good example of this on the wards of a large teaching hospital (University College Hospital, London) where members of different professions, including the play specialist, take turns to lead a ward round. The effect is as much symbolic as practical. It says that all the staff are there together, working for one common purpose: the good of children and young people. What is required to produce this sort of approach? The answer is professional leadership and vision.

4.150 A contrast can be found in the current approach to child protection. Given the high visibility of this area and the aversion to risk that pervades professional actions, professionals tend to retreat into their professional silos, secure in the knowledge that they have ticked the relevant boxes and ready to blame someone else if something goes wrong. It is an area crying out for leadership, common vision, and understanding and trust between the professionals involved. The Local Partnership can make a significant contribution.

4.151 It has become clear to me that training lies at the heart of making a better future for children and young people.[152] I have already said that those in general practice,

[152] The importance and potential of training was a major theme of my discussions with both the Royal College of General Practitioners and the Royal College of Nursing. It was also referred to by nearly every other person to whom I spoke, as well as in a large number of written submissions.

nurses as well as doctors, must, as a matter of urgency, receive appropriate training in children and young people's health and healthcare. This should be reflected in the Quality and Outcomes Framework and in the process of professional revalidation.[153] But the need for training goes much wider: there should be a common curriculum to which all those who come into contact with children and young people, not just health professionals or those working in NHS organisations, should be exposed. It should address not only matters specific to the care and welfare of children and young people, but also matters such as how to work in teams, how to see the child or young person holistically, an understanding of the development of children and young people, how to identify mental health problems, an understanding of what other professionals dealing with children do, and how local services are commissioned, co-ordinated, provided and held to account. It must be a central feature of this training that professionals should learn to understand their fellow professionals as a first step towards being able to trust and rely on them. Of course, the purpose of such training is not merely to build trust, but also to improve outcomes for children and young people as a consequence of such increased trust. Indeed, there is much to be said for the Local Partnership identifying a champion for the various professional groups whose job is to explain what the profession does and how it sees the world.

Recommendation 34: All those involved in providing services for children and young people, including but not limited to NHS services, should receive training together according to a common curriculum, developed with the involvement of the Royal Colleges and other professional bodies, a principal purpose of which must be to enable professionals to understand each other's roles and work together.

4.152 It has also become clear to me that an intrinsic element in the process of moving professionals from a default position of distrust to one of trust of each other is the need to show each of them how working with others will in fact make their job easier and, by extension, more rewarding as they can achieve more for the children and young people whom they serve. It seems that the natural propensity of professionals of all stripes is to assume that collaboration is some kind of betrayal of their tribal identity. In fact, collaboration is a mature response, recognising that the multi-factorial challenges presented by their responsibility for the welfare and well-being of children and young people can only be met by a multi-professional response (and professional here includes managers).

4.153 One aspect of the relations between professionals both within and across professions which causes significant concern is the difficulties associated with sharing information about children and young people and, on occasion, their families. The need to address the circumstances of children and young people holistically, to be aware of

[153] It was urged on me that the Quality and Outcomes Framework should be expanded to include a reference to participation in safeguarding and child protection cases.

the pathways of care that they follow both within the NHS and in contact with other agencies, and to plan services around the journeys they take, are fundamental premises in my approach to this review. These premises can be and often are undermined by a failure to share information. An example can serve to make the point. I heard from a number of young people about how frustrating and depressing it was to have to tell the same story to a succession of professionals, none of whom seemed to have passed it on to the next.[154] And I have already referred to parents and carers of disabled children who had to tell the same story on numerous occasions only to find that one specialist had not written to another, such that one parent ended up writing letters to consultants herself.

4.154 I have already stressed the importance of creating a climate of trust in which information may automatically pass from professional to professional. This may be an important task for the Local Partnership. It is not impossible to create such a climate. I have already referred to the example of the Family Justice Centre in Croydon.[155] I was equally impressed by what I saw in Sheffield. All those responsible for the care and well-being of children and young people had access electronically to a common database. The information was recorded in accordance with a protocol. Everyone, from the school health team, to the A&E doctor, to the health visitor, to the GP could check on the child or young person and also record information for the benefit of others. Clearly, one significant benefit this system provides is in the area of safeguarding and child protection. But its value goes far beyond this. If professionals are to be there for the child or young person as they develop and come into contact with various public services, then sharing information is essential. It allows the best choices about the care and well-being of the child to be made and it allows services to target those who most need help.

4.155 Of course, trust, though essential, is not the only factor necessary to facilitate the proper exchange of information. Two other matters are of particular relevance. The first is technical. Systems for storing and allowing access to information have to be aligned. This would mean that those entitled to enter data would have access to the data of other professionals. Currently, this may not be the case. As the NHS Confederation reported, the NHS's system of Connecting for Health does not recognise the systems used by Local Authorities. A health professional may be unable to gain access to records relating to the safeguarding of a child because the information is held on a different system or on premises occupied by another public service, such as the education department, as I encountered in Newham.[156] Or, as happened in Haringey, the hospital staff could gain access in principle to records on safeguarding, but could only do so in the presence of social workers.

4.156 Such a state of affairs is the opposite of integrated services: it epitomises services which have disintegrated. The solution lies in developing local networks for sharing data electronically, rather than simply seeking to create some overarching national solution. Protocols can be agreed locally as to what is to be stored and who may have access.

[154] View submitted at a meeting with young people.
[155] See paragraph 4.71.
[156] The benefits of the co-location of services again comes through.

National databases can be referred to when useful, but given that their creation has taken on the quality of the search for the Holy Grail (which, it needs to be recalled, has never been found!), it is better to think in less grand terms and get on with doing something which can be made to work locally. As it happens, the NHS Confederation has expressed the view that, of all local agencies, Children's Trusts have historically been the most successful in fostering the sharing of information between the various organisations that are a part of it.[157] This shows that progress can be made. It must be made faster, and more consistently, across and between all services.

Recommendation 35: There should be local networks through which services can share information electronically and protocols should be agreed by the networks to provide for this.

4.157 The other matter of concern is confidentiality.[158] This is not the place to explore the nature of confidentiality when dealing with children and young people (an exceedingly complex subject). Nor is it the place to seek to understand why the translation of information into electronic form surrounded with protection creates a level of concern not associated with the recording of information on paper, which routinely gets lost, is read by many, and the sharing of which is difficult at best. Nor is it the place to notice that, when asked, most members of the public, rather than those who claim to speak for them, say they are anxious that information be shared between professionals, recognising that it is in their interests that this be so. Of course, they wish for appropriate safeguards to be in place. Such safeguards are well understood and exist. Nor is it the place to notice that information is power and that professionals may be inclined on occasions to raise the flag of confidentiality to refuse access to 'their' data by others. Nor, finally, is it the place to remark that much of the controversy over sharing information relates to what is recorded, rather than to the fact of its being recorded. If a standard template were used by all that limits information to the factual and removes opinion and speculation, then objections to sharing would become less strong.

4.158 Instead, what I propose here is that there is a general understanding that confidentiality is a relative not an absolute obligation. That being so, local networks must agree on the protocol to be followed, share it with their local community (with the relevant arguments) and then get on with developing a system of sharing. Without it, services for children and young people will always be less good and children and young people, particularly in the context of safeguarding, will suffer. Of course, one part of such a protocol will include those circumstances in which respect for confidentiality has a very high priority, for example in the case of mental health problems or sexual

[157] NHS Confederation's submission to the review.

[158] It was put to me by senior officials that, as regards obtaining personal information in the context of providing a wide range of services for children, the NHS was rated as the most difficult organisation by professionals working in other agencies, with GPs being described as particularly difficult. A 'culture of confidentiality' was said to exist in the NHS and DH, with very limited leadership at senior level leaving professionals unsure of how to respond to requests for information, and therefore reluctant to share it.

behaviour in young people. But, even here, the objection of the young person usually relates to sharing information with family members not other professionals, including the school health team. Indeed, properly understood, the issue is largely one of privacy rather than confidentiality.

4.159 Before I leave this section about professionals, it is important for me to recognise one central and immovable point. The services provided to children and young people are delivered by professionals on the ground. They are at the centre of everything. Unless they are encouraged and empowered to adapt the culture in which their services are provided and received, nothing will change.

4.160 Thus, perhaps, the most important agents for change to advance the interests of children and young people are the professional commitment and ethos of those who serve them. Many professionals feel beleaguered or beaten down, frustrated that they cannot achieve what they signed up to do and what they have spent their professional lives trying to accomplish. Many professionals have turned inwards, seeing the outside world of 'the system' as somehow hostile and designed to frustrate them. Many do the best they can and settle for that, in the knowledge that it is not what they would wish. The system must reconnect with its professionals. As mentioned above, this applies to managers as much as to technical (in the case of healthcare, clinical) professionals.

4.161 At the heart of such a proposition is leadership and vision. At all levels, from the government and policy-maker to the nurse on the ward, the professionals must recognise in the changes that I am proposing a way of re-committing themselves to the design and delivery of services for children and young people. The natural conservatism of all professions will draw them towards a reluctance to change. The natural commitment to service should draw them out. School nurses must see that, by working with the general practice and the health visitor, they are doing, and doing better, what they, as school nurses, trained to do. They will be better school nurses, as well as provide a better service to children and young people. GPs must see that being at the hub of the service for children and young people is not a further burden for which they must negotiate appropriate terms and conditions (though these are not unimportant). Rather, it is the chance to become a more fulfilled GP, caring for families and young people and working collaboratively with others. GPs must see the collection of information as an affirmation of the care based on evidence which was at the heart of their motivation for joining the profession. Managers must see themselves as facilitating the provision of services around the needs of, and therefore for the greatest benefit of, those who use them. Surgeons in the hospital must see themselves as part of a pathway of care. That is, after all what they trained to be and now they can make it happen.

4.162 Changes in the care of children and young people will not take place without the engagement of professionals. Once professionals realise that what I am proposing allows them to be how they see themselves, good and fulfilled nurses and doctors, they will want to make sure that change takes place. Those who are proposing to change how healthcare services for children and young people are organised and provided would do well to bear this in mind. Whatever the scale or the type of the proposed change, ultimately it has to be delivered by those who work in and dedicate their lives to these services. The motivation and conviction of professionals, unlocking their passion for the services that they provide, are, I believe, the most powerful tools that exist to bring about improvement, especially in the current climate of financial constraint. It behoves us all to recognise and mobilise this motivation and conviction.

Workforce

4.163 Within the NHS, perhaps the greatest and most pressing need is for an increase in the workforce trained in paediatrics and the care of children. In the hospital sector, it is still the case that, apart from environments dedicated to paediatric care, the level of skill and expertise in dealing with children and young people is not what it should be. A concerted effort must be made by all the Royal Colleges, professional bodies and the NHS to address this weakness.

4.164 Government, employers and professional groups must make the development of the workforce a very high priority. Endangered species such as psychologists, who perform a crucial role in hospitals and in the community, speech and language therapists who can rescue a child from uncomprehending exclusion, and play specialists in hospitals, should not be seen as expendable luxuries to be got rid of when the money is tight. They are part of the necessary complement of staff. They are crucial to the experience that a child may have of care in and out of hospital, and thus of the attitude to healthcare generally that that child will carry into later life, for example in their attitude to the self-management of a long-term condition. The fear of the school dentist of 50 years ago, which persuaded generations of children that dentists were to be avoided, with adverse consequences for health, offers a cautionary parallel.

Recommendation 36: Government, employers and professional groups must address the need for more professionals trained in the range of skills required in the comprehensive care of children and young people as a matter of urgency.

4.165 It must be recognised that significant shortages of professionals trained to care for young people with mental health problems exist at a time when an epidemic of such problems lies beneath the surface of society. This gap must be closed. I am aware of the concerns expressed about resources. My answer is that if we really care about young people and if we want to reduce the burden on adult services in the years to come, action now is the only option. I heard pleas for increased numbers of specialists (particularly in the area of cognitive behavioural therapy)[159] and for more generalists, particularly school nurses. It is not my place to arbitrate among these pleas. These decisions must be taken at a local level, on the basis of an understanding of the needs of each community.

4.166 As regards general practice, I have pointed out the need to train GPs and others who work with them. This need is increasingly pressing, for two reasons. The current level of training is poor and getting worse. Secondly, if general practice is to be at the

[159] View submitted at a meeting with Lord Layard.

centre of arrangements for caring for children and young people, as I propose, such training is required as a matter of urgency. As one senior GP put it to me, 'Some GPs now don't even know how to hold a baby'. The temptation to refer children and young people elsewhere from lack of knowledge or confidence must be resisted by GPs. They will be able to resist it only if they are properly trained.

4.167 As regards the NHS's workforce more broadly, I have urged the development of joint curricula and joint training. This is something that the relevant Royal Colleges, professional bodies and regulators need to address urgently.[160] The purpose is obvious. Working in a team is a central feature of modern healthcare. Training together breaks down cultural tendencies towards professional isolationism. It also fosters an understanding of each other's role and contribution. And it sets the basis for a more holistic approach to the care of children and young people. Indeed, the ultimate goal must be to shift the focus away from single professional units and identities with their particular goals, to a single-minded concern only for the outcomes which are needed for children and young people: that is, work backwards and start with the child or young person, "I exist to provide for you", rather than forwards from "This is what I, as a professional, do".

4.168 Joint training is of particular benefit as regards safeguarding. Of particular importance is an understanding of what constitutes a risk factor. We know more about these risk factors than ever before, but this understanding, and how to apply it in making professional judgements, needs to be more widely taught to relevant staff.[161] It is clear that different professional groups use what appears to be a common language in different ways (for example, the degree of evidence called for to allow a view that abuse may be suspected). The value of training together is that these differences can be identified and a way forward found that puts the interest of the child or young person first, rather than any particular professional group's sense of what is right. By training together, professionals come to understand how their views of the world differ, how that affects their behaviour, how this might cause confusion or tension between them, and how this might be resolved. In this way professionals can understand how their differing perspectives can add to the richness of understanding particular cases and to the subtlety of agencies' response.

Recommendation 37: There should be joint training of professionals involved in the care and welfare of children and young people, according to agreed curricula, particularly in the area of safeguarding.

4.169 Equally, as regards safeguarding, different professionals operate different thresholds to justify action. Again, these need to be explicitly identified and a common

[160] Both the RCPCH and the Royal College of Nursing stress the need for broader programmes of education, to include such matters as safeguarding, in the case of nurses or, as the RCN describes them, 'the Child Health Nurse of the future'. While this is welcome, it still envisages the nurse being educated in isolation. The need to avoid these silos, whether in practice or in education and training, is what is being urged here.

[161] This was mentioned to me both by officials and independent experts working in the area.

approach agreed. Such a solution will be made easier should my broader proposals be accepted, given that policy will emanate from only one department of state and will be translated into action at the local level by a single Local Partnership that brings together all of the relevant organisations.

4.170 One of the consequences of an integrated approach to the workforce in providing services to children and young people is the quite proper reflection that some jobs are better done by this rather than that professional. One such example is the recognition that there is a difference between a health visitor and health visiting. The latter job may be carried out perfectly well by someone who is not a health visitor but is part of their team. Such developments are essential to produce an efficient and effectively integrated workforce. They will be resisted by those who think in terms of their professional identity rather than in terms of what all professionals are there to achieve: the best possible service for children and young people. The task of all who can influence the shape of the future workforce must be to redesign the workforce around the child or young person. The reverse has for too long been the story. One way of achieving this, which is worth considering, is to create not just an integrated approach but an integrated workforce for children and young people, whereby all those involved in health and healthcare in the local community are employed by the same organisation, preferably the Local Partnership. Such professionals might include the health visiting team, the school health team, community nurses and others. In this way, inter-professional barriers are broken down as organisational barriers which keep professions apart are removed.

Recommendation 38: Consideration should be given to the creation of an integrated workforce for children and young people, in which all those involved in health, healthcare and welfare in the local community are employed by the same organisation, preferably the Local Partnership.

4.171 I have referred several times already to the challenge of managing the care of young people as they pass to adulthood. It is clear that the process of 'transition' is both entirely artificial and, at the same time, entirely real.

4.172 The artificiality lies in the arbitrary boundaries drawn between the services offered to young people and those offered to adults, with all the unfortunate consequences that flow from this. As I have said, it is essential that local organisations come together to ensure that the young person can enjoy a continuity of care which ignores birthdays and concentrates on needs.

4.173 The reality lies in the fact that young persons are, of course, in a process of development and that the services offered to them need to reflect and take account of this. To begin to address this reality, I propose that there should be a cadre of professionals who are trained in both paediatrics and the care of young adults. These would be available to the Local Partnership to enable it to commission services which manage the process of growing up, putting the young person at the centre and addressing the needs of 16- to 25-year-olds.

Recommendation 39: There should be a cadre of professionals who are trained in both paediatrics and the care of young adults. Government, employers and professional groups should work together in order to ensure that such a cadre is established and receives appropriate training.

5. Conclusion

5.1 There is no doubt that many children and young people receive better care from the NHS than ever before. There is no doubt that up and down the land, every day, children and young people receive good care from good caring professionals. But there is also no doubt that services for children and young people could be significantly better. That is the premise on which I was asked to conduct this review.

5.2 The influence of cultural factors on the performance of the NHS is very great. If these factors are not identified and addressed, the scope for improving the services which the NHS provides for children and young people is limited. If they are addressed, a major step forward is possible. The long decades in which reality always fell short of rhetoric will be over. Children and young people, tomorrow's future, will get what they deserve and what we owe them.

5.3 I have adopted an approach in this review which seeks to address this historical problem. I have proposed that the care of children and young people must be seen in the round rather than from the narrow perspective of the acute sector (healthcare as intervention). I have further proposed that care should be unified and co-ordinated at two critical levels: as regards policy, in a single department of state; as regards the commissioning and provision of services locally, by a Local Partnership which, while it could take a variety of forms, must operate according to certain principles, the most important of which is that it be wholly dedicated to the needs and welfare of children and young people.

5.4 If services for children and young people provided by the NHS are to improve, the barriers to collaborative working, both within the NHS and between the NHS and other agencies, must be overcome. Services must be integrated within the NHS along pathways of care. They must interact successfully and seamlessly with other public agencies. The NHS is not an island. We fail children and young people if we perpetuate a system in which they (or their parents or carers) need to knock on the right door in search of care and risk going un-helped if they get it wrong. We fail children and young people if their needs and concerns are not at the centre of everything that is done: easy rhetoric but very difficult to pull off. Being held accountable by reference to the sole criterion of whether the outcome of the service provided was satisfactory will mark a new beginning: that the NHS intends to respond to children and young people, rather than expecting them to respond to the system.

5.5 We must invest. We must invest to save and we must invest because it is right to do so. To those who say that the times are not propitious for investment in anything, that disinvestment is the only way forward given the state of the public finances, I say the following. The new approach that I propose contemplates the integration of services, working collaboratively within the NHS and across the other agencies. Savings will be made through greater efficiency, through co-location and the benefits it brings, and through the joint planning and commissioning of services. They will also be made through the reduction of the current complexity which particularly surrounds the services provided by the NHS. A system that still relies on multiple appointments for different things in different places, or, worse, by returning to the same place, is expensive. It does not meet the standards that children and young people are entitled to expect. As regards early intervention and a shift towards health promotion and the prevention of disease, the pay-off is obvious. What has been lacking at times has been the political will.

5.6 Finally, at the centre of any system for providing services are the professionals. The challenge for them is to re-engage with the system so as to change it for the better. It cannot change without them. The prize at stake is the chance to be the professionals they want to be. The greater prize is services for children and young people that they and the NHS can be rightly proud of.

Annex A: Terms of Reference: Review of NHS Services for Children

1. **Goal:** to identify the cultural obstacles that inhibit sustained improvement in frontline NHS services for children, and in particular NHS action to safeguard children; and to make recommendations to support sustained improvement for the medium and longer term in outcomes for children receiving services.
2. **Context:** improving children's health and wellbeing, including action to safeguard children, are identified as clear priorities for the NHS, and policies and guidance are in place. But successive HCC [Healthcare Commission] and CQC [Care Quality Commission] reports and other evidence indicate that good practice is not always embedded effectively. While the NHS responds positively to specific initiatives and reports, short term improvements tend not to be sustained. Child health is established as a priority through the NHS Operating Framework more firmly than ever before, and a comprehensive programme of action is being put in place in response to Lord Laming's recent report on child protection. So it is important to take the opportunity to secure the cultural change that will lead to lasting improvements in outcomes for children through improvements in practice and in the leadership of organisations.

   The review will need to reflect the principles of change management in the NHS following the NHS Next Stage Review, and the focus on Quality, Innovation, Productivity and Prevention as key drivers as we enter tighter economic circumstances.
3. **The task** is to explore with staff and local leadership what are the cultural obstacles to improvement in outcomes to children, and how these can be addressed.
4. The **scope** covers:
   - dedicated children's services (including health visiting and other community services, paediatrics, CAMHS [child and adolescent mental health services]);

- services dealing with children as part of their wider responsibilities, including primary care, A&E, ambulance and out of hours services; and some aspects of surgery; and
- services working with adults whose condition may create pressures or risks for their families, including mental health, alcohol and substance misuse and domestic violence.

5. The review will need to explore with staff and local professional and organisational leaders the factors that inhibit change. This will need to be shaped by their views, but potential issues to explore include:
   - perceptions of health services' role in child health and wellbeing, and in safeguarding;
   - the challenges to professional practice and how these can be met;
   - challenges to leadership, especially given the disseminated responsibilities across the NHS on children's health and their healthcare and safeguarding and between departments of state/government departments;
   - the balance between personal professional responsibilities and wider team responsibilities across the NHS and LA [Local Authorities'] children's services for safeguarding;
   - wider social/cultural factors, for example concerning professional training and development, and the status of children and families.
6. The project should have a practical focus, and include workshops and discussions across SHA [strategic health authority] regions. A short report with recommendations for action should be submitted to David Nicholson by end March 2010.
7. **Wider engagement**. While the review is specific to the NHS, it will need to take account of the requirements for cross sector working on children and on safeguarding. At national level, the Government has recently put in place arrangements to strengthen cross sector co-ordination through creation of a cross-government National Safeguarding Delivery Unit, and the appointment of Sir Roger Singleton as National Adviser to Government on the Safety of Children. This project will be of interest to Sir Roger and the NSDU and appropriate involvement and sharing of insights will be agreed.

PART II

Regulation in the Public Sector

Regulation rarely has a good press. It's perceived as being 'in the way'. It attracts soubriquets such as 'red tape', 'bureaucracy', 'rules and regulations'. It is rarely spoken of warmly, as a way of keeping us safe or keeping people honest. Yet we never give a second thought to whether the medicine or the eye drops or the mascara we get from the chemists, or the lamb chop or chicken we get from the butcher, or the light bulb or plug we get from the hardware store are safe. We take it for granted that they are. We do so because the way in which they are produced and made available is regulated – regulated for our benefit.

The same is true in so many other walks of life. Your dentist, your doctor, your maternity nurse are all qualified. They have passed through a closely regulated system designed to keep you safe. The bus driver has passed her tests. The police officer has done his training. The firefighter knows which end of the hose the water comes out of. The solicitor knows what a will is. They've all been through a regulated system. If they fall down on the job they are disciplined, again according to a system of regulations.

Regulation is about managing risks. In the public sector where I have worked, it's about managing the risks that the public is exposed to. The greater the risk and the greater the fall-out if the risk becomes a reality, the more careful the regulation. It's about getting the best deal for the taxpayer, making sure that money is spent wisely and well. The public is entitled to the best value that their taxes can provide – what has become known as getting 'value for money' (or vfm). You will see how vfm is a central and largely misunderstood concept in regulation.

Regulation is also about promoting good practice and improvement in the provision of services to the public. Getting hospitals to collect and make public accurate and relevant data about what they are doing and how well they are doing it, for example, helps to reduce the risk of getting things wrong. It means that comparisons can be made between organisations so that lessons can be learned and improvements made in performance.

I am an unapologetic advocate of regulation. I have set up from scratch two major regulatory bodies – the Healthcare Commission and the Independent Parliamentary Standards Authority and been involved in a number of others. I do not accept the lazy caricatures. For me regulation, properly understood and properly designed and delivered, is a force for good. But I am the first to admit that there is a lot of regulation and a lot of regulators who don't see regulation as I do and so fail to take advantage of the opportunities to improve services that it provides. They behave like police officers keen to catch people out. They generate oodles of paperwork which takes organisations away from what they should be doing while largely failing to enlighten the regulators as to what may really be going on. They descend on organisations and claim to be able to make informed judgements about performance based on a glancing and superficial view. Such behaviour, which is far too common, feeds the caricature. Regulation has so much more to offer, as I argue and seek to demonstrate in this Part.

3

CHAI – Making it Better[1]

Introduction

These notes are not the standard text of a lecture. Rather, they reflect an attempt to share my thoughts with you as I and colleagues find a way through the challenges which face the creation of CHAI (the Commission for Healthcare Audit and Inspection[2]). As you know, CHAI will be established by the Health and Social Care Bill currently before Parliament and I was appointed the Chair in December 2002. We are due to begin operation in April 2004.

What follows describes 'work in progress'. It comes with a very significant health warning: it describes the process of my thinking aloud. Many decisions have yet to be made. There may be changes of direction, either because ideas advanced prove to be less sound than currently appears, or because external events (such as changes in the draft legislation) cause us to proceed differently.

I will address three themes: CHAI, CHAI and children, and some concerns for the future.

CHAI

CHAI is in the process of being built. It is a complex task. A new organisation, the role of which is not yet widely understood, has to be created.

An initial and very challenging question for those of us at CHAI (and for you) is about the making of policy and its effect on practice. How do you move from abstract analysis to practical action; from the architecture and structure of organisations to what happens on ward 5; from the concept of regulation to the nursing shortage on ward 8?

They seem, and are, worlds apart. Do they have anything to say to each other, or is CHAI just another political fix, prompted by the political need to be seen to do something, but in fact just another burden to the 'pbi' (poor bloody infantry)?

[1] This is the lecture that I gave at Great Ormond Street Hospital at the invitation of the Chairman on 24 September 2004.

[2] The title CHAI was wished on us by the Department of Health. Apart from being ugly, it was easy to confuse with the title of the organisation it replaced – CHI, the Commission for Healthcare Improvement. Within months, I persuaded the Secretary of State to allow us to go by the name of the Healthcare Commission.

The theory behind the creation of CHAI is, of course, that it can and will affect behaviour for the betterment of patients. My responsibility, with fellow Commissioners and staff, is to translate that theory into reality, or, if the evidence suggests it, and I underline this, having given it our best shot, to conclude that the theory is flawed.

I will give it my best shot, but I have an open mind on the larger question of whether regulators can bring about improvement, by which I mean create the necessary environment in which you can deliver improvement, since it must be obvious that sitting in an office in Central London I cannot directly improve how this or that patient is cared for.

I care about the treatment of patients. I care particularly about the treatment of children. But I don't look after them. You do that. So if CHAI is to achieve anything it needs your help. You, as clinicians, managers, and patients are the bridge between the abstract analysis and ward 5. You have to help me to understand what you do, what you want, what your ambitions are. You have to understand what I and my colleagues can do, what our role is, and help us. We will be listening.

Let me now set off on this journey from the abstract to the concrete: from my world to yours.

CHAI's Role and Responsibilities

First, a word about CHAI. CHAI is a new organisation, not yet formally in existence, but about to be created by legislation currently passing through Parliament. My colleagues and I enjoy the privilege, through the foresight of the previous Secretary of State for Health, of having some time, now down to six months, in which to get our thinking straight and our tackle in order. We exist only in shadow form, with no formal status. With the creation of CHAI, and its formal beginning in April 2004, the current Commission for Health Improvement (CHI) will cease to exist as will the National Care Standards Commission (NCSC) (responsible for the regulation of private health care), some of the functions of the Audit Commission will be passed over, and it is likely that the Mental Health Act Commission (MHAC) will be subsumed into CHAI informally. CHAI will also take on the second tier of the NHS' complaints procedure. So, I repeat, CHAI is a new organisation. Its portfolio of responsibilities is greater than any of the current organisations and is different in nature and perspective.

CHAI is charged under the Bill as it stands with a duty to assess the performance of those providing healthcare by reference to nationally determined standards laid down by government. The primary purpose of such assessment is stated to be so as to promote improvement. This is important. The goal is improvement.

How is CHAI to improve anything, bearing in mind that *you* deliver the service?

CHAI's Vision

CHAI published for consultation its Vision Document in July this year as the first step in the process. We made it clear that we were in listening and learning mode and that we wanted to hear from anyone who cared to comment. The process of consultation is complete and an analysis of the responses will be published shortly. It would appear from anecdotal evidence that the document has been well received, albeit there are real concerns about obtaining the information necessary to do the job as we envisage it.

I am not going to rehearse here what is in the Vision Document. I want instead to explain our thinking about how we take the vision forward: how we edge from the abstract to the concrete. I emphasise again that these thoughts are very much 'work in progress'. They are daily being discussed and refined. CHAI has yet to decide on them. I share them with you on those terms and with a view to inviting further comment from this most distinguished of audiences. Remember that the acid test is whether what we develop will help to improve the care of patients, including children, and to improve the ability of those who look after them to deliver that care.

Assessing Performance

There are four steps in CHAI's approach to creating the framework for assessing performance in the NHS (the private sector is subject to a separate regime, but the aim is to establish in time one system across the whole of healthcare).

1. The first step is the development and publication of the standards against which performance is to be assessed. The Bill makes it clear that these standards are for government to determine. They will include existing national standards, such as those contained in the various national service frameworks (NSFs), including the Children's NSF. Our hope is that the standards issued will be general in nature and over time fall into a number of discrete domains. These domains, it is hoped, will embrace the quality and safety of care, the quality of the patient's experience, the quality of clinical governance and organisational competence, and the quality of the arrangements made by organisations to work in partnership with other organisations which affect the health and welfare of members of the public. It is further hoped that as time goes on two further domains will be added: the national targets announced by government from time to time and which currently form the basis of annual ratings (suitably reduced in number), and local targets agreed by local communities. Clearly, the latter will be the product of sustained dialogue between clinicians, local government, the public and other interested parties and will respond to local needs and circumstances.
2. The second step is to develop criteria which will breathe content into the broad standards laid down. The formulation of these criteria is central to CHAI's vision for at least two reasons. First, the criteria will drive improvement. By identifying what organisations will be assessed on, CHAI will be signalling what it regards as important. Given the implications of being assessed, organisation will seek to satisfy the stated criteria. And, by seeking to satisfy these criteria, provided that we get the criteria right, attention will be drawn to those matters which, in the view of all concerned, encourage and promote improvement. Secondly, the criteria, if they are to signal what, within the various domains of standards, CHAI will be assessing, must reflect the concerns, ambitions and aspirations of those affected by the NHS: patients and professionals. Thus, in developing the criteria, CHAI will be consulting as widely as possible. To take an example of relevance to you

in Great Ormond Street, we would be anxious to learn what children, carers and professionals think should be the criteria by reference to which we should assess the extent to which the generic standard set out in that part of the Children's NSF so far published (relating to acute care in hospital) is being met in practice.

3. Once the standards and the criteria are in place, the next step is to devise means of determining whether the criteria are being satisfied. The 'holy grail', of course, is the identification of some key indicator which will tell the whole story, or a large part of it, without having to ask a lot of detailed questions. Until this is found, the next best thing is to ask what I call the 'cute questions' – those questions which will tell us whether the criteria are being complied with in a way which redounds to the benefit of patients. Formulating these questions so as to avoid, for example, measuring process where it is outcomes that are important will be a significant challenge. It can only be done by those with an intimate knowledge of how care is delivered, namely patients and professionals. So, CHAI will need to consult widely and take account of the experience and wisdom of patients and staff. The challenge, a challenge I have already issued to a number of audiences and which I issue to you here, is to help us to frame the 'cute questions' which tell us what we need to know; what we need to know in your and your patients' interests.
4. The final step is obvious, yet currently the hardest to deal with. If you ask questions, you want answers. Those answers will be in the form of data relating to those aspects of performance which we have decided are important. Those data will make up what we have termed 'intelligent information': information which, once collected and analysed, will allow the assessment of current performance in respect of the declared standards and criteria. To some extent, the data required to answer the questions already exists, although some may not always be recognised as data touching on performance of organisations in the NHS. Identifying the range of data currently available and its possible use in assessing performance is a task of the greatest urgency, as is the task of identifying gaps which need to be filled. Of course, while rapid progress is being made, there may be questions that on the basis of current data, we cannot answer. In such cases, ways of collecting such additional data and then analysing them, so as to amplify and enrich the corpus of intelligent information, must be devised as soon as possible.

Once we have established the basis of our system of intelligent information, CHAI's framework for assessing performance will be in place. It will allow for a model of audit and inspection very different from that currently in place. Let me describe very briefly the key features. Before doing so, I point out that I leave out here detailed discussion of another of CHAI's responsibilities: the assessment at a national level of 'value for money'. This is a task which CHAI will take over from the Audit Commission. The language of 'value for money', just like that of 'improvement' or of 'successful performance', is clearly evaluative. Thus, on the one hand, we must devise ways of measuring 'value for money', drawing on the considerable expertise of the Audit Commission. We must ask where the money has gone. With increasing amounts of tax-payers' money going into the NHS, some account must be rendered by CHAI as an independent body. But, we shall also be asking what does 'value' mean to patients and to professionals, so as to examine the deployment of resources and the nature of priorities. For, clearly, what is of 'value' to patients (just as what constitutes 'improvement' or 'success') may not be the same as that which managers, or government, or clinicians regard as valuable. In time, of course, such an analysis should have a direct influence on the emergence of targets.

Key Features of CHAI's Model

1. First, a point about **language**. CHAI will inspect, but inspection is a word which means different things to different people. Very often it is used as if it were synonymous with visiting: you inspect by visiting. This is how inspection is widely understood elsewhere in the public sector, for instance, in education and the social services. To CHAI, inspection is a generic term, describing all the various methods by which CHAI will assess performance. Thus, you inspect by examining data, by drawing on surveys, as well as by using visits. Putting it another way, visits will form part of CHAI's activities, but will not be the only means of assessment.
2. Secondly, in recognition of the fact that change and improvement can only effectively be made by those who are actually doing the job and receiving the care, CHAI will commit itself to **working with patients and professionals**. As I have said, it will consult widely on criteria and on what I have called the 'cute questions'. It will also empanel groups of advisers, both patients and professionals, to advise the Commission.

   Of course, such arrangements are largely self-evident. But two other features may not be and may, therefore, be worth setting out here. I will call them 'local targets' and 'local presence'.
3. **Local Targets**: Taking local targets first, as has been seen, national targets will over time, it is hoped, be subsumed into the standards by reference to which organisations are assessed, as one of a number of domains. CHAI would wish to see the development of local targets as a further domain. These targets, which would be in addition to but not detracting from the national targets, would allow local communities to spell out what they think are particularly important for their community and then develop a plan to meet these targets. CHAI's role would be to monitor and assess performance and report back regularly to the community. Such a development would also allow CHAI to adopt a more nuanced approach to assessment, recognising that one size does not fit all, and that different communities have different needs and aspirations. One particular example may serve to make the point: the public health needs and consequent strategy and targets of, say, Solihull are unlikely to be the same as those of Tower Hamlets.

   Of course, there is a larger goal than just a focus on targets in promoting such local involvement. This is the crucial goal of engaging local communities in the provision of healthcare. By such engagement, there is a real sense of common ownership of ambitions and achievements. Equally, there is less of a sense of being powerlessly subject to central diktat, whereby, in effect, management and discretion are taken away by Whitehall.
4. **Local Presence**: Turning now to the concept of the 'local presence', let me explain the evolving thinking. The idea is that, so far from directing assessment from the centre in London, CHAI will gradually devolve the role of assessment to teams

in local offices, the geographical remit of which could, perhaps, coincide with that of the current Strategic Health Authorities. CHAI will, of course, be separate from these authorities. The head of the local office will liaise closely with the providers of health care in the catchment area. CHAI's needs for information in answer to CHAI's 'cute questions' will be explained and assistance provided in answering them. The performance of organisations will be explained and reported back to the local community as well as to the centre. Comparative analysis will be provided by the centre which will give a national and international context to the local assessment. The aim will be to ensure the engagement of the local community (patients, public and professionals) in the performance of the providers of healthcare, whether in acute hospitals, primary care trusts, mental health trusts, or through community healthcare and public health. The head of the local office will be required to build a relationship of trust and understanding with the local community so as to promote a frame of mind in which the commitment to improvement across the whole range of standards becomes part of the operational culture of healthcare.

5. Next, CHAI's commitment to an approach to assessment which puts the patient at the centre means that it must concern itself with the patient's journey through the various stages of healthcare. It is not sufficient to concentrate solely on one organisation, or unit within an organisation. From a patient's perspective, he or she follows a pathway of care and it is the performance of all those along the pathway that is important, including, crucially, how at each point in the journey those responsible for care manage the process of receiving and moving the patient on. The experience of the Bristol Inquiry was that patients were most at risk when they were at the borders of care between one group, or institution, and another. CHAI will be particularly vigilant to monitor the patient's experience along the pathway of care and the quality of care delivered at all points.
6. Finally, monitoring the patient's journey and assessing the performance of those providing the care along it will not be limited to those providing healthcare. CHAI will be placed under a statutory obligation to collaborate with its new sister organisation, the Commission for Social Care Inspection (CSCI). The reasoning is obvious, even if it has taken a long time to translate it into action. Assessment of performance should not be something which stops at the city walls so to speak, such that the patient is then left to hope that some other body will keep an eye on what happens thereafter. This is to abandon the patient. It is a failure of public responsibility and accountability. So, from its inception, CHAI will work with CSCI to ensure that patients who move between the various providers of health and social care, both public and private, are properly looked after. It will do so by ensuring that among its portfolio of standards and criteria by which organisations are assessed, are criteria which specifically address the management and organisation of care of those who move between health and social care.

So far, I have explored the challenge of moving from the abstract to the concrete. I hope I have been able to show that, beginning with general concepts in the form of generic standards, you can move through a process of concretisation until, as the product of consultation and discussion, you arrive at specific issues, as, for example, how importantly patients value good communication, and how ward 5 is performing, both against its own ambitions and the achievements of other similar wards.

CHAI and Children

I am conscious that in a lecture delivered at one of the world's most famous hospitals for children, I have scarcely mentioned them. Forgive me, but I considered it important to set out our thinking on the design and architecture of CHAI before considering the specific question of where children fit into the scheme of things.

As I have said, the care of children is very important to me. It is 23 years since I broadcast, as my third Reith lecture, the lecture entitled 'Suffer the little children'. It is only two years ago that I explained to the press that the Chapter on children in the Report of the Public Inquiry into Paediatric Cardiac Surgery at Bristol Royal Infirmary was written 'in anger'. Since then, of course, we have had the Victoria Climbie inquiry and the subsequent publication two weeks ago of a Green Paper 'Every Child Matters' (on which more later).

Equal Citizenship

Let me first explain how the care of children fits into CHAI's general approach. The care of children has often been described (and, I interject, commonly treated) as a Cinderella service. Children have been and are categorised as vulnerable, as they are to a greater or lesser extent, because we make them so. Their care has thus been seen in the context of the 'needs of the vulnerable'. As such, disempowered by their very vulnerability, their voices and the voices of those who speak for them have often been shouted down in the scramble for resources. As increasing resources are made available, the need to choose between this or that group of patients will recede. But, it will not go away. Thus, the need for effective advocacy, and subsequent action, remains.

In that advocacy, for me it is unhelpful, and perhaps damaging, to talk of the 'needs of the vulnerable'. It conjures up supplicants, waiting in line for their needs to be met, and perhaps giving way to others with greater claims or capable of making greater fuss. Rhetoric and language are important here. The discourse must not be about needs but rights. Children have rights which properly demand to be met. They are not extravagant rights: food, shelter, safety from preventable hazards, education, healthcare. It is a comment on all of us that these rights continue to be denied to so many of our children, while this and that Declaration and Manifesto constantly proclaim that neglect will be a thing of the past. Proceeding from the premise that it is children's rights which we must be concerned with, CHAI's approach is to see the care of children as being an issue of equal citizenship. Children as citizens are entitled to equality of access to care and to a quality of care that equals that provided to others. This is their right. To continue to deny them this is to deny their fundamental rights as citizens. And, of course, this approach, based on the right to equal citizenship, is not limited to children. It extends equally to those who live at the margins of our society and, for whatever reason, have unequal access to the benefits which society claims to extend to all. They include the mentally ill, the infirm elderly, those with learning or other disabilities, or those discriminated against because of racial or ethnic background.

Adopting the approach to the care of the children based on equal citizenship has a further consequence. It necessarily entails that priority be given to those whose need is greatest, and this includes children and their care. This, then, must be a commitment made by CHAI. The justification for this commitment, if justification were needed, lies in a notion of justice that suggests that, if we truly value equality of opportunity, those most in need have first claim on our attention. So, my first message and challenge to you is to keep us to this commitment. And, of course, tell us how we could do better.

Criteria for Assessment

Secondly, in developing the criteria which will put flesh on the bones of the standards which CHAI will use to assess performance, in the case of children we will need the advice of children, carers, and clinicians. So, the second challenge, or invitation, is to work with us (as some of you are already doing) to get the criteria right. In the case of the NSF on acute care in hospital, although there is only one general standard, the NSF clearly points to the direction of travel we should be taking in developing criteria, in breathing content into that standard. We are working closely with colleagues in the Royal College of Paediatrics and Child Health to develop a 'tool-kit' which can be used by trusts for this purpose. Equally, as other elements of the NSF are developed this year and into the future, this process of consultation and deliberation must continue, so that the rest of the NSF addresses the things that matter to children, their carers and those who look after them.

Questions

Then, we come to the 'cute questions'. What are the questions which will really enable us to find out whether the care of children in this or that context really is satisfying the standards and criteria? Here again we crucially need your help and advice. It is patients, carers and professionals who know from their respective experience what we should really be looking for if we want to find out about the quality of care.

Answers

Finally, we need to be able to answer the questions. As we said about the Bristol Royal Infirmary, it was awash with data. What was lacking was information. The challenge is simple. Clinicians and managers must see the accumulation and sharing of data as a central duty. It can no longer be acceptable that organisations providing health care have only the dimmest picture of what is going on in the many corners of the organisation. Nor can it any longer be a defence to say that it is hard to find out. It can no longer be acceptable for clinicians to collect their data for what they see as their purposes, for example, research, but regard any other data about the performance of their organisation as not their business. It can no longer be acceptable that patients and carers are allowed only a partial picture at best of an organisation's quality and performance. All of these challenges have to be met. CHAI's role is to help you to meet them.

The Child's Journey along a Pathway of Care

You will recall that I referred earlier to CHAI's intention to follow patients as they journey through their various exposures to healthcare, sometimes called the pathway of care. You will recognise the importance of doing so in the case of children. One of the particular features of the Bristol Inquiry was the fact that it was as children moved from one form of care to another, from one building to another, even from one clinical team to another, that they were at increased risk. Equally, it was at such times that essential features of care such as communication with carers was at risk of breaking down. CHAI will be vigilant to monitor how effectively the process of care is managed. Thus, CHAI will not only be looking into the particular arena of care, the particular trust or even unit, but also at how the child gets there and how well the child's next move in his/her journey is managed and communicated. Of course, team-work is a crucial component in good care and CHAI will be particularly attentive to the way in which professionals are able to work together for the good of the child. Here again, we will need your advice to develop the right criteria and ask the right questions, so as to assess performance, share good practice and help improvement.

'Joined-up' Assessment

Collaboration and team-work become even more important when the care of children extends beyond healthcare to include social services and perhaps on occasions, the justice system. You will recall that CHAI will be under a statutory duty to collaborate with CSCI (the Commission for Social Care Inspection). This means that the assessment of performance must be seamless, such that the care of the child must be seamless too. That there is much to do was cruelly demonstrated by the case of Victoria Climbie, one of a series of tragedies which have continued to make the same point for decades. CHAI's intention is to work with CSCI and others to prevent as far as possible this blight on our society. CHAI, in other words, has the obligation and relishes the opportunity to engage in joined-up action at the operational, not just the political level.

Reducing the Burden of Inspection

One other feature of CHAI's role as a 'joiner-up' of organisations bears mention here, though it takes us away from the theme of children for a moment. The Bill now before Parliament casts on CHAI the duty to be the leading inspectorate in the context of healthcare. This duty translates into at least two concurrent activities which CHAI is currently analysing. The first is the rationalisation of the multiple requests for information currently placed on those who work in the NHS. It is an unceasing complaint that every day some form, or somebody, arrives requesting information on this or that, most of which, with just sufficient difference of emphasis to make it not suitable for the current request, was asked for yesterday, and which, unfailingly, will be asked for again tomorrow. This serves no-one. It distracts those caring for patients away from the task of doing so. It feeds an appetite for data, the feeding of which is an end in itself and seems to serve no other purpose. CHAI is duty bound to bring some order to this situation and it will do so, though it will take time and will not be easy.

Just as with requests for data, so with visits. The other way in which CHAI will seek to comply with its duty to rationalise inspection will be to co-ordinate and reduce the number of visits which organisations are subject to. Of course, visits have a purpose, and CHAI will use them, albeit selectively. But currently, there is a small army of agencies and bodies which presume to descend on the NHS without any apparent coordination. The burden of such activity, in terms of distraction, extra work and reduced morale cannot be overstated. CHAI will sort this out too, though again it will take time.

There are many other strands to CHAI's development which I could put before you, but I am conscious of the limits to your patience. Therefore, I refer you instead to CHAI's Vision Document. And, of course, as we develop ideas over the next months and years, we will continue to consult and listen and learn. Before I close, however, I want to say a couple of things about the recently published Green Paper and the status of children's care generally.

Some Concerns for the Future

The Green Paper 'Every Child Matters'

I begin with the welcome which all those interested in the welfare of children must extend to the Green Paper and its proposals aimed at making children healthier, safer, better educated and better able to get by in the world. Equally, the recognition that it is the whole child and all of the influences and agencies with which children come into contact that must command our attention, while self-evident and long overdue, is again very welcome. I recall also that it is a Green Paper and, therefore, seeking views rather than setting out a decided position.

Approach to Inspection

Those things having been said, there are some matters on which I entertain reservations. In doing so, I emphasise that I speak in a personal capacity. CHAI has not yet formally considered the Green Paper but will, of course, respond in due course. My principal reservation revolves around the way policy appears to have been made. In the case of Bristol while the central concern was children's healthcare, the response of government was to recognise the interrelatedness of health and social care and promote an integrated response. Nor was the response limited to children; it addressed issues across the whole of health and social care. In the case of the Green Paper, however, while apparently espousing the cause of an integrated response, the model chosen to be the basis for building a new approach is that of the inspectorates concerned with child protection. This has a number of implications for the healthcare of children.

Whither Children's Healthcare?

First, there is a real danger that, having at last, after Bristol, gained the attention of government, those concerned with children's health will see in the Green Paper a fragmentation of their plans and ambitions. The danger arising from the Green Paper is at least two-fold. First, the healthcare of children will remain, and thus, perhaps become isolated, in the Department of Health while all other activities relating to the care and welfare of children are to be centred in the Department for Education. Secondly, this picture is itself confused by the fact that some areas of children's healthcare will fall within the purview of the proposed new system of integrated inspection, co-ordinated from the Department of Education, while other areas, including acute services, would appear to be excluded from the perceived advantages of the new system. The almost arbitrary separation of areas of healthcare runs entirely counter to CHAI's approach, in which the assessment of pathways of care is so important. It leaves CHAI's ability to carry out its responsibilities to children, as CHAI judges best, in some doubt. I am sure that you would agree that it would be a sad day if the progress currently being made in relation to children's healthcare should be shipwrecked on inter-departmental divisions of responsibility, with all the opportunity for children to disappear through the cracks which are the inevitable product of such divisions.

Model of Inspection

My second concern relates to the concept of inspection which the Green Paper reflects and appears to endorse. I have already referred to the different meanings which can be and are attributed to inspection. In CHAI's case, as you have seen, we have a view that assessment of performance should be carried out through a variety of means of inspection, including but not limited to visits. The assessment, as I have pointed out at some length, should take account of the views of local communities and the criteria of assessment should be the product of continuing dialogue between the public, professionals, patients and government. The model of inspection which informs the Green Paper, however, is that of education and social services, centred on the periodic visit. It would be unfortunate indeed if the approach to inspection being developed by CHAI, and so far apparently welcomed, should have to be revised to fit another model developed for other activities with their own history and tradition. This risk exists not least because the Green Paper vests the role of leading inspectorate in Ofsted, notwithstanding the fact that the Health and Social Care Bill currently before Parliament vests in CHAI the role of the leading inspectorate in healthcare. Mine is not a point about hegemony. It is a point about clarity of responsibility and the use of models of assessment which are suited to the task. The model contemplated in the Green Paper may be appropriate in the context of Child Protection. I am not an expert and do not know. But, healthcare is simply too complex to be assessed by a visit every three years. Patients and professionals deserve better.

I have every reason to believe that as the proposals mature, a suitable way forward will be found. I merely raise the points here by way of giving notice both that CHAI must work wholeheartedly with others to make a success of the Green Paper's ambitions, and that I am determined that this will be accomplished without abandoning what CHAI's vision contemplates.

Funding

One final point. You will all know that the Children's NSF in relation to acute hospital care called for action but did not accept that any extra funding was needed to achieve the necessary action. I am afraid that I belong to an old-fashioned school of thought that says that there are occasions when 'money brings honey'. Again, speaking entirely personally, as a long-time observer of children's care, it has long been clear that in the case of children, things do not get better by wishing them so. I could understand, therefore, if professionals felt let down by the absence of dedicated funding following the first part of the NSF. They would probably think that some earnest would not go amiss.

Conclusion

CHAI's ambition is to make a difference for patients, for professionals and for the public. Its central concern is to promote improvements in healthcare and in public health. To do so, it needs your help. I invite you to join us on an exciting journey.

Postscript

The vision I describe for regulating the provision of healthcare was, at the time, revolutionary. Perhaps it was too much so. Certainly it was frustrated by government which constrained it with a straitjacket of targets, some motivated by politics rather than the welfare of patients, while other, more relevant goals were ignored. Equally, the vision was met with intransigent opposition from the managerialist classes. Both (rightly!) saw the approach as leading to a level of accountability which was far too threatening. The Healthcare Commission was abolished after five years, its abolition having been announced after only 11 months! It was replaced by the Care Quality Commission (CQC) which took a much more tender approach to those who managed the NHS, with predictably damaging results for patients. Once it was realised that things needed to change, a revised version of the CQC emerged. Its way of working, though an improvement, still differs greatly from the vision I offered.

4

The Healthcare Commission's Blueprint for Regulation[1]

Currently, there is much discussion of regulation. It is not just limited to the private sector where business has always had a fraught relationship with regulation. It now occupies much attention in the public sector, particular as regards the regulation of healthcare – those who practice it and the organisations which provide it. A number of premises seem to operate. Regulation:

- is something imposed from outside that which is being regulated;
- by definition is a 'burden', (burden being defined loosely as something which detracts from the efficient running of that which is regulated);
- being a burden, it inhibits the efficiency of the enterprise regulated;
- it is synonymous with inspection, meaning periodic visits to the organisations being regulated;
- as a consequence, should be kept to a minimum commensurate with achieving whatever goals are sought.

This fifth premise, of course, exposes at least two problems. The goals sought may not be clear, such that no amount of adjustments to the relevant regulation will suffice. Secondly, they may not be achievable, except through a kind of regulation which is undesirable according to the other premises.

Regulation, particularly in the public sector, has perennially reflected these premises and the attendant problems. However, whatever the plausibility these premises may have as regards regulation in other spheres, they have little relevance to the kind of Regulation contemplated by the Healthcare Commission (HC), both in its initial Vision and in all subsequent Plans. The HC's approach to Regulation is radically different in concept. It proceeds from a different set of assumptions:

- it is assumed that there is common agreement between government, those who provide healthcare, those who receive it, and those who pay for it through taxation, that it is desirable to improve the safety and quality of healthcare;

[1] This was an unpublished paper which I wrote in March 2005, two months before the Healthcare Commission began operations.

- it is assumed that there are a number of means of achieving this aim, each of which is not enough in itself (eg the provision of increased funds will not achieve the desired result without, among other things, careful management);
- it is assumed that one of the means (in conjunction with others) of achieving this aim is through the creation of a regulatory body, called, traditionally, an inspectorate (a loosely used and ill-defined term). A number of further points flow from this:
  (a) this inspectorate should be independent of government – independence being understood as a term describing a complex relationship, the prime characteristic of which is the power to look at what it, as well as others, chooses to look at and to report publicly what it finds
  (b) the role of government should be retained through stipulating some but not all of the standards of performance (reflecting the government's priorities) that the inspectorate will measure
  (c) the inspectorate should see itself as one of a series of mechanisms concerned with promoting improvement and seek to collaborate with others to maximise the efficiency with which it can carry out its regulatory role
  (d) the Inspectorate should not behave in such a way that it inhibits improvement in healthcare but rather seek to foster and contribute to it.

The HC has translated these assumptions into a radical approach which involves the following analytical steps:

1 The HC's principal statutory duty is to use its assessment of the performance of organisations in the NHS to encourage improvement in the provision of healthcare.
2 This duty is to be achieved taking account of the standards laid down (initially) by government.
3 The standards are grouped under Domains, such as Safety, Clinical Effectiveness, Focus on Patients. These Domains are the point of departure for assessing performance.
4 The Domains should be populated with those things which matter to two principal audiences: those who use healthcare services and those who provide them (without prejudice to the concerns also of the general public and of government). And, 'what matters' should be defined in terms of what promotes improvement in the provision of healthcare, so as to fulfil the HC's statutory duty.
5 The HC as an organisation does not know what promotes improvement.
6 By contrast, those who receive and provide healthcare do know. The HC must, therefore, develop its portfolio of things that matter by listening to those directly affected.
7 While there will be some differences between the matters chosen by the various audiences, there will be a significant degree of overlap: a common set of things that matter, both from a generic perspective and as regards specific areas of care or groups of patients.
8 Having identified the things that matter, appropriate means must be developed to discover whether they are being complied with.
9 Data must be collected to answer the questions posed by 8 above. The data need not be bespoke nor new data. Indeed, it should already be collected by an organisation,

if the organisation is managing itself appropriately. If not collected, it is the organisation which should change, not the data. As for those who complain that collecting the relevant data is a 'burden', it is only dysfunctional organisations, not geared to the service of patients, or a managerial class which seeks to avoid a mode of accountability which is concerned for patients, which complain.

10 The data will be routinely collected, allowing for regular surveillance of performance, with a view to alerting/assisting organisations encountering difficulties and sharing/celebrating good practice. Visits to organisations (the only meaning that 'inspection' has in the context of the HC's approach to regulation) will be for specific purposes, prompted by data, together with the occasional spot check and unannounced visit.

11 When Hospital Trusts understand what it is about their performance that the HC will assess, they will direct their energies to providing the data about that which matters, since rewards (and the opposite) will flow from the HC's assessment of their performance. (And, unlike the case of targets, data will be drawn from a range of sources, so as to avoid 'gaming').

12 If, therefore, the HC is assessing the right things, and it should be because it will be measuring the extent to which organisations are doing those things which the various audiences have said promote improvement, then trusts will, by responding to the assessment, be delivering the desired objectives and thus, by definition, promoting improvement.

13 Finally, those who have contributed to the identification of the things that matter, patients and those who provide healthcare, will recognise that the system of assessment does, in fact, reflect their interests and concerns and will, therefore, identify with and support it.

14 Of course, the approach is not static, but dynamic; kept under constant review and revised as appropriate.

The above outline describes a system of regulation which has at its heart a virtuous cycle of improvement. It is not imposed from above and from outside the groups whose interests are crucial. Rather, it is designed and therefore 'owned' by them. It is designed from the 'bottom up'. Improvement becomes both the purpose and the result of regulation. Talk of 'burden' becomes part of a different conversation, concerned not with the inherent nature of Regulation, but with a second order issue having to do with the detail of what data is needed and how it is best collected. Indeed, so far from being a 'burden', Regulation, as conceptualised here, is beneficial, serving to facilitate continuous improvement.

Moreover, based as it is on the collection, analysis and dissemination of data in the form of relevant and intelligible information, the form of regulation described also meets three other fundamental goals: it allows government and taxpayers to identify where and how well money is being spent; it allows those who provide healthcare to be held to account; and it allows the public and patients to inform themselves about the safety and quality of the healthcare available to them.

Of course, translating into practice what is described here is an extremely complex undertaking. This cannot be surprising given the size and scale of the NHS and the soon-to-be-integrated independent sector. But, the thesis is clear and remarkably simple.

There is a real danger, however, that this radical, indeed revolutionary approach to regulation will be lost in the diversions of amalgamations and mergers within and between healthcare and social care. The barriers between healthcare and social care are largely bureaucratic and deserve to be removed. Moreover, the shape of future healthcare, and its inevitable overlap with social care demand that they be removed. But, this should be done with due care and deliberation. It should not result in the lazy opting for inadequate systems of regulation which put at risk the possibility of building a system of regulation in which accountability and the real interests of patients and those who provide for them are lost or ignored.

Postscript

As I have said already in relation to the previous piece, the implementation of this approach to regulation was frustrated by a government bewitched by the siren calls of de-regulation (leading inexorably to the financial crash of 2008/09 among other things). The Healthcare Commission was abolished within 11 months of its creation! Also, meaningful standards for measuring performance and the analysis and publication of relevant data was a bridge too far for many thereby exposed to scrutiny.

5

The Safety of Healthcare: The Role of Regulation[1]

Regulation in the Architecture of Health and Healthcare

As regards the NHS, the government's policies of decentralisation and localism, the establishment of national standards of performance coupled to local decision-making, a budget in excess of £100 billion of taxpayers' money, and the performance management cascaded from the centre in Whitehall through regional Strategic Health Authorities, and Monitor in the case of Foundation Trusts, to individual trusts; and, as regards the independent sector, its interaction with the NHS and the principle of consumer protection, all combine to create the need for an independent watchdog:

- to provide assurance to the public about the safety and quality of care, currently through the Healthcare Commission's various activities and in the future through the Care Quality Commission's (CQC) system of registration, review and assessment;
- to hold the system to account;
- to promote improvement;
- to publish information allowing for comparisons across the system.

All of these fall to be achieved through the assessment of the performance of providers and commissioners of care; reviews of services and of care for certain groups of patients; and investigations, backed by powers and sanctions.

The Aim of Regulation in Relation to Safe Care

Healthcare is intrinsically risky. Mistakes will inevitably be made. A proportion of patients (though the number and identity are not known) will inevitably be harmed, of whom some will die. These are the facts of modern healthcare, as are the remarkable benefits now enjoyed by patients. In a significant number of the cases in which patients are harmed, the harm could have been avoided.

[1] This is an otherwise unpublished paper submitted to the Health Select Committee in March 2009 as the Healthcare Commission was about to be abolished and replaced by the Care Quality Commission.

The regulator, working with others, particularly the National Patient Safety Agency (NPSA), should be concerned to:

- emphasise the particular importance of seeking to secure ever safer care for patients;
- contribute to the prevention and mitigation of unsafe behaviour.

How Should the Regulator Achieve These Aims?

The regulator should seek to ensure that the safety of care is a high (the highest) priority in the system of registration and continuing assessment and review.

Assuming an information-led, risk-based system of regulation, for the regulator to contribute to improvements in the safety of care the following requirements need to be met:

- an analysis of what constitutes safe care in the various settings in which care is provided;
- agreed standards of performance which reflect this analysis and describe what good, safe care looks like;
- the design of ways of measuring (metrics) compliance with/departure from these standards;
- the collation and analysis of data (from all sources, formal and informal, including whistleblowers) required to inform these metrics;
- the reporting of what the analysis shows, including any intervention by the regulator in organisations, any investigation, and any necessary follow-up.

These are the building blocks which, taken together, enable the regulator to play its part in promoting the safe care of patients. If they are not in place, regulation and the regulator are less effective, and the patient is less protected. Each of the elements requires examination.

An Analysis of Safe Care

There is a growing body of evidence of what makes healthcare safe; what good care looks like. This needs to be understood, shared and adopted. Much of the evidence relates to the acute sector. There is, perhaps, undue emphasis on the operating theatre and the intensive care unit, as if it were there that the patient is most at risk. In fact, being more at risk does not necessarily mean that the patient is more likely to be avoidably harmed. This is demonstrated by the extraordinary success in reducing the incidence of avoidable harm in anaesthesia. It remains a high-risk field of healthcare, but through close, detailed analysis, not least of the design of equipment, errors and associated harm to patients have been dramatically reduced. The same analysis needs to be applied to all aspects of care in the acute sector.

An important feature of such analysis should be the adoption of a 'systems' approach, whereby care is understood as being provided within a system. Usually, things go wrong and safe care is compromised when systems break down. Crucially, the systems approach sets its face against the notion that unsafe behaviour and any ensuing harm can be explained simply by identifying individuals whose behaviour is the cause and are therefore personally responsible and should be blamed. Instead, it talks in terms of 'human factors analysis': what are the human factors in any particular activity which contribute to things going wrong? They may be the working practices, the morale, the team-working, incentives, equipment, resources, external pressures, or the interplay of all of these. Individuals may have done something wrong (though rarely intentionally), but to concentrate on this and not to see any individual as part of a larger whole, inevitably affected by a range of other surrounding factors, is to fail to understand how unsafe practices come about and so fail to be able to learn from them and limit their occurrence. The analysis of what makes care unsafe and how to make care safer must, therefore, be informed by the adoption of a systems approach.

Unfortunately, this approach, associated with the psychologist James Reason,[2] is only just beginning to influence thinking in healthcare. Blaming individuals is still the preferred option of the press and to a certain extent politicians and the public. By contrast 'human factors' is well embedded in the approach to safety adopted in a range of other areas where high-risk, complex activities are the norm, such as aviation, and the petrochemical, gas, and nuclear industries. Each of these industries now has an impressive safety record.

As has been said, much of the evidence on safe care and much of the current activity directed at improving the safety of care focuses on the acute sector. At first blush, this seems appropriate. This is where the action is, it is said, and where errors can cost lives. But, it is too unbalanced an emphasis for two reasons. First, around 90% of all contacts between patients and clinicians take place in primary care settings or through care in the community. To focus concerns about the safety of care largely or wholly on the acute sector ignores what happens elsewhere. Second, there is no reason other than to assume that a similar incidence of unsafe practice takes place outside the acute sector. And, if this is so, the incidence of avoidable harm, currently derived almost entirely from what happens in the acute sector, must be much higher than currently estimated. The risks are different, but there nonetheless. The effects, if care is unsafe, may be different but there are effects and they can harm patients.

It is one thing, of course, to assert this as something that must rationally be true. It is another thing to be able to demonstrate and document it. Again, there are at least two reasons why this is so. They interact with each other. First, there is a very significant gap in the data: we just do not know the incidence of unsafe practices outside the acute sector which cause avoidable harm. Secondly, not only is there a gap in the data, but the way in which the safety of care is conceptualised makes it currently very difficult to fill that gap. We refer here to the over-identification of unsafe care with 'incidents' (reported or otherwise) and 'near misses': ie things being done.

[2] J Reason, *Human Error* (Cambridge: Cambridge University Press, 1990).

In primary care and care in the community, however, unsafe care may take the form of omissions – failures to do something; not 'doing something' but 'not doing something'. Examples include a GP's failure to diagnose a condition warranting treatment, mis-diagnosing what is affecting a patient, such that the wrong treatment is given, or making a diagnosis later than should have been made, with consequent avoidable harm to the patient. The Healthcare Commission's work in dealing with complaints against Trusts provides a considerable body of anecdotal evidence of this state of affairs. In none of these circumstances is there an 'incident' in the sense of something being done leading to the harming of a patient, such as giving the wrong medicine, operating on the wrong site, or inserting a breathing tube incorrectly. An approach to safety, therefore, which is posited on the notion that unsafe care takes the form of 'incidents' and which then proceeds to quantify these incidents (concentrating on the acute sector), is important in contributing to the analysis and understanding of safe care, but only offers a partial and limited picture. This is now well recognised by the National Patient Safety Agency which is developing ways of capturing data on unsafe care in the form of omissions, with particular reference to general practice.

There is a view that omissions of the sort described are not properly understood as matters of safety, but rather reflect on the quality of care provided. The patient, on this view, suffers harm from a poor quality of care. On one level, this could be a matter of semantics. And, arguably, if it is, safety should have a wider meaning to embrace omissions which put the patient at unacceptable risk. But, this view should be resisted on other grounds. Quality of care exists on a spectrum on which the safety of care sits as the starting point: to emphasise its importance, it should not be shouldered aside by describing something as 'merely' a matter of quality (and, therefore, not requiring the concern devoted to safety). And, secondly, to categorise something as a matter of quality tends to suggest it is a matter of personal failure or competence, calling for some sort of response at the level of an individual. This runs counter to the systems or human factors approach set out earlier.

It follows that a true analysis of the safety of care, of the incidence of unsafe care, and the lessons for the former which can be derived from the latter, depend on coming to terms with what goes on in primary and community care as well as in the acute sector (and not forgetting the ambulance sector), and with omissions as well as commissions.

Standards of Performance

Put simply, the standards relating to the safety of care are the distillation of current opinion as to what constitutes good practice in the relevant area of practice. It is important to recognise that there must be a degree of flexibility in the standards, since it is unhelpful to adopt a position that 'one size fits all'. Some flexibility is required so that account may be taken of the context in which the standards are to be applied. In some geographical areas, there may be levels of disadvantage and deprivation such that the standards may have an aspirational element. In such circumstances it may be helpful to establish a 'benchmark' of current performance, as a way of applying the standards locally, since the term benchmark has within it an implicit assumption that what can be expected by way of performance can, and should, change (ie improve).

Once the initial benchmark is established, improvement can then be sought, monitored and identified and the benchmark set higher, always with a view to meeting the required standards, albeit in a measured way. This fits well with the regulatory duty to encourage improvement. What is sought is some standard or norm of performance, a description of what amounts to good practice, derived from observation of practice, not just nationally but internationally, against which actual performance can be assessed. And, in articulating this norm, due account can be taken of the surrounding circumstances in which the performance to be assessed takes place. This allows for a more nuanced approach. It allows due account to be taken of the difference in caring for a population and patients who suffer various levels of deprivation as compared with those who are more affluent and have more opportunities.

The fundamental basis of the approach is its reliance on good practice and the avoidance of risk. The question to be asked in arriving at the relevant standard is: what is required by way of performance so that a patient has care of good quality and will not be exposed to a risk of harm greater than could reasonably be expected? The aim, therefore, is to agree standards of performance which reflect the analysis of what constitutes safe care and which properly take account of the context in which care is provided and the risks involved. The regulator (and everyone else) is then interested in what can reasonably be expected of this or that service, taking account of all relevant circumstances. But, a caveat must be entered immediately. When talking of safety, the safe care of patients, the idea of a standard developed through a process of benchmarking with its inherent flexibility cannot be used to justify behaviour which falls below some accepted and agreed minimum of safe care.

What emerges is the notion that standards of safe care consist of three elements – certain non-negotiable requirements – risks that must be avoided, whatever the circumstances; the norms of current good performance as reflected in national and international practice and the general understanding of accepted risks; and incremental improvements in the avoidance of risks.

This idea of a scaled or layered approach is also reflected in how standards relating to safe care can be made to operate in practice. There will be certain standards which are generic, applicable in all circumstances, whatever the context and the area of healthcare involved. Then there will be standards particular to the area or specialty of care, child-specific in paediatrics, or specific to the care, for example, of those with diabetes.

From this approach, it will be clear that it becomes absolutely crucial who should establish the standards. Given the highly politicised nature of healthcare, government is an obvious contender. And, certainly, across the broad spectrum of health and healthcare it is entirely appropriate for government to stipulate that certain conditions be met in terms of what the NHS and the independent sector deliver. This has led government to issue targets and the Standards for Better Health, which the Healthcare Commission is statutorily obliged to 'take account of'.

There are significant drawbacks, however, from the perspective of the regulator, in the government's doing anything more than identifying a small number of targets from time to time, which reflect the declared priorities of an elected government. Going further than this should be avoided for at least two reasons. First, the choice of what to focus on is often (usually) politically driven. It may not, however, address the real challenges to safe care. 'Deep cleans' may have some effect on *some* hospital-associated infections, but are largely irrelevant as regards others, such that, if the time of the regulator were spent in assessing compliance with the programme of cleaning, it would, to that extent, be distracted from contributing to improvements in the safety of care more broadly. Furthermore, by not including the safety of care in its targets until 2003 (and then only as regards some hospital-associated infections), when targets were the medium through which government signalled the really important things that had to be addressed, it could be said that the government failed adequately to signal the importance of the safety of care in the scheme of things. And, again, while creating a significant regulatory machinery to address concerns over hospital-associated infection, other hospital-associated conditions, some of which, for example, venous thromboembolism (VTE) cause a much greater toll of avoidable deaths, have gone without mention until very recently, and, thus, from one perspective, perhaps, were seen as being of less importance.

Perhaps the strongest reason why government alone should not establish the standards of performance is that, to be successful in promoting incremental improvement in performance, they need to be recognised as relevant by the clinicians who are to apply them and whose performance is to be assessed by reference to them. It follows that the regulator also is not the body to establish them.[3] Certainly, government, and indeed the regulator, have a role to play in the development of standards, but as the regulator we take the view that their development must be led by clinicians (by which we mean the broad spectrum of healthcare professionals) in consultation with patients. Only then will they be accepted as clinically driven (in Lord Darzi's language), focused on and agreed by patients and owned by clinicians, rather than seen as imposed from above and outside.

This is why the question who sets the standards is important to the regulator. There are three reasons. First, the regulator wants to concern itself with what matters to patients and professionals; the standard must reflect their views on what is important as regards the safety of care. They are the experts. Secondly, the regulator is, as has been said, part of the overall architectural scheme for delivering increasingly safer and better care. If clinicians do not feel themselves genuinely engaged in the development of the standards that the regulator applies, they become disengaged. The regulator's task in promoting improvements becomes that much more difficult: the regulator is seen by clinicians as the agent of external power imposed upon them, rather than as assessing compliance with standards that they and their patients recognise and endorse. Thirdly, regulation, to succeed in the particular culture of healthcare, must be understood and accepted by those regulated, not least clinicians. To work alongside them and others in the development of standards achieves that goal and thereby improves the prospect that patients will be treated more safely. After all, few clinicians would wish to be associated with a quality of care regarded as substandard by their peers.

The Healthcare Commission has worked successfully with clinicians over the past three years in realising the approach set out above. The collaboration has led to a large

[3] NICE is currently seen as the organisation best equipped to develop standards. This accords with the approach taken here, given NICE's well-developed system of engagement with clinicians and patients.

number of specialist-specific standards, some of which deal with the safety of care. So as to ensure some degree of authority in what is produced by way of standards, certain principles were agreed and are followed:

- the standard must be grounded in up-to-date evidence;
- it must be accepted by the large majority of clinicians in the relevant field;
- it must have been agreed also by an appropriately constituted sample of patients;
- compliance with it must be measurable through the collection of data;
- a mechanism must exist whereby it can be reviewed and, if necessary, revised periodically.

One final point needs to be made. While there is a strong argument that government alone should not set the standards, neither should it be left to some local free-for-all to decide what standards they prefer to abide by. Apart from anything else, this would leave the regulator with no firm basis on which to assess performance except on the terms set by those being assessed. A mechanism, therefore, is needed whereby the standards which are put forward by the relevant professional groups are agreed nationally, and examined and endorsed, arguably by government and the regulator.

Measuring Compliance

Standards are only useful to the regulator (and all others concerned to assess performance) if compliance with them can be readily measured. This is the area described as 'metrics'. In an information-led system of regulation, measurement in the first instance is through the analysis of data. The system, crucially, is not wholly based on data. This would make it too mechanistic. It must be supplemented by 'softer' local intelligence and, where appropriate, targeted or unannounced visits to hospitals/trusts. The importance of such visits cannot be understated: suitably targeted, they provide an essential further element of insight into what is going on.

The development of metrics is to a large extent a matter of technical expertise, but there are a number of points to be made of a general nature.

First, the data necessary for the relevant analyses to be made must exist. In the case of the safety of care, it has been seen that in primary care there are significant gaps. Across the system of healthcare as a whole, historically the NHS has collected data relating to finance, workforce and the throughput of patients. Then, data to meet the demands of government relating to targets were added. There was also the data necessary to meet the requirements of the regulators, the Healthcare Commission and Monitor. And, with specific reference to safe care, there is the data which the NHS Litigation Authority calls for to set its risk assessment, and that which the National Patient Safety Agency asks for (rather than requires) through its system of reporting 'incidents' and 'near misses'. As regards the independent sector, the data required by the current regulator (the Healthcare Commission) addresses the question of whether a provider of services should be licensed rather than any specific focus on the safety of care (although serious untoward incidents must be reported).

From this picture, it can be seen that data about safety has not historically been a priority and that its collection to a degree has been the response to external factors rather than a very important end in itself. Evidence is now emerging that healthcare organisations are paying increased attention to safety. There is an increase in the reporting of incidents to the NPSA and the Healthcare Commission's inspection of compliance with the Hygiene Code has had a significant effect ('what gets measured, gets done'!). But, there remain significant gaps in the data available to assess, as a regulator, or as a manager, how safe care really is and what needs to be done by way of improvement (one example emerged from the Healthcare Commission's review of maternity services where it was found that only 17% of trusts collected data which would allow them to assess the quality and safety of care that women receive from the point of initial contact with the service to the provision of care after birth[4]).

One particular challenge as regards data is the capacity to keep track of patients (and professionals) as they move about and through the system of healthcare. The difficulties in exchanging data across the system remain a significant impediment to safe care and need to be addressed urgently. This was demonstrated once again in the 'care' of Baby P,[5] whereby he was taken to a variety of healthcare organisations, each of which remained largely unaware of previous encounters and, therefore, unable to respond to the unsafe care that he was receiving.

This must change if the safety of care is to improve. The regulator, as part of its duty to inform the public, must be able to know how safe services are and whether those commissioning services are insisting on such information. The recent resurgence of interest, on a national level, in audit is an important step. The regulator, as one of the mechanisms available to government to advance government's strategic goals, can then stipulate that it requires evidence that audit is being carried out, that the information on the safety of care figures prominently in the audit, that the evidence produced is reported to those needing to know, and that it is then acted upon. One particularly important aspect of this insistence on audit is the development of a culture among professionals of reporting and learning from things that have gone wrong. Such a culture, championed by NPSA, has been slow to develop, but progress is being made. It is crucial, not only for the critical reflection of professionals, but also for the regulator (as well as others), both as evidence that the safety of care is being addressed, and as a means of determining whether lessons are, in fact, being learned.

Meanwhile, the regulator should not rely solely on data generated by the NHS and the independent sector in its assessment of the safety of care. There are a very large number of organisations which, for one reason or another, hold data on health and healthcare. The regulator should, as part of its strategic approach to information-led regulation, continue to identify these sources of data and add them to its database, not least to give a broader and different perspective on the performance of trusts and services in the area of safety. One of the most important sources is, of course, the NPSA. A successful working relationship has now been developed between the Healthcare

[4] [At the time of writing, the shortcomings in maternity care at Shrewsbury and Telford Hospital NHS Trust revealed in the Ockenden Review (10 December 2020) suggest that lessons are still not being learned, with disastrous consequences.]

[5] Peter Connelly who died on 3 August 2007 aged 1 after sustained abuse.

Commission and the NPSA, allowing for the sharing of data, so that the regulator can act promptly and effectively when appropriate. Two further sources of data which are worth mentioning, since they are often overlooked, are, first, the views of patients and the public. These should be routinely collected by trusts and shared with the regulator, as they contain insights about safety which might otherwise be lost. Secondly, the regulator should routinely examine the data on complaints made against providers and commissioners of care for the same reason.[6]

Of course, insisting that data exist invites the question, data about what? The answer is of crucial importance. The regulator, to assess the extent to which trusts and services comply with standards of what constitutes safe care, must be interested in outcomes, what was supposed to happen and what did happen. Partly because of what has historically been seen as important to measure, and partly because to measure what the regulator is interested in would call for different data and a different mindset, the safety of care, when it has been measured at all by organisations providing care, has been measured by reference to whether processes and procedures have been followed, rather than on the outcome of care for the patient.

There are clear dangers in relying solely or too heavily on data about processes. They reflect what has come to be called a 'tick-box' mentality, by which is meant an approach in which following some process or procedure becomes the focus of attention rather than what is happening to the patient. The regulator, if it is to contribute to the improvement of care, must be concerned with what has happened as a consequence of some action or inaction. This is what needs to be measured. There will, undoubtedly, be circumstances in which the outcome will be too difficult to measure. In such cases, looking to processes may, if the right data is sought, serve as a proxy for the outcome. In such cases, such data may serve as the basis for the metric. But, the golden rule should be the pursuit of data on outcomes of care, and in the case of safe care, whether the outcome for the patient was that risks were managed and the care was safe. And, to drive home the point, an agreed understanding of what safe care looks like must be arrived at, as must the opposite, an agreed understanding of what constitutes a departure from the required standard such as to warrant attention (in short, what is, in the current jargon, a 'serious untoward incident'[7] and we would add 'omission').

The last question as regards metrics is what are they for? Obviously, in general terms, they are to measure whether the relevant standards have been met; currently, the Standards for Better Health and other related standards, but in future, the requirements for registration to be operated by the CQC. As regards regulation by the Healthcare Commission, there are two distinct purposes. The difference between the two has very great importance in the context of safe care. The first purpose of the metrics is to be able to conduct a retrospective audit of performance. This was the task given to the Healthcare Commission when it was required by Parliament to publish an annual review of the performance of NHS organisations. While important, such an approach is too limited. Certainly, it allows the regulator to describe what has happened, albeit with a time-lag of up to 18 months. In terms of safety, problems can be identified and calls to

[6] Of course, complaints may be an indication of good performance as indicating an openness and preparedness to listen on the part of organisations (by actually soliciting feedback).

[7] And later, 'never events'.

learn lessons can be issued. But, from the perspective of the patient who may have been harmed, it all may be rather too late.

So, the second purpose of the metrics is to allow the regulator to engage in regular or continuous surveillance of performance. Here the aim is to identify where patients are being exposed to unacceptable risks, so as to enable prompt action to be taken by the relevant organisation before they are harmed rather than report on the harm later. This notion of designing outcome-based metrics and mining the data on a regular basis to identify outcomes outside the expected and tolerated norm is, perhaps, the single most important development in regulation that the Healthcare Commission has been aiming at since its inception. Of course, throughout its existence, it responded to 'alerts' that all was not well. But, these were the product of a variety of sources, some more reliable than others, and if all were followed up, unnecessary burdens can be placed on those providing services which, on examination, turn out to be perfectly good. The difference now lies in being able to mine data to identify concerns otherwise unnoticed, and to check out those brought to our attention, before taking any action.

The capacity to carry out surveillance through mining data was reflected in the identification of Mid Staffordshire NHS Foundation Trust as being an 'outlier' in terms of the rate of mortality of patients receiving emergency care. The data, of course, only raises a question (several Trusts were identified as outliers, but in each case concerns were allayed after questions were asked. Mid Staffs, however, remained as a cause of concern[8]). The regulator can then go in search of the answer to the question, which is in essence a question about the risks that patients are being exposed to. And, if unsafe care is identified, pre-emptive, preventative action can be taken, not just by the regulator but by all those responsible for managing the performance of the trust or service in question.

When the regulatory system based on registration is introduced by the CQC, it may well be that the same approach to the use of data will be found to be useful. At the stage of registration, CQC will need to be satisfied that registration is justified, and that a significant number of the requirements to be satisfied address the safety of care. And, thereafter, CQC will be keen to keep under review, through the use of data among other things, the continued safety of the care provided by those registered.

Collecting and Analysing the Data

As has been seen, the data required to enable the regulator to do its job will be found in a range of sources. It should not be the responsibility of the regulator to collect data: this is the job of the various organisations, either within the NHS and the independent sector or outside.

The job of the regulator is to ensure that the data on safety which it needs to carry out its analysis is collected and made available. To those who complain of the 'burden'

[8] See the Healthcare Commission's Report, March 2009 and the subsequent Report of the Mid Staffordshire NHS Foundation Trust Public Inquiry, February 2013.

of doing this, as has been said, this should not, in fact, be a burdensome requirement: organisations and services should already be collecting data on safety so as to monitor their own performance. As regards data collected by organisations outside the NHS and the independent sector, the regulator should agree a system whereby it has access to what it needs and can influence what is collected, by, for example, a Royal College, the NPSA, the Health and Safety Executive, or the General Medical Council. The NPSA is a crucially important partner and relations between it and the Healthcare Commission continue to flourish.

The analysis of data to produce what the Healthcare Commission termed 'intelligent information' in its Vision Document (2003) lies at the heart of modern information-led, risk-based regulation. To this end, the regulator must have a significant capacity to carry out such analysis. This calls for investment in information technology and in highly skilled analysts. 'Informatics' is the brains of the regulator and over time should be warning, reassuring, and continuously monitoring the safety of care. It should be posing questions and prompting, where appropriate, the targeted visits when they will lead to answers.

Reporting, Intervening and Investigating

The regulator should work in public. One of its fundamental obligations, reflected in the law, is to make public its findings. Nowhere is this more important than in the case of reporting on the safety of care. Patients and the public are entitled to know how safe their care will be. They are entitled to know that care is safe and to be celebrated. Equally, they are entitled to know if it is not, not least so that they may demand that action be taken. There is a view which says that the regulator's reporting of unsafe care undermines patients' confidence in the NHS and the morale of those looking after them. It is not clear what is intended to flow from such an observation: the regulator exists to check up – this is the job it was given by government – and cannot shut its eyes or hold its tongue when it sees patients exposed to unacceptable risks. Moreover, it is clear from surveys of patients and the public that, so far from wanting to be protected from such information, they are anxious to have it, feeling empowered by it. That morale among staff may be dented is, sadly, an inevitable consequence of the reporting of failures. The responsible regulator will ensure that any report is fair, that it emphasises a 'systems-based' approach, and that any action taken as a consequence of its report pays particular attention, where necessary, to rebuilding morale among staff.

What the regulator may do, so as properly to inform the public, is now being supplemented by the decision of the NPSA to make public a profile of the level of risk of harm which attaches to services in every organisation in the NHS. This sits alongside and complements the contribution of the regulator. It focuses ever greater emphasis on safe care. It also can serve as the basis for regulatory action, should analysis of the data warrant it.

Reports of performance can take many forms – from the paper publication to the interactive website. The fundamental obligation of the regulator, of particular significance in the case of reports on the safety of care, is that whatever form a report may take, it is fair, accurate and comprehensible. If it is not, the regulator will have failed in its primary duty to the public.

On occasions, the regulator may reach the view that on the basis of the information before it, patients may be, or appear to be at risk. It may do so based on the reports of its regional and local staff who are its eyes and ears. The Healthcare Commission has introduced, for example, monthly 'risk summits' at which representatives of agencies involved in monitoring local public services share concerns and perceptions as to the risks that users of services, including patients, are being exposed to. This is a very important development, allowing the regulator to work with others to form a risk-assessment of local services.

Alternatively, as has been seen, the regulator will reach a view on the risk to safe care on the basis of the analysis of the data it has had submitted to it or as a product of its surveillance. Or, it may have had concerns brought to it by a whistle-blower, by staff, by management anxious for an outsider's view, or by other parts of the machinery of management and governance.

The regulator's first task is to assess the evidence that it has. It should be a fundamental rule that when safety is concerned, every expression of concern should be examined, however implausible or contentious it may be. The regulator's second step is to decide on what action to take. If it is clear that patients are at real risk of being harmed, immediate action to remove the risk is required. The precise nature of this action will depend on the circumstances, but the point of departure should be the welfare of patients and members of the public who might be affected. Their needs must be the first concern of all. Then, a plan must be agreed and put into action, the operation and outcome of which should be monitored by the regulator.

If the regulator is satisfied that there is no immediate threat of harm warranting action, the regulator should adopt a graduated response. The criterion should be what will be the most efficient and effective way of securing the safe care of patients. It may involve a visit from the regulator's staff, a review by outside peers, the drawing up of a plan in conjunction with others, or all of these. It will involve the relevant tier of management in the NHS, including the Strategic Health Authority, and Monitor as regards Foundation Trusts. Only rarely should a full-blown investigation be needed, prompted, for example, by the severity or scale of the risk and harm to patients, or the generalisability of the findings to the national scene or to all similar patients. Clearly, the results of any investigation must be published, not just so that what happened can be understood, but also so that lessons can be learned.

One of the beneficial effects of publishing a report is the opportunity to set out guidance on future conduct designed to secure safe care. In keeping with what has been set out earlier, any such guidance must be the product of engagement with all those involved in, and with, the area of concern. The Healthcare Commission has adopted this approach on a number of occasions, for example, in the case of maternity care, arising from the investigation into Northwick Park and the subsequent national review of maternity services. Moreover, in that case, not only was the guidance a prescription for future safer care, but it also brought together the three major professional bodies (the Royal Colleges of Midwives, Obstetrics and Gynaecology, and Nursing) into a collaborative venture, where their previous difficulties in collaboration had been one of the factors contributing to unsafe care. This is a particularly effective way for the regulator to fulfil its public duty to encourage improvement in the provision of care.[9]

Postscript

The Healthcare Commission was abolished in April 2009 and replaced by the CQC. On one view, the Healthcare Commission was turning over too many stones and revealing what was underneath. CQC adopted what it described as a 'light touch' approach to regulation. The Healthcare Commission's model of regulation and particularly the centrality of data gave way to an approach largely based on periodic visits. Incidents involving the safety of patients continued to attract public attention.

[9] [In my letter to *The Times* (12 December 2020), following the Review of Maternity Services at Shrewsbury and Telford Hospital NHS Trust, I lamented that the collaboration that the Healthcare Commission fought so hard for had clearly not survived very long.]

6

Value for Money – Who Says?[1]

The Independent Parliamentary Standards Authority – A Case Study

Introduction

Recently (on 14 July and later 13 September 2011) I appeared before the House of Commons' Public Accounts Committee. I was to be questioned on a report prepared by the National Audit Office (NAO) on the value for money provided by IPSA (the Independent Parliamentary Standards Authority) which I chair.[2] In opening the hearing, the Chair, Margaret Hodge MP, asked me what I understood by value for money. This was not the first time: in my many years working in public services, I have frequently asked and been asked whether this or that public body, including those I have been responsible for, provided value for money (vfm). My response has always been: 'it all depends on what you mean'. This response has ordinarily been seen as unhelpful. So, I have also had to frame a second response which meets the demands of what has become the conventional approach.

In what follows, I want to explore that first response. It will necessarily also involve a consideration of the second response. I will be wholly concerned with the delivery of public services and, thus, the notion of vfm in the public sector as it relates to the use of taxpayers' money. Vfm in the private sector requires a different analysis, not least to take account of the centrality of choice (for example, to put their money elsewhere) which investors and consumers have, but which has not ordinarily been a feature of public services.

Approaches to Understanding Vfm

There is a lot written about vfm. I am not going to take you down that path, though I may have to alert you to where it leads. At its simplest, vfm in the public sector means

[1] This paper was written for the Board and Executive of IPSA in November 2011 and subsequently published as an Appendix in my *Cleaning up the Mess – After the MPs' Expenses Scandal* (Biteback, 2019). Reprinted with permission.

[2] I was Chairman from 2009 till 2016.

achieving stated aims in a way which makes best use of taxpayers' money. At this level, vfm is a very straightforward notion, not calling for much theorising. At another level, however, it is has become an extremely complex idea. There is much theorising, much of it, unfortunately, unhelpful. What has emerged is what I have just described as the conventional approach to vfm.

According to this conventional approach, vfm is a term of art. It is talked of in terms of objectives to be achieved. These objectives are represented as being so clearly articulated, so carefully adumbrated, that they have all the qualities of certainties. They are, it is claimed, objective. Their presence or absence can be measured. As if to enhance this appearance of clarity and certainty, three words have entered the language as being the real keys to vfm: the '3 Es' – economy, efficiency, effectiveness. These words will tell you what is best as regards the use to which money should best be put. They have become the passwords to a world which is technical: a world which economists and accountants have claimed as their own. Vfm is a technical term. They are the designated technocrats.

The Problem of 'Value'

Of course, the problem which strikes anyone looking beyond the jargon is that the supposed certainties are no such thing. They are an illusion.[3] There are no objective certainties which allow precise calculation and objectively verifiable measures. The reason is obvious. 'Value' is a term of judgement. It is, unsurprisingly, an evaluative term! It does not describe something which can be stated as an objective fact.

Of course, attempts are made to square the circle by saying that it is not the word 'value' that we should be concentrating on, but the careful articulation of the objectives which lie behind it. According to this view, when we are assessing vfm, we are really assessing whether these clear, unambiguous and verifiable objectives are being met. And, it is said, these objectives can be stated with such precision that their presence or absence, whether they are being met or not, is merely a matter of factual determination. So, on this basis, vfm is about facts, objective evidence and certainties.

There are at least two difficulties with this gambit. First, referring to 'objectives' is no less a matter of aspiration or judgement than referring to value. Objectives speak to that which is sought after and desired rather than that which exists. Take the following example. A particular public service states that in the pursuit of providing value for money it will become more efficient by closing down 40+% of its operations (think railways and the Beeching Report). What lies behind the claim of greater 'efficiency' are a myriad unstated calculations/judgements about matters ranging from the relative cost of continuing to operate versus redundancy to the political fallout nationally or in a local community.

Secondly, setting the objectives down undoubtedly produces a list, but lists are always incomplete (irritatingly, they usually fail to include the very thing that crops up!).

[3] Commentators have recently added a fourth 'E' – equity, the meaning of which, of course, is no less elusive than the other three.

But, more significantly, such lists give only the illusion of objectivity, because the value decisions on which they are based, while central to the enterprise, are not revealed. The judgements are still being made. It is just that they are hidden and, to that extent, unaccountable.

The Key Question

The pursuit of value for money, therefore, needs to be addressed differently. The question is not one of the definition of vfm and its central constituent element 'value'. Nor is it one of reciting a list of objectives, without identifying what lies behind them. This is because any consideration of vfm represents a judgement. The really key question is whose judgement is the relevant judgement. It is not what vfm means, or what the objectives are; it is who decides what it means, or what the objectives should be. What may be of high value to some may be valued less by others. Choices need to be made. Who makes them is the key. It is that simple.

The '3Es'[4]

I have already mentioned the 3 'Es' as being central to decisions about vfm. You only have to look at these '3 Es' to get the point that I am seeking to make. Consider whether a public service is meeting the test of the '3Es'. 'Economy' is said to relate to the cost of the service. Is it economical? But, whose view is to be listened to in determining whether the cost which has been settled on provides the proper level of service? How do you take account of the *quality* of the service from a number of perspectives, of which the perspective of the recipient of any service, especially public services, is the most relevant? The same problem arises in the case of the other two Es. 'Efficiency' refers to what is got out for what is put in. Fine, but who decides what it is that should be got out, so as to judge whether you are efficient in getting it? 'Effectiveness' in turn is supposed to measure the impact, the effect achieved in any particular context. Again, fine, but, again, who determines which effect should be sought? A list of objectives may have been drawn up. But, who decided on the objectives and whose hand wrote the list?

In short, to the proposition that the 'value' in vfm consists of achieving the '3Es', you must ask: 'economical' at what cost as judged by whom; 'efficient' to what purpose as judged by whom; 'effective' to what end as judged by whom?

Those who dwell in the land of vfm are quick with a reply. As it happens, it takes the discourse into even more uncertain territory. It goes like this. Vfm is really about 'achieving the right balance between the 3Es'. Would it be cruel to repeat the question: the right balance in whose eyes, or, who sets the scale against which any balancing is to take place?

[4] See fn 3.

The Real World of Vfm

The unavoidable conclusion is that, when we talk of vfm, we are firmly in the world of value judgements. In the realm of public services, the world which I inhabit, the importance of this obvious conclusion cannot be overstated. It is literally about democracy. Public services are paid for by the taxpayer. They exist to provide particular specified services to the public. The services must be provided in such a way that the public gets value for money. It must, therefore, be at the heart of the democratic covenant between people and government that it is for the public to decide what value consists of, what they count as valuable in the services provided.

Enter the Public

The moment that this proposition is advanced, and it is clearly correct, the notion of vfm can no longer be claimed by economists or accountants as their unique preserve. It is clearly the preserve of the public. It is for the public to determine the v in vfm. But, the technocratic approach has another line of defence. Yes, the argument goes, it is quite true: we are talking about judgements. But, judgements about public services, including vfm, are vested quite properly in Government and politicians. They are elected to decide on how taxpayers' money is to be disbursed. In deciding on how it is to be disbursed, they have the best information and serve as proxies for the public. So, when Government or politicians pronounce on vfm, it *is* really the public after all who are deciding, albeit at second hand through their elected representatives. This is standard democratic territory. But, unfortunately, there is a catch.

Re-enter the 'Expert'

You will remember that I said that the conventional approach to vfm is to regard it as a term of art. Government and politicians have come to believe, or have been persuaded to accept, this approach. They have come to accept that vfm is a matter of expertise, best left to experts. They happily abdicate from their role as proxies for the public. They just 'follow the science' they say. They just pass the buck to others – the technocrats – particularly the NAO and until recently the Audit Commission. And these bodies, the 'experts' in vfm, see vfm technocratically, through the prism of the '3Es'. 'Value' takes on a limited meaning, relating to cost, price and output. The underlying value choices which, as we saw, necessarily inform the decisions made, are not made explicit by the experts. All is science and calculation. The choices cannot, therefore, be subject to scrutiny to ensure that they, in fact, reflect what the recipient of public services would choose as being important; that they reflect what the public really values and wants from the services. They may just as well, and most likely do, reflect what the *providers* rather than the recipients of the services value. This is particularly true when the resources available to provide a service are, as is usually the case, under strain.

Back to Real Vfm

Seen in the way that I have set out, vfm poses wholly different questions from those asked according to the conventional aproach. This is where things get complex. Seeking to reflect what the public values in the provision of any service is no easy task, even if it is the only right way to assess vfm. The public values different things at different times. And, of course, the public is not a homogenous entity. There will usually be several publics with several views.

Such untidiness, however, is the stuff of democratic discourse. It is an abiding feature of any public policy. Consequently, there should be established mechanisms to address the challenge posed: the challenge being to elicit, in the light of available evidence, a considered and broadly representative view on a matter of public importance, having to do with the delivery of public services, as regards which there may be no obvious consensus.

Democratic Engagement: The Example of NICE

One such mechanism exists in one of that most contentious of all areas of public policy – the NHS. Within the NHS, one of the most difficult challenges is to determine what medicines/drugs should be made available to patients through the NHS. Whether the words 'rationing' or 'resource allocation' are used, it is clear that, however much money is made available, choices will always have to be made as to what can be afforded and thus provided. And, such choices often have to be made against a background of the special pleading of single interest groups, the effective lobbying of the pharmaceutical industry and professionals, and the significant interest of the media. What is involved is a major issue of value for money. It could not be more explicit. Against the background of limited resources, does the purchase by the NHS of this drug for this group of patients amount to value for money for the NHS and thus for the taxpayer?

Since 1999 such decisions have fallen to be decided by the National Institute for Health and Clinical Excellence[5] (NICE). NICE was created by statute. You may think that by doing so, Government has conformed to the approach that I referred to earlier whereby issues involving vfm in the NHS are seen as matters for experts and so are passed to experts. But, NICE is different. Whatever Government might have had in mind, NICE has gone its own way. It has recognised the central issue of the democratic covenant. It has earned the admiration of countries around the world while routinely getting up the nose of Big Pharma, patients' groups and Government (thereby proving it must be getting something right!). It operates a complex system of assessing value, the basis of which is a calculation of QALYs (Quality-Adjusted Life Years). The calculation is driven by a regard for the values of the NHS and for the principle of the greatest good for the greatest number of the population as a whole. In this way, NICE explicitly recognises the evaluative nature of the exercise. The Q in QALY reinforces the fact. And, in

[5] Until 2005 the National Institute for Clinical Excellence.

its analysis of QALYs, NICE seeks to expose for scrutiny the underlying factors which bear on quality and which it bears in mind. All of them are judgements. All of them are available for debate and discussion (which routinely takes place). Admittedly, at one level, the calculation of QALYs appears to be formulaic and driven by econometrics. But, this calculation derives from a prior application of a series of judgements which are explicit.

So, when NICE talks of vfm, it overtly sets out what it judges the word value to signify. It takes two steps. The first is to be as clear as possible as to the values and principles which underpin the objectives sought; the values of the NHS. The second step is to decide whether, as regards any particular decision, the decision best accords with those values. This is where engaging with the public comes in. NICE takes account of a range of factors from a range of interested parties. But, so that the judgement made should not simply be that of interested parties and its own experts, NICE also provides for the element of democratic engagement the importance of which I emphasised earlier. NICE seeks advice from its Citizens' Council. The Council was created by NICE. Its membership consists entirely of members of the public. They meet to discuss proposed decisions of NICE (whether, for example, to approve the provision by the NHS of a particular drug). They hear the relevant scientific and economic arguments. They weigh the opportunity costs inevitable when the resources available are finite. Cost, price and output are parts of the story, but they are not the whole story.

The injection of the Citizens' Council into the system of deliberation means that a central contribution to the judgement of what is to be valued, the vfm provided by the NHS, is vested in the public, through the proxy of the Council, a public which has been informed and then is free to make up its mind.

A device such as the Citizens' Council is central to any really genuine appraisal of vfm. It cannot, of course, be used for every detailed issue of the day. And, of course, other mechanisms of democratic engagement, local and national, co-exist and are of central importance. But, as regards the vexed issue of vfm, true democratic engagement is at the heart of things. Vfm is not for technocrats.

This is not to say that there is no role for technocrats. Clearly, they do have a role, but it is a second-order role. What they can do, and it is of great importance, is to determine whether, once the choices have been made, the means of putting these choices into effect make the best possible use of the money available. Matters such as the ways in which contracts are let, staff are deployed, and money is accounted for are all part of this second order role. But, in the case of public services, the first-order issue, the values and objectives, and the last word on them, must be with an informed public.

IPSA and Vfm

I mentioned IPSA at the outset. As an organisation funded from the public purse, it must, of course, provide value for money. You will have gathered by now that, for me, the crucial question is not what value means in this context, but whose view of value should be determinative. Unsurprisingly, there is significant disagreement. The perspective of MPs, by and large, is that IPSA exists to provide what they regard as important and only if it does so is it providing value for money. And, given that in the minds of many MPs, IPSA does not give them the support (aka money) that they claim is their due,[6] IPSA, by that token, fails to provide value for money. The taxpayer on that reasoning is getting a poor return.

What MPs are doing is defining vfm in a way in which it is assumed, without discussion, that they are the arbiters of what constitutes value. They could be said to be making this assumption because they see IPSA's Scheme of Expenses and Costs as existing solely to do what they want. But, if that is their view, it is clearly wrong-headed. IPSA is not the servant of MPs, created to serve their needs, though this is a prevalent view. IPSA is an independent regulatory body. It exists to serve the public interest. Its role, among other things, is to ask whether what MPs argue for is, indeed, in the public interest. That is what regulators do as regards those whom they regulate.

There may be another basis on which MPs assume themselves to be the arbiters of value. They may claim, as I set out earlier, that, as elected representatives of the public, they are the public's proxies in ensuring that the public gets value from the taxes levied. There are at least two problems with this approach. First, there is, of course, a clear conflict of interest. Second, and equally clearly, such a view also represents an attempt to return to self-regulation[7] by the back door. But, putting aside these awkward truths, this role of proxies was, perhaps, what the Public Accounts Committee saw themselves as playing (though there were plenty of the other assumptions around, such as that IPSA is there to serve MPs and that MPs are IPSA's 'customers'). But, if this was how the PAC saw itself, as the proxy for the public, its response was to do precisely what I referred to earlier. It commissioned the NAO, as experts, to determine whether IPSA provided vfm. It defined vfm in technocratic terms and brought in the technocrats.

As it happens, the NAO's response was fairly complimentary of IPSA, given the difficult circumstances in which it was established and has had to operate. But, that said, the NAO's approach was at best problematic. Two particular positions that it adopted warrant comment. The first reflected the view that IPSA exists to serve the perceived needs of MPs, to 'enable' them to carry out their parliamentary duties (avoiding, of course, what will be recognised as the crucial question – who decides the nature of the 'enabling'). The flaw in this approach, its under-appreciation that IPSA is an independent regulator established to serve the public interest, is something that I have already dwelt on. The second position adopted by the NAO which is particularly problematic was its specific reflection on IPSA's preparedness to accept risk (IPSA's 'risk appetite'). IPSA could be more 'efficient' (save money), the NAO stated, if it were less risk-averse. In saying this, the NAO appeared to be defining value in technical terms, having to do with efficiency as it relates to the cost associated with risk. But, in fact, of course, it was making *its* judgement about the proper balance of risk and where the public interest and the public's appetite for risk should lie. By doing so, the NAO was challenging IPSA's view as to where the public interest lies. But, it is IPSA which is charged by Parliament to serve as the independent regulator. It is IPSA which, as a central part of that responsibility, must seek to determine and act upon what it, and it alone, judges to be in the

[6] [Written in the early days of IPSA.]
[7] Recognised as untenable after the Expenses Scandal of 2008–09.

public interest. Its judgement must be the product of some democratic engagement. It can be questioned if it is patently at odds with what an informed public is calling for. It should not be questioned, however, simply because others would wish for a different judgement.

I reach this view because it must be clear beyond peradventure by now that vfm is crucially something on which the public's view must be central. Compare the NAO's approach. It maintained that IPSA exists to serve the needs of MPs. This was what vfm meant: that what was done should be what best met MPs' needs. And, to assess IPSA's success in achieving this, the NAO looked inwards and commissioned a survey of what MPs thought of IPSA. The response was the predictable 'turkeys voting for Christmas'. The NAO did not ask itself how the *public* might assess vfm. It did not look outwards to gauge the views of the public: what the public might regard as being of value in the disbursement of their taxes as regards the expenses and costs of MPs. The NAO did refer to a survey carried out by IPSA. But, this was interpreted narrowly as showing an increase in the trustworthiness of MPs and Parliament. It was not viewed as central to the question of vfm. Of course, from the perspective of the public and of the Parliament which created IPSA to achieve that very result, this notion of trust is a defining feature of vfm.

For IPSA, trust between the electorate and the elected is THE value most sought after by the public and the most crucial feature of the public interest which it should seek to achieve. The extent of this trust currently is central to any assessment of the vfm provided by IPSA. IPSA was created as a response to a massive scandal which rocked the nation. Trust in MPs and our democratic institutions was at an appallingly low ebb. IPSA was created as an *independent* body whose task it was to replace failed self-regulation with real, effective regulation. Unsurprisingly, it was not welcomed in Westminster, once the dust had settled. Those who had enjoyed life for centuries without effective scrutiny and accountability, save of their own making, were suddenly being asked for receipts! The sunlight was too bright for some. Indeed, some even thought (and think) that IPSA is an assault on their very status as MPs, despite what Parliament may have thought in 2009.

This is the historical background (and it is a history which is barely a couple of years old). It should not be a surprise that, as an independent regulatory body, IPSA sees its principal aim as being to act in the public interest. The fundamental public interest was and remains, as surveys show, the restoration of trust in MPs. Nothing can be more important for democracy and, of course, for MPs.

So, the answer to the question whether IPSA is providing vfm does not lie in whether MPs or technocrats approve of what it does. The only answer is whether it is doing what a properly informed public wants it to do. This is so important that it is routinely ignored and why it is has been repeatedly emphasised here. Until this point is accepted, IPSA will continue to lock horns with those who, for whatever reason, choose to ignore it.

From IPSA's perspective, it must, of course, regularly satisfy itself that its sense of what the public values is sufficiently acute; that, for example, it has got the balance of risk about right. This is where what I called democratic engagement comes in. IPSA must routinely check to ensure that it reflects what an informed public wants. To this end, IPSA is working to establish ways of going beyond surveys to taking the temperature of informed public opinion on a regular basis. Now that IPSA has the responsibility also of setting MPs' pay and pensions, this need to stay close to informed public opinion takes on even greater importance.

By gauging and giving effect to the views of an informed public about what value they seek to get from their taxes, IPSA will truly be able to monitor whether it provides value for money. It will also serve as the only valid basis on which those who would expose it to scrutiny regarding vfm may properly judge IPSA.

PART III

Medical Law and Ethics: From Huntington's Disease to Covid-19

From being barely recognised as a discrete area of law, medical law has grown into a subject commanding its own library of texts, a much-studied course in Law Schools and a constant in the Law Courts. I wrote my first paper in the area in 1969 (it was about the concept of death). As modern healthcare developed and patients and healthcare professionals became more aware of their respective rights and duties, the role of law in regulating the delivery of healthcare became increasingly important. New fields of enquiry began to occupy lawyers and the law; not just the traditional areas – abortion and mental health – but everything from contraception to transplantation to care of the dying. Perhaps the most significant area of importance was not in fact an area of medical practice, though medical practice was the context. It was the notion of consent – consent by a patient to treatment – what consent means, who can give it and to what. It marked the embrace of the notion of autonomy and the slow ending of the paternalism which previously held sway.

The reference to autonomy makes clear the link between medical law (often more broadly described as health law) and medical ethics. If medical law was a new endeavour then it needed some philosophical roots to underpin and nurture it. The subject of applied ethics stepped in to meet the need. For some time, applied ethics had largely concerned itself with the rights and wrongs of warfare. The emergence of calls for an end to racial discrimination and for civil rights for all injected new interest and gave the field a boost. Modern medicine supercharged the field. Ethical disputations had long been around. But they had largely been regarded as the province of theologians, fretting over abortion. Suddenly philosophers climbed on board and medical ethics went from being a backwater to being a staple on university curricula and, with varying degrees of rigour, on the front pages of newspapers and on TV screens. Indeed, I made two series of six programmes in the late 1980s for BBC TV: each attracted audiences of over three million.

In the section which follows I offer a glimpse of the breadth and range of medical law and ethics, from wrestling with what to do when a patient's care goes wrong and she is harmed, to when if ever a doctor should breach confidence, to clashes between parents, their children and their doctors, to the current (as I write) Covid-19 pandemic.

7

Huntington's Disease and Confidentiality[1]

Introduction

In the early 80s I made a series of BBC TV programmes about medical ethics (*Doctors' Dilemmas*). The programmes were based on real stories. They exposed problems which strategists now call 'wicked problems' – problems to which there is no right answer, just less wrong ones. The programmes were concerned to demonstrate the importance of principles and reasoned analysis; to show that rigorous examination of how to respond to ethical conundrums wasn't just the stuff of head-in-the-clouds seminars but the daily bread and butter of clinical practice. One week it was the care of patients suffering from anorexia, the next the allocation of scarce resources (kidneys for transplantation), and another adolescents and consent to treatment. There was also a programme about the duty of confidentiality that healthcare professionals owe to their patients. When could or should they break this duty?

At around this time I was doing some work on a disease called Huntington's Chorea/Disease. This is a disease caused by an abnormality in a single gene. At between 30 and 50 years of age, people who have inherited the gene begin to show symptoms. The disease is incurable and leads to physical and mental deterioration culminating in death. If you have the faulty gene, there is a 50 per cent chance that you will pass it on to a child. Once the gene was identified, patients began to have to decide what they wanted to know (if there was a history of the illness in the family) and doctors had to work out what to tell them. Because of its late onset, patients and doctors also began to have to work out whether to have children and if they had already had a family what to tell their children.

Clearly, this was a minefield in terms for confidentiality – should you tell a child about her mother's/father's condition? To do so would plunge the child into enormous anxiety – should she be tested or not? Could she live with the certain death sentence of a positive diagnosis? Was the mother entitled to insist that her doctors keep the information secret, ie confidential, or should they reveal it? As it happens, we decided not to make a programme about Huntington's Disease – it seemed too esoteric.[2]

[1] This is an unpublished paper that I wrote in November 2019, reflecting my continuing interest in medical law.

[2] We chose to make a programme about a rather more mundane example of confidentiality – the infidelity of a husband, the infection of his wife with chlamydia, and the doctor in the middle. Both of them were his patients. The husband had insisted on confidentiality. The wife was at risk of considerable harm. What should the doctor do?

Well, over 30 years later, a court found itself wrestling with Huntington's Disease and the question of confidentiality. In February 2020, the High Court (in the *ABC* case[3]) had to consider whether to keep a patient's secrets or reveal them to others. A daughter brought a legal action because her father's doctors did not tell her that he suffered from Huntington's disease. The father, who was detained under the Mental Health Act having murdered her mother, once his condition was diagnosed, had told his doctors that his daughter was not to be informed. She was not told, but learned inadvertently of her father's condition from one of the doctors treating him. She was being treated by another team but under the general auspices of the same NHS Trust. By the time she became aware of her father's condition she had become pregnant. She was found to have the disease. There is a 50 per cent chance that she has passed it on to her child.

Analysis

It is principle of medical ethics and medical law that there is a duty of confidence owed by a doctor to a patient: that the doctor will not reveal to others information confided during the medical consultation. It is not always understood, however, that in English law, this duty is not absolute (unlike in certain European countries). There are circumstances, in other words, in which a doctor is quite properly entitled, and in some cases obliged, to break a patient's confidence by telling others. The justification derives from a doctor's concomitant duty to seek to protect others who may predictably be otherwise harmed.

These others may be the doctor's patients. In my TV case,[4] the wife was also the doctor's patient. She could suffer harm by contracting chlamydia. In the *ABC* case, the daughter was receiving treatment at the Hospital Trust, though from a different team, and the father's doctors knew of her since he had forbidden them from telling her. She has contracted Huntington's Disease. She said that she has suffered harm in that she was robbed of the chance to make an informed choice about whether to continue her pregnancy.

Alternatively, those put at risk may be members of the general public, where, for example, a patient tells the doctor of his intention to harm someone or has a dangerous, transmissible disease.

Ethics

Taking ethics first, the question appears to be: when may the doctor break confidence? In fact there is a prior question. If the patient reveals to the doctor something which has the potential to bring harm to others, and asserts that the information be treated as confidential, it is open to the doctor to advise that the information is such that s/he cannot be bound to keep it secret. The patient will then have to decide how best to

[3] *ABC v St George's NHS Foundation Trust* [2020] EWHC 455 (QB).
[4] See fn 2.

proceed, ideally with the help of the doctor. It appears that in the *ABC* case the father's doctors tried to persuade him to reveal the truth to his daughter but, having failed, regarded their duty of confidence to the father as paramount.

Assuming that the doctor does not opt to refuse to go along with the patient and that the patient continues to forbid disclosure is that the end of the matter? No. The general view is that, as a matter of ethics, the doctor may break the duty of confidence owed to the patient if s/he believes that others may be put at risk of harm if not informed of the risk that they are exposed to and of which the doctor has been made aware. It may be that the doctor should seek to persuade the patient to reveal the information her/himself to those who may be affected, but ultimately the doctor may do so. Indeed, the doctor may be obliged to break confidence (ie *should* do so) if the circumstances are sufficiently egregious. If the doctor acts honestly and in good faith, the breach will be judged to be justified. Equally, a decision not the break confidence may be justified, even if harm to others follows, if, at the time, the doctor judged it right to preserve the confidence. One such justification may be the desirability of maintaining a relationship of trust with the patient where on balance the doctor judges it is warranted. In medical ethics, therefore, professional judgement, drawing on principled analysis, is central. Professional guidelines issued by the GMC and various Royal Colleges (in respect to their particular areas of expertise) endorse the view expressed here.

Law

What about medical law? Unlike medical ethics, the approach is somewhat different. Given the existence of the duty of confidence (which is one element of the duty to protect another person's privacy) the doctor must not ordinarily reveal a patient's confidences. Just as in medical ethics, however, since the duty is not an absolute duty, there may be circumstances in which the doctor *may* inform others, provided the disclosure can be justified.

But, in contrast to ethics, there's another, separate question that has to be asked: are there circumstances where the doctor *must* inform others of what has been revealed, ie is under a duty to breach confidence, on pain of legal liability if s/he fails to do so?

Modern medical law would suggest that the importance of this second question lies in the fact that the law does not now leave the answer to the doctor alone or to doctors as a whole. Crucially, by contrast to medical ethics, the starting point in modern medical law is that professional judgement may be relevant in answering the legal question but it is not determinative. Ultimately, it is the law through a decision of a court which will decide.

That's the starting point. How far does it get us? How should the courts proceed? Historically, the courts have been slow to involve themselves in the nuanced and complex interplay of the doctor-patient relationship in the consulting room. There are, of course, certain landmark cases where lines have been drawn.[5] But, in cases like the one under consideration, a court will need strong evidence of harm or the risk of harm

[5] Most significantly in *Montgomery v Lanarkshire Health Board* [2015] UKSC 11.

to others before stipulating that there is a duty to breach confidence, rather than an ethically-grounded choice. The court should tread carefully. Patients need to able to tell doctors uncomfortable things. And doctors need to be able to reflect carefully on the extent of their responsibilities, without the shadow of legal action hanging over them. That said, the devastating consequence associated with certain genetic information, as illustrated in the current case, may suggest that disclosure in such a context is called for – that there is a duty to breach the confidence.

The *ABC* Case

What did Mrs Justice Yip make of this challenge in the *ABC* case? We're concerned with whether the law recognises a duty to breach confidence such that the father's doctors in this case had a duty to inform the daughter of her father's condition despite the father's direction that she not be told.[6] Well, the judge's answer is a bit of a dog's dinner.

In essence, she found that the Trust through its doctors did owe the daughter a duty, ie we were in the territory of 'must' rather than 'may'. But what according to the judge was the duty? According to Mrs Justice Yip, the duty didn't consist in breaking confidence and telling the daughter. Instead, it was to 'balance her [the daughter's] interest in being informed of the genetic risk against her father's interest in preserving confidentiality in relation to his diagnosis and the public interest in maintaining medical confidentiality generally'.[7]

In effect, Mrs Justice Yip has appeared to decide that there was some kind of duty lurking here but that, taking account of the various guidelines on ethics promulgated by professional bodies and the regulator (the General Medical Council) the extent of the duty rests on the decision of the doctors, either those caring for the parties or more generally, the medical profession at large through their guidelines. If this is right, doctors when challenged can simply say that they gave their mind to the problem, considered the relevant guidance, did the necessary balancing and then decided in X or Y way. An issue deeply concerned with the welfare of patients and the responsibilities of medical professionals becomes, in Mrs Justice Yip's hands a procedural matter – have the doctors done things by the book? It would appear that, to her, the law is not concerned with the outcome, just the process.

To confound things, however, having decided that all the doctor has to do is balance things, Mrs Justice Yip then offers a couple of paragraphs which will have doctors and those advising them scratching their heads or tearing their hair.

She writes:

> If a defendant has conducted a balancing exercise properly [sic] in accordance with professional guidance and has reasonably [sic] concluded that disclosure should not be made, they will have discharged their duty. No liability can then arise even though others may have taken

[6] For our purposes here I leave aside the other questions which arose – who were the appropriate defendants – the particular doctors or the Trust as employers – and whether the daughter could establish that she would not have become pregnant or would have had an abortion.

[7] Note there was no reference to the countervailing public interest in protecting her health.

> a different view, allowing considerable latitude to clinicians faced with a difficult decision where the competing rights of two individuals are concerned. …
>
> If a defendant has not conducted a proper [sic] balancing exercise (applying the *Bolam* test) the court will have to go on to consider what the defendant would have done if the exercise had been properly [sic] performed. If, on a balance of probabilities, the defendant would have disclosed, a potentially actionable breach will be made out. If the defendant would not have disclosed, the court will have to consider whether such a decision would have been negligent [? a breach of duty], in the sense that no responsible body of medical opinion would have supported it (applying *Bolitho*).

It's hard to find your way through these two paragraphs. The first just echoes the notion of 'balancing' and effectively says 'over to you, doctor'. The proviso that the doctor has to do the balancing 'properly' is challenging without further guidance. Merely referring to *Bolam* (what doctors as a group ordinarily do) doesn't get us far, since it appears to be circular, ie he's done the balancing if he's done what doctors of whom he is one ordinarily do.

But then, Mrs Justice Yip goes on to consider what happens if the doctor hasn't got his 'balancing' right. She states that he's in breach of his duty to disclose the confidence to the other party, if 'on the balance of probabilities, the defendant *would*[8] have disclosed …'. But who's to say what the doctor *would* have done, except the doctor himself and he may not in fact have disclosed the information even after carrying out a 'proper balancing exercise'? If she means *should* have disclosed, then Mrs Justice Yip is doing what she says should not be done, namely imposing the court's view of what to do rather than respect the views of medical opinion.

There's more. If the defendant having failed to do the 'proper balancing' would *not* have disclosed the information, the court would have to consider whether this is a breach of duty (negligence). Again, who's to say he would not, though at least the judge, in referring to 'no responsible body of medical opinion', seems to avoid imposing her own view, even though no other view is available.

I confess that I am not confident that I understand Mrs Justice Yip's analysis. What I am more confident about is that it cannot be right. It is right that the law should not stipulate a hard and fast rule, Yes or No, because circumstances differ and context is all. But, the law should do better than simply hand the problem back to doctors and revert through the back door to the long outdated mantra that 'doctor knows best'. The law should do more than talk of 'balancing' without either identifying the relevant scale against which to balance or proposing a mechanism for doing so.

The way forward in a case such as this and others, posing the most difficult of ethical, legal and practical challenges, must be that there is put in place a mechanism which will ensure not only that the doctor has given her/his mind to the question, but that s/he engaged in reasoned analysis and (crucially), the reasoned analysis is one which others would regard as plausible.

It is this last factor which is most important. It contemplates some kind of sounding board. In the case of the care of severely handicapped babies, that sounding board has become, faute de mieux, the court. But this is a sign of the law's failure. Resort to the

[8] My emphasis.

courts must be avoided at all costs, given the time, expense and general distress involved. Rather, the law should support the idea that the hospital, clinic or whatever must have in place a body to which problems such as this may be taken. Ethics Committees may serve this purpose if properly and carefully constituted, with the membership reaching beyond medical professionals. They would meet the law's obligation to do the balancing that Mrs Justice Yip calls for, but crucially they would address both process and outcome.[9] And, it would follow, that, endorsed by the courts as the right way forward, their decision would be final (subject to any challenge by way of judicial review). A healthcare professional who ignored their decision would be subject to disciplinary action.

No-one says such dilemmas are easy to solve. To avoid resort to the law and courts, alternative ways of working through these immensely challenging questions must be developed which can then be endorsed as the way forward. Doctors, nurses, hospitals and clinics all need to be properly equipped to engage in the necessary careful reflection. This was the point I was trying to make in the TV programmes nearly 40 years ago. Doctors and others need to be able to carry out the required reasoned analysis, recognise when to take advice and know whom to turn to. It should be a central part of their training. It is in their interests and in the interests of patients. Inviting the courts, after the event, to be a party to the difficult conversations which are the stuff of medical practice, is not the right way to go.

[9] In the *ABC* case, an Ethics Committee did consider the issues raised, but rather than being seen as a legally endorsed mechanism to resolve the case, it became just another piece of evidence about 'balancing'. In the case of severely handicapped babies, the institutionalising in hospitals of a process of mediation is a recent response designed to avoid recourse to the courts.

8

Reflections on Charlie Gard[1]

Charlie Gard is not a 'case'; he's a very sick little boy. But his case – how to respond to his condition, he has a rare genetic condition and has suffered brain damage – has attracted world-wide attention. His parents, his doctors and nurses, Great Ormond Street Hospital, have all found themselves in a maelstrom of attention, opinion, concern and worse, stretching from the White House to the Vatican. The issue at stake is whether to continue to seek to keep him alive or whether to allow him to die. His parents insist that he be treated on the proposition that while there's life there's hope. His doctors advise that further care is pointless and that he may, in fact be suffering, such that he should be allowed to die peacefully.

About 20 years ago, I was just about to leave for the airport in Auckland when I got a 'phone call from lawyers. It was 7.00 in the morning. Would I meet them urgently in half an hour to advise on a case? I said of course, provided I could catch my plane.

A boy had suffered a catastrophic injury while being operated on: his neck had been broken. Though alert and talkative he was paralysed. His parents had told his doctors that they wanted care to be withdrawn (he was on a ventilator) so that he could die peacefully. He wasn't terminally ill but they thought it best if he died given what the future would hold.

There was no previous case in New Zealand. My advice was that the parents' views were not the last word; the lawyers should go to court, ensure that the child was separately represented by a lawyer, and that the only question for the court was what was in the child's best interests. The advice was followed. The child was made a ward of court, was cared for and lived on.

I'm sure that those now involving themselves in the case of Charlie Gard would applaud what happened in Auckland. But if they do, they would have to recognise the consequences. They would have to acknowledge a number of things which have been part of our approach to the care of children since the nineteenth century.

The first is the most fundamental. As a society, we must choose how to decide such heart-breaking cases. Of course, each child is different but do we accept that there should be principles and rules, whatever the circumstances, which should guide us as we try to work out what's best? We can, of course, reject such a view and choose to go with the heart and emotions. But if we do, whose heart should prevail when there are conflicting views and, where there is conflict, how do you resolve it? Alternatively, we can reason

[1] First published in *The Guardian*, 26 July 2017 in response to the publicity and litigation surrounding the care to be provided to the little boy, Charlie Gard. Reprinted with amendments.

our way through, cold as this may appear. We can accept the idea of principles and rules. And, if reason is to prevail, you need to analyse how to proceed.

These are the steps. The first is to recognise that children do not belong to their parents. They are not things. They are not property. They are people with all that this description entails. Secondly, when an appeal is made that parents have rights over their children, it is important to step back and examine the language used. We need to remind ourselves that parents do not have rights regarding their children, they only have duties, the principal duty being to act in their children's best interests. This has been part of the fabric of our law and our society for a long time. Thirdly, if we concerned with the language of rights, it is, of course, children who have rights; any rights that parents have exist only to protect their children's rights.

Now, in giving effect to a child's rights, the parents' views as to their children's interests should usually be respected. But parents cannot *always* be the ultimate arbiters of their children's interests. If parents, for example, insist on subjecting their child to a particular diet, which, in the view of others with acknowledged expertise in the subject, will cause the child harm, we do not stand by. We intervene to safeguard the child

When such concerns arise, there has to be a mechanism to decide the circumstances in which parents' views should not prevail. That mechanism has to be a trustworthy and independent source of authority, sometimes a local authority, but ultimately, as ever in a civic society, a court. The court's sole concern is for the child and the child's interests. Evidence and views, including, particularly, those of the parents, must be listened to. The court must then decide and, crucially, make its decision and reasoning public, exposing it to scrutiny and holding it to account. The court is not infallible. That's why we allow for appeals, a kind of second thought. But, ultimately, we are not in the realm of there being a right answer. We are in the realm of judgement, reasoned judgement, and we look to the courts to provide this.

This process depends, of course, on acceptance of the supremacy of reasoned argument over passion and the acceptance of the independence and authority of the courts. Campaigns against the courts, whether led by tabloid newspapers, organised through social media, or exploited by sectional and religious groups are increasingly a feature of modern discourse. It is one thing to comment on or criticise a particular decision, it is a very different thing to attack the institution of the courts. Here, in Charlie Gard's case, the call is to keep the courts out; they don't understand. Only the parents should decide: let passion prevail. Those behind such calls should reflect on what they wish for in case they get it. A whole system designed to address dispassionately the rights and interests of children would be pushed aside. And they should think of the little boy in Auckland.

9

Doing What's Best – Who Says?[1]

The notion of being concerned with the interests of patients is not new. It is as old as medicine. What is new, or relatively new, is the question: how is that concern best dealt with? Put another way, who is the best judge of a patient's interests? For almost the whole of the history of modern medicine, this question was not asked because the need to ask it was not recognised. A patient's interests were best judged by the doctor. That was part of what a doctor did. Patients knew nothing of clinical matters. How could they be expected to decide what was good for them? Indeed, it was cruel to impose this burden on them.

Times have changed. A better-educated population, exposed through a variety of media to the idea of choice and impressed by the language of rights, began to see themselves differently. They were no longer passive receivers of goods and services, grateful for whatever came their way, but consumers with choices who were entitled to expect good quality and to complain if they were not satisfied.

In relationships between professionals and clients, of which the patient-doctor relationship is one example, the accommodation of this change has not been easy. The consumer may be king in Tesco's, but not in the barrister's chambers, the accountant's office, or the clinic. The professional, let us concentrate on the doctor, is the one who knows. The patient's interests are safe in the doctor's hands. They would not be safe in the hands of the uninformed patient.

Of course, to arrive at such a conclusion demands the adoption of a very crude notion of knowledge. In fact, as all but the most recalcitrant now recognise, there are at least two bodies of knowledge which are relevant to the exchanges between doctor and patient: the doctor's and the patient's. Both are experts in their own fields: the doctor in clinical matters; the patient in his/her experience, feelings, fears, hopes, and desires.

This is the context in which the question, who is the best judge of the patient's interests, began to be canvassed as a question which should be asked and which required an answer. The emerging answer was that caring for a patient requires both parties to recognise and respect the other's area of expertise. The doctor knows what the operation on the ankle involves and what the likely physical consequences will be. The patient will know what it feels like to face the prospect of a limp, or of never dancing or playing football again. Together they can pool their knowledge and choose the way forward.

[1] This is an unpublished paper written in February 2012 reflecting my continuing interest in the place of the patient in exchanges about healthcare.

The language of partnership becomes the currency: not a swing of the pendulum from doctor-power to patient-power, but a relationship of interactive partnership.

To some, this development is wrong-headed. It is caricatured as the approach which appeals to the assertive Guardian reader, who is already well able to take care of her/himself. It has no resonance, they say, with the vulnerable, the disadvantaged or the excluded: indeed it disempowers them by placing a burden of participation on them which they cannot bear. This sounds like the old argument, patients cannot really know what is best for them, under a new guise. It suggests that only a certain section of the population need to be actively involved in their healthcare because the rest have no view to express on what they want or hope for. Merely to say this is to recognise that it is as offensive as it is untenable. The disadvantaged may need more time or more explanation, but they have their needs, their fears, their dreams, and their hopes like the rest. And like the rest, as citizens and as equals in their humanity, they have their claim to engage in their care.

My personal experience of hearing the stories of parents during the Bristol Inquiry confirmed me in the view that good medical care must involve patients and carers as well as professionals. It also confirmed me in the view that, these days, most professionals do not seek intentionally to exclude patients. Rather, they genuinely believe that they are involving them (often mistakenly), or they do not know how to do so, or they find the whole business too emotionally taxing. The lesson which we should draw from this is so simple that it is usually overlooked. We should not criticise nor blame professionals. Instead, we should help them through the barriers which prevent them seeing their patients as interactive partners. The place to start is at the beginning of professional education, but it is a process that continues through the whole of a professional's career.

How does this sit with the current growth industry of what is called PPI ('patient and public involvement', with apologies to the English language)? Some of what is written under this banner purports to talk of the patient's experience, but in fact describes what the patient experienced, ie was exposed to, rather than what the patient experienced, ie felt. In so doing, it continues to regard the patient as a passive recipient, albeit while using the smart new language. Other writing tends towards the strident assertion of patients' rights, relegating the professional to the status of a technician, there to take orders. Neither of these polar opposite positions advances the interests of patients nor, equally important, since their interests are intertwined, those of healthcare professionals. The 'middle way', exemplified by the writing of Angela Coulter,[2] is the only sensible way.

A mature culture will settle on sharing power and responsibility, on a subtle negotiation (not in a legalistic sense, but in the way we negotiate our way through life) between professional and patient as to what each wants and what each can deliver. This is the culture which we should work towards, helping each other as we go.

[2] Eg *Engaging Patients in Healthcare* (Open University Press, 2011).

10

Ethical Issues in Transplantation[1]

I am delighted and honoured to be invited to give this Inaugural Lecture in memory of Bill Hoffenberg.

I knew Bill first through his very significant role as President in involving the Royal College of Physicians in the ethics of research on human subjects. The College led the way in developing thinking in this country in an area which had been hitherto neglected. Under Bill's leadership, the College produced a Code which served as the starting point for all that followed: no-one could say now that the area is neglected, nor should it be. The College was also greatly involved in wrestling with the determination of death, in the face of developments in artificial respiration and intensive care. Here again, under Bill's leadership, the College produced a set of guidelines which led the world. I had the privilege and pleasure of working on them with Bill and other giants, such as Professor Brian Jennett, and considered myself very fortunate to be involved.

Out of the involvement in the determination of death grew the interest in transplantation. We were all keen to point out that they were entirely separate subjects: death needed to be determined in some circumstances, whether transplantation was an option or not. But, that said, the growth of interest in transplants and the hopes that transplantation held for people otherwise very sick and often destined to die before their time, drew many to the subject. Of particular interest to Bill and those he gathered around him, were the ethical challenges thrown up by the possibilities of transplantation. This was typical of Bill: he was a deeply moral man who saw medicine as a moral as well as a technical endeavour. Through his enthusiasm and that of colleagues such as Robert Sells and Janet Radcliffe Richards there was created the International Forum for Transplant Ethics. We met regularly, sometimes in the UK, sometimes in Europe or North America. It was a serious business. Papers were circulated, discussed, re-thought, re-circulated. Many ended up in *The Lancet* and the like. All the hot topics of transplantation were taken on.

What characterised these meetings, apart from the fact that we were all volunteers and made the time within our day jobs, was the sense of camaraderie and fun which Bill did so much to engender. We were serious, indeed very serious when it came to matters such as the link between executions in some countries and transplants. But we were also good friends, enjoying each others' company. Indeed, when I was in Australia on one occasion I made a side trip to the Gold Coast north of Brisbane, just to touch

[1] This is the unpublished Inaugural Hoffenberg Lecture established in memory of Sir Raymond Hoffenberg which I delivered in March 2010.

base with Bill and Margaret, because I so liked and admired him. We talked of his enthusiasm for the new South Africa and what he was doing to help Mandela's government to meet the massive challenges of health and healthcare. I remember walking on the beach with him, this big bruiser with the broken nose (the product of boxing, not rugby), and thinking how much he had done to humanise medicine and make ethical issues a central part of the discourse. He was, if I may use a very English term, a very nice man.

He was also a giant of a man in spiritual as well as physical terms. No-one reading L Ross Humphreys' biography[2] can come away without a sense of wonder at all he achieved. A fierce opponent of apartheid, he was made subject to a banning order which put an end to his career as a doctor and teacher. He, like many others, was forced out of his beloved South Africa. When he left in 1968, over 2000 students came to the airport in white coats to say their farewells – that was the measure of the man. Leaving your home with a family to start again would overwhelm many. But this man just went from strength to strength. A Chair in Birmingham University, a distinguished career in research, the summit of his profession as President of the Royal College of Physicians, and the President of Wolfson College Oxford.

He threw himself into the issues of the day with energy and intellectual rigour: they included the prison medical service, medical ethics – from research, to euthanasia, to transplants, to torture. His condemnation of research on South African miners showed him at his most humane and courageous, as his previous mentor in South Africa attacked him and only later and grudgingly apologised. And, of course, he was deeply involved in the politics of healthcare as the NHS struggled to come to terms with the Conservative Government's view on life in the 80s. And finally, as in all good stories, the wheel came full circle. Apartheid collapsed, Mandela began the task of guiding South Africa out of the darkness of the previous decades and Bill was invited back to help. You can imagine the pleasure that gave him.

And, before I close this tribute, may I share something with you that I found out only recently? Why was Sir Raymond known to all as Bill? Well, Bill had a sister, Elaine, who, at the age of four, Bill being three, developed an imagined attachment to one Billy Ryan who went to the school next door. Unable to make contact with the real Billy, she converted her brother into a surrogate Billy. The rest is history.

This evening I am invited to explore some of the ethical challenges thrown up by transplantation. I shall do so in very general terms. I shall do so with one eye on the legacy of Bill Hoffenberg.

Let me indicate the topics I'm going to touch on. They are:

- the determination of death;
- the allocation of organs;
- strategies to increase the supply of organs;
- commerce in organs;
- transplants and state execution.

[2] *Hoffenberg: Physician and Humanitarian* (Royal College of Physicians, 2010).

Each of these topics deserves a lecture, or a series of lectures, in its own right. Here I will fly high and fast and hope not to be thought too perfunctory. I will be looking at the various topics from the perspective of asking what is the right way to think about them, as a guide to asking what we should do about them.

Before an audience such as this, I do not need to rehearse the development of transplantation over the past 50 years since the first transplant at Peter Bent Brigham Hospital in 1954. I notice in passing that corneal grafts anteceded the development of organ transplants as we think of them, but they need not detain us here this evening. Transplantation is now an accepted weapon in the armamentarium of treatments in response to patients suffering from the failure of one or more organs. It was not always so. Acceptance was not guaranteed. The first heart transplant, as some will recall, provoked considerable public concern, on two grounds, both of them ethical.

The first concerned the experimental nature of the procedure. On the death of the first and subsequent early recipients, the question was asked whether it was ever right to use very sick people as, effectively, guinea pigs. This is not, of course, a problem particular to transplantation and it continues to raise its head. The ethical response which emerged was one of the early examples of the rise of autonomy as a fundamental guiding concept in medical ethics. The argument went that if the patient was made aware (informed) of what was at stake – his current condition, the proposed intervention and the likely outcome – then the transplant was ethically justifiable. The fact that the patient was close to death made the issue appear easier. There was no real choice: it was certain death against the faintest of hopes of continued existence for some unknown period of time. The counter argument that the patient was being used as a mere means to an end, ie the development of this area of surgery and that such use of him was contrary to the public interest, did not get very many takers. It was his life, his body, his heart, and he could do what he liked with it. Of course, such a claim is question begging: there are and should be limits to what it is proper to do with your body. Was agreeing to a heart transplant one of them? But, as I've said, this strand of argument did not gain much currency. Autonomy ruled.

The Determination of Death

The second ground of public concern which attended the early heart transplants was a concern that has dogged transplantation ever since, even though as I've said, strictly speaking, it is entirely unrelated to transplantation. It may be as well to recognise it early on and deal with it. I refer to the determination of death. This is not the place to explore the issue in depth. Indeed, if I do, it would mean that, again, it has captured the discourse about transplants. So, instead, I will offer a series of propositions, which move from the scientific to the ethical.

First, whether people/patients are dead is a question which has to be answered in certain circumstances, quite apart from any question of transplantation. It arises because a patient's vital signs can be maintained independently of the patient's current capacity to do so. At some point the question must be asked, out of concern for the patient, for the patient's family and friends, for the staff caring for him/her and for the proper use of scarce resources, whether the patient has died.

Of course, the determination of death is not a scientific question, though an understanding of medical science is important. It is an ethical question, a question not about the meaning and determination of death, but about the meaning of life. We must understand what we regard as being alive, so as to settle on an understanding of death. I cannot rehearse here all of the arguments. By way of shorthand, the philosophical has been intertwined with the scientific. The debate, which still runs hot in some quarters, centres on the brain versus the heart. These serve as surrogates for on the one hand a conception of being alive which looks to a continued capacity to sustain vital functions, the irreversible loss of which constitutes death, and on the other one which looks to the complete absence of vital functions, the cessation of heartbeat. In the UK, after careful deliberation, the former definition was adopted, as long ago as the late 1960s. The scientific criterion chosen to establish death was the irreversible loss of brain stem function. The continuing commitment to this approach was signalled only last year again in the latest update by the Royal College of Anaesthetists' Working Group on Brain Stem death. Elsewhere, as is well known, the commitment to a definition based on the presence or absence of heart beat, or the rather curious half-way house based on the absence of all cerebral function, are still argued for.

As we shall see, this discourse continues to have implications for the practice of transplantation. But, I repeat, of itself it is an entirely separate ethical and scientific discourse, arising not from the development of transplantation but from the development of techniques of intensive care. That said, the two issues have been brought together in a debate which I ought to notice here before moving on.

The argument is as follows. A patient is near death and will not recover (assume the facts). The patient's organs would be suitable for retrieval and transplant. Can the patient's treatment be managed differently so as to ensure that the organs are kept as viable as possible for transplant, even if that means that the nature of the patient's care changes, more in the interests of the organs than the patient? The initial answer should be, No. The patient is living until dead and thus is owed the same duty of care as any other patient. To modify treatment so that its purpose is not to put the patient's interests first is, on this reading, unethical and probably unlawful. Some find this an unfortunate conclusion. It means that organs may deteriorate in the process of dying and not, therefore, be usable for transplant.

A modification to the hard line advanced above has therefore been advanced. It has something of the Jesuitical about it, but can, I think, be defended. It is described as the non-heart-beating transplant, meaning that the patient's organs are removed after death and the cessation of heartbeat, but measures are taken in advance of death to ensure that the organs remain viable for transplant. The argument is that the general rule is sound and should be followed. The basis is the duty always to act in the patient's best interests. But then, enter a more subtle point. What if the patient had signed a donor card or expressed a documented wish that his organs be used for transplant? In these, and perhaps other circumstances in which there is evidence that the patient was willing to donate his organs, it may be in the patient' best interests to manage his care so as to give effect to his wish, if he is inevitably going to die.

I can see the power of this argument in terms of advancing the cause of transplantation in the context of scarcity. It needs to be said, however, that it is an approach which must be adopted with great care and monitored scrupulously.

I now have to grasp a nettle which has been around for some years. How does this argument affect the question of what is known as elective ventilation. This involves a decision to place a person who has suffered massive brain damage and whose prognosis is hopeless, on a ventilator in an ICU to ensure that his heart, for example, is not irretrievably damaged during the process of dying for around 48 hours or so until brain-stem death takes place. Developed in Exeter in the late 80s, it was discontinued in 1994 on the basis of legal opinion that it was unlawful. The unlawfulness lay, it was said, in the fact that the patient had not consented and that the intervention was non-therapeutic and thus not in the patient's interests.

Can we deploy the argument that if the person was registered as a donor, he had indicated his willingness to be taken to the ICU and ventilated? My answer is no: the argument cannot be deployed. The reason is that consent to elective ventilation must be specific and cannot be assumed from a general agreement to be a donor. This is because elective ventilation carries a risk, albeit small, that the patient will not die but enter a persistent vegetative state. It is unlikely in the extreme that someone would explicitly agree to take this risk, both for his own interests and for those of his loved ones. Certainly, no such consent could plausibly be implied. Thus, I still hold to the position I took when asked in the 80s: elective ventilation is both unethical and unlawful.

There are, of course, other ethical objections, having to do, for example, with the use of a bed in an ICU for two days and thereby potentially denying care to others, and the use of the scarce resources involved. I do not rely on them here but note them.

The Allocation of Organs

Now, let me turn to the next of the issues that I mentioned earlier: the allocation of organs. Of course, we must begin by asking why this is an issue to be discussed. As you all know, we ask it because, within varying degrees, there are not enough organs to transplant into those who could benefit from a transplant. So, since the advent of transplants, choices have had to be made. And, choices call for criteria. Given what's at stake, sometimes the patient's life, always the possibility of improved health, the criteria need to be ethically justifiable. You can, of course, and some did and do say that there is nothing of ethics here: the criteria guiding the choices are wholly medical. But, even if 'wholly medical' intrinsically meant free of ethical content, which is difficult to sustain, the proposition does not hold water, as I sought to suggest many years ago.

We are in the world of rationing and there is no escape. This is not something bad, of itself: all health care is rationed to a greater or lesser extent. What occupies us is the consequence of not being selected for transplant and the consequent need to have a system of allocation which is ethically sound.

Let's remind ourselves of the strategies which have been rehearsed for allocating what is a scarce commodity. I confine myself initially to organs retrieved from the dead. Initially, age was frequently used: an unstated rule that very young patients and those over 55 would not be considered for transplant. There were some plausible medical justifications, having to do with the likely success of the transplant, but the reasoning was essentially ethical: that a chance of life or better health should be given to those who could still derive the greatest benefit from a transplant – could enjoy a fruitful and productive life. Or, more crudely, were not past it. The reasoning was not, however, altogether about fitness for a transplant. Transplantation before a patient had been put on dialysis was almost unheard of at that time. It was in fact the scarcity of dialysis machines that was largely responsible for the rationing. Nephrologists tended not to offer dialysis to the over 55s. Such patients, therefore, did not get into the transplant queue.

As results improved it became clear that selecting recipients on the basis of age was a pretty desperate strategy and was increasingly hard to defend medically. Other approaches were mooted, on the assumption that the prospective recipients were otherwise equal both in terms of the likely success of the transplant and the prospects of benefitting from it. A lottery was proposed, as was queuing, that quintessentially British device. The wheel has turned again, prompted by increasing understanding of the reasons for success and failure. Now, allocation is made on the basis of a number of physical criteria, so as to ensure the best possible match between the recipient and the person from whom the organ has been obtained. We are back to the position in which ethics can be sidelined in the minds of some.

But, insisting on the best possible match means that the person who could, perhaps, benefit but is pipped by someone with a marginally better match, loses out. The consequences could be fatal. Unsurprisingly, this person doesn't want to take no for an answer. Re-enter ethical debate.

Faced with a shortage of organs for transplantation, a range of responses can be made to the person who cannot gain access to the needed transplantation. The state can take action to increase the supply, or the individual can take action. These twin approaches can and do, of course, co-exist.

The state can do a number of things aimed to increase the supply of organs. It can also take action with the aim of limiting the supply, if the proposed means of increasing supply are considered ethically undesirable.

Increasing the Supply

In Britain, the access to organs for transplant has been based on the fundamental premise that they should be freely given. The ethic is one of solidarity and collective concern for the welfare of all. It was the inspiration behind the National Health Service and is reflected in the Richard Titmuss' seminal and hugely influential work on blood donation, *The Gift Relationship* (1997). It is no surprise that it was the approach adopted in relation to organ donation. People were encouraged to carry donor cards. When need began increasingly to outstrip supply, the response of the state from time to time has been, in effect, to urge more people to carry donor cards and enrol on the voluntary donor register. This was the fundamental message which emerged from the Organ Donation Taskforce which reported at the beginning of 2009. The principle of the gift, characterised by voluntary donation, was endorsed. This principle was to be surrounded by a series of administrative measures to make it work better. But, from the point of view of the state, it was to remain the central ethical pillar of the system. The fact that it had not produced the goods over the past decades was shrugged off: we just have to try harder was the message.

There are, of course, other things that the state could do. They are deemed to be ethically contentious. Let's look at some of them and then take a view.[3]

Presumed Consent or Opting Out

Currently, the system established by English law is that, broadly speaking, an organ may only be removed from a deceased person for the purpose of transplantation if that person, prior to death, has indicated an intention to donate the organ for that purpose. Carrying a donor card, or 'opting in' through registration are the ways in which that intention is signalled. As we all know, this system has increasingly failed to bridge the gap between supply and need. Presumed consent, or opting out, represents an alternative. The state, through its law, would establish a system whereby a deceased person is presumed to consent to the removal of an organ, if otherwise suitable for transplant, unless a contrary intention has been expressed. Clearly, the notion of presumed consent is an oxymoron, and, as such, is capable of being confusing. The term opting out, therefore, is seen as preferable. In contrast to the current system which requires members of the public to opt in, that is, positively to indicate their agreement to the removal of organs for transplant, opting out would shift the onus and allow the state to assume that an organ may be removed unless an objection has been registered during the deceased's lifetime. The result under both terms is the same. The required conduct is the same, a positive act of refusal, but to some the language of 'opting out' sends a more acceptable signal: that the decision is in the control of the citizen.

I must here declare an interest. I first advocated 'presumed consent' nearly 30 years ago. I have never seen any reason to change my mind. Indeed, I have never understood the objections raised. Clearly, there are administrative issues, which would need to be addressed. And, there would be the need to respect certain beliefs. This latter concern can readily be met by focused information and a suitable time-scale before implementing the system. But, over the years, other objections have been raised. They have included references to the rights of the family, the rights of the deceased, and the interests of those caring for the dying potential donor. To my mind, none is ethically persuasive. Indeed, they could be said to be ethically perverse. For me, the most critical ethical concern is for the patient who could benefit from the organ. His or her claim to the organ, which will otherwise be burned or buried, should be recognised by the state as far stronger that any other's. The deceased has no claim, unless s/he has opted out (the claim is that of the executor). As for the family, its claim that the organ be destroyed rather than used to benefit another does not rest on any sense of ownership: the organ does not belong to them. It can only rest on a claim that their sensitivities should prevail. And, while ordinarily, the state should seek to respect such sensitivities, the state also

[3] [Things have moved on, thankfully, in the years since I gave this lecture. I set out in a postscript the current (2020) situation. What I say in the lecture, however, remains of interest as exploring the ethical arguments in play as policy shifted.]

has an obligation to those who are ill and could be made better. Rescuing the living, in my book, takes precedence: it should be the ruling ethical principle.

It came as a surprise to many, therefore, when the Taskforce that I just referred to, having deferred a decision in its original Report, subsequently announced that they opposed opting out. It came as a surprise and a huge disappointment. To the members of the Taskforce volunteering was the only game in town. More donor cards had to be carried: despite decades of evidence that donor cards alone had not reduced the shortage of organs. Even more surprising was the reason given. It was that those caring for patients whose organs might potentially be used after death for transplantation opposed opting out and their view was accepted. This opposition was based on the fear that their relationship with the patient's family and loved ones might be compromised, that they may not be trusted to devote their total commitment to the patient because the possibility of transplanting the patient's organs was on their minds or in the background. This is, of course, a legitimate concern. But there are at least three responses.

First, it is expressed as a concern or fear. It is not expressed as a proposition of fact. No evidence is adduced that families have taken or would take this view, if the situation were appropriately managed. Secondly, if it is a real concern, the response ethically is to ensure that all means are used to dispel any concern or fear, so that the family may be reassured, rather than use it to prevent the introduction of a policy which is otherwise ethically justified. Thirdly, it is of some concern that the ethics and policy of transplantation should be decided by one particular clinical constituency. Of course, the views and values of those caring for a dying patient deserve respect. But, in my view, the challenge is for them to adapt and help others to do so, rather than veto change because it might be temporarily challenging.

But, presumed consent, or opting out, remains off limits in the UK. Ethically, this can be regretted.

It could be objected that I have failed to acknowledge that there are, in fact, two types of opting out: 'hard' and 'soft'. 'Soft' opting out refers to the practice that, while the law allows organs to be removed without seeking permission, in fact the family are asked for their permission. This is the practice in Spain. Obviously, the notion of 'soft' opting out is a subterfuge. It undermines, even frustrates, the policy behind the law. That said, I do not object to this ethical fudge, provided two criteria are met. First, it must be understood that it constitutes a temporary accommodation, allowing for the gradual shift in culture. Secondly, the number of refusals must fall over time. Otherwise, the needy patient will see the claims of compromise and 'pragmatism' once again raised as barriers to meeting his need.

Mandated Choice

The Chairman of the Royal College of Physicians' Ethics Committee recently urged the adoption of a policy called mandated choice. This would again require action by the state. It contemplates that each citizen should be required to register an answer to the question whether s/he is willing to have his/her organs removed after death for transplantation. Much hangs on the answers allowed. In some early examples of this policy, the citizen was given only two choices: Yes or No. Such an approach was thought to be too limiting and thereby not sufficiently respectful of the individual, who may, for example, support the notion of transplantation, but may be ill-at-ease in making a decision in his own particular case. For this reason, a third possible answer was added, namely, Ask my relatives. This answer allows the citizen to avoid the question, without undermining the possibility that his organs could be used, on the say so of his relatives.

The Royal College's proposal was not widely welcomed. This is understandable if only the two answers were allowed, because it is then just a variant of opting out and so attracts the same opposition. The addition of the third possible answer makes it essentially the same as the existing system,[4] whereby, in the absence of any expression of intention by the patient, the relatives decide. To that extent, it's hard to understand why it would be opposed. Equally, given that it largely reflects the current system in the absence of an express wish to donate, it's hard to see how it would improve the supply of organs.

The Israeli Option

One recent innovation is the position adopted in Israel. There, priority in access to an organ for transplant will be given to those carrying donor cards. As a rationing device, its intention is political. It is clearly intended to increase the number of citizens who carry donor cards. In terms of ethics, it constitutes a continued commitment to the principle of voluntariness and social solidarity. It merely goes further in its commitment by rewarding those who demonstrate through active engagement their solidarity, rather than just passively supporting it. It could be said by critics that it discriminates against those who are unaware of the policy. The answer lies in placing on the state the obligation to use all appropriate means to make the law known. It also discriminates against those who oppose the removal of their organs for transplant, but who may, if they come to need a transplant, ask for one. To them, the response must be that social solidarity means what it says. In the context of scarce resources, it is entirely defensible to prefer first those who are prepared to give as well as to get.

Designated or Conditional Donation

This term is used to refer to the situation in which a person before death indicates his willingness to be an organ donor but seeks to specify the person, or class of persons, into whom the organ may be transplanted. The stated intention is that the organ should go to that person, or group, and no other. When this circumstance arose in recent cases, the decision was taken that the specific designation should have no force. The reason given was that organ donation must be seen and operated as an altruistic endeavour (the Gift principle again). Laying down conditions, designating a recipient, violated this principle and so could properly be ignored.

I must say that I find this reasoning unpersuasive. Certainly, it would be desirable for organ donation to be based on altruism. But, this does not mean that it must

[4] Human Tissue Act 1961, s 1.

be exclusively altruistic. It will be a relatively rare case in which someone will seek to direct who may receive his/her organ. If the direction is expressed in some negative form, eg barring donation on religious or racial grounds, then it will be ethically legitimate to prohibit such a bar, based on principles of fairness and hostility to adverse discrimination.[5] But, this need not necessarily rule out all forms of designation. Indeed, designated donation is deemed entirely acceptable from an ethical standpoint in the case of a living donor who provides an organ for a relative (or even a friend). If it is ethically acceptable among the living, it is not at all clear why the intervening death of the designating party changes anything.

It may be said that to allow designated or conditional donation limits the pool of available organs. But, this is obviously not the case. It increases the pool and reduces the number waiting. What then of the argument that the designated donor has allowed the favoured recipient to jump the queue: that there are potential recipients who have waited longer and are just as good a match? My response is that, if, once the organ is available, it is then given to the person on the waiting list rather than the designated person, this not only offends a general principle of our society that we should seek to respect the expressed views of the deceased, but also gives greater weight to the principle of the queue than to the expressed wishes of the donor. And, of course, allocating resources by reference to the queue, while a long-established British principle, itself ignores any special circumstances which may make a particular case more ethically compelling than that of the person who is first in the queue. We let the mother with her child jump the queue, just as we let someone join the queue when the person he is joining says that 'she is with me'.

Commerce in Organs

We enter now a very complex area, replete with ethical challenges. And, in contrast to what has gone before, the discussion here is about transplants from living donors. This is not to say that transplants from the deceased cannot raise concerns about commerce. Rather, it is to say that the problems in practice largely relate to living donors.

It will be clear that the British approach to transplants, based on altruism and the notion of the Gift Relationship, would have difficulties with the notion of a trade or commerce in organs. Indeed, such commerce is unlawful in the UK, under the Human Tissue Act 2004. But what of the ethics?

I begin by noticing perhaps the most important element in the discussion, though superficially somewhat at a tangent. I refer to the internet. No consideration of commerce in organs can ignore the powerful coming together of an unmet need for organs and the desperation that comes with it and the creation of a virtual global market. Notions such as transplant tourism and trafficking in organs have entered the debate. But before I address them, let's look briefly at the arguments surrounding commerce: the sale of organs.

[5] In a case in Sheffield in 2000 a racist condition attached to a deceased donor's donation was rejected, and see Cronin and Price, 'Directed Organ Donation' (2008) 1:3(3) *Clin Ethics* pp. 127–31.

Classically, objections are raised against commerce because of the circumstances in which it arises. Someone seeks to raise money by selling an organ, let's say a kidney. (Suicide donation, where the person offers himself for surgery in the knowledge that it will be fatal, though not unknown, and carried out willingly for perhaps the financial benefit of a family, must on any analysis be unethical: it necessarily involves the person taking the organs in an act of killing.) The argument has it that, under normal circumstances, no-one would be willing to part with a vital organ, even though he can function perfectly well, for example, on one kidney. The only reason, therefore, that he is doing it is out of a need for money. The argument immediately lurches to the conclusion that he is being exploited. Exploitation, it is said, is wrong. So, such commerce is unethical.

The difficulty with this argument, which, I repeat, I pursue so as to set the parameters for the wider discussion to follow, is that it does not take account of the fact that much of what people do who have no or limited money could be described as exploitation. They work in dangerous jobs, live in unsafe places in an environment which has many dangers. They make their way through these hazards. Choices are rarely open to them. In such a context, if someone were to say that a person could earn enough money to get a house or educate his children by agreeing to have his kidney removed, he may well jump at the offer. It's not what he might want, but little of his life is. At least it brings a significant reward. And, I assume in this scenario that the operation will be properly carried out, the person treated till ready to be discharged, and then properly followed-up.

On this, somewhat idealised, version of events, a case can be made that the purchase of the person's kidney is not unethical. Both parties recognise their respective needs and reach an accord. This would compel the argument that there is nothing intrinsically unethical in commerce in organs, provided that the conditions having to do with the welfare of the donor are met. Nor would the clinical team be behaving unethically. The person has made his assessment of his needs and has made his decision. The surgery admittedly is carried out on a healthy person and is mutilating. But this is no different from consensual live donation where no payment is involved. The patient's consent and the general public good served by transplantation provide ethical cover.

The difficulty is that this idealised picture is not what we are currently dealing with. Through the internet those needing organs, often in countries where there is no or a very limited transplant programme, seek out those who will secure organs. It is largely the domain of the wealthy sick. The organs are secured from the (relatively) healthy poor. Trafficking in people and organs is the order of the day. The reality is one of exploitation, of the very poor being tricked or trapped into 'giving' their organs, of illegal operations (since many countries, particularly in the middle and far east ban commerce), of botched operations, of people left with no after-care, and of the rich clutching at a chance of life denied their poorer fellow citizens.

This may also be something of a caricature. But, it is certainly close to the truth of what has happened over the past few years. Ethically those involved in recruiting 'donors', in operating on them, in then abandoning them, and in oiling the wheels of the enterprise have much to answer for. In terms of ethics, and here I mean a universal ethic, they are to be condemned. What they do is wrong. What should be done about them and the practice they are part of is a separate question. Clearly, given the international nature of the trafficking, only international action will do. The recent Declaration of Istanbul is one example of such action.[6] But, ultimately, such trafficking will only cease when the supply of organs meets the need. In the meantime, the greatest force for limiting trafficking is the clinical professions. They have already shown remarkable leadership. They should continue, making it clear that someone who carries out a transplant in the circumstances I have described deserves condemnation and rejection from the ranks of caring clinicians. And because this is the reality of commerce in organs, rather than the arm's length agreement between two consenting parties which is the theoretical model of the commercial exchange, commerce in organs has no place as a response to scarcity.

But, is there a way round these objections? Would commerce be acceptable if it was controlled by the state? The supply of organs could be increased, but, through the engagement of the state, exploitation could be avoided, the welfare of the donor could be addressed as could the quality of the organ removed for transplant. These are the justifications advanced. How to respond?

There are two ways in which the state could be involved. The first is through what economists call a monopsistic market, whereby there is only one purchaser. This could be the NHS, which is largely the case with pharmaceutical products. The NHS would purchase the organ at an agreed price and make it available, free at the point of need, in accordance with the overarching principle of the NHS. The same approach to allocation would be followed as is now the case: there would just be more organs to allocate, it is said. And the rich would fare no better than the poor, at least in the receipt of organs, because the organ would be free.

The rich would donate fewer organs than the poor, however, because they would have no financial reason to donate. The risk or reality of exploitation would still remain. Moreover, and this may be the fundamental objection to the introduction of such a policy, it would constitute an abandonment of the principle of the gift. I am prepared to depart from that principle in the case of 'opting out', where the organ is removed from someone who has died. But, to do so as between the living donor and donee is to take the state into troubling and troubled waters. It would commodify us. It would constitute an admission that altruism, coupled with the far less contentious 'opting out', cannot deliver all that we need. It would mean that the state was prepared to see its more economically vulnerable citizens expose themselves to a serious non-therapeutic intervention out of need (and make no mistake, it would only be the needy who would be persuaded to come forward by the financial motivation). I cannot see, therefore, that this form of state involvement in creating a market for organs is ethically acceptable. I leave aside the additional question of whether the removal of an organ for payment would be lawful. I would only add that the law recognises limits to that which a person may consent to. Those limits reflect a sense of the public's view as to what should be regarded as morally permissible. I would hazard that a court would find the surgery unlawful.

Another way in which the state can become involved is to allow for commerce in organs but seek to regulate the market, through such conditions as fixed prices for organs, quality control, and safe care for the donor. Those who believe in the market as a solution to our problems, the perfect regulator of our affairs, have recently argued

[6] The *Declaration of Istanbul* was agreed at the 1st Summit on Organ Trafficking and Transplantation Tourism, Istanbul, May 2008. It declared that organ trafficking and transplant tourism should be prohibited.

strongly in favour of a regulated market in organs. Supply will be increased, waiting lists will disappear. Supply will be brought into contact with demand through the agency of money.

There are at least three difficulties with this approach: the supplier; the purchaser; and the context. As regards the context, it is one of significant scarcity (which will never be completely eliminated) in which the scarcity threatens the life of the person wanting the transplant. The supplier is someone who needs the money and sees or has no option but to submit to surgery. We are back to the exploitation point. It is fine for commentators to say that the operation is standard and the loss of a kidney poses virtually no threat to continued health (and partial liver, partial pancreas and partial lung transplants are now also routine in many centres). For my part I would be more persuaded of their concern for their fellow humans if they were at the front of the queue to have their kidney removed.

As regards the purchaser, he is by definition able to pay the price. The principles of fairness and equal access to care which inform the approach to healthcare in the UK fall by the wayside. The rich inherit the earth, sponsored by the state.

And, as if these difficulties were not enough, there is a further difficulty with this approach. In the context of scarcity, regulated markets soon spawn unregulated markets (commonly known as a black market). The state ordained safeguards are sidestepped or simply ignored as needy donor (wanting money) pursues and is pursued by needy donee (wanting a transplant). Even with a well-staffed and vigilant inspectorate, the black market will thrive. And with it, the problem of the exploitation of the economically vulnerable already alluded to will, if anything, be exacerbated. The recent experience of Iran offers clear evidence of this.

Organs from the Executed

I have left till last the grisly issue of transplanting organs from the recently executed. Allegations have been made that this is a practice carried out in a number of countries. I do not intend to spend a great deal of time on it. Capital punishment is outlawed throughout Europe. This is because capital punishment is judged to be ethically indefensible in a civilised state. It follows that states which continue to practice capital punishment already take themselves outside the league of the civilised, at least in this respect. Of course, some argue that each nation has the right to determine its policy in this as in any other area. The answer is that, unless we are to accept a notion of unbridled subjectivity in moral affairs, nations' rights are circumscribed by the need to pay due respect to certain transcendent norms. The rejection of capital punishment is one such norm.

This means, of course, that the consideration of the ethics of using the organs of the recently executed never gets off the ground. It cannot be justified, because capital punishment cannot be. And that is where the argument should be focused. That nations may base their policy of execution on the need to meet the demand for organs for transplant is merely a further illustration of the wrongness of state execution. Thus, in my book, it is not worthwhile to complain about the links between execution and transplantation. To do so misses the bigger point.

Conclusion

I recognise that, not least for reasons of time, I have not addressed all the myriad ethical challenges thrown up by organ transplantation. Equally I recognise that I have given but a poor imitation of the analysis and argument that Bill Hoffenberg would have offered you. But, I have felt hugely privileged to be invited to add my voice to the many who remember this fine man. And, if I may end on what some may see as a controversial note, and I can see him in mind's eye egging me on, I would leave ringing in your ears the need to introduce a policy of opting out at the earliest opportunity. Bill came round to supporting the idea and I know he'd want me to remind you.

Postscript

Wales was the first to catch up with the argument. The Human Transplantation (Wales) Act 2013 introduced the system of deemed consent/opt out which came into effect on 1 December 2015. England and Scotland then both introduced opting out in 2019, the English system to come into effect in May 2020 and the Scottish from March 2021.

The three countries' laws each provide that everyone over the age of 18 will be considered to be in favour of donating their organs and tissue unless they have opted out, they have appointed a representative to act for them after death, or they belong to an excluded group, eg are under 18 or lack the mental capacity to consent.

These changes have been a long time coming and are very welcome. Bill Hoffenberg would have been pleased.

Northern Ireland still retains the 'opting in' system though the government agreed in July 2020 to consult on the introduction of an opt-out system.

11

A Collection of Children's Hearts[1]

Introduction

The Chief Executive of Birmingham Children's Hospital asked me in February 2014 to carry out a review of the Hospital's policy relating to its collection of children's hearts and to advise as to future policy and practice.[2]

The Hospital has a collection of children's hearts (currently totalling 1969). All of these hearts were removed and stored prior to the passage of the Human Tissue Act 2005. The period covered is 1939–2002. No hearts were removed and stored between 2002 and the coming into effect of the new procedures under the Act in 2005. That Act provides as its central principle that consent is required before tissue may be removed and stored. It also sets out what may be done with the tissue and lays down specific procedures to be observed. It established a system of regulation operated by the Human Tissue Authority (HTA), including the licensing and inspection of premises and monitoring compliance with the Act. Its provisions regarding the authorisation of removal and storage of organs do not apply to those hearts in the Hospital's collection which were collected before the Act came into force. It is expected, however, that the underlying principles of the Act regarding use of tissue would govern any use made of hearts removed and stored before the Act.

During the hearings of the Public Inquiry into paediatric cardiac surgery at Bristol Royal Infirmary in mid-1999, evidence was given that a number of Hospitals, including Bristol, had retained the hearts of children who had died of congenital heart disease. Parents and families were unaware of the practice whereby organs were retained by pathologists, usually after a Coroner's inquest, rather than returned to parents. It was described as being common practice at the time, amid confusion as to what it was that parents had consented to in agreeing to an autopsy, and to a lack of clarity in the law. Once revealed, the practice caused considerable concern among families and the wider public.

At the invitation of the Chief Medical Officer for England, the Inquiry conducted an inquiry within the Inquiry and published a Report in May 2000.[3] The Report

[1] A Review commissioned by the Chief Executive of Birmingham Children's Hospital NHS Foundation Trust and submitted in December 2014. It was widely circulated though not formally published.

[2] I am very grateful for the advice that I received from Professor Bob Anderson, Mr William Brawn and Dr Andrew Cook.

[3] *Removal and retention of human material, Interim Report, The Bristol Royal Infirmary Inquiry* (Stationery Office, 2000).

recommended changes in practice and law regarding the removal and subsequent use of human material, principal among which was the need to obtain consent before an organ could be retained after death. This was echoed in the subsequent Alder Hey Report.[4] In advance of a change in the law, a Special Health Authority was established to address the question of returning organs which had been retained without permission and to advise on appropriate regulation and legislation. It was recommended that those Hospitals holding collections of children's organs should seek to identify the parents and relatives of the children whose organs (largely hearts) were retained, with a view to obtaining either retrospective consent to continue to hold them, or to handing over the organ to be buried or cremated according to the family's wishes.

In response to this recommendation and to the considerable attention from the media, Birmingham Children's Hospital (BCH) sought through appropriate means, including the media, to contact the families of those children whose hearts formed their collection so as to seek their wishes. A number came forward, broadly in three waves at the end of 1999 and in early 2000. After the publication of the Alder Hey Report there was a further wave of enquiries. In all, the Hospital had received 1146 enquiries by October 2001. Some parents and families claimed the heart so as to dispose of it in accordance with their wishes. Others asked the Hospital to retain the heart but surrender it on the death of a parent. Others indicated that the Hospital could retain the heart in its collection. The number of hearts in the collection fell to around 1980[5] from the original total of 2055. The Hospital has not made any public call for families to make contact for a number of years, but a handful of family members continue to come forward with requests or instructions (eight in the past two years).

The collection is carefully stored in a room in the Hospital's mortuary. The temperature is controlled and the preparation of formalin in which the hearts are stored is routinely checked. The hearts are stored in transparent containers in batches of about 20. Each heart has a tag naming the deceased child and, where applicable, a number relating to the Coroner's inquest. The Hospital does not allow the hearts to be removed from the Hospital, but they are routinely used for the education and training of cardiologists and surgeons.

This Review

The Review was prompted by exchanges between the HTA and the Hospital in April, May and June 2013. After a routine inspection, the Chief Executive of the HTA wrote to the Hospital advising that, although the Hospital was not in breach of any regulation in maintaining the collection, since the hearts were collected before the HTA came into existence, the Hospital should consider whether the collection was too large and whether some hearts might be disposed of. No indication was offered as to what might constitute an appropriate number. A helpful guide relating to disposal was made available.

[4] *Inquiry Report (The Redfern Report)* (Stationery Office, 2003).
[5] Currently 1969.

Given that the Hospital was not in breach of its licence to store organs, nor of the relevant regulations, it may be thought important to determine the basis for the HTA's advice. The stated reason was a concern that the Hospital might attract unwelcome and critical comment from the media and elsewhere if knowledge of the collection was made known.[6] It may seem odd that the HTA was offering what in effect was advice on handling the media. But, the advice offered makes a larger point: there was a significant public outcry after the Alder Hey Report such that the issue of retaining children's hearts can still attract considerable attention and rekindle the sense of scandal that accompanied the initial revelations.

In the light of the exchange of correspondence with the HTA, the question of the future of the collection was considered by the Hospital's Ethics Advisory Group. In the Minute of its meeting on 4 July 2013, it is reported that the Group, having considered the various arguments, '... was unable to give definitive advice'. Subsequently, the Deputy Chief Executive wrote to Mr Bill Brawn, the leading paediatric cardiac surgeon at the hospital, advising that, in the absence of clear guidance from the Ethics Group, he and his senior colleagues had agreed a number of guidelines. These were to be followed until outside advice was received. The Deputy Chief Executive advised that the collection should be used 'to provide benefit for future generations of children and young people with a heart problem'. 'That said', he went on, 'the education and training process should always be organised and delivered in such a way [as] to treat the organs with [the] dignity and care they deserve'. The guidelines stipulated that the organs should only be used for training and education, should not be transported away from the Hospital, that no incision be made in the organs until advice had been received, and that other methods of assessing the collection, such as the use of photography or MRI scanning may be used provided no damage is done to the organ. This is the background against which I was invited to conduct this Review.

The Hospital's Chief Executive asked me to undertake the Review so as to advise her how she should act in the light of the HTA's letter and subsequent exchanges. The issues raised involve questions of ethics against the background of the surrounding social and political context. In formulating my advice, I have spoken to a number of the staff at the Hospital and been shown the collection. I have also spoken to experts from a range of disciplines, the Medical Director of the British Heart Foundation, and representatives of parents and relatives of children with congenital heart disease. I am immensely grateful to them for the time that they gave me. I also wrote to a number of other Hospitals which, it was thought, have similar collections of hearts dating from the period prior to 2005. I am grateful for the responses that I received. (The letter that I wrote to the Hospitals and the responses are set out in Annex I.) Should my recommendations be accepted by the Chief Executive, I urge that every effort be made to work with other Hospitals in pursuing what I recommend.

[6] The Chief Executive of the HTA wrote in her e-mail to Dr Gray at the BCH, that '... these are existing holdings being stored on licensed premises and therefore there is no regulatory or statutory breach. However, T[sic]he size of the collection and the nature of the material make it of potential media interest'. There followed a number of recommendations, the first of which was that '... the trust prepares lines to take in readiness should the matter ever come to public attention'.

The Way Forward

The Options

Before offering my view as to what the Hospital should do, I set out the options available and the relevant arguments.

(a) Dispose of the collection completely.

This course of action is not, in my view, appropriate.[7] The collection is of considerable value as a tool for educating and training those who are, or will be, caring for children with congenital heart disease. It would be a great loss to such children and their parents and families if the collection were not available for these purposes. I therefore discount this option.

(b) Dispose of a number of hearts, so as to reduce the size of the collection.

There is no obvious reason why reducing the size of the collection, of itself, just to make the collection smaller, would make any difference to the appropriateness of having the collection. It is hard to see why a collection of, say, 500 hearts is ethically justifiable while a collection of close to 2000 hearts is not, except to notice that the larger the collection the greater the potential attention from the media and others (this latter point looks as if it was behind the HTA's view). Any argument for reducing the number must rest on more than volume.

One argument could be that there are several examples of a particular congenital abnormality, making it possible to dispose of all but the one example. Alternatively, it could be argued that some of the hearts have been so affected by the process of storage that they are no longer of use for education and training.

As regards the argument that some hearts in the collection could be disposed of as constituting duplication, it is flawed, quite apart from the fact that it rests on the assumption that disposal of some, if not all, the hearts is a good thing in itself. The flaw lies in the fact that, although a number of hearts may be categorised as having the same congenital abnormality, the precise presentation of the abnormality may be different. It is of the first importance from the perspective of education and training to appreciate that such differences occur and to understand the implications for care and treatment. Equally, the surgical responses to the abnormality may have varied, allowing lessons to be learned.

As regards the argument about the possible degradation of some hearts beyond a point at which they could be of further use in education and training, I am led to believe that the condition of some hearts has, in fact, deteriorated over time. It is a matter for expert opinion whether this is so. However, given the possible forms of research which may be undertaken, which I will refer to shortly, it may be that the heart could still be of value for research purposes, despite its condition. Clearly, should any heart be deemed, after expert evaluation, not to have any further value for any of the purposes of education, training or research, the Hospital may decide that it

[7] My colleagues and I concluded in the Interim Report (see fn 3), (p 19, para 63) that 'We can also hope that … ways may be found whereby existing archives of human material, which could hold the prospect of help for future children, can remain in existence'.

should be disposed of. In such circumstances, the HTA has a detailed set of guidelines concerning the disposal of organs which I would expect the Hospital to observe.

(c) Continue to hold the collection in its current form and preserve it, but not make it available for use of any kind.

It is hard to see how this approach could be justified. The collection would simply be a drain on the Hospital's resources without providing any benefit. One justification offered is that the collection constitutes a historical record, an archive, of children's hearts, preserved as they were when the child died. As a historical record, it may be argued, it would be wrong to tamper in any way with that record. The difficulties with this approach are plain. Historical records, or archives, by their nature, serve a purpose. They exist to allow others to have access to them. (The precise nature of that access is a different question which I will address shortly.) Secondly, whatever the reasons behind starting and then continuing the collection, it is most unlikely that those responsible contemplated that the collection be treated like some relic, to exist but nothing else. It is much more likely that, from the outset, the collection was begun and maintained to advance knowledge and understanding about heart disease in children and how the care of children with heart disease could be improved.

(d) Allow the collection to be properly catalogued.

The classification of the different forms of congenital abnormalities has long been an issue of concern among clinicians. Obviously, if clinicians are, for example, going to discuss the merits of one form of treatment over another, they must be able to agree that they are talking about the same condition. The classification of conditions, therefore, is essential. Yet, until very recently, consensus among clinicians and anatomists about classification has been elusive. Now, through the International Nomenclature Committee, international agreement has been reached. The cataloguing of the collection at the Hospital according to the international system is now almost complete. Subject to what follows, this development could allow clinicians to share experience with others, secure in the knowledge that they are all discussing the same condition.

(e) Allow the collection to be used for the purposes of educating and training cardiologists and cardiac surgeons specialising in the care of children (and, increasingly, as the care of children improves and they survive into adulthood, clinicians also caring for adult patients).

It is likely, as has been said, that this was the reason which lay behind the creation of the collection in the first place. The advantages of such use are clear. Equally clearly, if the collection is to be protected for the future, access to it must be appropriately regulated. This would mean, for example, that use must be properly supervised and that hearts are not removed from the environment in which they are preserved.

(f) Allow the collection to be used to carry out research.[8]

There are various forms of research which might be contemplated. Some are not currently envisaged, since, by its nature, research often constitutes doing

[8] The benefits to be gained from having access to a collection were described by Professor Anderson over 14 years ago in his evidence to the Bristol Inquiry. He was, of course, describing practice before the revelations

> something not done before. The arguments in favour of allowing research are merely an extension of those already identified as justifying the use of the collection for the purposes of education and training. Research in the past has led to improvements in the outcome of care for babies and children with congenital heart disease. Research in the future would do the same. Tomorrow's children would be better cared for, and their prospects of survival and better health would be enhanced, as a result of the information and knowledge gained from research.

There are two principal objections raised against the notion of conducting research on hearts in the collection. The first simply states that all and any use of the collection is objectionable. This has already been referred to, the counter-arguments noted, and the argument rejected. The second objection is more elusive. It is that, while education and training may be acceptable, research is not. What lies beneath this objection is some sense that it is wrong to interfere with the hearts, ie go beyond looking at them. There are different responses to this second objection. They need to be considered separately. They involve an understanding of the various forms of research which may be contemplated.

- First, the process of classification and cataloguing the collection may itself be a form of research. It is hard to see, however, what objections could be raised. No interference is called for. The only ground must be that classification facilitates use of the collection and any such use ought not to take place. Such a view has already been noted and rejected. It might be the view held by those who see the collection as a historical record only, but even then it is hard to sustain since it is in the nature of historical records to be catalogued.
- Second, research may involve what is called imaging – using MRI, or other scanning techniques – to create an image of hearts in the collection. The purpose of such an image is clear. Those involved in education and training, and in seeking to understand more about congenital disorders, can generate a picture of the morphology of the heart, thereby allowing clinicians to get a better sense of how the various conditions present themselves. Apart from handling the heart so as to produce the image, there is no interference with the heart.[9] There would, however, be a need to remove the heart, albeit temporarily, from its storage. This would need to be done under appropriate supervision and after clear demonstration that the heart will not suffer damage through the process. Once the process is complete, it should be returned to storage as soon as possible.
- Third, research may involve actual physical interference with a heart. This could take a variety of forms. It could involve removing the surgical patches on the heart so as better to see how the abnormality presented itself and what the surgical response was. Research could also involve removing a very small piece of tissue for research into any genetic component of congenital heart disease.

at the Inquiry about the lack of parental involvement. While the practice has changed, the principles may still apply. He explained: 'We retain the hearts because we examine them for the purposes of our research. We demonstrate them. We make them available for others to study …'.

[9] But see my comment later, under Recommendations, on the implications of techniques involving staining tissues.

Apart from those who are uncomfortable with any use of the collection, the first two forms of research that I have set out are not seen as problematical. They are seen as extensions of education and training.

It is the third area of research that causes some to be more circumspect. The key to the concern appears to lie, as I have suggested, in the notion of interference: that the heart is being interfered with. It is not clear why this should warrant concern. It may be that there should be a clear rule that no research should be carried out which destroys the heart or renders it less useful to others subsequently engaged in education, training and research. But, if the heart is not going to be destroyed or irreversibly damaged, what lies behind the objection to interference?

The answer must clearly be in the realm of feelings rather than reason. The key is a notion of respect. The object being interfered with is the heart of a child who was once alive. Concern for respect, therefore, relates to respect for that child, and its parents and family, not for the heart itself. And, out of respect to that child, great care must be taken to honour the memory of that child and not dishonour it. So, the question becomes: does conducting research which involves interfering with a deceased child's heart dishonour that child, or the memory of that child. In my view, under the right conditions, conducting such research does not dishonour the child. Indeed, honouring the child's memory may, in fact, lie in carrying out research for the benefit of future children, so that the child's death was not completely in vain.

But, honouring that child also means that any research must be carried out with respect, and according to a strict protocol of rules. Principal among the rules must be a clear requirement that any proposed research must have a valid scientific justification, that this justification is agreed by a suitable panel of experts, and that the research will be carried out with appropriate respect and sensitivity to the interests of families and the wider community. Any such rules surrounding research would have to be sufficiently clear to indicate what is allowed, without delineating it in too detailed a fashion, so as to allow clinicians and researchers to adapt to new possibilities.

These are the options as to the way forward. I will now set out my recommendations. They are addressed to the Chief Executive who commissioned this Review.

Recommendations

1. Given the circumstances under which the hearts were collected and stored, the Hospital should consider whether to make one further effort to raise awareness of the collection among parents and families of children who died as a consequence of congenital heart disease, so that they may come forward to discover whether their child's heart is part of the collection, and if so, to take possession of it, or otherwise give instructions as to what should be done with it.
2. Should the Hospital decide to make this further effort, it should use its long experience of engaging with the local community to determine what it judges to be the most appropriate means.

3. After an appropriate time, perhaps three months later, the Hospital should hold a Memorial Service to remember the children who died and whose hearts remain in the collection.
4. The Hospital should then introduce the policies set out in the recommendations which follow.[10]

Storage

5. The Chief Executive of the Hospital may wish to consider establishing a Group or Committee with responsibility for overseeing the collection.
6. The collection should continue to be kept under the same conditions as currently prevail, with the same regard for its careful storage: in a temperature-controlled environment, with the formalin preparation routinely monitored.
7. The hearts should not be stored in batches. Each heart should be stored separately. This would improve the opportunity to use the hearts for education and training, and enhance the process of classification and archiving. It would also constitute a recognition of the individuality of each heart.
8. No hearts should be disposed of currently. The fact that the collection includes several examples of a particular abnormality is not, of itself, a reason for keeping one example and disposing of the rest, since each heart, and abnormality, is unique in its presentation. Moreover, even if the heart is in a poor condition for whatever reason, this is not a reason for disposing of it, given the possibilities of its use in research in genetics leading to further developments in treatment in the future. It may be appropriate to revisit the issue of disposal in due course.
9. Those hearts in the collection which the Hospital holds on behalf of parents or families who have come forward and identified the heart as being that of their child should be kept separate and not be available for any form of use unless explicit consent for that use has been given.

Classification and cataloguing

10. The collection should be classified and catalogued according to the criteria established by the International Nomenclature Committee. This work has been begun and should continue. Funding, if necessary, should be sought from appropriate bodies.

Use

11. Hearts in the collection should be made available for use in the education and training of clinicians. There is advantage in allowing the heart to be moved from the store, and this should be permitted so that it can be displayed in an educational forum. To provide for this removal, there must be in place strict rules concerned the proper care of the heart outside the store and for documenting any removal and return of a heart. This practice is already followed at Great Ormond Street Hospital (GOSH) and advice on its operation should be sought from colleagues at GOSH.
12. Hearts should be made available for the purpose of photography and imaging, viz the use of MRI and other forms of imaging, with a view to using the images for

[10] As regards all that follows, the HTA should be advised.

the purposes of education and training and for research. The process of imaging must be carried out in such a way and according to the same rules as referred to in paragraph 11.

13. The process of imaging should also be used for the purpose of 3D printing, to create an exact replica of the particular heart which can then be examined and used for training and research outside the storage area.

Research

14. The hearts in the collection should be available for research, subject to the relevant provisions of the HTA and to specific rules which I set out below.
15. The responsibility for ensuring that the rules on research are observed should be borne by such person as is so designated by the Chief Executive of the relevant Hospital or centre.
16. Research may take the form of observation or invasive intervention. Research by way of observation, eg imaging, involves the same principles as imaging for education and training and requires no further regulation.[11]
17. Research by way of invasive intervention is justified provided that the following principles are followed:
    - all proposals for research should be approved initially by a Research Committee, as well as by the relevant research ethics committee;
    - to obtain approval, it must be shown that the research is scientifically valid and is likely to contribute to improving care for patients in the future;
    - research which would destroy, or significantly degrade, a heart in the collection should not be permitted.
18. Forms of research involving intervention may include:
    - removing patches, and other similar interventions, to examine the abnormalities and the surgical response to them;
    - careful dissection of the heart, which should be permitted provided the dissection is carried out by a suitably qualified person and does not destroy or interfere with the overall anatomical structure of the heart, and provided, therefore, that the heart's value for education and training is retained. Where dissection is proposed, the heart should first be subject to appropriate imaging so that it can be printed by 3D printing and thus preserved in its original state, as well as subsequent to any dissection;
    - taking a very small amount of tissue so as to undertake research into the identification of any genetic factors in the cause and incidence of congenital heart disease.
19. Any dissection which would effectively mean the destruction of the heart should not be permitted, since, over time, this would lead to the destruction of parts of the collection.

[11] There are techniques for scanning and for histological examination which call for staining the tissue. Such a procedure, though providing additional information, could render the heart of less use subsequently for the purposes of education and training. It would be for the relevant research committee to take a view as to where the balance lies when considering a proposal for such research. The ethics committee can then take account of this view when reaching its decision.

Collaboration

20. Those responsible for the collection in Birmingham Children's Hospital should establish links with the University of Birmingham, particularly the Medical School, so as to develop in Birmingham a centre for education, training and research in congenital heart disease, and subsequently, a programme of research, both locally and nationally. Currently, research in cardiology appears not to be a priority for the Medical School. But, given the opportunities for research and collaboration represented by the collection, given the very significant programme of activity and research in cardiac surgery at the Hospital and its international standing, and given the possibilities for research and understanding arising from the fact of a very demographically varied population in Birmingham, the Medical School should, in collaboration with the Hospital, consider whether it should expand its research efforts to include the causes and treatment of congenital heart disease. In this context, it should be remembered that an increasing number of patients with congenital heart disease now grow up into adulthood, such that the need to be educated in and to understand congenital heart disease extends beyond paediatric specialists.
21. Links should be established with other centres holding collections, with a view to establishing a national database of hearts with congenital heart disease, classified according to the criteria of the International Nomenclature Committee, and with a view to establishing, in conjunction with relevant professional organisations such as the British Congenital Cardiac Association, a national centre for carrying out research according to the principles I have set out.
22. The Birmingham Children's Hospital, with the University of Birmingham, should seek to establish a system of international collaboration with centres in other parts of the world with similar archives, such as Toronto, Chicago, Pittsburgh and Gainesville, with a view to establishing an international national database and to developing and enhancing international collaboration in education, training and research in congenital heart disease. The use of imaging and 3D printing will greatly facilitate such collaboration.

Collections established since the Human Tissue Act 2005

23. A number of Hospitals have begun collections since 2005, pursuant to the provisions of the Human Tissue Act. My brief in this Review is to consider collections which predate the Act. But, clearly, any activity carried out, beginning with classification, should be extended to include hearts retained after 2005. The provisions of the Act contemplate the use of tissue for education, training and research, such that what I recommend as regards the pre-2005 Act collection falls within the spirit of the Act and could be carried forward as regards post-2005 collections. The greater the scale of the collections, when considered nationally and internationally, the greater the opportunity for a step-change in research into congenital heart disease.

Funding for research

24. The process of classification and cataloguing, which is at different stages in different centres, requires resources, as does research. Hospitals and University Departments

may be able to provide some funding. But, funds will also be needed from outside bodies. Clearly, funders such as the British Heart Foundation should be approached. But, projects must be 'fundable', that is to say that they must be well-led, scientifically valid, and judged by peers to have real prospects of benefitting future children.

Annex 1
Other Centres

Letter

Dear

I am currently carrying out a Review for Birmingham Children's Hospital of their policy relating to their collection of hearts of children who died from congenital heart disorders. There are close to 2000 hearts in the collection. All of them date from the period prior to 2001 during which, on occasions, hearts were removed and retained without the knowledge and consent of parents or relatives. The Hospital has made every endeavour to contact the parents or relatives of the children whose hearts are in the collection so as to make whatever arrangements are requested, but there still remain around 2000 as regards which they have received no contact.

Currently, the hearts are stored in appropriate conditions and used for the purposes of education and training. The possibility has also been raised of carrying out research, provided appropriate rules are in place. This is one of the matters that I will be considering.

My review, as I have said, is concerned with collections which predate the change of policy after 2001 and the subsequent passage of the Human Tissue Act. Clearly, if I were to come to the conclusion that it is justified to use this and similar collections in a number of specified ways, it would follow that the collection could be added to any collection that your Trust has created since 2001 so as to increase the overall size of collections and thereby enhance information and understanding.

I understand that you have a similar collection to the one in Birmingham at your Trust. I wonder whether you could confirm this and, if it is so, let me have a description of the collection and the arrangements that you have in place for managing it.

The collection at Birmingham is currently being classified and catalogued according to the system established by the International Nomenclature Committee. I am keen to discover whether other collections have been or are being similarly catalogued. Perhaps, you could advise me in the case of your Trust. Such cataloguing would allow for the creation of a national database, according to commonly agreed norms of classification. Clearly, such a local and, if possible, national database would benefit education, training and, if appropriate, research. It may also provide a stimulus to the development of international collaboration on a systematic basis.

I look forward to hearing from you.

Yours Sincerely

Responses

Glasgow: NHS Greater Glasgow and Clyde has a collection of approximately 500 paediatric hearts. The collection is stored in the Mortuary of Southern General Hospital. It is kept by the Pathology Department and transported to and from the Cardiology Department for courses of training and education. The collection is regarded as an 'invaluable resource' used to train staff in several medical specialties. The Pathology Department would support the development of a national database and has already had preliminary discussions with colleagues in Scotland and London.

St George's: St George's (the University and the NHS Trust) do not have a collection of paediatric hearts, though it has a collection of adult hearts which pre-dates 2001.

Great Ormond Street Hospital: GOSH has a collection dating back to at least 1940. It contains over 2600 hearts and lungs. It has been catalogued according to the criteria of the International Committee on Nomenclature and scanned into a local database. The collection is currently used only for observational study, but guidance would be welcome on any use for research. The collection is in daily use for education and training. Scanning for 3D printing has begun and a prototype 'app' is being developed (which could be developed further if funding were available) so that images can be accessed for the purpose of education and training. There is enthusiastic support for a wide range of collaborative activities with other centres.

Newcastle: The Institute of Genetic Medicine is exploring ways of establishing closer ties with the paediatric cardiologists and cardiac surgeons. Significant progress has been made in 3D printing of hearts for use in education, training and potentially research. There is strong support for the development of cataloguing collections and of establishing local and national archives (including virtual archives) and data-sets.

Leeds: Inquiries have recently begun about the collection, in response to my letter.

Alder Hey: A response has been promised shortly.

Guys and St Thomas': There is a collection of 'hundreds' of children's hearts which are stored in pots in the old mortuary at Guys. They have not been used for the purpose of education or training for at least a decade. They have not been catalogued.

No responses at the time of submitting this Review had been received from Brompton, and King's College London.

12

Safety and Blame: Learning from Mistakes in the NHS[1]

NHS, Clinical Negligence and £83bn

There is something of a fervour for reform, especially radical reform, what with iconoclasts storming the barricades of 10 Downing Street and Brexit looming. Consider, then, the following. If ever there was an issue looking for radical reform it is the exposure of the NHS to liability in negligence, currently[2] estimated at £83bn.

It has long been argued that a disruptive, game-changing approach is the only way to address the problems lying behind this extraordinary burden on the taxpayer. While it has long been said that this cannot go on, it still goes on.

In one of my Reith Lectures of 40 years ago (1980) I argued for just such a radical approach. I went so far as to invoke Henry VI – 'First … let's kill all the lawyers'. I pointed to the fact that patients harmed while receiving treatment could only receive the financial support that they might need (other than state benefits) by proving that their doctor or nurse (and/or the clinic or hospital employing them) had been at fault. This had led, I argued, to a search by patients for someone to blame and a concomitant resistance from healthcare professionals to admit any error, when doing so might damage their reputation and career. I argued that the consequences of this approach were that errors were not admitted, lessons were not learned, errors continued, and patients continued to be harmed. In the task of seeking to improve the safety of patients, litigation and the search for someone to blame were, sadly, part of the problem rather than of the solution.

My approach was applauded the following day in a Leader in *The Times*. Nothing happened, save excessive ventilation on the part of lawyers representing themselves as defenders of the rights of patients. The Pearson Commission's Report[3] two years previously had, of course, exposed the hopeless inadequacies of the civil law of negligence in securing financial support for plaintiffs and in deterring accidents. The Report had been ignored. My proposal suffered the same fate.

In my Report on the Public Inquiry into Bristol Royal Infirmary almost 20 years later (2002[4]) we returned to the theme. I repeated the arguments. The intervening years

[1] Unpublished memo submitted to Cabinet Office, January 2020.
[2] Writing in 2019.
[3] *Royal Commission on Civil Liability and Compensation for Personal Injury*, 1978.
[4] *Learning from Bristol: The Report of the Inquiry into Children's Heart Surgery at Bristol Royal Infirmary* (2002).

had made them even more compelling, not least because of the series of Inquiries which had exposed the failure of the NHS to learn from errors and the pernicious role of blame. Though the Government of the day accepted virtually all of the Inquiry's recommendations, those concerned with getting rid of negligence litigation as the route to financial support for patients and addressing what to do when things go wrong were not accepted. As it was put to me at the time by senior civil servants in the Lord Chancellor's Department, 'We believe in blame'!

When I chaired the Healthcare Commission, I continued to argue that meeting the needs of patients who had suffered harm should not depend on showing some failure in the conduct of healthcare professionals. The culture of litigation and blame, I argued, continued to prevent lessons from being learned. Mistakes were repeated. The culture of healthcare remained one of defensiveness. Taxpayers' money continued to be dissipated in lawsuits which benefitted only a fraction of those in need of support. Healthcare professionals felt increasingly beleaguered. The realisation that accidents are inevitable and should be seen as an opportunity to learn continued to be drowned out by a discourse of blame and shame. The wealth of scholarship associated with the psychologist Professor James Reason and his Human Factors approach[5] continued to be pressed on all who might listen. But, 'the system' went on blithely, piling up the cost both financially and in terms of human misery.

I have spent much of my career concerned with policy relating to healthcare. Getting it right for patients and professionals has been an abiding passion. I have seen from the inside the stranglehold that lawyers exert over a system which should be putting the interests and needs of patients first. The introduction of a radical alternative to the outdated, arbitrary and scandalously expensive system of clinical negligence remains unfinished business for me.

A radical approach involves the following:

- An understanding that in an often highly complex technologically driven activity (modern healthcare) it is inevitable that things will go wrong on occasions and that patients will be harmed.
- A relentless pursuit of safe care predicting and eliminating as far as possible practice that compromises the safe care of patients – the work of James Reason has led the way.
- An effective regulatory system to manage the risks involved in healthcare. The system must be based on the accumulation, analysis and sharing of data on all aspects of performance in the delivery of care. Data would prompt targeted inspections. I was beginning to embed this approach while Chair of the Healthcare Commission (2003–09) having sought the advice of the distinguished Cambridge biostatistician David Spiegelhalter (now Professor Sir David). The aim was to replace the old, discredited system of occasional inspection visits to institutions. Mid-way through developing this approach, the Commission was abolished as part of Gordon Brown's 'bonfire of regulation'. It was replaced by the Care Quality Commission which reverted to 'light touch' visits, with initially disastrous results.

[5] See eg *Human Error* (Cambridge University Press, 1990).

- A radically different response to when things go wrong and patients are harmed. Currently, if a patient needs financial support as a consequence of what went wrong, apart from state benefits, the patient must look to the institution and/or healthcare professional. This involves the search for negligence as being the basis on which money can be obtained. The patient therefore must find someone to blame. The institution/healthcare professional will be keen to defend its/their reputation, save in egregious cases which are settled quietly without the public and future patients being aware and no guarantee, nor ability to check, that lessons have been learned.

  The different approach would separate the needs of the patient from the conduct of the institution/professional. The **patient** would receive such financial support as is required, when required (rather than in a lump sum). The money would come from some form of statutorily created fund paid for from general taxation. The fund would be administered according to strict criteria. There would be no need to engage lawyers. Estimates of the cost depend on the criteria adopted but would be nowhere near the current £83bn liability.

  As regards the **healthcare professionals** involved in what went wrong, the question to be addressed is whether the professional should continue to work at the particular institution and, if so, under what circumstances, eg re-training. This would be for the institution to decide. Whether the professional should be entitled to continue to work at all as a doctor, nurse, or whatever would be a matter for the relevant professional body's disciplinary system. In the case where the **institution** is involved, the relevant regulatory body would determine the appropriate response, eg internal review, replacement of leadership, special measures, or some sort of amalgamation with another institution.
- The separation of the two issues, the needs of the patient on the one hand and the professional's and institution's conduct on the other, would mean that the patient would receive financial support promptly. A concurrent analysis of what went wrong would be conducted without the threat of blame and consequent tendency to cover up. Lessons could be learned and shared which would reduce (though not eliminate) further occurrences of harm.

According to recent reports, the Secretary of State is said to be concerned (unsurprisingly!). Those of us who have been calling for change for decades would love to be surprised. We can hope.

Postscript

Nothing came of the then Secretary of State's (Jeremy Hunt) concern. He was replaced on the election of Boris Johnson as Prime Minister. Then Covid-19 struck. Reflections on litigation and healthcare have once again fallen off the radar. As it happens, given the costs associated with Covid-19, this may just be the time for the reflections to be taken up again.

13

Deprivation of Liberty and Medical Care[1]

Ordinarily, no-one may be deprived of her liberty without lawful justification. This is a proposition that goes back centuries in English law. The question to be considered here is whether there are circumstances which justify depriving someone of his liberty (ie without his consent) for the particular purpose of providing medical care? Notice the word justify. It means that a justification must exist for what would otherwise be unlawful. The default position, in other words, is that deprivation of liberty for the purpose of compulsorily treating someone is not permitted unless it can be justified.

The apparently simple question posed above is not at all simple to answer. It involves poring over exceedingly complex statutory arrangements added to by large helpings of equally complex Codes of Practice and judicial decisions. It also involves picking a way through a minefield of ideological conflict between (somewhat roughly stated) civil libertarians on the one hand and healthcare professionals, particularly psychiatrists, on the other. Both see themselves as guardians of the interests of citizens/patients. Both seek ascendancy in the political disputes which have characterised the past several decades as Parliament and courts have wrestled to attempt to square the circle.

Parliament's efforts have produced a series of laws which largely please no-one and are repeatedly revisited as the conflict ebbs and flows. Bodies such as the Law Commission and Select Committees add their views to the mix. Reference to human rights has become increasingly prominent. Language, its use and the nuances of meaning, dog every step taken. Social scientists, meanwhile, try to discover what in fact is happening behind the screen of formal law and procedure. Add in the decades of neglect by the NHS of those with problems of mental health, where the issues under consideration principally arise, together with the continuing under-resourcing of whatever care there is, and it is no surprise that healthcare professionals express concern or worse. The patient who is the centre of all this tension and argument too often is the outsider, included only when decisions have already been reached.

In this short piece it would be unwise to attempt to offer anything other than a brief introduction to the circumstances in which someone may be deprived of liberty in medical practice. To gain a thorough and comprehensive understanding the reader should refer to: P Fennell, *Mental Health: Law and Practice* (Jordans, 2011), L Gostin et al (eds), *Principles of Mental Health Law and Policy* (OUP, 2010), and J Laing and J McHale (eds), *Principles of Medical Law* (OUP, 2017).

[1] First published in *Medicine*, June 2018. Amended version reprinted with permission.

Mental Health Act 2007

What does deprivation of liberty mean in the context of medical practice? Conventionally, it refers to when a person's freedom of movement is taken away without consent with a view to treating that person. This is usually taken to refer to the circumstances in which the provisions of the Mental Health Act 2007 are used so as compulsorily to admit a patient to hospital. It applies where the person is suffering from some form of mental disorder. But before examining these circumstances further, it is important to notice that there are other circumstances in which a patient may be deprived of liberty.

Mental Capacity Act 2005

The Mental Capacity Act (MCA) 2005 authorises the detention of someone for the purpose of treating a *physical condition* if *the person is incapable of giving consent to treatment*.

As in all matters relating to the care of the mentally ill and vulnerable, the law as set out in the MCA is complex. There are two conditions to be met: incapacity to give consent, and treatment limited to a *physical condition*. An example would be performing hip surgery on an elderly, confused and uncomprehending patient after a fall. It does not extend to treatment for *mental disorder*.

The treatment allowed by the MCA necessarily, of course, involves limiting or *restricting* the person's freedom of movement, at least while the treatment is being delivered. But does it go further and permit a person to be *deprived* of her liberty? The distinction between the two (restricting and depriving) may appear semantic but it is important. The importance lies in Article 5 of the European Convention for the Protection of Human Rights and Fundamental Freedoms. Article 5 says nothing about *restricting* liberty, but it makes it unlawful to *deprive*[2] someone of liberty *unless authorised* either by a court or by *statute*. Does this exception include the MCA?

In its general application, the MCA provides a defence for the doctor or other who treats a person without consent because the patient is incapable of consenting: basically, the MCA provides that the treatment is lawful if the person, had she been competent to consent, would have consented. But this defence of presumed consent is not available where the person to be treated has been *deprived* of liberty, rather than just having her liberty (temporarily) *restricted*. When a person is *deprived* of his liberty for the purposes of treatment, a defence under the MCA still exists, but it is much more limited. It was created to address the problem which arose in the case of *R v Bournewood Community and Mental Health NHS Trust, ex p L*.[3]

[2] Whether someone lacking the capacity to consent is deprived of liberty, rather than her liberty being restricted is judged objectively and depends on the particular facts. This is not wholly satisfactory as it leaves those caring for them having to make fine judgements. It also may be said to be a triumph of legalism over a more generous approach to the care of incapacitated people, or put another way, a win for the civil libertarians over the carers!

[3] [1999] Appeal Cases 458. H was admitted 'informally' (ie not under formal statutory powers) to a psychiatric hospital for treatment judged to be in his best interests. He was compliant. The European Court of

The MCA created a statutory framework to allow for the *deprivation* of liberty and treatment of incapacitated patients. The provisions, it should be noted, only apply to adults detained in hospitals or care homes (who are not there by virtue of the mental health legislation). They do not apply to children under the age of 18. Further, as has been said, they apply only to treatment for physical illness: they do not apply to treatment for a 'mental disorder', albeit that treatment for a mental disorder has been given an increasingly broad meaning, such that the boundary at the edges is by no means clear.

The MCA sets out three situations in which detention (deprivation of liberty) of an incapacitated person for the purposes of treatment may be permitted:

- when authorised by the Court of Protection;
- when authorised under specific safeguards called the 'Deprivation of Liberty Safeguards';
- when detention is needed so as to provide emergency or life-sustaining treatment in advance of obtaining a decision from the Court of Protection.

The first and last of these three conditions are straightforward. As for the second, the Safeguards provide two layers of protection for the person unable to consent. First, the general principles governing the treatment of such persons apply: that the proposed treatment is in the person's best interests so as to protect him from harm, that the treatment is both necessary and proportionate, and that there is no less restrictive alternative. Secondly, the detailed safeguards themselves provide a further layer of protection.[4]

MHA or MCA?

As has been said, there is another and separate statutory regime whereby a patient may be deprived of liberty – the Mental Health Act (MHA) 2007. What is the relationship between the MHA and the MCA? Which statute should be used in a particular case? The courts, in cases that have been brought before them, have made it clear that it is for professionals to decide. This is fine, as long as they can work out the basis on which to decide!

The **MHA** is the appropriate route for the treatment of those with a 'mental disorder'. It should also be used if a patient is objecting to treatment of any kind, which is judged to be necessary in his interests, whether he has the necessary capacity to consent or not. The **MCA** is the appropriate route if the patient could not consent and needed treatment for a physical illness.

But there are a host of situations which fall outside these two positions. Apart from being required, by the MHA's Code of Practice in relation to a mental disorder, to decide on the basis of which, for the patient, is the least restrictive course of action,

Human Rights decided that he had been deprived of his liberty contrary to Article 5(1) of the European Convention for the Protection of Human Rights and Fundamental Freedoms such that the treatment was not lawful.

[4] Set out in section 4 of, and Schedules A1 and 1A to, the MCA.

the professional is basically on her own. To that extent, the professional is always at risk of being judged (by hindsight) to have made the wrong decision, either because a court judges that compulsory detention and treatment under the MHA was not justified so that the professional acted unlawfully, or that it was justified and the professional's failure to do so resulted in harm to the patient or others which the professional was responsible for. To put it mildly, this is an uncomfortable position to be in.

As between the two statutory regimes, understanding and applying the MHA in the context of deprivation of liberty is more challenging. The MHA gives certain specified persons,[5] supported by recommendations from two doctors, the power to apply for a patient to be admitted compulsorily to hospital (ie to be deprived of his liberty) for assessment (section 2) and for treatment (section 3).

Section 2 describes admission for *assessment*. Admission can be up to but may not exceed 28 days and is not renewable. Although the admission must be for assessment, this does not mean that the patient may not also be treated. Indeed, the treatment may be part of the process of assessment. The grounds for admission are that the patient:

- is suffering from mental disorder of a nature or degree which warrants the detention of the patient in a hospital for assessment; and
- he ought to be so detained in the interests of his own health or with a view to the protection of others.

Clearly, professionals have a wide latitude in making their determination. Though these things tend to go in cycles, the current climate of aversion to risk suggests that professionals will err on the side of compulsory admission. Importantly, a patient admitted under section 2 has a right to apply to a Tribunal to be discharged within 24 days of the admission.

Section 3 describes admission for *treatment*. The patient may be detained for a period of up to six months. The grounds for admission under section 3 are that the patient:

- is suffering from a mental disorder of a nature or degree which makes it appropriate for him to receive medical treatment in hospital; and
- it is necessary for the health and safety of the patient or the protection of other persons that he should receive such treatment; and
- appropriate medical treatment is available.

Detailed provisions are set out in the Code of Practice relating to such matters as the meaning of 'nature or degree', the 'health and safety of the patient', and the 'protection of others'. Of particular importance is the provision relating to the availability of appropriate treatment.[6] One particular concern relates to the meaning of 'available': whether, for example, it means locally available or available somewhere, and whether it means that it is available in theory or is actually available. Another concern is the threshold for detention and the effect of shortages of hospital beds. In the face of such shortages, there is a risk (and some evidence) of compulsory detention being used to obtain a hospital bed.

[5] The patient's nearest relative or an Approved Mental Health Professional (AMHP).
[6] See Laing and McHale (eds), *Principles of Medical Law* pp 595–98 for a detailed analysis.

This not only distorts the general availability of beds, but also constitutes a misuse of the powers under section 3 and, thereby, an abuse of the rights of any patient so admitted.

It is important, so as to comply with the law, that the powers under the two sections are used for the purposes set out. There is another contingent reason why this should be so. A patient admitted under section 2 for assessment has a right to apply to a Tribunal. If after assessment, section 3 is invoked, the patient has a further right to apply. By contrast, if the route for admission is straightaway to invoke section 3, the patient has only one right to apply during the six months of detention.

In addition to sections 2 and 3, by section 5 of the MHA, a nurse or doctor may restrain and thereby detain a patient who has been admitted consensually and informally and then seeks to leave. Effectively, this allows professionals to respond to emergencies when it is not possible or practicable to resort to sections 2 or 3. It is important to understand that this power may not be used to detain and treat without consent just any patient whom the doctor or nurse think ought to be treated. The purpose of the section is to detain the patient so as to allow an assessment under the MHA to be carried out. That said, the provision is sufficiently broad to offer only limited protection to patients.

Central to the operation of the statutory regime set out in the MHA is section 63. It provides for the power to treat detained patients without their consent, provided that the patient is in fact detained, that the treatment is for a mental disorder, and that it is sanctioned by the doctor in charge. Treatment under sections 56 to 63, however, which are concerned with a number of forms of treatment, some of which are controversial (ECT) or otherwise tend to be irreversible or may have long-term effects, is subject to additional conditions intended to safeguard the interests of patients.

It will come as no surprise, given what has gone before, that Prime Minister announced an independent review of the operation of the MHA in October 2017. The review will be conducted by Sir Simon Wessely, former President of the Royal College of Psychiatrists.

Postscript

The Report *Modernising the Mental Health Act; increasing choice, reducing compulsion* was published on 6 December 2018. The then Secretary of State welcomed the Review's recommendations as 'increasing patient rights and improving the way the Act works for people'. He stated that the Government 'will consider the Report and its Recommendations …'. It is 'our intention to reform mental health law'. The Government 'will bring forward legislation when Parliamentary time allows'. Until 'time allows', the law is as stated above.

14

Rights and Values in Health and Healthcare[1]

I am delighted and honoured to be invited to deliver one of this year's Tanner Lectures. Health and healthcare offer a huge canvas on which to sketch out some thoughts. I have chosen to concentrate on a set of issues which occupy one small corner. That said, they are issues which currently pose significant challenges and which will increasingly do so in the future.

People and Their Stories

May I introduce you first to some people and their stories.

First, there is Dan James. He was paralysed from the neck down as a consequence of an accident while playing rugby. Two years after the accident, he travelled to Switzerland, to the organisation called Dignitas.[2] There he died, in circumstances which have come to be known as 'assisted suicide'. He went to Switzerland, because to assist him to die in the UK would have constituted a crime. He went because he took the view that he had a 'right to die' and that this was a fundamental human right, arising from and the necessary corollary of his right to life and his right to a private life, and was perhaps the most important right left to him. He went because he also accepted that, should he petition the court in England to recognise his claim to this right, he would be denied.

Secondly, there is Debbie Purdy. She went to court to seek a declaration that if, following the example of Dan James and others, her husband helped her to travel to Switzerland so as to be assisted to die, he would not be charged with the crime of aiding and abetting a suicide. The Court of Appeal rejected her application as a matter of strict law.[3] The Court went on to say, however, that it thought it most unlikely that her husband would be prosecuted on the basis of the facts before them. A typically English fudge, you might say, whereby the letter of the law is kept intact, while what one scholar famously called 'under the counter deals with death'[4] were made. But underlying the

[1] This was one of the Tanner Lectures on Human Values delivered each year at Brasenose College, Oxford University. It was delivered on 21 February 2009 as a contribution to the theme 'Meeting the Challenges of the 21st Century: Human Rights in the 21st Century', and published by the College.

[2] See, *The Times*, 18 October 2008.

[3] *R (Purdy) v DPP* [2009] WLR (D) 62.

[4] D Daube, 'Transplantation: Acceptability of Procedures and the Required Legal Sanctions', in Wolstenholme (ed), *Ethics in Medical Progress* (Ciba, 1966).

fudge, there was a re-affirmation that the right to respect for private and family life as set out in Article 8 of the European Convention on Human Rights, and incorporated into English law by the Human Rights Act 1998, did not incorporate a right to be assisted by others to die. Thus, the prohibition against aiding and abetting a suicide in section 2 of the Suicide Act 1961 remained law until Parliament decides otherwise.

My third story is about people who need some form of organ transplant, for example, a kidney, a liver or a heart, but cannot obtain one because there are not enough organs to meet the need. Organs are largely obtained through voluntary donation and the subsequent concurrence after a person's death of her family. For a variety of reasons, this system does not produce a sufficient number of organs. After many years of trying to make the system work, a taskforce was charged in 2008 with examining what changes could be made. The Chief Medical officer for England had nailed his colours to the mast[5] by advocating what has come to be known as 'presumed consent', whereby a deceased person can be presumed to have agreed to the removal of organs for transplant unless the person has explicitly stated otherwise. Aware of the toll of ill-health and death arising from the current system, and of the economic consequences, the Prime Minister publicly declared himself in favour of 'presumed consent'.[6] He was disappointed, therefore, when the task force advised against it.[7] To many, including this writer, people were being denied the opportunity to gain access to life-saving, or life-enhancing, treatment for not very persuasive reasons and, to that extent, their right to life was being denied or put at risk.

Next, I introduce a group of patients who have advanced cancer of the kidney(s). A drug exists which can extend the life of these patients for some months and is made available to patients in a number of countries. The National institute of Health and Clinical Excellence (NICE) has the responsibility of determining what medicines given its inevitably limited resources the NHS should purchase for prescription to patients. Using its established approach, NICE recommended that the drug in question not be purchased, on the grounds that it did not offer sufficient value for money: if it were prescribed within the NHS, something else of greater value to patients in the NHS would have to be foregone (the opportunity cost). Patients and those supporting them object that NICE's approach, concerned as it is with some idea of the general good, violates the individual right to life of each patient, in the sense that it denies them the chance to live that much longer.

May I now introduce Christopher Reeve, an American known to many through his cinematic role as 'Superman'. After a riding accident, he was paralysed from the neck down. He dedicated his life thereafter to promoting research into spinal injuries, with a view to developing techniques to restore function. The most fruitful line of enquiry was thought to involve the use of stem cells. To do so calls for research on embryonic stem cells. While such research was being pursued in other parts of the world, it was banned in the United States in institutions in receipt of federal funding. The ban, strongly advocated by President Bush during the eight years of his Presidency, was justified on the

[5] Chief Medical Officer for England, *Annual Report on the State of Public Health* (Department of Health, 2006).

[6] See, *Daily Mail*, 13 January 2008.

[7] Organ Donation Taskforce, *The Potential Impact of an opt out system for organ donation in the UK* (Department of Health, 17 November 2008).

grounds of the right to life, not of those who had been injured (including many injured in wars in Iraq and Afghanistan), but of the embryo. Drawing on a particular strain of Christian thinking (or, more cynically, with an eye to politics), the President ruled that the state's duty to preserve the 'sanctity of life' extended to include the life of the embryo. Using the embryo for research was, therefore, a wrong which it was the duty of the state to prevent.

I turn lastly to an elderly person, alone and neglected in a side room in a hospital (it could equally be a nursing home). No-one comes, or they come after a long wait, when she rings the bell. Her food is put on a table where she cannot reach it and is later removed, accompanied by a comment (it is not a question) such as 'not hungry, then'. She has a right to dignity, but her enjoyment of that right is gradually being stripped away. Such a denial of her rights may not appear to count as much as a right to life, but, for her, it is about all she has.

Real People, Real Problems

All of these stories are about real people with real, concrete problems. As you will know, there are countless more played out each day up and down the land. While most may not be as dramatic, they are all important: to those caught up in them and to the analyst who seeks to find a way through the ethics and law which form the backdrop. They include such dilemmas as: does the doctor tell a patient the truth about his condition (and should it be the whole truth or a partial account?), and if so, how should she do so; is an abortion the best solution in this woman's case, indeed, is it ever the right solution; under what circumstances, if any, can a patient's confidences be divulged to others?

The Need for Answers

All of these, and there are so many more, are ethical challenges. They are concerned with notions of rights and values.[8] And, most critically, they call for answers. We are not in a game in which the answers depend on the careful application of reason, but nothing actually turns on what is decided. We are in the real world of healthcare in which the answer has very real consequences for real people. We are in a world where the views of patients and professionals jostle with each other and with those of the wider community.

The Discourse of Rights

We are also in a world where the language of human rights has become the prevailing discourse. In the context of healthcare, the rights in play are those of the patient.

[8] See my earlier Darwin Lecture at Cambridge University, in which I described the coming 21st century as 'the century of bioethics': 'The Medical Frontier: Emerging Legal and Moral Dilemmas' in L Howe (ed), *Predictions: 1991 Darwin Lectures* (Cambridge University Press, 1992).

The question for us, then, is the extent to which this discourse has, in fact, meant that concern for patients' rights has shaped the way in which decisions about healthcare have been made.

Before going further, I emphasise that I am concerned here with health and healthcare. I remain a cheerleader for the principles of human rights and their application to the world that we live in. But, I wonder aloud in this lecture whether healthcare is a special case, exposing the weaknesses of recourse to the discourse of human rights in achieving the desired ends for patients.

In the context of healthcare, the discourse of rights might be thought to have been intended to empower patients. The question I seek to explore is whether it has in fact done so. It is clear that there is enormous symbolic importance in resorting to the rhetoric of rights. But, are its effects limited in fact? Is the cynic right that, in healthcare, whatever may be true in other spheres of life, the patient has been and is empowered only if what the patient wants is acceptable to those with the real power of decision-making? And, if there be any truth in this cynic's view, what is it about healthcare that makes it so? Is it ultimately the intimate relationship of professional and patient, whereby rights have to give way to values, in this case the values of the professional attending the patient?

Why do I sound this equivocal note? Consider two distinct contexts: what I will call 'outside the consulting room', and 'inside the consulting room'.

The Discourse of Rights in Two Contexts

Outside the Consulting Room

What I refer to here is the extent to which the discourse of rights and values is embedded in and informs the general socio-political discussion of healthcare. At least two major problems exist. First, in so far as a concern for rights is a concern for the individual, this sits very uncomfortably with the overarching value of the National Health Service, the vehicle through which healthcare is provided to the large majority of people in the UK. The NHS constitutes a commitment to collectivism, to a welfare state in which the claims of individuals are set against some understanding of the needs of the community. An obvious example is the notion of the waiting list: queuing to receive treatment in the knowledge that there is a limit to the service available at any particular time and that treatment will be allocated on the basis of need, as judged by others, rather than the demand of the individual patient. The reality becomes one in which the individual asserting his rights finds that he has to share his purist space with others.

The second problem is one of language. The discourse of rights, like any discourse, involves interpretation. It must engage with the inherent uncertainty of language and meaning. One way of expressing this is that the position you take depends on where you start from.

Looking back at some of the stories I referred to at the outset may help. In the case of the group urging NICE to approve the drug which might extend their lives, their appeal was to their right to life. In the case of 'presumed consent' to organ transplants, again the appeal was to the right to life. And Debbie Purdy, as did Diane Pretty whose case had been decided seven years previously,[9] was asserting a right to autonomy to choose to die as a necessary extension of her right to a private life, as well as (though this was not part of her case before the court), of her right to life, and to be free from inhuman and degrading treatment (which is how she saw her current state). Each case rested on an appeal to rights. To each of the people involved the case was open and shut. Yet in each case, the decision went against them. The drug was not made available for prescription on the NHS,[10] 'presumed consent' was not introduced, and Mrs Purdy did not get her ruling.

Inside the Consulting Room

Here I refer to that intimate space occupied by the patient and the professional. Increasingly, healthcare is practised in teams and by teams. But, it is still characterised symbolically and actually by the private and confidential exchanges between the patient (or a proxy) and the professional.

Inside the consulting room, two particular problems with the discourse of rights are evident. First, the language of rights sits uncomfortably with the historic cultural assumptions of the clinical setting: the deep-rooted idea of the professional's clinical freedom and the emphasis on the professional's duty of care rather than the patient's rights. Secondly, resort to the discourse of patients' rights often provokes a backlash, at least from those who claim to speak for professionals, particularly doctors. What about the rights of the professional and the duties of the patient, they ask.

One example of this phenomenon of backlash in practice is the advocacy of sanctions against patients who fail to keep an appointment. The doctor can keep the patient waiting but she must not be kept waiting! Or, translated into the language under review here, the patient has a duty to show up on time but no right to be seen promptly, if there on time. A second example relates to the NHS Constitution, recently promulgated to celebrate the 60th anniversary of the NHS and soon to have statutory force.[11] The Constitution explicitly embraces the language of patients' rights, though the rights are no more than those already set out in law. In their responses to the consultation on the Constitution, a significant number of professionals and their organisations argued for additions or amendments to the Constitution to set out explicitly what they referred to as the rights of professionals and the duties of patients.

Against such a background, you may think that it requires a particular kind of patient to be assertive and lay claim to her rights, the more so, given the disequilibrium of power and information between the two of them. You might almost say it would, in fact, be hazardous to do so for all save the card-carrying *Guardian* reader!

[9] *Pretty v United Kingdom* (2002) 35 EHHR 1. In particular, Mrs Pretty argued that section 2 of the Suicide Act 1961 violated her right to life under Article 2 of the European Convention on Human Rights as well as her right to a private life under Article 8. Regarding her right under Article 2, she argued that it protected not only the right to life but also the right to choose whether or not to go on living. The court rejected her arguments.

[10] The approach adopted by NICE has since been modified.

[11] Health Bill 2009.

Enter Choice

What do I take from this analysis so far? To me, it is obvious that because of the elusive quality of language and the socio-cultural backdrop to the provision of healthcare, simply to point to rights is not going to get very far in empowering patients. Indeed, the more you observe, the more it becomes clear that in understanding, interpreting and applying the discourse of rights, what is happening is that a position is being taken, choices are being made.

So, it becomes important to understand what conditions the choices made. What values are at play?

Choices and Values

There are, to me, two orders of choices. Some are taken in the spotlight, as it were, in the form of legislation, judicial decision, the actions of organisations, or the reports of the media. In such cases, we can usually see more clearly why certain choices have been made. In the spotlight, it is clear that attempts to reflect the aim of empowering patients, the fundamental goal of an approach based on human rights, are made. Individualism and self-determination are given prominence. Government talks of a 'patient-led NHS'[12] and draws up a Constitution for the NHS.

In the Spotlight

But, even in this context, in the spotlight, there is clearly tension between the notion of an individual's right to X on the one hand, and other claims to Y and Z and the claims of others. The choice which is made depends not on the assertion of any particular right but on what are seen to be the relevant values in play.

So now we are in the territory of values. Admittedly, the choice may reflect values which are explicitly rights-respecting values. I have in mind such values as truthfulness, honesty, equality, or respect. But even these can, of course, work as much against as for any particular individual in any particular situation of tension between her and another. But, more tellingly, the values at play are just as likely, as we have seen, to be those of the 'common good', or the needs of the wider society, or reflect political considerations, or be those of a particular group able to exert power. All of these may work more obviously against respect for rights and the empowerment and self-determination of the individual.

The stories that I began with offer illustrations of the resort to values which in effect, negated the reliance by individuals and groups on the assertion of their rights.

Dan James, the young rugby player left for Switzerland, aware that respect for his rights as he saw them would founder in the face of some sense of the collective good in upholding the ban on assisting death, *whatever the circumstances*.

[12] 'Creating a patient-led NHS' (Department of Health, 2005).

Diane Pretty, who set the scene for the later case of Debbie Purdy, took her legal case all the way to the European Court of Human Rights (ECHR). She was, as she saw it, asserting her right to self-determination, albeit she was asking that it be asserted through a proxy on her behalf, ie that she be helped to die. But her claim of self-determination was trumped by the Court's resort to the social value of paternalism. She was, the Court held, 'vulnerable', or more accurately, belonged to a class of people who by virtue of their condition were vulnerable (it was accepted that she herself could not be regarded as vulnerable). And, being vulnerable, she and those like her, the court went on, needed protection from those who would exploit them and, perhaps, even bring about their deaths without their truly wishing it. Diane Pretty had, therefore, to be protected from herself; protected from the exercise of what she saw as her right.

The difficulty with the ECHR's approach is profound. Preferring, for unstated reasons, the value of preserving life over any individual's claim to have her life ended (in carefully constrained circumstances, it should be added, and set about with safeguards), the Court took two steps. First, Diane Pretty was, or was made to stand for, the class of the 'vulnerable'. But, such a view ignores the fact that people are not themselves vulnerable. It is society, its values and the way it organises itself that make people vulnerable. They are made vulnerable because their rights are not being respected, for whatever reason. Then, secondly, the Court held that being 'vulnerable' she needed the law's protection. But, if the first proposition is accepted, what this second step translates as is the following: we will not protect your right to self-determination, because we have already failed to protect your rights more generally, thereby rendering you vulnerable, and, therefore, susceptible to our preferred choice – paternalism.

In the case of the drug for advanced kidney cancer, NICE decided against approving it for prescription through the NHS. NICE did so because, as an organisation, it was created to allocate scarce resources (there will always be limits to what can be afforded). It does so in accordance with a transparent analysis of the clinical effectiveness and cost-effectiveness of a drug, a process that also calculates the opportunity cost entailed in approval. Had the patients' group prevailed, a system based on the value of achieving the greatest benefit for the greatest number would have been under challenge from a system based on individual rights, according to which, if a drug exists and a patient can show that she might benefit from it, it is her right to receive it. This is not the current system. At present, the choice is made not on assertions of rights, here the right to life, but on the basis of values captured in the notion of the common good.

What about the ban (since lifted by President Obama) on research on embryonic stem cells? The prevailing view is that such research holds out real prospects of being able to respond therapeutically to paralysing spinal injuries, from which recovery is currently not possible. In terms of rights, the argument was advanced that such research should take place and to ban it infringed the right to life of those disabled by spinal injuries. The ban, however, grew out of a different perspective of the world. It grew out of the religious beliefs and values of a powerful minority who had the ear of President Bush. These values have it that life is sacred, and must be protected by the state, from the moment of conception. To take stem cells from an embryo, thereby ending its existence is, on this view, a sin to be denounced. Faced with this choice, the President sided with the Christian right. Another way of framing the objection is that the embryo has a right to life. If this position is taken, despite the well-rehearsed analytical counter-arguments,[13] the question becomes one of preferring one claimed right over another. And, the choice as to which claims should prevail is resolved by reference to values, in this case those of the Christian right.

What about the example I gave of those dying for want of a transplant and the call for a system of 'presumed consent'? Here the arguments mounted against introducing this approach were not couched in terms of rights, or even overtly of values. Instead, 'presumed consent' was rejected to a very large extent because of the exercise of influence of a powerful group, specialists in intensive care. Clearly, a range of arguments was advanced, including comparisons with other countries which had and had not adopted 'presumed consent'. But, in my view, the views of the intensivists were crucial. Their values prevailed. They claimed that concern for the common good, as they saw it, should prevail over the claim of a patient to an organ from a dead body. Lying behind this claim, however, were another set of values, those of this particular group of professionals and what they were comfortable with.[14]

It became clear that they did not want to operate a system of 'presumed consent' because of the tensions and difficulties that would arise in dealing with grieving relatives. Better and easier to operate a system which gave the relatives a veto over obtaining organs for transplant than having to advise that the organs would be removed on the basis of 'presumed consent'. Intensivists argued that the latter system '… might erode public confidence'. So it might, but arguably, starting from a different position, they could have said that they recognise the challenge regarding the public's confidence and would work to overcome it. It was also said that 'Clinicians were anxious about the potential negative implications …. [It (presumed consent)] could threaten the trust that patients and their families have to have in them'. Notice the words 'potential' and 'could'. By contrast, by retaining the current system, many patients will (not may) die for lack of a transplant. But, the choice was made to prefer the position advanced by the intensivists. The discourse of rights again is trumped by recourse to some set of values, described pre-emptively as the common good.

My final story was about the right to dignity. Here, there was no disagreement about the right and the values underlying it. The problem lay in getting the right respected. The elderly woman was a prisoner in a system which did not appear to place her right to dignified care on the same level as other values. She was trumped by concerns for such values as cost-effectiveness in planning levels of staff, or efficiency in terms of who received most attention: the ill needing treatment taking precedence over the bed-bound, lonely hungry woman who does not need any particular treatment and is not going anywhere. Again, the discourse of rights fails to empower the patient because the choice is made to pay lip-service only to her right to dignity, in the face of what are seen to be more pressing claims.

Of course, these tensions between rights and values in the context of hard choices are well-recognised. In healthcare, although the language of rights is gaining ascendancy, resort to the values of the common good or the politically pragmatic is never far away, especially in the context of this icon of collectivism, the NHS.

[13] See, eg, 'The Moral Status of the Embryo' in I Kennedy, *Treat Me Right* (Oxford University Press, 1992).
[14] See Chapter 10 above.

Consider the NHS Constitution: in its section on 'NHS Values' there is an instructive example of an attempt to square the circle, to have your cake (rights) and eat it (choices based on the common good). It reads:

> Everyone counts. [Is this individualism, a commitment to rights?] We use our resources for the benefit of the whole community [enter the common good] and make sure that nobody is excluded or left behind. ['nobody'? Are we back to individualism?] We accept that some people need more help, that difficult decisions have to be taken [so far so good, but on what basis?] – and that when we waste resources we waste others' opportunities.

Out of the Spotlight

You will remember that I said that there are two orders of choices. The second set of choices are those made away from the spotlight, in the everyday practice of healthcare. How are choices made here? What values are at play, what conditions the choices made, the position taken? Again, I offer what is, perhaps, a jaundiced view. Let us assume that patients may in fact make choices, taking seriously for a moment the Department of Health's rhetoric of a 'patient-led NHS' or 'personalised care'. Let us assume that the patient recognises the notion if not of rights then at least that she has a choice. It is my view that even in such circumstances, the disequilibrium of power and information between her and the professional profoundly affects what in fact will be decided. This imbalance in power, intrinsic in any client-professional relationship, but much more pronounced in the case of healthcare given that the patient is or may be ill, will condition what choices are made. So will the way in which any choice, if offered or raised, will be put to the patient. Moreover, and crucially, the values at play in conditioning the choice are likely to be those of the professional. He may take on what superficially appears to be the role of a neutral guide. In fact, he is very likely to proceed from a position of paternalism, benign perhaps, but paternalistic nonetheless. The consequence is that, if the patient exercises any choice, she will do so on terms that the professional's blessing is sought or even required. Whose choice is it by then? What values are at play? Certainly not those of respect for patients' rights, of a patient's self-determination and empowerment.

Whither Rights

On this view, which I have admitted may be jaundiced but is born of long years of experience, we have moved a long way from the idea of patients' rights, travelling through the land of choices to the values underpinning those choices. Indeed, we are almost at the point where empowerment and self-determination, which lie behind those rights, become not something that is the birthright of all patients, but a status that the professional endows (or does not) on the patient.

The intrinsic uncertainty of the discourse of rights, the choices it calls for, the conflicting values at play, the context in which choices are made and the values brought to bear, all combine to challenge the role that rights-based language may play and plays in healthcare. Beyond the considerable symbolic significance of the rhetoric, you are left with the question whether in fact talk of rights greatly contributes to the empowerment of patients.

Back to the Real World of Healthcare

So, bringing all the threads together, where does this leave us in the real world of healthcare? Well, it does look as if healthcare is a special case as regards the actual implementation, rather than the rhetorical acceptance of human rights. Admittedly, there are some areas of healthcare that have attracted laws, or judicial decisions, or guidance which pronounce on what patients can expect from healthcare. Patients' rights may be mentioned, but as we have seen, they are then often argued away by reference to competing claims and values. As far as they go, these laws and other public utterances do, at least provide us with some sort of landmarks. At the same time, there are areas of healthcare that attract limited attention and where there are few landmarks: areas such as the determination of death, the practice of mass vaccination, or the sharing of medical records across professional groups. These seem to pass without great attention even though human rights are also significantly engaged.

But, even when there are landmarks along the way which refer to, while perhaps not actually giving precedence to patients' human rights, everyday practice, which is what we are all interested in, works, on my analysis, in a different way. What happens in that intimate space between the patient and the professional is decided by reference to two factors above all. The first is the ability of the patient to be heard. The second is the choice made by the professional, reflecting the professional's values (while, perhaps, considering those of the patient). What becomes crucial, then, is the professional's moral compass; her understanding of whatever landmarks exist, and her personal moral hinterland. Rights, the rights of patients, by this time are firmly in the back seat.

So: How to Respond?

So, how do I answer the question I posed at the outset: how should we respond to the kind of dilemmas I set out and the myriad others?

At the level of the general, it may be helpful to separate what might be called the 'softer' less politically charged rights such as dignity and look to various administrative and institutional mechanisms to ensure that these rights are respected. Independent regulatory bodies, such as the recently created Care Quality Commission, explicitly committed to safeguarding the rights of patients, particularly those less able to fend for themselves, can be a powerful force for patients. They can seek to ensure that those charged with the care of patients pay due respect to what I've described as these softer patients' rights. So can those bodies charged with the overseeing the competence and standards of the various professions.

As regards the 'harder', often politicised issues, such as rights in the context of allocating resources or of a dissonant criminal law, whereby people are exposed to criminal liability if not prepared to be protected from themselves, perhaps some national body, a Council of Bioethics could be established.[15] This would allow the ventilation of points of view and guidance from a body, acknowledged to be independent of sectarian influences. Such a body exists in most developed countries, but government has steadfastly resisted the call to set one up in the UK. The reasons are not clear but probably reflect an unwillingness on the part of government to relinquish power in the highly political environment of healthcare and a rather conservative professional response, nervous at being 'told what to do' by 'outsiders'.

As for everyday practice, the challenge is one of education. Professionals should be educated, trained and sensitised in moral reasoning. They should be made aware from the outset of embarking on their careers that healthcare is a moral enterprise in which the realms of right and wrong, fair and unfair co-exist with the world of science and technology. They should understand and become comfortable with the notion of patients having rights. After all, the National Health Service is supposed to serve patients, albeit that there has never been a strong tradition of a kind of service in which it is the patient who sets the terms, rather than the professional. This needs to change if the idea of patients' rights and such edicts as the NHS Constitution are to have any real meaning.

This process of education and sensitisation should be repeated regularly throughout professionals' lives. They should not, as is too often the case, be sent out into the world of practice with a set of stock answers, or worse, unanalysed prejudices. Moreover, in their dealings with patients, they should be encouraged to make their values explicit, while recognising the rights of their patients. Therein lies the opportunity for real engagement between patient and professional. And to those who say this is far too highfalutin an approach for a busy surgery on a Thursday morning, the answer is that it can be done, indeed, is already done by the better professionals, and if done, makes healthcare more successful, not least by being more respectful of patients.

I should close, however, with a warning. Education, moral analysis, debate and discussion are all very well, but they are abstract. Talk of rights and values can seem to many professionals as being remote from the untidy, complex reality of humanity which they daily confront. To enter the operational DNA of professionals these notions have to be connected to a world recognised by them. And, in that real world, healthcare professionals often struggle to make any relevant connection between abstract reasoning and the human condition before them.

I leave you with the following, taken from a radio programme that I made in August 1977.[16]

Dr Carrington (not his real name) was a psychiatrist in Southern California. He had a progressive lung disease. He had become permanently dependent on a respirator. After consistently struggling to stay alive, he decided that he wanted all further treatment to cease so that he could die. He was assessed by a psychiatrist and judged to be lucid and competent to make such a decision. He asked for the respirator to be turned off. His physician said that it would be easier for Dr Carrington and for him

[15] There is, of course, the Nuffield Council on Bioethics, of which I was a founder member and chaired for five years, which is an independent body funded jointly by the Nuffield Foundation, the Medical Research Council and the Wellcome Trust, but it and its expressions of view have no formal standing.

[16] And see Kennedy, *Treat Me Right* (Oxford University Press, 1992) pp 308–10.

(the physician) if, rather than do that, he injected him with a high dose of morphine and gradually turned the respirator down. He did this and Dr Carrington died.

Here is part of my interview with the physician.

> Kennedy: Do you think you behaved entirely ethically in your treatment of Dr Carrington?
>
> Physician: Well … I'm not sure. I've gotten away from … Let me put this in a less than shocking way, gotten away from thinking of everything in so-called ethical terms, because it confuses me. I know that giving a man on a ventilator morphine in high doses, enough to cause general anaesthesia, is risking his life, and it distracts me to think about whether or not it's ethical. I felt like there was a … a more concrete and unifying decision, that … that decision was what are Dr Carrington's chances of being alive in any sense whatsoever, in having any human experiences, away from the hospital and away from this ventilator? And once that decision was made, then I felt that there was sort of humane behaviour was required.
>
> Kennedy: What would you say to the commentator who said, 'My, here's another case of the doctor playing God?'
>
> Physician: Well … you see, I don't have a concept of God in that sense. I feel like the situation in which Carrington was in is what God does and that I'm part of that situation, and that he was going to die, and that there was nothing that I could do about it. And as a matter of fact, what got Carrington and myself to that situation on the last day was my giving up trying to play God, and I'd really reject that. I feel that sometimes I do try to play God when I do try and keep people alive beyond reasonable times. But he was to die. I don't think there is any question about that, and I feel like we gave him a good shot at staying alive. I think he got good medical care and was kept comfortable, and God decided he should die, and I couldn't prevent it.
>
> Kennedy: What would you say to the lawyer who would analyse what you did and what many other doctors, I'm sure, do every day, and would say, 'This looks like homicide – killing by injection'. What would you say to that?
>
> Physician: I could make no comment
>
> Kennedy: Do you think it would be an insensitive response?
>
> Physician: I think it's a response that has nothing to do with my interaction with Carrington. I think it's looking at a single event out of context. I think his comment is true for what he has to say, in the sense that, you know – I always conceive of interactions with lawyers as answering questions, and that's not a question. All that is, is a comment. And I think his comment should stand for what it is. It's not an important comment as far as I'm concerned.
>
> Kennedy: But don't you feel uncomfortable, you as a member of the medical profession, don't you feel uncomfortable if there exists in the wider world a set of rules which would condemn as one of the most heinous crimes that which you regard as the most humane of conduct?
>
> Physician: It's a really uncomfortable thing. It's terribly uncomfortable to be trapped in this situation in the first place. The second place is that probably one of the reasons that physicians feel threatened by these kind of laws is that, without the law, I can cruise along and maintain my patients' comfort and my sanity to the best of my ability. When the law starts coming along, it brings in another factor that has to be contended with. I trust myself. Now the legal system always thinks that there are people around who shouldn't be trusted, and I think that's right, and that's what there's laws for. Homicide isn't far away from that. But this was not a circumstance of homicide. That's all there is to it. Sure, injecting high doses of morphine, or low doses of morphine in a patient like this, contributes to his demise, but so does turning off the respirator, so I don't think there's any difference really.

15

Sumption's Gambit – Give Me Liberty and Give Me Death[1]

Lord Sumption has presented himself as a reluctant commentator on the policy of lockdown: 'Somebody has to speak up for rationality, objectivity, and a sense of proportion, and for the millions whom the lockdown is propelling into utter misery and ruin. It is a sad reflection on the current hysteria that it should have to be me' (*Spectator*, 19 May 2020). But, that said, he's on the barricades again, this time writing in *Prospect*.[2] Before examining what he says, it may be worth noting that words such as 'hysteria' may have difficulty in passing the test of 'objectivity' (and, for that matter, the other two principles that Sumption claims he is speaking up for).

Sumption pins his colours in his piece in *Prospect* to the proposition that '[t]here is something endearingly absurd about the argument that house imprisonment is necessary for freedom'. In part this appears to be because, as he goes on, 'law is an instrument of state coercion'. This, of course, is a strangely limited view – law facilitates as well as coerces, as Sumption must know well – but the assertion helps to set the scene of state versus individual which is Sumption's preferred battleground.

Lockdown is justified by governments across the world as a means of preventing the spread of infection, thereby ensuring that healthcare services are not overwhelmed and that, wherever possible, deaths are averted. Sumption's response seems to be that, at least as regards the UK, the government over-reacted because the threat is not anywhere near as great as we were led to believe, and, that being so, it is 'wicked' (his preferred word in his *Sunday Times* article of 17 May 2020) to deprive people of their liberty.

To justify his stance on the nature of the threat, Sumption cites the data currently available, claiming the numbers of those affected is tolerably low. But, as the President-elect of the Royal Society (a statistician!) has pointed out, there are 'extraordinary amounts of uncertainty' as regards all of the data. What Sumption is doing is pulling out a snapshot. It serves his argument but cannot be passed off as anything other than a snapshot. It tells us nothing about any possible second or third wave, any reappearance of the virus towards the end of the year, any mutation in the virus that may undermine the success of any vaccine. To pray in aid provisional and deeply uncertain data as if they clinched the scientific and political arguments is, at worst disingenuous, at best, to adopt one of Sumption's preferred adjectives, incoherent.

[1] Written in early May 2020, a version appeared online in thearticle.com. Though the central argument still holds, clearly things have moved on as regards Covid-19 such that I have added a postscript.

[2] 26 May 2020.

But Sumption doesn't stop there with 'the data'. To justify his description of the government's response to the pandemic as 'hysteria', he asserted in an interview with the BBC a few days ago that this particular pandemic was not a particularly significant one in historical terms, as if tens of thousands of deaths, let alone the even greater number made ill, and the risk of many more deaths unless action were taken to slow down the rate of infection, were things any reasonable government should shrug off as a little local difficulty. Moreover, to make his point more pointed, Sumption is keen to assert that, in any event, a great many of those who had died had been suffering from underlying illnesses from which they would have died soon anyway. As he said in his BBC interview, 'The overwhelming majority would have died. A bit later, but not much later'. It may be said that there are two approaches available to us as a society as regards the vulnerable ill – that they be cared about and for, or that they be left to die, if a suitable opportunity for doing so arises. Sumption clearly appears to favour this second option.

A second charge made by Sumption is that the government's response is 'incoherent'. If the virus is going to be with us for some time, as the government advises, according to Sumption the government has only two options: permanent lockdown or no lockdown. Since the former is not a plausible policy, the latter is the only coherent approach. Of course, there is a middle way, sometimes compared with moderating the flow of water from a tap – turn the tap off (lockdown), turn the tap on or let water through in a trickle (easing lockdown), turn the tap off again if the rates of infection undermine the capacity of the NHS to provide all of the services which people expect. This middle way may not suit Sumption's too-convenient binary approach but it's the approach most careful governments have endorsed.

Of course, all of these points are really the preamble to Sumption's principal beef – that people should be left to make their own choices without the intervention of the state. The same arguments have been routinely deployed in the case of vaccination, seatbelts, or smoking. Here they are deployed as regards infection with Covid-19.

Like the militia in Michigan, Sumption wants to make his own choices. He wants his freedom back, even if every step he takes, everything he touches, poses a risk to others. His response? They can avoid him, and, if they are really scared, they can stay at home. But this is a very myopic view of the world in which Sumption would seek to move around. It overlooks the millions who provide the services which he enjoys in his liberty and whose work means that they can't stay at home – the nurses, the doctors, the cleaners on the hospital ward, the ambulance driver, the bus driver, the tube driver, the security guard, the postal worker and delivery driver, the police officer, the care home worker, the construction worker, the supermarket staff. Whether obliged to do so, or through a sense of duty and to follow their conscience, or to feed their family, they cannot exercise the free choices available to the Lord Sumptions of the world. His prescription for the world only addresses his world: it does not address their worlds.

Sumption could, of course, carry a note addressed to the world at large saying 'I don't need you, I'm exercising my liberty'. But, the nurses and doctors would still look after him and his fellow 'freedom fighters' should they land up in hospital, because they have a different, more generous view of the interlocking nature of society. And, by looking after them, by doing what is right, they are put at risk because of the risks he and his 'freedom fighters' choose to take.

A final point – Sumption is not writing as Lord Sumption, the neutral judge. He is writing as a political commentator. While judges are entitled to respect for their judicial pronouncements, it is always important not to transfer that respect automatically to pronouncements in the world of public affairs. The traditional view was that judges, with a few notable exceptions, once retired, kept their views on public affairs to themselves. Sumption has decided on a different tack, presenting himself as a public intellectual. He is, of course, a polemicist. That being so, the fact that he was once a judge of the Supreme Court lends no greater weight to his views than if he were still a don in an Oxford College going on at High Table about the state of the world.

Postscript

By the autumn of 2020, we were in the grip of a second wave, much of the country was in lockdown, the number of deaths had reached circa 60,000, and intensive care units were coming under pressure. The ambivalence of the government in seeking to keep people healthy while seeking also to open up the economy, schools and universities left England[3] with the worst of all worlds and the highest number of infections and deaths in Europe as well as the worst performing economy.[4] This is one of the two false dichotomies peddled by Sumption – health versus economy. The other is that society has to choose between saving the lives of the 'less valuable' (as he describes them) and liberty. But there should not need to be a choice. That there is or may be is a reflection of the failings of the Government's response. With proper planning and prompt action, there would have been no need to contemplate choosing some patients for death. Hospitals would not have been overwhelmed. Care homes would not have had patients dumped on them. Some patients would not have made it but many more would not have fallen ill.

The lamentable failure to observe the basic principles of public health in responding to pandemics – track, trace, isolate – owes much to hapless leadership and the decision to hand the responsibility to management consultants (at great expense) rather than relying on the well-established network of local public health experts.

Yet Lord Sumption still advances his libertarian line as in his recent (27 October 2020) Freshfields Lecture.[5] He still holds to another of his preferred binary positions – elderly vulnerable or unaffected, whereas it is increasingly clear that Covid-19 is affecting people of all ages in a variety of ways, some of which are significantly disabling. He talks in his lecture of being surprised that the word 'libertarian' should be a ground for criticism – aren't we all in favour of liberty? He must not have noticed how 'liberty' shades into 'licence' and also have forgotten Jeremy Bentham's trenchant aphorism that

[3] The other three countries of the UK have followed differing paths with differing outcomes.

[4] Wolf (*Financial Times*, 24 November 2020) showed that economies have been less badly affected and begun recovery more quickly if governments took rapid and tough action to suppress the spread of the virus (including lockdown).

[5] He seems to have overcome his reluctance to 'speak up', given his regular appearance on radio, television and in newspapers. Even as I write, a letter from him (rehearsing the Sumption line) appeared in *The Times*, he graced the airwaves of the Today programme, and appeared (disastrously), on a Sunday morning TV debate running his line that some lives are 'less valuable'. He's obviously the 'go to' guy if you want 'the other side'.

'your freedom to swing your stick ends where my nose begins'. Sumption could say, of course, that Bentham's view cuts both ways but the problem is that the person holding the stick is an individual. The nose belongs to the rest of us. The clash is between self-regarding individualism and a collective solidarity. Like it or not and I'm sure he wouldn't like it, Sumption's repeated reference to 'hysteria', (he does so again in the lecture) serves as a lightning conductor for those who inhabit the darker reaches of the internet – Covid-19 is a hoax, a conspiracy of government/doctors/global capital/Bill Gates (tick as preferred), the product of the 5G telecommunications network, a device of government to rob us of our freedoms, and so on. In fact, it's a pandemic which is busy killing people for as long as it's allowed to run free.

By January 2021 (as I write), the death toll has reached over 1500 *a day* (100,000 in total), intensive care units, particularly in London, are overwhelmed, patients with less chance of survival are being triaged for death, and the third wave and mutations of the virus (which I referred to in my initial piece) have become an existential threat. Countries throughout Europe (even Sweden, for long the poster boy of the libertarians) have imposed lockdowns and stringent public health measures. The United States, of course, led by Trump the 'denier-in-chief' goes its own way – 425,000 dead and counting. There, the watchword is 'Liberty'.

PART IV

Inquiries and Reviews

There was a time when, if in some affair of state things had gone wrong or bad things had happened, governments ordered up a Royal Commission to look into it. It no longer happens. It's said that Mrs Thatcher saw them as outmoded. The last one was 20 years ago (into reform of the House of Lords). Their place has been taken by Public Inquiries, plus a plethora of other Inquiries and Reviews not carrying quite the same heft.

Public Inquiries have become the resort du jour of campaigners, injured and disgruntled citizens and the media. The fact that there is no clear criterion as to whether to establish one or not means that it can cover (or uncover) a multitude of sins. It has meant that the Public Inquiry has been seen by many as the preferred route to the truth, indeed, the only route. Distrust of authority and, in particular, of government fuels the public's conviction that a Public Inquiry must be established to 'get to the bottom of' this or that.

Government is often prepared to go along with the pressure. Yes, there's a risk of embarrassment as evidence emerges and is splashed on TV and in the press, but Ministers know that by the time the Inquiry reports, they will usually have moved on, many outside the Westminster bubble will have forgotten what happened, and Government can already begin to put measures in place to allow them to argue by the time of the Report that if there were a problem, it's already been solved.

You may think this is excessively cynical. My experience teaches otherwise. You do the Inquiry or Review, you set out the Recommendations, a grateful government thanks you and accepts your wise words, and then with few exceptions, the world carries on as before. The principal reason is that it is usually an organisation's culture which lies behind its failings, whatever the particular events. And cultures are very, very hard to reform or change absent the kind of leadership which has been lacking in government and public services for some time.

This is not to say that Public Inquiries and Reviews are worthless. They serve a valuable purpose in analysing events and identifying factors which led to whatever is being inquired into. From this grows understanding and an appreciation of lessons which, if learned, can help to prevent something similar in the future. And, as an educator, you would expect me to point out that, by inviting the public in and exploring what happened in public, you at least give the public the opportunity to see for themselves what was and is done in their name. This is a somewhat more modest goal than the ambitions often expressed when a Public Inquiry is set up. But, in my view, it is more realistic.

In what follows I examine why Public Inquiries are set up and how they might be run. I also describe some Reviews rather than full-scale Public Inquiries that I chaired where the focus was more narrow. The Review I carried out into the surgical practice of

Mr Paterson was one of my most challenging assignments. I worked alone (with support from a few dedicated members of the Hospital Trust's administrative staff). I assembled a group of women with breast cancer who had been operated on by Mr Paterson. At first suspicious since they had been let down for so long, they grew into an invaluable source of insight into what had happened and what they had gone through. I spoke to many witnesses – away from the Hospital, in a reception room in a hotel, with refreshments and counsellors on hand. Gradually I built up a picture of years of senior executives and staff looking the other way while Mr Paterson damaged the lives of so many. Then I wrote it all up as a story, beginning at the beginning and ending (at that point) with Mr Paterson's expulsion from the Hospital. Following my Review, he was erased from the medical register and then prosecuted. Found guilty of unlawfully wounding patients, he was sent to prison initially for 15 years, increased to 20 years on appeal.

The victims got some element of closure. The Hospital Trust, having not really grasped the enormity of their failure, was taken over by another. Mr Paterson was taken out of circulation. But, did my Review and its Recommendations signal an end to the sort of circumstances which allowed him to prosper for so long? I doubt it. Until the culture changes, until boards of directors and senior executives remember that serving the needs of patients is what they exist for, there will continue to be some bad hospitals and medical staff, and patients will continue to be harmed unnecessarily.

16

Public Inquiries: Experience from the Bristol Public Inquiry[1]

Introduction

This paper first emerged as a Lecture given at the Royal Free Hospital in London on 7 February 2002, in honour of the late Lord Jacobovits.[2] I knew Immanuel Jacobovits and had benefited greatly from his advice and wise counsel. His particular interest in medical ethics (it was the subject of his doctoral dissertation) brought us together. I had the privilege of working with him and of being entertained in his home. We worked together for a number of years in a group formed at King's College London to discuss medical ethics. The group brought together Protestants, Catholics, Jews – and lost souls such as me. I learned to admire Immanuel not only for his wisdom and erudition, but also for his kindness and enthusiasm for intellectual challenge and debate.

There is a story attributed to Lord Jacobovits which goes as follows. Three men, doomed by their doctors to die within three months, were asked how they would spend the time left to them. The Scotsman answered that he would cheerfully squander his savings on all the pleasures which he had previously denied himself. The Frenchman spoke of the utter abandon with which he would dine and wine to his heart's content. And the Jew simply said, 'I would look for another doctor to get a second opinion'. As Lord Jacobovits explained, this story illustrates the perennial refusal of the Jew to regard anything as final or inevitable. This has meant that even in the darkest days, when Jewry was threatened with doom, the Jew, refusing to accept finality, has consulted his faith for a second opinion.

The gloss that I would put on the story is that it reminds us of our duty constantly to search for truth and understanding; a duty which marks us out as moral beings, whether Jew, Christian, Muslim, Hindu, or whatever. That is what the Bristol Inquiry, in its small way, was about.

After the Jacobovits Lecture, I dedicated my Presidential address to the Bentham Club in the following month[3] to the same subject. In December 2004, I gave evidence

[1] This chapter appeared in *Law, Medicine and Ethics: Essays in Honour of Lord Jacobovits* (Cancerkin, 2007). The full title is 'The Public Inquiry into the conduct of children's heart surgery at the Bristol Royal Infirmary between 1984 and 1995'. Reprinted with permission.

[2] As it happens, on his birthdate.

[3] 22 March 2002.

to the House of Commons' Select Committee on Public Administration, as part of its examination of Public Inquiries.[4] In this paper, I draw on all of these.

Bristol

From 1998 until 2001, I chaired the Public Inquiry into the conduct of children's heart surgery at the Bristol Royal Infirmary between 1984–1995. The Report of the Inquiry was published as *Learning from Bristol* (2001).[5]

The establishment of the Inquiry was announced in Parliament by the then Secretary of State for Health, Frank Dobson, on 18 June 1998. As Chairman, I sat with three others.[6] The first formal, public hearing was on 17 October 1998, when I set out the procedures that the Inquiry would follow. The hearings in public began on 16 March 1999 and ended with the final submissions from interested parties on 9 February 2000. The final Report of the Inquiry was published in July 2001, a separate Report having been published in May 2000.

Background

In this paper, I seek to make some general observations about the circumstances which might determine whether to establish a Public Inquiry and how it might be conducted. In 2005, Parliament passed the Inquiries Act. Given the very general nature of its terms,[7] I am persuaded that the views expressed here remain worthy of exploration.

Inquiries which are the subject of this paper come in many shapes and sizes. They effectively defy characterisation, in that they are:

- creatures of Government at the whim of government, usually central government. I will not be examining inquiries set up, for example, by local authorities or local hospital trusts, although some of the points made may apply,
- statutory (derived from a specific statute) or non-statutory,
- public or private,
- widely variable in terms of:
  - terms of reference
  - subject matter
  - perspective (eg that of the public, the consumer, the patient, the taxpayer).

[4] See, the Select Committee's Report, *Government by Inquiry* (February 2005).
[5] CM 5207 (1).
[6] Professor Sir Brian Jarman, Mrs Rebecca Howard and Mrs Mavis Maclean.
[7] Section 1(1) provides: A Minister may cause an inquiry to be held under this Act in relation to a case where it appears to him that – (a) particular events have caused, or are capable of causing, public concern, or (b) there is public concern that particular events may have occurred.

A Starting Point

The first question that requires attention is whether there are some issues which should be the subject of a Public Inquiry, all other things being equal, and some that should not be. This question is pertinent because of recent events in the UK. The suicide of Dr David Kelly, a scientist who specialised in biological and chemical warfare, prompted the Government to set up a Public Inquiry, under Lord Hutton. The basis of the British government's decision to go to war against Iraq, though not the subject of the Inquiry, inevitably formed the backdrop.[8] To some, Lord Hutton's Report was a vindication. To others, it was a 'whitewash'. The subsequent Report of the Inquiry conducted by Lord Butler into other aspects of the circumstances surrounding the decision to go to war suffered a similar fate.[9] Clearly, those with fixed views were not to be moved by forensic examination of evidence. More important, in terms of the general good of the body politic, a distinguished judge became to some, overnight, a 'lackey of Government', and a distinguished public servant was praised or reviled, not by reference to what he had said, but whether he was seen to be 'for' or 'against' the Prime Minister. Respect for and belief in a particular constitutional mechanism, the public inquiry, were put at risk, not because of the merits or otherwise of the mechanism, but solely based on whether the answer arrived at was the 'right' one.

A Distinction between Two Types of Issue

In the light of this recent experience, I would propose that it may be plausible and helpful to draw a distinction between two types of issue. The distinction is not, perhaps, clearly delineated. Indeed, it may be more helpful to talk in terms of a spectrum of issues, some falling largely towards one end and others towards the other. But, that said, there is, I submit, a distinction which can be made between:

- those issues that directly involve the action or inaction of government, present or past, which I will call TYPE A; and
- those that do not directly involve the action or inaction of government, which I will call TYPE B.

Type A

Recent examples of this type would include the Inquiries carried out by Sir Richard Scott,[10] and those just mentioned, conducted by Lords Hutton and Butler. In this sort of case, my view is that the establishment of a Public Inquiry is not the right approach.

[8] Lord Hutton, *Report of the Inquiry into the Circumstances Surrounding the Death of Dr David Kelly* (January 2004).

[9] Lord Butler, *Review of Intelligence on Weapons of Mass Destruction* (July 2004).

[10] *The Inquiry into exports of defence equipment to Iraq*, 1996 (Cmnd HC 115) (Sir Richard, later Lord Scott, a Lord of Appeal in Ordinary).

No matter who is appointed to chair the Inquiry, the political nature of the issue means that some, from the outset, will never accept the Inquiry's findings, as a matter of party politics, whatever evidence is adduced. The Inquiry, and the Chair's role in it, is impossibly compromised from the beginning.[11] The situation is even worse if the Inquiry is chaired by a senior judge. Not only will the judge as Chair be compromised from the outset, but, given the nature of the issues under consideration, s/he will, at the same time, inevitably have been drawn into the party political arena. As a consequence, judicial independence, both in theory and in practice, will be seriously undermined.

In my view, the only forum in which issues of this type can properly be examined is Parliament. It is for Parliament itself to deal with them. That its current procedures do not allow it to do so effectively does not serve as a reason for passing what is ultimately a political responsibility elsewhere. Rather, it casts on Parliament the duty so to revise its procedures that it can examine the type of issue under consideration. After all, by doing so, it would be doing no more than carrying out one of its principal roles, subjecting Government to public scrutiny.[12]

Type B

Recent examples of this type would include such Inquiries as Lawrence,[13] Paddington,[14] Bristol,[15] and Shipman[16] [and the current (January 2021) Grenfell Tower Inquiry]. The Inquiry into BSE[17] may be said to sit in the middle of the proposed spectrum, since it concerned the conduct of Departments of State, but its remit went significantly beyond the actions and inactions of the Departments involved.

My position is that it is on issues falling under Type B that the discussion of the merits of and justification for Public Inquiries should focus. Consequently, I shall concentrate on Type B in what follows.

Criteria for Establishing a Public Inquiry

To the person seeking a guide to the circumstances in which a Public Inquiry should be set up, the first point of reference would naturally seem to be to some formal criteria. Indeed, if they existed, the previous discussion about types of Inquiry would have been unnecessary. In fact, however, very few criteria exist and, where they do, they tend to be very general. They are to be found in the few cases which have come before the courts

[11] [Sir John Chilcot's Iraq Inquiry (2016) seems to have escaped this fate perhaps because, by the time he reported (after seven years) the world had moved on and passions inflamed a diminishing number of breasts.]

[12] [The current (2020) call for a Public Inquiry into the governments' response to the Covid-19 pandemic should, on this reasoning, be resisted. Of course, unless Parliament can come up with an alternative mechanism, a Public Inquiry may be the only option, flawed as it is.]

[13] *The Stephen Lawrence Inquiry* (February 1999) Cm 4262-7.

[14] *The Ladbroke Grove Rail Inquiry* (June 2001).

[15] See fn 5.

[16] *The Shipman Inquiry* (2002–05).

[17] *The BSE Inquiry* (2000).

in which the issue has been addressed, in the writings of academics, and in the Bristol Report itself:

- public confidence and trust in government or a public service cannot otherwise be restored (*Bristol*, *Walshe* (Walshe K, Higgins J, '*The use and impact of inquiries in the NHS*', (2002) BMJ 325: 895-900);
- the integrity of the system of justice is under challenge (*R v SoS for DEFRA, ex p Persey* [2003]);
- misfeasance by government (*Persey*);
- a major disaster with loss of many lives (*R v SoS for Health, ex p Wagstaffe* [2002], *Walshe*);
- an issue of significant importance is involved which also raises matters of wider public concern (*Bristol*);
- a Public Inquiry will bring added value, ie the issue cannot be examined as appropriately in any other way that is less expensive, less elaborate, and more speedy (*Bristol*);
- new or poorly understood issues of major public concern are involved (*Walshe*).

Applying the Criteria – Deciding on a Public Inquiry

If Public Inquiries of the sort that I am discussing are the creatures of government, then, clearly, it is government, in one form or another which decides whether to set one up. The important question, of course, is what persuades government to do so. It will be obvious from the criteria just set out that there are no rules, or even guidelines, to which government can be held accountable, or must follow. The reality is that Public Inquiries quite clearly live in the world of politics. It is quintessentially a political decision to set one up: a decision born of the political calculation that there is something to be gained and more to be lost by not doing so. Talk of guidelines or rules, therefore, misses the point. What is important is political pressure and political calculation. Section 1 of the Inquiries Act 2005, makes this poignantly clear by purporting to legislate on the circumstances in which an Inquiry may be set up and giving up immediately. The section reads:

> (1) A Minister may cause an inquiry to be held under this Act in relation to a case where it appears to him that–
>
> (a) particular events have caused, or are capable of causing, public concern, or
> (b) there is public concern that particular events may have occurred.

The Chair

The first step, once it has been decided to hold a Public Inquiry, is to appoint a Chair. S/he will, thereafter, need to be involved in all that follows, from framing the terms of reference onwards. The appointment of the Chair will ordinarily condition the way in which the Inquiry is both perceived and how it is conducted. Thus, it is a very important decision. Ultimately, it is a matter for the Secretary of State or Minister whose Department is establishing the Inquiry.

The person appointed must be of sufficient standing and have sufficient experience of and expertise in the subject matter of the Inquiry to command the respect of all those affected by it. Furthermore, s/he must understand issues of procedural fairness and due process and what constitutes evidence. This suggests a background in law.

Should the Chair sit alone? I have no doubt that the Chair should sit with others, perhaps two or three, who bring necessary additional skills and background. The reasons are obvious. No Chair can be the repository of all knowledge and wisdom. There is everything to gain from collective debate and discussion, particularly when the issues at stake are both complex and highly charged. Moreover, collective decision-making makes it less easy for those unhappy with the Inquiry or its findings to attack the person of the Chair, rather than address what the Inquiry finds or recommends.

If, as I would urge, the Chair always sits with others, the status of those others must be agreed at the outset. There are two options: they can be advisers to the Chair or full members, with an equal say in the conduct and outcome of the Inquiry. Which of these options is the more appropriate will depend on a number of factors. Certainly, my view is that, if it is thought that the Inquiry will last for more than a few months, those sitting with the Chair should ordinarily be equal members. It seems to me unreasonable to expect them to give large amounts of their time, yet remain only advisers, whose views can be discarded at the Chair's say-so.

While discussing the role of Chair, I would add one further point on which I feel strongly. In my view, the Chair of a Public Inquiry should not be a judge. The reasons are two-fold. The first is of some constitutional importance. Judges are seen and expected to be independent of other branches of government. To involve them, even after they have retired, in the chairing of Public Inquiries, usually into matters of considerable public and often political disagreement, is to risk bringing their independence into question. This is the more so because, as a necessary feature of the conduct of a Public Inquiry, they cannot call on the authority and respect which they can claim in the conduct of legal cases, surrounded as these are by rules and precedents and the possibility of appeal.

The second reason is of a different order. Judges have spent their lives in courtrooms. They see issues in binary terms, as being right or wrong, true or false. They are used to and rely upon a set of procedures at the heart of which is the proposition that there is a single truth and that it can be elicited by the application of forensic skill. Examination and cross-examination by counsel are what they are used to. Whatever the suitability of this approach, or what lies behind it, to the conduct of a Public Inquiry, this is how Public Inquiries conducted by judges tend to turn out. The Public Inquiry becomes a court of law. And, as I will hope to show in a moment, this is precisely what Public Inquiries should not be. Courts of law and the procedural approach associated with them lack the subtlety and sensitivity required of a Public Inquiry. Judges, only really at home in courts, equally, therefore, do not naturally bring to a Public Inquiry the range of skills required.[18]

[18] Sir Leslie Scarman's conduct of the Brixton Inquiry (*Scarman Inquiry into the Brixton Riots*, 1982) is often cited in rebuttal. In my view, it merely serves as the exception to the rule. It is interesting to note that the Inquiries Act 2005 seeks to occupy a middle ground. While not stating that judges should not be appointed as Chairs, Ministers are required, by section 10, to consult, in the case of England, the senior Lord of Appeal in Ordinary [now President of the Supreme Court] or the Lord Chief Justice, if they propose to appoint a sitting judge as chair, or even as a member of the panel, of an Inquiry.

Terms of Reference

The terms of reference of an Inquiry have an elusive quality. They set the terms of the Inquiry, yet, at the same time, they may well serve only as a signpost to where the Inquiry will go. This elusiveness is easy to understand. The terms are the first step in getting the Inquiry on its way. They reflect the concerns which gave rise to the Inquiry and the goals which it is hoped will be achieved. But they are necessarily the product of only partial understanding; after all, the Inquiry has not yet begun, and when it does, the evidence may lead in a variety of directions, only some of which could have been predicted. So, the terms must retain for the Inquiry a degree of flexibility. They should not be too restrictive. But, flexibility holds dangers either for Government, or for the Inquiry. The Government does not want the Inquiry rampaging about, turning over every stone it comes across. The Inquiry does not want to be stuck with an impossible task, or one which would take a decade to do properly.

The answer lies in careful thought and careful drafting. The answer also lies in the close engagement of the Chair. While, on the face of things, the terms are for Government, they must be acceptable to the Chair, who will, after all, have to do the work. The Chair must, of course, understand and accept the broad sweep of Government's ambitions for the Inquiry. But, the Chair must also ensure that the Inquiry has a degree of room for manoeuvre which will allow the Inquiry to respond to the story as it unfolds. Of course, both Government and Chair can agree on narrow terms and then stick to them. But, this often ends in tears, with the Chair having to defend a report or recommendations which seem limited by saying that 'I was not asked to look at this', or 'that was outside my terms of reference'. This is not a satisfactory outcome, least of all for the taxpayer who will have footed the bill.

What are Public Inquiries for?

My Approach

Here I am concerned to explore perhaps the question which is, at the same time, the most important, yet one of the least examined. Public Inquiries must serve some purpose. What is that purpose (or are there more than one)? And, equally important, is the purpose unique to Public Inquiries, because, if it is not, alternative ways of meeting the purpose warrant consideration?

In what follows, I draw on the approach that I adopted in the case of the Bristol Inquiry.

Background to Bristol

First, it may help if I set out very briefly what Bristol was about. The then Secretary of State for Health, Frank Dobson, announced to the House of Commons in July 1998 that in the wake of the disciplinary hearings before the GMC and the representations of many parents, he had decided to establish a Public Inquiry into the conduct of paediatric cardiac surgery at Bristol Royal Infirmary during the years 1984 to 1995.

The Inquiry's terms of reference were: 'to inquire, make findings as to adequacy of care, reach conclusions concerning action taken, **and** … to make recommendations to help to secure high quality care across the NHS' (my emphasis). This second part of the terms of reference meant that the Inquiry not only had to discover what went on in Bristol. It also had about as wide a brief as could be contemplated to apply what it learned to reshaping the NHS. The breadth of this second mandate went far beyond what would normally be the case. Terms of reference ordinarily, if they call for recommendations at all, call for more focused recommendations arising out of the particular circumstances under review. The challenge given to the Bristol Inquiry was intended. We were being asked to think about the future shape of the NHS and healthcare generally. Perhaps Government did not predict how far we would cast the net, but we made it clear from the outset that we accepted the challenge and would be casting our net very widely.[19]

Next, the Inquiry was a Public Inquiry. It need not have been. The Secretary of State had a number of other options available. He could have ordered that an Inquiry be carried out in private by some outside figure, unconnected with Bristol, or even healthcare. This was a common response to calls for inquiries.[20] It was rejected in the case of Bristol, since it was clear that the parents with whom the Secretary of State was dealing, and those supporting them, had no confidence in anything carried out in private. They wanted everything to be in the public domain as a guarantee of accountability.

For the sake of completeness, it was open to the Secretary of State to ask the Commission for Health Improvement,[21] or the relevant NHS Trust (the United Bristol Hospital Trust) to conduct an investigation, or inquiry. Given the high profile that the events had gained, these were never serious options.

The fact that a Public Inquiry was chosen as the appropriate response had consequences which I will now seek to address and analyse.

Purpose(s)

What I had to ask myself is: what was I being asked to do. Once I was able to answer that question, I could then go on to deal with the second question: how was I going to do it. And, critically, in addressing these questions, I had to remind myself at all times that I was not being asked to be a judge, nor was I presiding over a court.

So, how did I answer the first question: what was I being asked to do? I took the view from the outset that a Public Inquiry, any Public Inquiry and not just the Bristol Inquiry, is intended to serve not one, but a number of purposes. Moreover, it was clear

[19] I do not, in this paper, describe the content of the Inquiry's Report and Recommendations, but they did amount to a systematic analysis of, and blueprint for, all aspects of healthcare.

[20] See, for example, *The Allitt Inquiry* (Department of Health, 1994).

[21] The Commission was established under the Health Act 1999 and abolished in 2004, when the Commission for Healthcare Audit and Inspection (known as the Healthcare Commission) came into being, by virtue of the Health and Social Care Act 2003.

that achieving these purposes would be challenging, not least because they did not all complement each other. Indeed, meeting one might, unless carefully managed, mean failing to meet another.

The following were the purposes that I identified:

- discovering 'the truth';
- achieving catharsis for those affected by the events in Bristol;
- holding people and organisations to account;
- beginning a process of healing;
- learning lessons for the future;
- prescribing what should be done in the light of the lessons learned.

Two other factors should be mentioned. Although they are not strictly purposes, they significantly condition all aspects of a Public Inquiry. They are:

- value for money – the Inquiry must be conducted in a way which uses public funds to best effect to achieve what the public wants out of the Inquiry;
- all due speed – given that time means money, that those affected need an end to the burden that the events under inquiry and the Inquiry itself represent, and that government needs advice so as to introduce any necessary measures as soon as possible, the Inquiry must be conducted with all due speed.

Having set out these purposes in general terms, it may help if I examine each one in turn.

Discovering 'The Truth' or Establishing 'The Facts'

This purpose is both the most commonly cited and the most misleading. It is usually said, at the establishment of a Public Inquiry, that the Inquiry will 'get to the bottom of things'. Indeed, I gave this pledge myself. But, this must not be thought to be the same as 'discovering the truth'. The reason is simple, yet hard to grasp by those raised on the (spurious) certainty of a courtroom's black and white. In the examination of complex events, involving many people, over a long period of time, there are, in fact, many truths, not just one; many accounts, each with its own claim to validity. In the context of interactions between doctors and patients, what the patient heard may not be what the doctor said, but it is no less true for the patient. In a courtroom, where one 'party' has to 'win', such an approach cannot be admitted. In a Public Inquiry, where there are no 'parties', no 'winners' and it is understanding rather than a binary approach to reality that is important, the acceptance of multiple truths is a crucial first step.

Thus, discovering 'the truth' becomes discovering the layers of understanding and perception which prompted the actions and reactions of those involved. There may be circumstances in which it matters that, for example, a meeting was on a Friday rather than a Monday and that this can be established unequivocally. But, there will also be many more circumstances in which recollections will differ and where the fact that they differ is more important than resolving the difference. This is a complex notion, alien to the instincts of those used to the courtroom. But, unless it is grasped, the Inquiry will founder at the first hurdle and will convert itself into a trial.

Even when there is a grudging acceptance of the notion of multiple truths, the pursuers of certainty, those who would discover 'the truth', will play what they see as a trump. They will refer to 'the documents'. My response is to caution: 'beware of documents'. They introduce a dangerous air of certainty. In an urge to find something to rely on as 'fact', that something has been written down and is regarded as a record clearly seems to fit the bill. But, anyone who has had the slightest connection with the real world of how organisations, large and small, work will tell you that the documents rarely, if ever, tell the whole story and sometimes tell you the wrong story. Decisions are made, deals struck, confidences passed on in corridors, offices, and lifts without any documentation. Nuances are negotiated; agreements are reached that the minutes were not intended to mean this or that; concessions are made and agreed as 'not for the Minutes'.

Documents provide an illusion of certainty. To rely on them exclusively as the (or even a) historical record of what may have been happening is to make a serious mistake. To give them some elevated status, as 'the best evidence', is equally a serious mistake. They are part of the story, but only part, and they belong in a context.

I have already referred to the way in which organisations work in practice. They are organic entities, with complex informal structures grafted onto and often more important than any formal structure. Discovering 'the truth' must take account of this complexity and structure. That a memorandum records something as agreed does not mean that everyone involved in fact agreed. That a memorandum was marked as circulated widely does not mean that it was read, or understood, by all those named. And so on.

One final point is worth making. It should be clear that I would replace 'Discovering "the truth"' with 'Facilitating understanding' as more clearly reflecting the first purpose of an Inquiry. It follows that, in the conduct of an Inquiry, all of the evidence sought by the Inquiry, the questions it asks, the witnesses it hears from, must all be designed to achieve this end. In the case of Bristol, and I think it is generally the case, as I will explain more fully later, understanding was more likely to flow from examining the 'systems' underlying how the organisation worked. This is the story, how the organisation works in all its complexity, which is the story that any Inquiry should concentrate on. This is the story which the Inquiry should focus on in the evidence it chooses to examine, because this will facilitate understanding.

It is tempting to some, of course, to concentrate their attention on the behaviour of certain particular individuals and seek to explain everything in terms of their failings. But, chasing down some individuals who can be singled out will not facilitate understanding, though it may feed some atavistic appetite. By contrast, a recognition of the need to focus on 'systems', informed by the work of such pioneers in the analysis of failing organisations as Professor James Reason,[22] is of crucial importance. It was an absolutely crucial guide to the pursuit of understanding in the case of the Bristol Inquiry.

Catharsis

It is often overlooked in the forensic hurly-burly which attends the setting up of a Public Inquiry that the Inquiry is about people; people who have died, been injured or survive,

[22] Professor Emeritus of Psychology, University of Manchester is a world-renowned expert on human error and 'human factors' theory.

and their families, friends and relatives. The psychological and emotional weight of the Inquiry, the memories it brings back, the hopes and despair it engenders, must never, for one moment, be forgotten by those conducting or involved in it. The response must be to seek to create through the medium of the Inquiry the circumstances in which catharsis can take place. In the case of Bristol, this meant catharsis for individuals, for example, parents of children who had died and the doctors and nurses who had looked after them. It also meant catharsis for groups, such as the nursing and medical staff at the hospital, all of whom felt the shadow of the Inquiry hanging over them. And finally, it meant, if possible, catharsis for a whole community, since the events which gave rise to the Inquiry had traumatised the whole city of Bristol.

Catharsis, in my view, is a noble purpose for a Public Inquiry. It is a necessary step on the way to understanding. It has implicit in it an element of theatre. It allows the opportunity for feelings to be expressed. It licences expressions of sadness, of anger, of sorrow, and of happiness, in an environment and context in which such displays are not seen as being out of place. As will be seen, meeting this purpose significantly affected the way in which the Bristol Inquiry was conducted.

Accountability

It is a legitimate expectation and, thus, a proper purpose of a Public Inquiry that organisations and people should be held to account for the events which gave rise to the Inquiry. It is crucial, however, to have a clear understanding of what accountability means and what function it serves. In my view, accountability contemplates the existence of a system or set of principles and rules which are known by those regulated by them and by reference to which they understand they are to be held account. It does not consist of some after-the-event attribution of blame, on the basis that something has gone wrong and someone ought to 'carry the can'. The function served by accountability is, of course, to affix responsibility where this can fairly be achieved. But, more important, its purpose is to contribute to an understanding of what happened and to seek thereby to prevent similar occurrences in the future, not least by devising mechanisms which will achieve this end. One such mechanism will, of course, be a proper system of accountability, by reference to which, all those in an organisation will know what is expected of them, whom to report to, and by what criteria their performance will be judged.

This rather careful notion of accountability does not, of course, sit well with calls for heads to roll, nor with blaming the most readily identifiable or prominent individuals. In the case of Bristol, two doctors had been 'struck off' the medical register and another had had limitations placed on what he was allowed to do and then dismissed by the hospital which employed him.[23] Here, therefore, were three ready-made candidates for blame and, in the views of some in the press and elsewhere, there might be more.

But blame is not a mechanism for systematically assuring and determining accountability. It is a serendipitous approach, picking out some individuals without reference to

[23] The doctors were the two surgeons carrying out paediatric cardiac surgery and the chief executive of the hospital trust.

their interaction with others and to the context and systems within which they worked. It also profits from the perspective of hindsight, a perspective no fair system of accountability can adopt. That there may be individuals who should be blamed is a given in any Public Inquiry. But, it must also be a given that any blame flows from and is the consequence of a proper approach to accountability. It cannot be the starting point.

Once again, an understanding of what the purpose that I have called accountability really means significantly affected the way in which the Inquiry was conducted. The organisation of the evidence was specifically choreographed, so that the Inquiry, and the public following it, could obtain as full an understanding as possible of the way in which the care of children with congenital heart defects was organised in the relevant period. Only then were the surgeons and the doctor who was the chief executive of the hospital trust, who were heretofore the sole objects of obloquy, called to give their evidence. In this way, there was a context. Accountability could properly be attributed to organisations and individuals against the background of the circumstances in which they worked.

I would add one further point. Blaming three or more individuals for what happened in Bristol might have satisfied some. It would not have achieved a great deal by way of understanding any underlying systemic problems. Nor would it have necessarily protected the lives of children, or other patients, in the future. The reason is obvious. Take the three or so individuals out of the hospital, covered in blame, and replace them with three others. The result will be that they will encounter some or all of the systemic difficulties faced by the previous three: in the case of Bristol, a situation which saw care split between two sites; too few cardiologists who were not available in the operating theatre; poor equipment; insufficient facilities in intensive care; shortages of trained nursing staff; poor arrangements for providing covering care at night; dysfunctional management; and poor leadership. Unless these underlying issues were properly understood and addressed, the risk that the pattern of poor care would be repeated was high. Against that background, merely to blame three doctors, as if that would solve everything (or anything) can be seen to be a nonsense.

Healing

I have already said that catharsis may a first step on the way to healing. But, healing is also an end in itself: an important end or purpose. It should be recognised clearly as one the principal goals of an Inquiry. That said, there is a real risk that an Inquiry will take too narrow a view of its role. It may simply see its function as being to hear and weigh the evidence, deliberate on its conclusions and recommendations, write its report, and then dissolve itself. To do so overlooks what is so obvious that it is so easily overlooked.

For those touched by the Inquiry, their lives in one way or another have been irrevocably affected by it. When the Inquiry leaves town, they continue to live their lives. If those lives are lives in which they are shunned by others, or remain fixed in grief, or stuck in defence and denial, the Inquiry has failed them. This is because the Inquiry should seek to promote understanding. Part of that understanding is an understanding of how others may feel and why some may have done what they did. And with that understanding comes the possibility of healing. The Inquiry has a duty to seek to heal broken lives, so that there can be life after the Inquiry.

Learning Lessons

A central function of any Public Inquiry is to enable lessons to be learned. This is self-evident. Less evident is that lessons cannot be learned unless the Inquiry begins its inquiry with an open mind. Having a view at the outset of what the appropriate conclusions should be, therefore, is best avoided! Instead, the Inquiry must not be led to premature evaluations because of previous speculations, or even the findings of other bodies. Lines of enquiry should not be discounted or discouraged because they do not fit current assumptions. Everything is grist for the mill. This is a fundamental principle of fairness.

It might be objected that my earlier reference to adopting a 'systems' approach constituted a conclusion which the evidence was then made to fit, with the consequences that the lessons extracted were the wrong ones. My answer is that the 'systems' approach was adopted to prevent the too-early adoption of conclusions based crudely on blame. Blame was not excluded. It was merely considered after the evidence was assembled rather than conditioning what evidence would be assembled.

Prescribing

Once the lessons thrown up by the Inquiry have been extracted, the Inquiry has the function of prescribing, or making recommendations. The scale and scope of the recommendations may be set out in the terms of reference. It cannot be doubted, however, that recommendations should be made.[24] Government, having set up the Inquiry, is clearly interested in gaining as much benefit as possible from it, and one of the obvious benefits are recommendations for future action.

The Government does not, of course, have to accept the recommendations and will not do so if they fail to subscribe to some fairly obvious criteria. In my view, these are that any recommendations should be:

- practical;
- achievable;
- understandable;
- affordable;
- modest.

Perhaps only the last of these warrants any explanation. By modest, I mean that an Inquiry should avoid recommendations in the form of some grand gesture or iconic

[24] One of the several odd features of the Inquiry under Sir Richard Scott (see fn 10) was that he made no recommendations.

statement. Recommending the appointment of some all-powerful 'Tsar' in the context of healthcare is, perhaps, a good example of something to avoid. A series of modest steps which can be readily put in place is usually to be preferred. This is without prejudice to mapping out a new architecture as the vision of where these modest steps should be leading. Such a vision is often essential. But, the recommendations should address how to get there not merely recommend that there is where we should be.

How to Meet these Purposes?

If what I have set out above are the purposes to be served by a Public Inquiry, the next question is, how should the Inquiry set about meeting them.

In my view, there are two necessary steps. First, the Inquiry must adopt a set of guiding principles. Then, it must adopt an approach to the conduct of the Inquiry which translates these guiding principles into practice.

But, it might be asked, is there not a set of guidelines, or some sort of Manual, prepared by Government, setting out 'How to conduct a Public Inquiry'? Surely, it cannot be for the Chair to work it out for himself, with all the risks of getting it wrong that this may entail. The answer is that, at the time when I was asked to carry out the Bristol Inquiry, there was no such guidance. It was very much a matter of 'DIY' (do it yourself). Clearly, this can be a little unnerving. It can also cause those in charge to take refuge in past practice, which may not readily transfer to current needs, or to the familiar, such as adopting the approach used by a court. As it happens, I found it entirely liberating. It meant that, having taken the counsel of wise colleagues, I could reflect carefully on what the Inquiry was there to achieve (which I have already set out) and then design an approach to meet these purposes.[25]

Guiding Principles

The following seven principles guided the conduct of the Inquiry:

- rigour;
- openness;
- accessibility;
- accountability;
- fairness and appropriate procedure;
- serving different publics;
- explain what the Inquiry is *not* addressing.

[25] The recently enacted Inquiries Act 2005 goes some way to fill the gap I refer to, but the provisions of the Act are couched in very general terms. They still leave a great deal to the discretion of the Chair, eg, section 17(1) provides: ' … the procedure and conduct of an inquiry are to be such as the chairman of the inquiry may direct'.

In this next section, I will explain how the Inquiry addressed each of these. But, first, I need to emphasise that nothing can be achieved by way of translating principle into practice without the creation of the team which will be responsible for doing so. By 'team', I mean the senior members of staff who will manage the conduct of the Inquiry. Paraphrasing Mrs Beaton, 'First create your team'.

This involves the following steps:

- identify the Inquiry's needs. These may range from legal advice, to communications, to Information Technology, to statisticians, to researchers. The needs will vary over time and must be anticipated so that work is never held up while staff are recruited.
- recruit the best available talent. The system of recruitment should be transparent and open. The only criterion for selection should be the ability to do the job in question to the highest possible standards.
- encourage challenge and debate. The team must see itself as a team and work as one. Strategy, tactics and decisions should be discussed openly and vigorously. Decisions once taken should be adhered to. Delegation of responsibility and clear lines of reporting and accountability must be established from the outset.
- share the vision which informs the approach to the Inquiry. It is crucial that the team understands and feels part of the vision. They, in turn, can then ensure that every member of staff also feels part of it.

Let me now revert to the principles that I just set out.

Rigour

There is no shortcut to understanding. In the case of Bristol, the Inquiry was concerned with a period of twelve years and with events which took place not only in the wards and operating theatres of a hospital in Bristol, but in places ranging from Whitehall to South Wales to Birmingham. The number of people who might conceivably be able to assist the Inquiry was very large.

In such circumstances, there is no alternative but to throw the net as wide as possible and slowly draw it in, selecting and discarding as you go. The watchword is rigour. The Inquiry must be rigorous in establishing what it wishes to know and in tracking down any information that may assist it in this process. Equally, the Inquiry must identify what it needs advice on and draw upon the best experts.

Let me describe, by way of illustration, how this principle was translated into practice in the Bristol Inquiry.

The Best Evidence

The process of gathering evidence took months before the Inquiry began its formal hearings. This process was crucial. It meant that the evidence could be analysed and areas of importance identified, so that the hearings could then focus on these areas in a structured and efficient manner. Around 900,000 pages of documents were scanned into the Inquiry's data-base. There were two principal sources. First, the medical care of 1,800 children was scrutinised. This involved examining 2,056 medical records, amounting to 3,497 files, and a total of 673,963 pages. Secondly, 42,071 other documents were identified as relevant, drawn from 30 sources and amounting to 219,828 pages. The Inquiry continued to receive further evidence, right up until the end. It was assessed, and where relevant added to the material that the Inquiry took account of in reaching its conclusions.

The Inquiry wanted to hear from all who could help in reaching a view on the events at Bristol Royal Infirmary over the relevant period. Some were easy to identify: the parents of children with congenital heart defects who had been treated in Bristol, and members of the staff (nurses, doctors and managers) who had been involved in their care. As the net was cast more widely, others were identified as being possible sources of information and insight.[26] So that the Inquiry did not overlook anyone, calls for witnesses were issued through NHS organisations and a range of newspapers. The Inquiry even sought to identify every junior doctor and trainee who had worked in Bristol over the relevant period to understand what they had seen and heard during their few months spent there.

To ensure that the formal hearings conducted by the Inquiry were tightly focused and addressed matters identified as being of significance, the Inquiry identified those witnesses whom it wished to hear from and those whose written evidence would suffice. Those witnesses who were to be called were required to prepare a Witness Statement. Appropriate advice was made available, either through legal advisers or through the Inquiry's own legal team, to enable the Statements to be drawn up. The Inquiry's lawyers then read each Statement and advised whether any reference to another person could reasonably be regarded as critical of that person. If it could, the Statement was sent to the person named, with the invitation to comment on what was said.

Clearly, this process called for careful planning, so as to avoid delays. The advantages were enormous. Crucially, the Inquiry proceeded on the basis of written evidence, rather than oral evidence. This encouraged greater focus and was much more efficient in terms of the time taken. Secondly, before a witness gave evidence, the Inquiry had had the opportunity to review the evidence and had been made aware of what might be contested. This allowed attention to be focused where it was needed. Thirdly, and very importantly both for the process of the hearings and their tone, the existence of comments from those referred to in Statements meant that the Inquiry's counsel could put all the sides of any proposition to the witness, thus obviating the need for cross-examination by a phalanx of other lawyers. At a stroke, the Inquiry was confirmed as an Inquiry rather than a court of law.

The emphasis on rigour from the outset paid dividends. In what was called Phase 1 of the Inquiry, the Public Hearings lasted 9 months (96 days of actual hearings), during which time the Inquiry heard from 577 witnesses, including 238 parents.

The Best Advice

The Inquiry recognised the need to be advised on a range of issues by the best experts. The issues ranged from clinical matters, to managerial practices, to statistical analysis.

[26] Appendix 3 of the Report sets out a complete list of those who gave evidence, whether orally or in writing, to the Inquiry.

Clinical matters alone covered a huge range of areas on which the Inquiry needed advice, including all aspects of cardiac care and surgery, intensive care, anaesthetics, paediatric nursing, and counselling.

To make sure that all respectable ranges of opinion were heard in areas where disagreement was common and legitimate, the Inquiry ensured that all interested parties had a role in proposing suitable experts. Once selected, it was established as a first principle that all of the experts were the Inquiry's experts. They advised the Inquiry. They did not appear on behalf of any person or group appearing before the Inquiry. This was a crucial decision, not immediately welcomed by legal representatives. It reflected again the fact that the exercise was a Public Inquiry, in which the Inquiry decided what it wanted to hear, from whom, and in what way. It was not a court of law where 'sides' were drawn and everyone who appeared was on one side or the other. In the Inquiry, there were no sides. Everyone, including (indeed, especially) experts, was called by the Inquiry to assist the Inquiry.

Some of the problems posed by the Bristol Inquiry called for extremely complex research and new thinking. In at least two areas, the development of statistical tools to analyse rates of mortality and the creation of a way of reviewing a sample of case-notes, the Inquiry broke new ground. The work undertaken is still the subject of learned papers.[27]

The Inquiry also commissioned papers so as better to understand certain issues. These ranged from a history of the law and ethics relating to consent to treatment, to comparative analyses of safety in healthcare and in such industries as oil, nuclear power, railways, and aviation, to research on leadership and management. As with all other material seen by the Inquiry, they were shared with all those appearing before the Inquiry, who, on occasion, offered additional helpful comments which, in due course, were put into the public domain.[28] Many of the papers were commissioned for Phase 2 of the Inquiry. In this Phase, the Inquiry held seven Seminars for invited experts, at which the Inquiry explored areas of importance in guiding the Inquiry towards recommendations for the future. A total of 150 participants attended and 180 papers were submitted.[29]

Openness – A Public Inquiry Works in Public

Working in public was a central principle of the Inquiry: it was after all a Public Inquiry. In essence, it meant that the Inquiry made clear from the outset how it intended to work, made known the documentary and other evidence it received, held hearings in public, and made the transcripts of the hearings available to all. The purpose is obvious. I and my colleagues were carrying out a public duty. We should do so in public, so that we could properly be held to account. If the public saw the same material as did the Inquiry, the public could challenge views or conclusions, if they thought that they were

[27] See eg, DJ Spiegelhalter, R Kinsman, O Grigg, and T Treasure, 'Risk-adjusted sequential probability ratio tests; applications to Bristol, Shipman, and adult cardiac surgery' (2003) 15 *International Journal of Quality in Healthcare* 7.

[28] Annex B of the Report.

[29] Ibid.

not supported by the evidence. This seems to me to be an elementary principle of due process. It surprises me that it is not universally accepted.[30]

The following were some of the ways in which this principle was translated into practice.

- The Inquiry held what it called a 'Preliminary Hearing' in October 1998 which every person and organisation with an interest in the matters falling within the Inquiry's terms of reference were invited to attend. Many parents and relatives of patients treated at the BRI during the period attended. Lawyers were also present representing various groups and a wide range of organisations. The purpose of this Preliminary Hearing was to allow me as Chairman to explain the ground rules of the Inquiry: the timetable, the process for collecting evidence, and the procedure to be adopted during the hearings. One crucially important feature of the Inquiry which was made clear at this Preliminary Hearing was that there were no 'parties' appearing before the Inquiry. It was not an adversarial encounter, on the model of a trial before a court. It was an Inquiry in which the Inquiry decided what needed to be known. Those providing evidence did so with the sole purpose of assisting the Inquiry. It was not a purpose of the Inquiry (although it might be a side-effect) to hold the ring between adversaries, all intent on stating their side of the story. The Inquiry recognised no 'sides'.
- After detailed examination of the various areas of importance emerging from the evidence, and after taking the views of all those interested in the Inquiry's work, the Inquiry published what it called an 'Issues List'. As the name indicates, the list set out the issues on which the Inquiry intended to concentrate.
- After further review of all the available evidence, the Inquiry prepared a 'Core Bundle' of documents in the form of a CD. Initially, it consisted of 15,000 documents which the Inquiry regarded as central. Over time, as further evidence became available, it was added to the 'Core Bundle'. The purpose of producing the bundle was to indicate to those involved and particularly legal representatives the evidence that the Inquiry was particularly interested in and as regards which witnesses could well be questioned during the hearings. The bundle was made available to legal representatives, but, since it was only intended as a procedural aid and since the documents involved would be made public as the Inquiry proceeded, it was not at that point put into the public domain.
- The date for the start of the hearings was fixed for March 1999. This meant that six months could be spent collecting, analysing and sharing the evidence which the Inquiry was to hear and consider. Moreover, the timetable of the hearings, which occupied the following nine months, was carefully planned, so that the Inquiry could hear and consider evidence in an ordered and sequential manner, dealing with each issue in turn. It also meant that witnesses were made aware of when their evidence was required and, as regards those called to give oral evidence, when they would be

[30] But compare the views expressed by Lord Justice Simon Brown in *R v SoS for DEFRA, ex p Persey* [2003] and the deeply equivocal provisions in section 19 of the Inquiries Act 2005. Of course, most of the circumstances contemplated as warranting privacy, even in a Public Inquiry, involve matters which I would categorise as falling into Type A (ante) and thus not matters properly for a Public Inquiry.

called. This last point was crucial. Given that the Inquiry would wish to hear from a number of doctors and nurses still working at the Bristol Royal Infirmary, it was essential that their appearances were planned well in advance, so that the care of patients was never put at risk.

- All of the evidence seen and considered by the Inquiry was seen by all those involved in the Inquiry and was made public. Conversely, the Inquiry did not consider any evidence that was not made public.
- The Inquiry invested a considerable amount of its resources in the latest information technology (IT). The investment was one of the most important decisions taken by the Inquiry and was hugely influential throughout. The IT served a number of functions. In the context of what is being discussed here, openness and working in public, three functions in particular are worth mentioning. First, in the preparation for the Inquiry, every document which might serve as evidence was scanned (saved electronically) into a central system. Each document was then given a unique identifying code. Whenever it was required by the Inquiry during the hearings, it was simply displayed on large television screens which were hung from the ceiling around the Hearing Chamber. (A separate set of screens showed whoever was speaking, by means of voice-activated cameras in the ceiling). Quite apart from the efficiency this brought to the proceedings, it meant that the public, which included patients, families and relatives, were able to see what the Inquiry could see. This apparently simple procedural device was of immense significance. It empowered the public by letting them in. Traditionally, in, for example, the course of a trial, documents would be pored over by lawyers, witnesses and the judge, with everyone else an onlooker of the process, but not of the document. In the Inquiry, everyone could read paragraph 3 of the letter, or whatever, at the same time as the Inquiry was reading it, and as lawyers and witnesses were offering interpretations. Not only did that further enhance accountability, but it served to make real what, to the public, would otherwise be abstract discussions. The second function served by IT was that it allowed the Inquiry to transmit the hearings to three separate locations some distance from Bristol (in Devon, Cornwall and South Wales). In this way, families and others interested in the Inquiry, were able to follow the hearings without having to travel to and stay in Bristol. Recordings of the hearings, week by week, were also kept at these locations, so that those who may have missed any were able to view them later. A third function was that, through the use of technology called 'LiveNote', which constitutes a transcript of the hearings which is transmitted instantaneously to a computer screen, the Inquiry was able to publish on its website a transcript of the day's hearings within an hour of its finishing. This particularly assisted the Inquiry in clearing up or clarifying matters which were identified from study later in the day of the day's transcript. (An additional benefit of 'LiveNote' was that lawyers could follow the hearings from their chambers and offices in real time. Not only did this save money, in that they did not have to travel to attend, but it meant that they could raise matters, by e-mail, for example, as they arose, which could then be dealt with).
- One particular use of IT warrants separate mention. This was the creation of the Inquiry's website. It proved to be a very important source of contact and communication

during the Inquiry. General information was made available and a regular Newsletter appeared, as did a series of commonly asked questions and responses to them, which were regularly updated. More formally, as part of the procedure adopted by the Inquiry, the statements of witnesses were posted, as was the Transcript of each day's hearings. By the time that the hearings ended in December 1999, the website had received over one million 'hits', and had been awarded the Department of Health's annual prize for the best website in the area of healthcare.

Accessibility: Physical Arrangements

While they were only a part of what the Inquiry did, the hearings were undoubtedly the most important part from the point of view of the public. It was critical, therefore, that the hearings were accessible. And here, what I am discussing is not accessibility to what went on. I have already referred to that, for example, in describing the use of IT. What is being considered here is accessibility in the sense of being able to attend, and, as important, *feeling* able to attend. Those affected by the events at the Bristol Royal Infirmary were ordinary people, not used to and perhaps inhibited by the formality and ceremony, as they might see it, which might be expected to surround a Public Inquiry. If the Inquiry was to be really accessible, very considerable thought and effort had to be put into the physical arrangements. The following are some of the more important elements of those arrangements.

Location

There were three factors which guided the Inquiry in choosing the location for the hearings. The first was that the hearings should be held in Bristol, where the hospital and staff were, and where many of the parents and others affected by the Inquiry lived or were based. Secondly, I directed the Inquiry's staff to look for a location for the hearings which was convenient in terms of transport, for those travelling within Bristol and from outside. In the event, the building chosen was close to the railway station and was easily reached by public transport. Thirdly, I directed that the building should be nondescript and functional, but should not be any sort of official or municipal building, far less a court. The reason was obvious. It was important that the public should feel comfortable and not be intimidated by their surroundings. Moreover, it was equally important that one group involved in the Inquiry, whether the Panel or the lawyers, should not feel more comfortable and more 'at home' than anyone else. On this reasoning, holding the hearings in a court or Town Hall would have been totally inappropriate. Some would have felt excluded or less confident in such surroundings. As a consequence, they might even think that the Inquiry had already 'taken sides', by holding the hearings in a place associated with authority or the exercise of power, authority and power which the families of the children who had died, in particular, felt that they were fighting. They had after all, campaigned for two or more years for a Public Inquiry to be held, with a number of disappointments along the way. To be even handed to all, and to retain the confidence of all in the integrity and impartiality of the Inquiry, attention to such apparently unimportant matters as the location of the hearings, therefore, was, in fact, of the greatest importance. Its importance lay in its symbolism as well as its utility.

The location chosen was an ordinary office block. The Inquiry rented three floors, removed all internal walls and designed each floor to meet its needs.

Architects and Designers

To translate the vision of how the various floors should be configured, architects and designers were employed. One floor had to be designed to accommodate the large number of staff, including lawyers, para-legal assistants, IT specialists, researchers and administrators. These were all in one wing. In the other were the offices of members of the Panel, the Inquiry's counsel (there were three), the Secretary to the Inquiry, and other supporting staff. On this floor there was also a secure area in which documents were stored. Another floor had to accommodate the needs of various groups representing patients and parents, plus their legal representatives to hold meetings. The principal floor housed the Hearing Chamber. There was also a meeting room for the Panel, dedicated facilities for the press and broadcast media, rooms equipped with screens to allow those who did not want to sit in the Hearing Chamber to follow proceedings, and a family room with facilities for young children.

The Hearing Chamber

Much thought was given to the design of what was, in the minds of many, the most important room, the theatre, in which the Inquiry was to be played out. I spent a number of days with architects explaining not only how the Chamber should be designed but what the principles were which informed the particular approach that I wanted. In essence, I envisaged that there should not be some central raised podium on which the Panel sat, above and, to a degree, aloof from the rest. Instead there should be a wide arc, or semi-circle, of places for the public. Facing the centre of this semi-circle, and the central focus of the room, should be the table and seat for the witnesses. After all, it was the witness who was important and whom everyone was there to hear from. Off to the left and at a tangent to the witnesses' table was the long table at which the Panel sat. Off to the right were the two tables for the Inquiry's counsel. Behind them and tucked into one side of the room were the tables for the many other counsel and solicitors who attended from time to time. Importantly, I made it clear that there should be no barrier between the front row of seats for the public, which curved around the room and went behind the Panel, and the Panel and witnesses. This created a degree of intimacy. More significantly, however, in the context of an Inquiry which attracted great anger as well as sorrow, it signified trust that the Hearings were open to all and that, in return, everyone attending would behave respectfully. This trust was never once threatened, let alone betrayed, even when the Inquiry took the evidence of those who, to some, had been responsible for their child's death. The Hearings were conducted calmly, followed attentively by audiences ranging from a handful (when some important but less interesting evidence was taken) to more than two hundred, with every seat taken. This need for an atmosphere of calm, which I thought would be crucial to the success of the Inquiry, persuaded me also to spend half a day with what, in other contexts, would be called 'soft furnishings'. Given the anger, frustration and sadness of many of those who would be attending the Inquiry, I decided that one way of inducing calm was through the colours used for the carpets, the backs of chairs and other fittings. Soft, autumnal colours, such as rust and leaf green, were chosen, not just for the Hearing Chamber, but throughout the family and other rooms on that floor. It may be thought that attention to this level of detail is something of a distraction for the Chairman of a major Public Inquiry. I would profoundly disagree.

Arrangements for the Media

It must always be remembered that the media are interested in the matters which prompt a Public Inquiry and seek to write and broadcast about it. The Inquiry should assist them in this activity. To this end, dedicated facilities were made available, including a room set up for television interviews and a news-room with state-of-the-art technology. By putting these arrangements in place, the Inquiry fulfilled its responsibility to the wider audience, interested in following the progress of the Inquiry.

Witnesses

As has been said, the witnesses were the most important people in the Hearings. The Inquiry wanted to hear their stories. As important, the Inquiry wanted to give them an opportunity to have their say, to be heard, to have the sense that they had been listened to and their views understood. Some witnesses were used to the public stage. The very large majority, however, had probably never spoken in public and certainly had never been exposed to the attention which sitting at the witnesses' table attracted. If the Inquiry was to benefit from their evidence, therefore, there was a need to ensure that, as far as possible, they were not overwhelmed by the occasion and their surroundings. In part, this was accomplished by briefings about the Inquiry and its procedure. But there were two specific measures taken in relation to the physical arrangements. First, every witness was given the opportunity, and most took advantage of it, to visit the Hearing Chamber in advance of giving evidence. They were given the chance to sit at the witnesses' table, get a sense of the place and have the seating arrangements explained: where the Panel were, where the Inquiry's counsel, who would be asking them questions, were and where their counsel, should they have one, would be. Though this could not wholly remove the anxiety felt by most, it was a helpful arrangement. Secondly, the witness, if looking straight ahead, looked out at the front row of seats in the middle of the arc of public seating. That being so, this row was always reserved for members of the witness' family, supporters or friends. This meant that witnesses could always find a familiar face, should they wish to.

Accountability

The Inquiry, while seeking to hold others to account for the events at the Bristol Royal Infirmary, had to be accountable itself for how it conducted itself and what it did. It could not expect of others what it did not practise itself. To meet this duty of accountability, the Inquiry adopted, in particular, two practices.

Openness

As has been said, the Inquiry worked in the open. What it saw and heard by way of evidence, the public saw and heard. There can be no more simple, yet demanding, principle of accountability. The evidential basis on which any view reached by the Panel was arrived at was made explicit. In this way, any view could be challenged. As it happens, none was.

Feedback

At all stages in the Inquiry, and particularly during the Hearings, the Inquiry's staff and legal advisers sought feedback from all those affected by or involved in the Inquiry. Comments ranged from concerns about aspects of procedure, to timetabling of witnesses, to communication with various groups representing parents or patients. All comments, positive and negative were communicated to the Panel and, wherever possible acted on. It is self-evident that an essential feature of feedback is that the Panel should make it known that the comment had been received and what action, if any, had been taken (and the reason for not taking action). The Inquiry sought always to observe this principle, even to the point, on occasions, of announcing at the start of a day's hearings specific actions that had been taken. One particularly useful device was the Inquiry's website and the regular Newsletter it produced for families involved in the Inquiry.

Fairness and Appropriate Procedures

The Inquiry had to be even-handed and fair to all. It also had to find its way through a great mass of evidence and do so efficiently and expeditiously. To square this particular circle, the Inquiry developed an approach to working which was original in a number of respects. In large part, the originality lay in the determination of the Inquiry to hold a Public Inquiry (stressing both of those words), and not fall back on the familiar, but unsuitable, approach of a court, or of certain other Inquiries. It is fair to say that some of the proposals concerning procedure which I advanced were greeted with less than enthusiasm by advisers. But, to their credit, they were prepared to give them a fair wind and were converted. The following are, perhaps, worth noting.

Written Statements and Comments

It was important, both in terms of fairness and efficiency that the Inquiry knew what witnesses wished to say, so as to decide whether they should be called to give oral evidence. It was also important that anyone referred to by a witness in any adverse manner should be made aware and have the opportunity to comment. As has already been noted, the Inquiry established a process whereby the statements of witnesses who were not to be called were made available on the Inquiry's website, together with the comment, if any, of someone identified by the Inquiry's lawyers as having been the object of criticism in the statement. The same procedure was adopted as regards witnesses who were to be called to give oral evidence, save that the statement and any comment was not put onto the website until the witness had given oral evidence. The purpose of this procedure was obvious. The Inquiry would know, in advance, the contribution a particular witness would make and so could schedule the witness' appearance accordingly, (given that the evidence was divided at the outset into blocks, covering different topics). Moreover, anyone referred to would have the opportunity of responding to what was said, in advance of the witness' being heard. Not only was this fair to all, but it allowed the Inquiry to take account of and explore differences of view when questioning witnesses. Moreover, it meant that the Inquiry could avoid a procedure known as the issuing of 'Salmon letters', named after Lord Justice Salmon who chaired the Royal Commission on Tribunals in 1966.[31] The purpose of 'Salmon letters' was to put individuals on notice should they have been criticised in evidence. It was a procedural response to the evidence heard, designed to ensure fairness. I took the view that it reflected an approach which equated Public Inquiries with judicial proceedings. It was, therefore, inappropriate and, moreover, unnecessary. Fairness could be maintained in a far more coherent and sensible way. In effect, the 'Salmon letters' procedure introduced an unnecessary formal step into the proceedings, which commonly provoked legal to-ing and fro-ing. By getting witnesses to reveal and confront their various accounts well in advance, everyone knew where they stood. There was no need to have resort to some additional, and time-consuming, and, frankly, out-dated procedural mechanism.

Inquisitorial Rather than Adversarial

It is often said that Public Inquiries are inquisitorial by nature. But the reality often is otherwise. One explanation is that those chairing Inquiries are usually unfamiliar with how to translate the idea into practice. Moreover, since they are very commonly judges, their first instinct is to revert to what is familiar and convert the Inquiry's proceedings into a courtroom. And courtrooms, in England, are not characterised by an inquisitorial approach (with the exception of the Coroner's court). Rather they are characterised by what can be described, perhaps a little provocatively, as a gladiatorial approach. The gladiators are the lawyers, usually counsel. The judge watches and gives the thumbs up, or down, at the end. Lawyers provide a further explanation to why the proceedings, though theoretically inquisitorial, soon take on an adversarial quality. This is because lawyers also are familiar with courts and the procedure of courts. It comes as no surprise that they will seek to treat the Inquiry as if it were just another court. And their position is not just born of professional preference and comfort. It also rests on a fundamental premise, particularly of counsel, that there is only one way to discover the truth and that is through the cut and thrust of examination and cross-examination. Leave aside the fact that we have already seen that the concept of a single 'truth' may be self-delusionary, the approach misses the point of what the Inquiry is seeking to do. It is not seeking to paint a picture just in black and white; that something happened and something else did not, that someone did wrong. It does not occupy a binary world of right and

[31] Cmnd 3121 (1966).

wrong, good and bad. What it is trying to do is understand, and understanding rarely comes in black and white. Furthermore, whatever else may emerge from gladiatorial contests, understanding rarely does. A Public Inquiry should pursue its responsibilities in a calm and measured way, encouraging witnesses to tell their stories, and listening. It is not assisted by those who would turn it into a form of combat, in which witnesses are exposed to the forensic skill of lawyers, but something fundamental – the possibility of understanding, healing, moving on – is lost.

No 'Parties'

In keeping with its inquisitorial approach, the Inquiry made it clear that there were no 'parties', no 'sides', to advance their particular view of events. Witnesses were called by the Inquiry and were the Inquiry's witnesses. They were there to assist the Inquiry. They were not there to score points in their own favour or against others. Legal representatives initially found these challenging propositions. They were used to taking sides on behalf of a client. But, gradually, they understood.

Experts were the Inquiry's Experts

Just like other witnesses, experts also were the Inquiry's experts. They gave evidence to assist the Inquiry in its task. They did not appear so as to advance the position of this or that person or organisation. They were advised as to the assistance that the Inquiry needed and gave their evidence accordingly, whether in the hearings or in the conduct of the several analytical studies carried out by the Inquiry. Again, this was unfamiliar territory to legal representatives. They were used to experts appearing for one 'side' or another. They urged that the expert should brief them and then they would question a particular witness, or advise the Inquiry, in the light of what they gleaned from the expert's briefing. I indicated that the Inquiry wished to hear from the experts and did not wish to hear their views 'second hand', through counsel. I went further and said that the Inquiry would benefit from experts taking part in the hearings at the same time as other witnesses, so that the Inquiry could test arguments as they were put, and witnesses could refer to experts as peers, sitting alongside them, in discussing areas of technical expertise. This they did, and the Inquiry would sometimes listen spellbound as expert and witness discussed matters of significant complexity, whether such and such was the correct response to a particular anatomical anomaly in the heart, or why paediatric intensive care was different from the care of adults, or how a particular statistical conclusion could be arrived at. In fact, the system worked very well and counsel became advocates for it. Moreover, quite apart from giving the Inquiry the benefit of a wide range of expertise, the advice of the experts could be offered in a thoughtful and enquiring way, rather than be the product of some forensic fencing match. And, in addition, there was a wider significance in the way that the Inquiry used experts. Put simply, in their discussions in public, they made it plain how complex the issues facing the Inquiry were. They made it plain that honest professionals could legitimately differ. It was important for the public to see this, not least to dispel the notion that all that the Inquiry was dealing with was a simple story of good and bad.

Role of Counsel to the Inquiry

Counsel to the Inquiry, of whom there were three (a QC and two junior barristers), played a vital role in the Inquiry. Their first engagement was in the organisation of the huge amount of material which the Inquiry collected. They prepared the 'Issues List', in consultation with the Panel, and liaised with all the other groups and organisations involved in the Inquiry. Secondly, it was their responsibility, as members of the independent Bar, to give the Inquiry legal advice. This was a continuing duty which lasted until the Inquiry published its Report. Their third, and by far their most prominent duty, was to take witnesses appearing before the Inquiry through their evidence. Because the Inquiry already had both the witness' statement and any comments from others, counsel to the Inquiry could ensure that the Inquiry heard both the witnesses' account, any challenges to it and their responses to these challenges. Counsel, therefore, had a role which was outside their experience. It was quite different from what they were habitually asked to do in a court. They were asked to be truly the counsel to the Inquiry, taking no sides, exploring and challenging what was said and assisting the Inquiry in any line of questioning that the Panel wished to pursue. They performed the role brilliantly.

Role of Legal Representatives

The role of counsel to the Inquiry had a significant effect on the role of those representing groups and organisations involved in the Inquiry. Prior to and after the hearings, their role was not dissimilar to that ordinarily played by lawyers. But during the Hearings, it was very different. I had decided, when planning the procedure which the Inquiry should adopt, that the Inquiry would work most efficiently if its time was not taken up by each witness being subjected to questioning by the various counsel appearing before the Inquiry. The Inquiry was interested in hearing what it judged important, not what might suit the needs or interests of a particular client. The procedural mechanism adopted was to insist that questions be put by counsel to the Inquiry. The role of other legal representatives, therefore, was to relay to counsel to the Inquiry any questions or observations which they wished the witness to address. The legal representatives were not, therefore, ordinarily called upon. This saved a very considerable amount of time without impairing the Inquiry's commitment to fairness. Three exceptions to the norm that they should speak through counsel to the Inquiry were allowed by the rules drawn up. First, they could claim a short period of time at the close of a witness' evidence to clarify any uncertainties in the evidence. Initially, this right was asserted quite frequently by the various lawyers. But, over time, as they came to understand that their role was to assist the Inquiry and not to make partisan points, the legal representatives grew increasingly content to rely on counsel to the Inquiry. Indeed, it became common for legal representatives to pass notes to counsel to the Inquiry during his examination, asking for this or that point to be clarified or dealt with and this was duly done. The result was a remarkably efficient use of time. The second exception was that legal representatives could address the Inquiry before the day's hearings began, if there was some matter which had been touched on during the previous day's evidence and which, in their view, required further elaboration or comment. This was not, however, an open-ended right of address. The legal representative had first to persuade counsel to the Inquiry, and then the Inquiry, that the matter needed to be raised by addressing the Inquiry rather than through a written submission. Given that the Inquiry dealt with large volumes of paper, another written submission would be no great imposition, and, being part of the proceedings, I undertook that any such submission by way of clarification would be published as part of the record of the Inquiry. In the event, this second exception was rarely exercised. The third exception was the possibility of cross-examination. I will discuss this in greater detail in the following section. Before I close this section, however, I might add that the response of the various legal representatives to this determination of their role was mixed. Some, who really wanted to turn the Inquiry into a court and put certain individuals on trial, accepted the procedure with varying degrees of reluctance. Others saw the virtue of it and responded extremely helpfully. They were helped by the extraordinary fairness and sheer hard work of counsel to the Inquiry, who left no stone unturned in their efforts to accommodate their colleagues.

Role of Cross-Examination

I have just referred to the role of cross-examination. The approach of the Inquiry warrants particular attention. It is, perhaps, helpful to notice two propositions by way of introduction. The first is that there is no *right*, as such, to cross-examination of witness (usually by lawyers) in a Public Inquiry. The Inquiry must, of course, behave fairly at all times. This does not, however, mean that cross-examination must inherently be embedded in the procedure adopted by the Inquiry in the conduct of its hearings. Fairness to all can be achieved through a variety of means. The second introductory proposition is that lawyers (especially barristers), used as they are to courtrooms, take for granted that they will be allowed to cross-examine witnesses. They tend to be convinced that only through this forensic technique, in which they are masters, can 'the truth' emerge. The position of the Inquiry was simple. It wanted to hear witnesses telling their stories, rather than have the story filtered through the interventions of their legal representatives, who might seek to gloss over this, or over-emphasise that, out of their perception of what it was good for the Inquiry to hear. The Inquiry wanted to conduct the Hearings with expedition. It did not want to be drawn into adversarial dogfights. And, it was convinced that proper understanding of the role of counsel to the Inquiry, and proper collaboration between them and those representing others, would mean that counsel to the Inquiry could pursue all lines of enquiry of interest to others without the need for cross-examination. This approach was not welcomed by some legal representatives. They wanted to have their 'go' at witnesses and seemed unwilling to accept that this was not the purpose of the Inquiry. Moreover, they appeared to cleave to the perhaps naïve view that 'truth' and its opposite would emerge from this particular form of jousting. The Inquiry was pressed to indicate more clearly the circumstances under which cross-examination would be allowed. A direction was duly handed down that an application, which had to be in writing, to cross-examine a witness would be considered by the Inquiry if two conditions were satisfied. The first was that the particular legal representative making the application had brought certain matters to the attention of counsel to the Inquiry as warranting exploration when a witness gave evidence. The second was that counsel to the Inquiry had failed to explore the matter, adequately or at all. In the event, no such application was ever made.[32] The Inquiry's Hearings lasted for 96 days. There was not one minute of cross-examination. The impact this had on the way the Inquiry proceeded, both in terms of the expedition of its work and its atmosphere and tone, was, in my view, hugely important. Moreover, by the end of the Inquiry, it was recognised by virtually all legal representatives that the procedure had been both fair and appropriate.

The Use of IT

The importance of IT to the Inquiry has already been discussed. What may be added here is its contribution to the fairness and expedition of the hearings. By scanning all relevant documents into the Inquiry's database, it was possible to ensure that the Inquiry, and particularly its legal team, could have access to all the relevant evidence collected at the earliest possible stage, and in a manageable form on computers. The creation of a CD containing the 'Core Bundle' achieved the same effect for both the Panel and the legal representatives of all those involved in the Inquiry. Witnesses' Statements, and Comments on them, were equally added to the database and were thus accessible to those involved. Once they began, the hearings were effectively 'paper free'. Counsel to the Inquiry, and other legal representatives on the occasions on which they addressed the Inquiry, were simply able to identify the unique code given to each document for it to be transmitted onto the computer screens of the Panel, other lawyers and onto the screens available to the public. It was estimated that, by not having to search through shelves of box files to find the relevant document and then pass it around to all, but instead being able to move on at the press of a button, the Inquiry was able to accomplish anything from a quarter to a third more work on an average day of Hearings.

Meeting the Needs of Different Audiences

The Inquiry had many audiences: they were in Bristol, in the South West and Wales, in Whitehall, throughout the UK and in many other countries. They consisted of patients, families of patients, doctors, nurses, managers, local and national leaders in clinical and related areas, politicians, commentators and, of course, the media. It was important for the Inquiry to recognise the differing interests and concerns of this range of audiences, and to seek to respond to them. It did so in a variety of ways, the more important of which were the following.

Patients and Families

Patients and their families reflected a spectrum of opinion about what had happened in Bristol, ranging from strong support for the surgeons and other staff responsible for the

[32] A request was made to recall a witness, when the Inquiry revealed the extent to which tissue had been removed from children who had died. The request was denied. Recalling the witness would not have added to the Inquiry's understanding, although it would have allowed some the opportunity to pursue further an issue which engendered very strong emotions.

treatment of congenital heart disease during the period, to vehement and angry condemnation of them. At the beginning of the Inquiry, these groups were at loggerheads. They had different legal teams and had distinctly different hopes and expectations of the Inquiry. To ensure that the various views were heard and understood by the Inquiry, regular meetings took place between all groups and the Inquiry's staff. The meetings took place not only in Bristol, but in a number of locations in the South West and Wales. They continued up to and after the conclusion of the Inquiry and the publication of the Inquiry's Report. The Internet was also used, not only to publish documents and the daily transcript and to relay the hearings to other locations, but also, through its dedicated website to publish such things as regular Questions and Answers, the timetable for the coming months, updates on progress, and a newsletter. The aim was simple. It was to ensure that lines of communication were established and maintained, out of respect for the concerns of families and out of a desire to respond to any needs that they might have. One measure of the success of these measures, building on the extraordinary sense of fairness of the families themselves, was that, by the time that the hearings were completed, the leaders of the two principal groups of parents walked together to lay a wreath at the hospital in recognition of their common sense of loss and the understanding that the Inquiry had given them. One other measure taken by the Inquiry bears mentioning. Aware that many of the families attending or giving evidence would find the experience painful and distressing, the Inquiry took the advice of specialists in responding to the needs of grieving parents. All members of the Inquiry, from the Panel, to counsel, to administrative staff, to receptionists were given intensive training. The aim was to produce an atmosphere of calm and understanding, so that anyone attending the hearings could be helped while they were there. During the hearings, the Inquiry also employed specialist counsellors who made themselves known and were available to give support and advice, if asked.

Legal Representatives

As has been explained, the Inquiry depended on the understanding and cooperation of the many legal representatives involved. This was particularly so during the early stages of the Hearings, when the unfamiliar approach being adopted by the Inquiry could have created tensions. There were, therefore, very regular, often daily, meetings between counsel to the Inquiry and other lawyers and I, as Chairman, regularly responded to requests for assistance or clarification. It is right to record that, overall, the various lawyers responded with very great professionalism. Certainly, the Inquiry could not have proceeded as effectively as it did without their help.

Media

As has been made clear, the Inquiry recognised the important role of the print and broadcast media in taking the Inquiry to the wider public. The Inquiry established a dedicated team from the very beginning of the Inquiry. Their role was to assist the media. Just as in any major public event, this took many forms, from briefings, to interviews with staff (though not with the Panel once the Inquiry began), to press releases, to support in explaining or clarifying this or that point. Practical arrangements were also made for the currency of the hearings, including a dedicated press room and a television studio for interviews. The difference from other public events was that the Inquiry lasted for almost three years. Thus, the team had to sustain the level of assistance, which called for stamina and patience. Also, they had to prepare for the surges of interest which happened, for example, when a particular witness appeared, culminating, of course, in the final release of the Inquiry's Report. This was a complex affair, not least to avoid leaks, and had to be choreographed against the background that, to observe the requirements of Parliamentary privilege, the Secretary of State first had to present the Report to Parliament. His statement to Parliament was transmitted to the press conference in the Queen Elizabeth II Conference Centre in central London, and the moment that he sat down, I was able to introduce the Report and respond to questions.

Government

The government of the day was interested in the Inquiry for a number of reasons. They had set it up and agreed the terms of reference. The conduct of one of the major Departments of State, the Department of Health, and a major public service, the National Health Service, was under scrutiny. Government recognised, indeed it was explicit in the Inquiry's terms of reference, that the Inquiry would not limit itself to the circumstances of paediatric cardiac surgery in Bristol in the 80s and 90s. It would ask what the events of Bristol said about healthcare and the NHS generally and what lessons for the system as a whole could be learned. And finally, government was interested in what the Inquiry might recommend, for both good and less good (or more obviously political) reasons. That is to say, it needed to understand and be able to respond responsibly to the Inquiry's Report, and, as all governments would wish to do, to demonstrate that it was already doing (or had done!) what was recommended. The Inquiry recognised the legitimate interests of the Government in the conduct, findings and recommendations of the Inquiry. The Inquiry also recognised that the government, in the form of the Department of Health, might attract criticism for its involvement in the events of Bristol. The Inquiry, therefore, had both to liaise with Government and keep it at arm's length. After all, the Inquiry was established as an *independent* Public Inquiry. Two issues needed careful attention. The first is the notion of independence. There may be some purists who think that there is a line which can be drawn, recognisable to all, which indicates what is for Government and what for the Inquiry. But, such people have little familiarity with the real world. Governments set up Inquiries, they allocate funding (which comes from the taxpayer), they are interested in the efficiency of the Inquiry, and are interested in, because they will be affected by, the outcome of the Inquiry. It is obvious, therefore, that independence is a subtle and complex issue. It fundamentally depends on trust on both sides. Government must be confident that the Inquiry will alert it to matters which are the proper concern of Government, and the Inquiry must behave responsibly in this context. At the same time, Government must also have the confidence not to seek to influence or affect what the Inquiry examines, how it proceeds, and what findings and recommendations it makes. In the case of the Bristol Inquiry, this trust was successfully built and sustained, notwithstanding the high public profile which the Inquiry acquired.

The second issue is one which needs to be resolved at the outset of any Inquiry: whose is the Report? It may be thought that the answer is obvious. An independent

Inquiry must necessarily produce its own Report. The difficulty is that this response is question-begging. It does not answer the question; for whom is the Report being produced? If the Report is being produced for Government, then certain things follow. The Government may decide not to publish the Report, or to publish it only in part, or in an abbreviated form. The Government may decide to publish it, but with a response or rebuttal. Clearly, any of these responses has the capacity to diminish the value of the Report as an independent Report. In the case of the Bristol Inquiry, I was in no doubt that the Inquiry had been asked to Report to the public. The technicalities of first reporting, through the Secretary of State, to Parliament did not detract from this. Accordingly, this was established at the outset. Although there were occasions in which the Government would have wished to exercise more control over the dissemination of the Report, if not its content, the initial position prevailed. The Report was shared with Government, as with others, under strict procedures of confidentiality. Nothing was leaked by anyone. The Government's conduct was exemplary.

Interested Groups

Beyond those people and organisations immediately involved in the Inquiry, there were a range of other groups who were concerned to follow the Inquiry. There were professional bodies, Departments of State other than the Department of Health, NHS Health Authorities, and various other national and international organisations. To meet their needs, a dedicated liaison team was established which operated for the duration of the Inquiry.

Explain What the Inquiry is Not

Many, particularly families affected by the events at the Bristol Royal Infirmary, invested in the Inquiry a range of expectations which it could not meet. From the first days of the Inquiry, the team responsible for communications sought to make it clear what the Inquiry could and could not do, pursuant to the terms under which it was established. The message was reiterated and reinforced regularly by me during the hearings and afterwards. But, merely to say something, and to say it frequently, is not necessarily to ensure that those hearing what was said were, in fact, listening. Some saw the Inquiry as being a means of obtaining financial compensation for the wrongs that they had suffered. Others expected, or hoped, that the Inquiry would be able to impose some sort of professional disciplinary sanction on some of the clinicians. Some even wondered whether the Inquiry could impose some criminal sanction on those who they saw as having behaved wrongly. The only answer was to keep repeating that the Inquiry was a Public Inquiry, explaining what this meant, and that it was not a court of law, nor a disciplinary tribunal. It could not award compensation nor impose disciplinary sanctions. The importance of explaining this, of explaining not only what the Inquiry was but what it was not, lay in the Inquiry's aim to meet the purposes which it was there to achieve. Catharsis, healing and learning could not be achieved unless everyone came to an understanding of what the Inquiry could and could not do. Disappointment at unrealised expectations would lead to frustration and anger. Thus, expectations had to be managed repeatedly.

Make a Video!

In the hope that the Inquiry's approach might be of interest to others, a production company was commissioned to make a video illustrating all stages in the Inquiry, for the purposes of sharing thinking across government

Due Speed?

The Inquiry took 2 years and 9 months, from the announcement by the Secretary of State to the publication of the Report. This is a significant period of time. It suggests that Governments should think long and hard before deciding that the creation of a Public Inquiry is the right response to a particular pressing issue. Careful thought needs to be given to whether the sort of criteria set out earlier are satisfied and whether pressure from whatever source should be resisted. That said, the period of time spent inquiring into the events in Bristol may not have been excessive, given three particular factors.

The first was the nature of the task. To review the care of over 1800 patients over a twelve-year period, and subject it to a form of rigorous analysis not previously seen, was an immense undertaking. Secondly, it was the Bristol Inquiry which drew attention to the practice of removing and retaining the organs of patients who had died. Parents were rightly shocked. They had been unaware of the practice. The Chief Medical Officer for England, Sir Liam Donaldson, invited the Inquiry to prepare an analysis and report, not only on what had been done in Bristol, but also on the relevant ethical and legal background. This occupied over six months of the Inquiry's time in the beginning of 2000. It required the redeployment of a great many staff and, given the complexity of the issues, a great deal of the Inquiry's attention. A third factor was the judgement that, while the Inquiry should proceed expeditiously, it should not proceed at a pace faster than the capacity of those involved to understand what was unfolding. In other words, if a fundamental aim of the Inquiry was to promote understanding, this would need time.

Value for Money?

Did the Inquiry provide value for the money spent? This ultimately must be for others to decide. And, of course, it is not just a question of the financial outlay, but also the contribution made to meeting the various objectives that the Inquiry set for itself, particularly to promote understanding so as to contribute to learning for the future.

In financial terms, the Inquiry cost the taxpayer £14 million over the almost three years of its life. In another first for a Public Inquiry, the Inquiry published its accounts in its final Report. IT and legal representation were the two largest items of expenditure. That said, the investment in IT undoubtedly brought significant savings. Equally, the engagement of lawyers in the months leading up to the hearings, when so much preparatory work was done and much of the groundwork laid, meant that the hearings proceeded extremely smoothly and expeditiously.

The output of the Inquiry was two major Reports. Beyond that, the Inquiry has had a very significant impact on the shape of policy about healthcare and the NHS.

Learning and Prescribing

The lessons and the prescriptions are set out in the Inquiry's Reports. The Interim Report was published in May 2000. Entitled 'Removal and Retention of Human Material', it was 60 pages long, had 2 Appendices and made 69 Recommendations.

The Inquiry's Report was entitled, appropriately, 'Learning from Bristol'. It was published in July 2001. It was 528 pages long and had 4 Appendices, which together ran to around 12,000 pages. The Report made 198 Recommendations of which the Government accepted all but a handful.

Postscript

It may be worthwhile to raise one matter by way of postscript. It can be captured in the question 'What happens next?' I raise this as a point of general constitutional importance. In general terms, once an Inquiry has presented its Report, it ceases to exist. It has no residuary powers. Its staff move on to new things, as do the Panel and all the various experts and advisers. Given that the Report has been formally presented to Parliament, the conventional procedure is that, in due course, the Government will produce its response. It may, of course, already have indicated its position, but a formal, considered response sets out the Governments position in detail.

Thereafter, it is for Parliament and interested individuals to monitor what actions, rather than words, have emerged from Government. If Government chooses not to act, which is, of course, its prerogative, there is a danger that the issues identified as warranting attention go unaddressed. One way of avoiding this inertia, would be to introduce a procedural mechanism whereby, after the publication of the Report of a Public Inquiry, the Government of the day would be required to report to Parliament after six or twelve months, what action, if any, had been taken and the reasons. Another approach is for the Chair to signal that s/he will review the actions taken in response to the Report after six or twelve months, in the light of which a further Report would be made public.

17

The Paterson Review[1]

This is a tragic story. It is not a story about the whole of the NHS. It is about something that happened in one corner of one Hospital Trust in one part of the NHS. But, it has lessons for the whole of the NHS.

It is a story of women faced with a life-threatening disease who have been harmed. It is a story of clinicians at their wits' ends trying for years to get the Trust to address what was going on. It is a story of clinicians going along with what they knew to be poor performance. It is a story of weak and indecisive leadership from senior managers. It is a story of secrecy and containment. It is a story of a Board which did not carry out its responsibilities. It is a story of a surgeon who chose on occasions to operate on women in a way unrecognised by his peers and thereby exposed them to harm.

The Review was commissioned by the Board of Heart of England NHS Foundation Trust (HEFT, the Trust). It is specifically concerned to identify the lessons which the Trust can learn from the way in which it responded to the concerns raised over time about Mr Ian Paterson's surgical practice. It is informed by the papers received from the Trust and the interviews held with patients, staff and others. Special thanks are due to the many patients whom I spoke to and who wrote to me. I learned much from their experiences and insights. They deserve to have the opportunity to understand what was happening in the breast unit while they were receiving treatment. I hope that this Review provides that opportunity.

The Review seeks to set out the facts as clearly as possible and to comment on them. The aim is to allow those who read it to come to an informed and considered view and reach their own conclusions. If there is to be any real understanding, so that lessons can be learned, it is important to avoid focusing on the 'name and shame' approach. When things go wrong, it is mistaken and naive to imagine that one person or group was solely responsible. Instead, the focus must be on the systems in place which brought about what happened.

In this Review I draw attention to features of the system which contributed to what happened. They include: the role of the Board; the approach and way of working of the Executive; the culture of the Trust; the ability to voice concerns and be heard; the level of communication within the Trust and between the Trust and others; the role of

[1] This is the Executive Summary of the Review the full title of which is: Review of the Response of Heart of England NHS Foundation Trust to Concerns about Mr Ian Paterson's Surgical Practice: Lessons to be Learned and Recommendations, also known by the short title, the Kennedy Review. It was made public by the Heart of England NHS Foundation Trust on 19 December 2013.

confidentiality; and, perhaps most crucially, the place of the patient's perspective. It is these factors which must be addressed if anything is to be learned.

The Review begins with the appointment by the Trust of Mr Paterson as a surgeon in March 1998. He had been the subject of an investigation and suspension two years previously by his then employer, Good Hope Hospital, and had been required to undergo a period of supervised practice before recommencing laparoscopic surgery. The Trust was advised of this prior to his appointment. On his acceptance of the appointment to the Trust, his relations with his colleagues at Good Hope became increasingly difficult. Matters came to head and he was asked by the Chief Executive of Good Hope Hospital to leave without completing his period of notice.

He is described as charismatic and charming and was much-liked by his patients. He was not, however, a team-player in an area of care which is absolutely dependent on clinicians working efficiently and effectively as a team. The team suffered as a consequence, as did, inevitably, the care of women with breast cancer. In July 2011, Mr Paterson's registration with the General Medical Council (GMC) was made subject to conditions for eighteen months. In October 2012 he was suspended by the GMC and the suspension remains in effect. He was suspended by the Trust in May 2011. His pay was stopped in November 2012.

Women with breast cancer undergo surgery as the principal form of treatment. Depending on their condition, they have some form of localised surgery, not amounting to a mastectomy, or they have a mastectomy. A mastectomy is defined as the removal of breast tissue so as to leave a flat chest wall.

Fellow clinicians and nurses in the breast care team became concerned about Mr Paterson's surgical practice. One of the particular concerns was the amount of tissue left behind on occasions after what was described as a mastectomy. Concerns were such that, towards the end of 2003, one clinician, Dr Stockdale, a consultant radiologist at another Trust who was part of the clinical team, carried out an audit of 100 patients. The audit called into question Mr Paterson's clinical competence and suggested that, by leaving behind tissue, women on occasions may have been exposed to an increased risk of a recurrence of their cancer. The Trust's senior managers responded by asking a senior clinician, Mr Wake, to carry out an investigation. A Report was prepared and submitted in January 2004. It made a series of recommendations. It was taken to be principally concerned with making the Multi-Disciplinary Team (MDT) work better. In fact, it made a number of other recommendations about Mr Paterson's surgery which were not acted upon. Surprisingly, it only referred in passing to one of the central concerns – that, on occasions, Mr Paterson was leaving behind tissue after carrying out what was supposed to be a mastectomy – and made no recommendation on the matter.

The Report overlooked a crucial issue: the issue of consent. Women were giving their consent to a mastectomy. But, on occasions, a variation of a mastectomy was being carried out; what became known later as a 'cleavage sparing mastectomy'. This was not a recognised procedure. Women did not consent to it in any properly informed way. Whenever Mr Paterson intentionally chose to leave behind tissue, while saying that he was carrying out a mastectomy, he was in breach of his obligation to obtain consent from his patient. Had this lack of proper consent been identified and dealt with properly by senior managers in 2003 or earlier, as it should have been, events would probably have taken a different course. But, despite being referred to by concerned clinicians in

2003 and again by an external expert in 2007, the question of lack of consent was not formally raised by senior managers until mid-2011.

The Trust's response to the Mr Wake's Report was to seek to improve the working of the MDT. The concerns over Mr Paterson's clinical competence went unaddressed. Mr Paterson continued to operate as before for nearly four more years. The oncologists who were based in another Trust felt ignored. They had expressed their concerns and supplied evidence. They felt that no-one at Mr Paterson's Trust was listening. Like many clinicians who spend their time looking after patients, they regarded the management of the Trust as remote. They had little understanding of it or contact with it. As a consequence, their attempts to provoke action from those able to take action were ineffectual.

They were faced by an awful ethical dilemma: what to do about the patients whom they were seeing who were supposed to have had a mastectomy but had not, in fact, had one, but, rather, had only had a 'partial mastectomy' (a contradiction in terms). The dilemma was resolved on occasions by compensating for the 'partial mastectomies' that some women were receiving. Some patients were referred back to the surgeon for more surgery (which, of course, should not have been necessary had a mastectomy been performed). But, as regards other women, the decision was taken, on occasions, to depart from standard practice and treat them with radiotherapy as if they had not had a mastectomy (as was the case).

The alternative course open to the oncologists and other members of the team would have been to down tools and refuse to treat those patients who had not been operated on correctly. They did not feel able to do this. They had raised concerns already and been told that the procedure raised no increased risk and that only fatty tissue was being left behind. (The breast care nurses, who had also expressed concern, received the same assurance from Mr Paterson.) The culture in the Trust was not conducive to raising concerns about a leading surgeon, particularly as the oncologists were not surgeons and were from another Trust. Their desire to do the best for the patient in front of them prevailed over making a stand. The result was less than optimal care for women and a festering sense of frustration and anger among the clinicians in the breast care team.

They could have raised the issue with the senior managers of their Trust, but did not do so. They could, when all else failed, have reported their concerns to the professional regulatory body, the GMC. They did not do so. In the circumstances, they should have done.

The QA (Quality Assurance) Visit of 2004 led to concerns being expressed about the MDT and surgical practices. In a follow-up meeting, three months later, concerns were reiterated. But, the QA team can only recommend. Action is for the Trust. The Chief Executive, Mr Goldman, rightly pressed managers for reassurance about the matters raised and was given such reassurance. The National Cancer Peer Review in 2005 painted a picture of a harmonious MDT delivering a good service. It is hard to reconcile the two opinions. Staff may have been seeking to put on a good 'show', though that is unlikely. It is more likely that the Review simply lacked rigour.

Senior managers saw Mr Paterson at the time as a highly effective surgeon performing efficiently, enabling the Trust to meet its targets. The memory of what the 2004 Report had been about faded. It became the received wisdom that it just concerned matters of man-management. The Board, which is responsible for the care and welfare of all patients in the Trust, was not at this time made aware of any of the concerns raised, nor responses to them. They were told the good news from the Report of the Peer Review in 2005. They were not told of Mr Wake's Report, nor of the less favourable views expressed by the initial and follow-up QA Visits in 2004, and the recommendations which followed. Good news was preferred to true news.

A further QA Visit took place in 2007. It reported that progress had been made. The Report was only four months before the Trust launched an investigation into Mr Paterson's surgical practice. The discrepancy can be explained, in part, by the absence of input from oncologists and the concentration of the Visit on technical problems confronting the holding of an MDT across three sites. That said, the Director of the West Midlands Cancer Intelligence Unit (WMCIU) who led the QA Visit, continued, at the same time, to raise concerns that had reached her concerning Mr Paterson's surgery.

Relations between Mr Paterson and other surgeons were unsatisfactory. A long-serving fellow-surgeon left. Another surgeon left within a few months of her appointment. Potential new recruits had been put off by Mr Paterson's behaviour, save for one appointment in 2003. It appeared that Mr Paterson wanted the lion's share of the work for himself. When the Trust decided to make a new appointment in 2007, Mr Paterson was excluded from the process of selection, despite his being the leading surgeon, for fear that he would again put off any applicant. This is just one example of how senior managers behaved towards Mr Paterson. Rather than confront him, they preferred to work around him.

The culture of the organisation at the relevant time was hierarchical and seen by some as oppressive. Inappropriate behaviour by consultants went unchecked. Speaking out about concerns was not easy, particularly for younger members of staff. The Board was passive, responding to what it was told by the Executive rather than actively exercising effective governance.

The new surgeon appointed in 2007 soon began to raise concerns about Mr Paterson's surgery after seeing some of Mr Paterson's patients, under the newly-introduced system of cross-cover. The senior managers decided to launch an investigation. They did so using the Department of Health's disciplinary procedures, working through the HR Department. This decision was to have profound implications for years to come. Principal among them was that, thereafter, everything relating to the management of the concerns about Mr Paterson was covered in a blanket of confidentiality. Communication within the Trust was impeded. Patients were unaware of concerns about the surgeon in whose hands they were placing their hopes for the best possible care. Mr Paterson's colleagues did not know what was going on. Others, including those responsible for managing staff working in and around the breast unit, could not answer the questions these staff put to them, because they could not get answers themselves. They felt undermined. Rumour, gossip and speculation filled the gap left by the lack of information. Members of the Board were in the same position. They did not see any of the Reports commissioned by the Executive and received only one formal briefing between 2007 and 2010. When there was a report to the Board in November 2010, it was triggered by the imminent publication of a story in the media.

The second important implication of pursuing an investigation through the disciplinary procedures was that senior managers worked within the approach adopted by the Department of Health's National Clinical Assessment Service (NCAS). This approach concentrated on identifying the measures necessary to reintegrate Mr Paterson into the team and make sure that his surgery met appropriate standards. The perspective, therefore, was that of the clinician and his needs, all set out in an Action Plan.

There was another perspective which could and should have been adopted: that of the patient. Had that perspective been adopted, the question would have been: how can we act in the best interests of patients. This may have caused senior managers to require Mr Paterson to cease operating on women with breast cancer until the concerns that had been swirling around for several years could be calmly analysed. This perspective did not appear to be understood, far less adopted.

The Board was informed that an investigation had been launched but received no further formal notice of progress. There is a device under the disciplinary procedures whereby a Non-Executive member of the Board is appointed to 'oversee' the investigation. If it was intended to provide it, this device failed to provide the Board with any assurance concerning the investigation. The Non-Executive did not once report back to the Board. Thus, the Board was entirely in the hands of the Executive. As a consequence, the Board could not effectively hold the Executive to account as to the conduct or outcome of the investigation or any action taken.

The senior management established a two-part investigation: matters of interpersonal relations were investigated by a physician from the Trust. An external, independent expert investigated Mr Paterson's surgery. Both Reports made a series of recommendations. The most important was that Mr Paterson must cease immediately from carrying out two surgical procedures: the so-called cleavage sparing mastectomy (csm) and 'shaves after mastectomy'. Mr Paterson agreed to do so at the end of December, 2007.

An Action Plan was drawn up for Mr Paterson in consultation with NCAS. One element of the Plan was that Mr Paterson's surgery be observed by a distinguished external surgeon. This expert made his observations unaware that there had been a series of previous Reports, and that concern had been expressed about breast tissue being left behind after what was described as a mastectomy. He should have been told. What had already been said would have provided a context in which to carry out his observations, but the claims of confidentiality meant that he was denied it. Nonetheless, he submitted a Report which was critical of aspects of Mr Paterson's surgical practice. The critical comments went beyond Mr Paterson's previous performance of 'partial mastectomies' to include his surgical technique more generally. In particular, it referred to Mr Paterson's surgery as needing to be 'less rushed' on occasions.

The receipt of this Report could have served as another opportunity to require Mr Paterson to cease operating while the concerns being expressed were even more closely examined. This is what at least one outside expert thought should have been done. It was not done. Mr Paterson continued to operate until mid-2011, subject to the conditions placed on him at the end of 2007. He did not observe these conditions on occasions and was eventually excluded from the Trust.

Having decided not to require Mr Paterson to cease operating, senior managers had to turn their minds to the patients whom he had already operated on. Their view appeared to be that, while Mr Paterson may have been carrying out an unrecognised procedure, it was not clear that the procedure was harmful. (This view overlooked the fact that the absence of consent, in the case of csm, already harmed patients, as did the need for further operations in the case of 'shaves after mastectomy'.) Given that it was an unrecognised procedure and involved leaving behind tissue on the chest wall, the view taken was that the procedure known as csm could pose a risk. This led to a pursuit of data to determine whether there was, in fact, a risk of harm, and, if so, what that risk was. At the same time, senior managers also sought to address a second question: if there might be a greater risk of a recurrence of their cancer, should any of Mr Paterson's patients, and, if so, who, be recalled by the Trust. In response to this second question, senior managers embarked on an approach which involved identifying those patients whom they thought might be most at risk and recalling only them.

This approach was hopelessly flawed. First, any woman who had had tissue left behind was necessarily exposed to an increased risk of recurrence. So, at the very least, all patients who had had csm or 'shaves after mastectomy' had to be recalled. But, there was no means of telling who had had csm. It was proposed to identify patients by examining their records and notes. But, the records did not identify who had had a csm: the operation was always recorded as a mastectomy. Photographs and other records equally would not identify the relevant patients. Three independent experts brought in to advise said as much. Their advice was not heeded. The only plausible approach was to recall all the patients who had been operated on by Mr Paterson for breast cancer. This was the view expressed by a number of clinicians. It was not accepted by senior managers. They embarked on a limited recall.

The reasons why senior managers chose the route of a limited recall, despite the fact that it was misbegotten, are complex and not entirely clear. They include:

- a failure, initially, to appreciate the scale of the issues involved;
- the tendency to approach the concerns about Mr Paterson's surgery as being technical, requiring an analysis of data about outcomes (even though such an analysis was impossible: the number of csm operations performed was unknown, as was the total number of patients Mr Paterson had operated on, in both the NHS and the private sector, and without a total number it is not possible to calculate a rate of recurrence and compare it with the rate of other surgeons);
- the sheer managerial implications of a mass recall of patients; and
- a desire to contain and control the fallout from the concerns and thereby protect the reputation of the Trust. Containment became a dominant objective over time, but it became impossible, not least when stories began to appear in the media.

The selection of patients to be recalled, apart from being flawed as an approach, was also affected by the fact that Mr Paterson was involved in the process of selection. If all the patients had been recalled, there would have been no need to involve him. A process of selection, however, meant that he was consulted as to whether this or that patient had undergone a csm. Given Mr Paterson's refusal to accept that csm exposed patients to any greater risk of harm, the process of selection was fraught and led to an even greater worsening of relations in the MDT.

Initially, 12 patients were identified for recall. But, even as they were identified, patients began to present themselves at clinics who had not been selected for recall, but needed further examination. The period between 2009 and 2011 was a period during which the limited recall unravelled, as more and more patients needed to be examined.

The process of recalling patients was dogged by delay. Not enough resources were allocated to do the job properly. The burden of examining patients fell largely on the shoulders of one surgeon who already had a full clinical load. The delay meant that the some patients may have been put to even greater risk by having to wait before being recalled or seen. It also greatly added to the anxiety of women, many of whom thought they had been cured and now were plunged into the uncertainty of a possible recurrence.

Members of staff within the Trust remained largely in the dark about what was being done. Confidentiality, as a consequence of the HR process, was cited as the reason. Outside the Trust, Regulators were advised of the recall in 2009 and were updated in 2011. By contrast, other bodies, particularly the Cancer Screening Service responsible for referring patients to the Trust, were not aware of what was happening until alerted by the media in 2010.

A new leadership team took over at the end of 2010. The decision to recall all patients was made soon afterwards. It was the right decision. Again, not enough resources were allocated but it was successfully completed by early 2012.

The fact that the recall was managed and operated by staff who had previously looked after them at the Trust created difficulties for some patients, and for some nurses. Efforts were made to engage outside specialists, doctors and nurses, but with very limited success.

The Trust invited patients to complaints resolution meetings at which senior managers sought to set the record straight and apologise. The senior staff acted with commendable sensitivity. Despite the effort to be open, however, these meetings were dogged by the repeated assertion, in response to patients' questions, that concerns had surfaced in 2007 and that the Trust had acted promptly to require Mr Paterson to cease carrying out csm and 'shaves after mastectomy'. It was not accurate that concerns had only surfaced in 2007, but those advancing this view did so unaware of the full history. They had not been adequately briefed.

The way in which the Trust worked contributed to this inability to recall, and uncertainty about, the past. The Trust appeared to have worked informally for a good many years. There were serious gaps in the organisational memory of the Trust. This was a significant lapse in good governance. In particular, the Board, which is responsible for all that goes on in the Trust, was never adequately told formally of what was going on in relation to Mr Paterson's surgical practice until towards the end of 2010, seven years after concerns had been raised by some of the team caring for women with breast cancer. Nothing ever showed up on the Trust's Risk Register, a remarkable fact given what has subsequently occurred.

The new leadership has sought to correct this state of affairs, through regular updates. The Board cannot discharge its responsibilities if it is not properly kept informed. It should have been informed at least by 2004, after Mr Wake's Report of his internal investigation.

Alongside the process for recalling patients which they established, the second element of senior management's approach to the concerns about Mr Paterson's surgical practice centred for several years on the pursuit of data. The pursuit of data might be seen, at some point, as some sort of displacement activity: wrestling with the very human problem of the patient could be postponed while the technical issue of data, which the clinician-scientist is more comfortable with, can be resolved. One of the lessons of history from the many occasions when things have gone wrong in the NHS, is that senior managers and doctors who are reluctant to confront what is actually happening, take refuge in the call for ever more data. The view was that data was needed to establish whether Mr Paterson's surgical practice exposed patients to an increased risk of harm. (The issue of consent, which did not require data, was simply overlooked and not pursued formally till mid-2011.)

Data was relevant to address two central questions: should Mr Paterson be required to stop operating on women with breast cancer; and which patients should be recalled. As regards recall, the only plausible strategy was total recall. As regards his continuing to operate, there was enough evidence to suggest that Mr Paterson should have been stopped at least by 2007, if not before. Indeed, if the issue of consent had been identified, as it should have been, a reason to require Mr Paterson to cease operating had existed for several years earlier. Equally, if Mr Wake's Report had been taken seriously, a proper analysis of Mr Paterson's performance would have been instituted over the next six months. This analysis would have built on the audit that Dr Stockdale had already carried out in 2003. It is very likely that the result would have been that Mr Paterson would have been required to stop operating on women with breast cancer by the end of 2004 at the latest. That did not happen. By 2007/8, in any event, data was emerging which appeared in the Report of the West Midlands Cancer Intelligence Unit (WMCIU) in 2009 to suggest that Mr Paterson's overall surgical performance was poorer than that of his peers as well as the fact that patients undergoing certain procedures were at a significantly higher risk of recurrence.

The WMCIU's Report, and subsequent iterations, were not received by senior management with the seriousness that they deserved. The Reports warned of significant risks to certain groups of patients who had been operated on and advised senior managers to act on this. They should have acted promptly. Instead, the Trust continued to state that the process of collecting and analysing the data on csm was still going on, but that, otherwise, Mr Paterson's overall performance was within accepted standards.

In fact, as regards Mr Paterson's overall performance, the standard that senior managers referred to had been undermined by data as early as 2005. Senior managers had been advised of this by the WMCIU on several occasions from 2007 onwards. Nonetheless, the Trust repeated the assertion that his overall performance was within accepted standards, such that the GMC, on the basis of the Trust's assurance, did not impose conditions on Mr Paterson's registration when dealing with complaints against him at an interim stage in 2010. It was several months later that he was suspended by the GMC and excluded by the Trust, and then on the basis of his breach of the agreement of 2008 and failure to obtain consent, rather than on the basis of his surgical practice.

While being a tragic story, this Review is also a story of the Trust now seeking to put the past behind it; to make a fresh start. It has begun that journey with a determination to be open and to understand and learn from past events. The scale of the challenge, however, cannot be overstated. Some staff feel let down. Many patients, past and present, feel betrayed. Their capacity to trust clinicians has been tested to destruction. The Trust must do all that it can to reach out to them and to the wider community. It must say it is sorry for the past. It must work to rebuild confidence for the future.

It is not the role of this Review to hold people to account. That is a job for others. What the Review seeks to do is to establish what went on as clearly as is possible, so that others can reach informed judgements. Certainly, there are matters which do need to be addressed:

- Senior managers did not respond effectively to concerns expressed about Mr Paterson's surgical practice until late December 2007 and then their response was neither sufficiently robust nor rigorous.
- Other clinicians in the breast team, fellow surgeons, oncologists, radiologists and pathologists, continued to work with Mr Paterson for years. They did not go to the GMC or the regulator, even though they felt that they were getting nowhere in the Trust. The oncologists worked in a separate Trust so could have gone to the senior managers of their Trust.
- The breast care nurses went along with Mr Paterson's assurances that there was no need to be concerned at what they were seeing, even though their training had told them that a mastectomy involved a flat chest wall.
- The process of gaining consent from patients was trivialised and patients as a consequence were sold short.
- Mr Goldman, as Chief Executive, appeared to leave things to others while clearly being closely involved behind the scenes.
- Senior members of the Executive decided to instigate an investigation into Mr Paterson's surgical practice under the disciplinary procedures. In doing so, they ensured that concerns would be investigated in confidence and from the perspective of the clinician rather than the patient.
- Mr Cunliffe, as Medical Director, in conjunction with Mr Goldman, clamped down on communication, sought to contain the fallout, chose not to stop Mr Paterson from operating on women with breast cancer, and chose to initiate a very limited recall.
- The Board was excluded from access to information by senior managers and made no formal effort to assert itself and become involved.
- Those responsible for Safety and Governance did not play any formal or prominent role in the Trust's response to concerns about Mr Paterson's surgical practice, despite the nature of their responsibilities.
- The Board and Executive did not meet proper standards of good governance. The Trust's 'organisational memory' was impaired through informal ways of working.
- The designated Board member 'overseeing' investigations did not formally keep the Board advised.
- The Trust's approach to audit and collecting data was patchy and poorly administered.

All of these matters are not above comment. I have commented on them. But, they make up only part of the story. The real story is about the leadership and management of the Trust over the years.

Winning back the confidence of patients, staff and the community will be a very significant challenge for the Board. To begin to meet the challenge, the Board must demand of its senior Executives that they identify what is relevant in determining that the care provided to their patients is safe and of good quality. The Executive must be required to provide routinely all the necessary information to determine whether such care is being delivered. Standards already exist nationally. It is open to the Trust to expand on these so as really to get under the skin of the Trust's performance. Patients and clinicians must be engaged in developing such standards. Information on how it is meeting the standards must be published routinely, not just to let everyone know how the Trust is doing, but also as a way of signalling that the Board accepts that it is accountable.

Not only will this bode well for the future but it will serve as one of the ways of indicating the Trust's determination to learn from the past.

This is a Review of the care of patients. It is fitting that the last word should go to one of Mr Paterson's many patients whom I spoke to, whose metastatic cancer is now widespread:

> '... some of us will always have rotten bad luck and carry on and the disease will develop, that is going to happen, but rotten bad luck is easier to live with than the thought that your surgeon may have damaged you .... You have this gnawing suspicion that maybe if you had woken up with a nice flat chest wall the day after the operation, maybe you would be feeling well now, but I'm never going to know', Mrs Shena Mason.

Postscript[2]

Mr Paterson was finally excluded from the Trust in 2011, his registration was suspended by the GMC in 2012, and he was removed from the register of medical practitioners in 2017. In the summer of 2017, in relation to his private practice, he was tried and convicted on 17 counts of wounding with intent and three other counts of wounding, as well as counts of fraud. He was sentenced to 15 years' imprisonment on 31 May 2017. The sentence was subsequently increased to 20 years on 3 August 2017.

Spire Healthcare, the private sector hospital group, paid out £27.2m by way of compensation. As regards the NHS, a settlement was reached with 750 claimants in the amount of £37m.

A further Public Inquiry chaired by the Bishop of Norwich reported on 4 February 2020. It relied on the Kennedy Review as regards the NHS and added further information about Mr Paterson's practice in the private sector.

Subsequently, in an Editorial I wrote for the Royal College of Surgeons of Edinburgh in November 2017, I highlighted some lessons from the Paterson case.

No-one is an Island

On one level, Mr Paterson can be compared with another doctor who earned notoriety, Dr Shipman.[3] Both were clearly highly exceptional characters: they fitted in on

[2] As regards the private sector, Spire commissioned a Review by Verita which can best be described as perfunctory and which was made public in March 2014 and there was a later Public Inquiry which, apart from relying on my findings in relation to the NHS, reported in detail about Mr Paterson's surgery in the private sector (*Report of the Independent Inquiry into the issues raised by Paterson's Surgery* (DHSC, February 2020)).

[3] A General Practitioner who was found guilty of murdering 15 of his patients. The total number of victims is thought to be around 250.

one level; on another level their behaviour was a daily denial of what doctors up and down the land stand for. So, it could be said that Mr Paterson was so off the spectrum of expected, even predictable behaviour that nothing can be learned from the harm he caused. This would be wrong. Mr Paterson was part of an organisation. It is proper to ask what the organisation knew of his practice, when they knew it, and what they did.

Working in a Team

All surgery involves a team. Nowhere is this more true than in the case of breast cancer. Mr Paterson was not a team player. He was a bully, prone to ignore his colleagues or belittle their views. The Multi-Disciplinary Team's meetings were dominated by him.

The team, the central element in the care of the patients, was not working. This was made known to the senior executives of the Trust. They allowed the concept of teamwork to be undermined. The reasons were not clear: they may include not wanting to stand up to Mr Paterson, preferring his views as a well-known surgeon to those of others, or satisfaction that targets were being met. Whatever, the reasons, when teams do not work and corrective action is not taken, patients are harmed.

Knowing What to Do

The nurses and fellow doctors were concerned but did not raise their concerns with others. That they did not is a comment on the culture of the Hospital, a culture which is not unusual. Staff are loath to challenge the powerful. Senior Executives rarely create an environment in which staff feel safe to do so. And, when they do, staff do not seem to be aware of the openings available to them and, as important, their duty to avail themselves of them

The radiologists and the nurses could have engaged the regulators, the Care Quality Commission and the GMC. They did not. Their training and the culture that they found themselves part of, did not contemplate such action. They saw their duty as being to do their best for their patients. But, they interpreted this duty too narrowly. Doing the best for the patient meant doing something about Mr Paterson, rather than coping with what he was doing. Doctors need to learn from this. But, regulators need also to learn that they must be much more visible and accessible. They must make it clear that they are there to protect patients and should be engaged when concerns arise and those inside the Trust do nothing. If they are not, patients may be harmed.

Training for Leaders

Mr Paterson was able to continue to put patients in harm's way for years for a variety of reasons. One of the principal reasons was that colleagues in senior roles were not prepared to stand up to him. Members of staff who could have done something took the path of least resistance. They worked around him. This of course was fine by him because it left him in his own bubble, free to do as he wished. The lesson which comes through strongly is that those who find themselves in positions of leadership must be prepared for the role. They must receive appropriate training. It is unrealistic to expect someone without such preparation to stand up to someone with Mr Paterson's personality. And so it proved for years. And patients were harmed.

What about Consent?

It did not occur to the Trust's senior executives, even when they were aware of Mr Paterson's practice, to put two and two together and realise that there was a fundamental issue of consent at stake.

Women had agreed to a mastectomy. When they had not had one, their agreement, or consent, had been acquired through false pretences. The information that they had been given, that they would be having a mastectomy, was false. They had not given valid consent. In legal and ethical terms this lies at the heart of Mr Paterson's wrongdoing – his violation of women's right to be informed and to choose what should happen to their bodies.

The lesson is an unhappy one. Consent is increasingly trivialised. It is seen as an administrative chore. 'Consenting' a patient is a common expression, despite its illiteracy and complete disregard for the fact that it is the patient who consents and the doctor who seeks permission. Until there is a proper understanding of the role and place of consent in medical practice, the opportunities for abuse will continue to exist. And patients will be harmed, if not by the procedure, then by the failure to obtain their consent.

18

Inquiries in the NHS: What's the Point?[1]

I'm delighted to be invited to deliver this year's Marsden Lecture in honour of William Marsden. He was remarkable man.

He founded the Free Hospital in 1827, first in Hatton Gardens, then in Gray's Inn, and finally here in North West London. I remember as a student walking from my digs past the old cottage-hospital-style buildings on my way to the George and the Roebuck (the two local pubs). They (the buildings not the pubs!) were replaced in the late 60s by the present building.

The hospital received its royal title from Queen Victoria in 1837 on her accession to the throne. It had been generously supported from the outset by royal patronage and, very importantly, by the Worshipful Company of Cordwainers – shoemakers to you and me.

Marsden's idea for the Free Hospital's foundation anticipated by over 100 years what finally emerged as the NHS. He founded it on the basis that the 'only passport [to admission] should be poverty and disease', which became, in 1947 with the creation of the NHS, 'service free at the point of need regardless of ability to pay'.

Very early on, the Free's principles were put to the test when London was hit by the great cholera epidemic of 1832. All of London's hospitals closed – except the Free Hospital. It stayed open: the same openness as was seen nearly 150 years on when it opened its doors to a sufferer from the ebola virus, while panic reigned elsewhere.

In 1842, the then Duke of Cambridge organised the raising of funds and presented Marsden with a marvellous silver statuette as a testimonial to the Royal Free's first 15 years. On one side was inscribed the parable of the Good Samaritan, a reminder again of the values of service and duty which were the inspiration of the Victorian reformers and of the founders of the NHS.

There were times, readily recognisable to those who run the hospital today, when Marsden would gladly have traded in the silver for some cash. He regularly needed money, as the number of patients rose and the need for beds grew. Without royal patronage and the support of the Cordwainers, things might have been different.

Marsden was inspired to act and establish the Free Hospital by coming across a young woman who was dying on a doorstep. He took her to a number of hospitals, all of which refused to take her. He then took her to his home, where she died three days later.

[1] This was the unpublished Marsden Lecture given at the Royal Free Hospital (Royal Free London NHS Foundation Trust) on 20 November 2014.

180 years on there are still people, young and old, lying and dying on the doorsteps of our city. I am a trustee of a charity, Pathway, founded three years ago,[2] which dedicates itself to providing health care and support to the homeless of London and elsewhere. The Royal Free gladly agreed to participate in the programme. William Marsden would have been pleased.

Now, to my topic.

Inquiries in the NHS

From time to time, something bad happens in the NHS and the cry goes up for an Inquiry, almost always these days, a *Public* Inquiry. The call used to be for a Royal Commission, but they were effectively abandoned as a way of addressing public concerns by Mrs Thatcher, not least because they took so long and were too broadly focused.

Now, the call is for a public inquiry: nothing less will do; nothing less can be trusted.

There's usually some back story since not all or even most circumstances in which something goes wrong end up with such a call. The back story tends to be: something bad has happened/is happening/is said to have happened; the particular hospital or Trust does not manage things well; it goes into denial; it obfuscates; it clamps down; communication is poor, or worse; the media latches on – human interest stories beckon; politicians are lobbied; they apply pressure; pressure mounts.

While the back story is important, there is something else which has increasingly conditioned the response of those affected by what has happened and which leads them to call for a Public Inquiry. Above all else, it is the growth of what can be called a culture of distrust, particularly of institutions and those who speak for them. In part, the hospital in question has brought it on itself by its behaviour. In part, there is a general cultural trend in which hitherto conventional forms of discussion, based on argument and evidence, have been overwhelmed by the new rules of discourse through social media – if someone says it, it's true. Calls for evidence are seen not as means of establishing some proper understanding, but as part of the establishment's way of controlling those who would speak out. Conspiracies swarm across the internet and people get caught up in them. The default position becomes – bad things have happened, there is a cover-up. A wrong has been perpetrated, there are people who are to blame, they should not be allowed to get away with it. The focus is on individuals not systems where it usually should be.

On top of these, what may be called non-rational, forces, there are also rational grounds prayed in aid of a call for a Public Inquiry: a search for the truth and for some for sort of accountability, and a conviction that these will only be achieved through some independent examination of what went on.

Since Public Inquiries are set up by government, however, it is clear that the **ultimate** determinant of whether, in fact, a public inquiry is set up is what politicians

[2] [Still going strong at the time of writing and soon to go into partnership with the much larger charity, Crisis.]

decide in the often frenzied and always muddy world of politics – in our case, the politics of the NHS.

So, returning to our question, at a crude level, if the decision whether to set up a Public Inquiry is political, the point of it must, at some level, *also* be political. A benevolent commentator would say that the political point or purpose is to commission some independent review which will arm the government with the means to address similar problems in the future. To the less benevolent, edging towards the cynical, the political aim is to get something out of the headlines and off the agenda for a period, during which time the Minister will have moved on, and the government can do things to make it look as if, by the time the Inquiry reports, it is able to say that problems have been exposed but thankfully the government has already taken, or is in the process of taking, action. A secondary political purpose, in this cynical vein, is to nail the previous government for failings, if circumstances are sufficiently convenient.

As in all things political, there's a bit of both the benevolent and the cynical in most decisions (as was the case in the decision to ignore advice and set up a Public Inquiry into what had gone wrong at Mid Staffordshire NHS Foundation Trust[3]).

But, if the political decision is taken to set up a Public Inquiry, the question – what's the point – does not go away. It still has to be answered in a second order way. This is because, to politicians, the political issue has been resolved. There is going to be an Inquiry. Now they can get back to work and someone can get on with it [albeit finding the 'someone' is not always easy, as the events relating to the proposed inquiry into the sexual abuse of children showed![4]].

So, the someone has to ask herself the question, what am I supposed to be doing, what's the point of a Public Inquiry? You may be forgiven for thinking that with so many Inquiries flying about, there is some file in some cupboard in the Cabinet Office telling the chair what to do and how to do it. No such file, in fact, exists though there is now some guidance. So, the Inquiry is set up, the chair is appointed (or not!), the terms of reference are set out and then you are left to get on with things. (The terms of reference, by the way, do not indicate the point of the Inquiry, though they may broadly circumscribe the task.)

Where did that leave me when I was asked to chair a Public Inquiry? I went into a corner, read and thought a lot, and decided on my own notion of what the point is.

In fact, I decided there were six points:

- discovering the truth
- catharsis
- holding to account
- healing
- learning what went wrong
- prescribing – making recommendations
- plus value for money and all due speed.

[3] Report of the Mid Staffordshire NHS Foundation Trust Public Inquiry published on 6 February 2013.

[4] The first two people named as chair withdrew after allegations that they were too closely associated with 'the Establishment'.

These points or purposes are each important. Some overlap, others seem mutually incompatible. The challenge is to get the balance right.

I don't intend to go through them now,[5] though they do give you one answer to the question posed – what's the point of a Public Inquiry.

They are all important purposes. They are what a well-established and well-run Inquiry can achieve. But they need to be unravelled in our pursuit of an answer to our question. They can be divided into three categories. We can call the first category, the **forensic** purpose – the first purpose in my list. We can call the second category, the **social** purpose – the next three in my list. And, we can call the third category the **remedial** purpose – the last two in my list.

Now, setting up an Inquiry just for what I have called the forensic purpose is a valid reason for establishing an Inquiry, the aim being independently to get to the bottom of things. There is a valid point or purpose. It may not, however, justify the full apparatus and accompanying time and the many millions of pounds in cost of a Public Inquiry.

Equally, what I have called the social purpose, alongside the forensic purpose, is a valid reason again for setting up an Inquiry and gives the Inquiry a point. But, again, you may well wonder whether a careful forensic examination of a particular event or set of events, plus what some have called 'psychotherapy on a grand scale' warrants the cost, time and effort associated with a Public Inquiry. Certainly, I pursued these objectives in Bristol and found it very rewarding. but I didn't regard them as the principal reason I was there.

So, are these forensic and social purposes the point of a Public Inquiry? Most would say not. The point of a Public Inquiry to most, as it was to me in Bristol, would be defined by the remedial purpose – the learning and recommending. This is what a Public Inquiry is really about. The other purposes are a necessary preliminary and a desirable add-on.

So, does this remedial purpose, incorporating the two aims of learning and recommending, give a Public Inquiry a point which the forensic and social purposes may not quite themselves provide as sufficient justification? Is this the key to answering the question?

There was a time when you could have said yes. There were Public Inquiries which did indeed identify lessons previously unknown or barely grasped, and make important recommendations.

But there came a time when observers began to notice something. Wherever the hospital, whatever the subject matter, the lessons and recommendations were the same.

Over time, in the NHS it had become increasingly clear what makes things go wrong.

We **know** what puts patients at risk. We **know** what upsets patients in their interaction with staff. We **know** what causes so-called junior staff (and hierarchy is, of course, one of the problems we know about) not to complain. We **know**, we **know**, we **know**. Public Inquiry after Public Inquiry has identified the same problems and advanced the same solutions. Protocol after Protocol has spelled things out. The literature is full of what to do.

[5] See Chapter 16.

Just as it became increasingly clear what makes things go wrong, so it became increasingly clear, as I have said, what needed to be done.

But, what also became increasingly clear is that in some parts of the NHS what needs to be done is not getting done. The lessons are not learned and the necessary actions are not taken.

So, we wait for another disaster and hear the inevitable calls for yet another Public Inquiry.

But, what would be the point?

Of course, we can't prevent politicians bending with the wind, but if you want to achieve more than what I have called the forensic and social purposes, there *isn't* a point in having another Public Inquiry. The lessons are only too well known. Why spend time and millions of pounds saying what's been said before?

Rather than Public Inquiries, what is needed is action and the most critical action, echoing through Report after Report, is the need for effective leadership – leadership at all levels.

Take hospitals, for example. They are complex organisations. Leadership is everything. And, leadership is what is failing in those hospitals where things go wrong and where there are calls for a Public Inquiry.

Don't get me wrong. Things go wrong in the best run organisations. What I am talking about when I refer to things going wrong are systemic failures (as for example in the case of Maidstone and Tunbridge Wells NHS Trust and the outbreaks of the bacterium Clostridium Difficile[6]); failures of the system of leadership to deliver what is needed and what is well-recognised as being required to ensure that patients are well cared for and staff perform to their best; leadership to produce the right culture – a culture of care and caring.

There is a need to confront an inconvenient truth: that the state of leadership in parts of the NHS gives real cause for concern. I could cite many examples of systemic failures of leadership but here I just mention one – bullying – one of the most common and most corrosive problems in hospitals.

Commitment to the principle that the NHS is a service, there to serve, too often bends and often breaks in the face of bureaucratic procedures and self-serving attitudes. Leadership prepared to confront this state of affairs is too often lacking. Patients and staff get the wrong end of the bargain.

We need to acknowledge that the NHS is a political enterprise. We need to recognise that politicians blithely set targets and talk the language of shame and blame, ably assisted by the media. This reality constitutes an enormous challenge for leaders, particularly against a background of the differing agendas of different regulators,[7] and of financial constraint.

The challenge is made the greater when the calls for a change of culture are picked up by those who underestimate the complexity that such a change involves. The rhetoric of cultural change is used but often what is proposed is the greater use of regulators as police rather than what regulators should be. There is even the proposed resort to the

[6] Healthcare Commission's Report of the Investigation into C Diff outbreak at Maidstone and Tunbridge Wells NHS Trust, October 2007.

[7] Monitor and the Care Quality Commission [at the time].

criminal law (mentioned many times in the Executive Summary of the Report on Mid Staffs[8]). Then, there is the preoccupation, almost obsession, with whistleblowing, not recognising that it is essentially a defeatist approach, the very opposite of what a good leader should tolerate. Good organisations empower individuals to speak out. They do not build systems to enable the frightened to expose their concerns in circumstances of secrecy. Good hospitals, through good leaders at all levels, deal with the challenges that the NHS throws up.

In other parts of the NHS, outside the hospital, the care of patients teeters on the edge of safety and humanity.

Another Public Inquiry could be around a thousand corners.

But what would be the point?

We know the problems. We know the answers. We don't have to discover them again. We have the lessons. We don't have to spend years and millions finding them out again.

We just have to implement them. And, only good leadership, from the top to the bottom, will get us there.

How do you make good leaders? They don't grow on trees! That's another lecture![9]

[8] See fn 3.

[9] See the work of The Staff College: Leadership in Healthcare (Staff College), a national charity dedicated to developing leaders and helping them to deliver better outcomes. Its faculty comprises experienced leaders who have led large, complex organisations in the NHS, Defence, Business and Education. [I was a founding member].

19

Appraising the Value of Innovation: A Review for NICE[1]

1. Introduction

1.1 I was asked by Sir Michael Rawlins, the Chairman of the National Institute for Health and Clinical Excellence (NICE) in February 2009 to undertake a study in response to the views expressed by Sir David Cooksey in January 2009 in his *Review and Refresh of Bioscience 2015*.[2] Sir David wrote that 'Currently, the perceived problem for UK industry is that NICE appraisals do not operate in a way that is supportive of innovation, or uptake and access to medicines and therefore dissuade companies from investing in the UK'.[3] As a response to this 'perceived problem' Sir David offered Recommendation 16. This reads:

> There should be an independent inquiry to assess NICE's long term impact on cost, access to, and uptake of, medicines in the UK. There should also be an independent review of the way in which NICE values medicines so that the current economic evaluation is complemented by clinician, patient and research inputs on the value of innovation from their perspectives.[4]

1.2 The study that I was asked to undertake was intended to respond to the second of these recommendations.[5] I take it as a condition of my study that there is a perceived problem concerning innovation. It is for others elsewhere to determine whether this is so.[6] Subsequently, in its response to Sir David's review, the government rejected the

[1] This is an extract from a study commissioned by NICE and presented to NICE's Board, then released to the press on 22 July 2009.

[2] 'A Report to Government by the Bioscience Innovation and Growth Team' (Department for Business, Enterprise and Regulatory Reform).

[3] ibid, p 43.

[4] ibid, p 51.

[5] NICE's evaluations centre on the cost-per-QALY (Quality of Life Years) of any product judged against an upper threshold of [then] £30,000. If the cost were greater, without good reasons NICE would not recommend that the NHS pay for the product.

[6] Two points can be made. First, rather than tinker with the NICE's system to privilege innovation of a certain kind, it could be argued that there needs to be a fundamental re-examination of what science should pursue and how it should be pursued, and of the business model adopted historically by the pharmaceutical industry, premised on the pipeline and the 'blockbuster' drug. Second, it is important at all times to remember, as a matter of national policy, the importance to health and healthcare of health promotion and the prevention and avoidance of ill-health, and the myriad factors beyond the reach of the NHS which contribute to ill-health which should be addressed. It is, of course, a matter of balance, but this need for balance must never be overlooked, for shorter term considerations.

first recommendation, that there be a root and branch inquiry into NICE, deeming it not '… the right way of addressing the specific issues his report raises'.[7]

1.3 The terms of reference that I was given were:

to carry out a short study of valuing innovation aimed at addressing the following questions:

- What approach should be adopted by NICE to ensure that innovation is properly taken into account when establishing the value of new health technologies?
- Should particular forms of value be considered more important than others?
- How should innovation in health technologies be defined?
- What is the relationship between innovation and value?

1.4 It was agreed that I would begin work on the study in mid-April. I was asked to prepare a report which could be considered by NICE's Board at its meeting scheduled for 22 July 2009. In keeping with Sir David Cooksey's recommendation, it was also agreed that I would conduct the study wholly independently of NICE. The views and recommendations are mine alone.

1.5 What follows is that part of the Study which addressed the issue of innovation. In earlier sections of the Study I put innovation in the wider context of NICE's overall assessment of health technologies. This entailed consideration of two preliminary questions:

- What should be taken into account in establishing the value of new health technologies (health technologies are defined as drugs, medical devices, diagnostics and surgical procedures);
- Whether particular forms of 'value' should be regarded as being more important than others.

1.6 Once I had considered them, I was able to move on to innovation.[8] I asked:

- How should 'innovation' in health technologies be defined and how should its relationship with 'value' be described?

1.7 I made as my starting point the poignant comment of a representative of a patients' group at one of the Workshops I organised. She remarked that there had been a lot of talk about health economics and theoretical models, but not enough about what patients such as she wanted and needed. This captures the heart of the dilemma which NICE was established to address. The NHS exists to look after individuals (and those who care for them) when they need it. But, in the context of a limited level of resource, decisions have to be made as to how much of that resource may be spent in any particular set of circumstances. It is a zero sum exercise – with a limited amount of money, what is spent on X cannot be spent on Y.

[7] 'Government response to review and refresh of bioscience 2015 report' 7 May 2009. It is worth saying that the role and performance of NICE has regularly been examined by a variety of bodies, not least the House of Commons Health Committee in 2001–02 and 2007–08.

[8] I invited written submissions from interested parties and held workshops. The papers submitted and the proceedings of the workshops were published on NICE's website.

1.8 NICE decides whether the NHS should pay for this or that particular drug or product. The basis of NICE's system of appraisal is simple: something will be approved for use by the NHS if the improvements to health offered to patients are expected to exceed the cost to health that is inevitably forgone elsewhere in the NHS as a consequence of any associated costs, all within a fixed budget. Behind this simplicity lies much complexity, and yards of books, learned articles, papers and other material. The claims of both those who make themselves heard and those who are not heard must all be weighed. And weighing means analysis, policy (and health economics). It is not uncaring, despite the complaint of patients I referred to above. Indeed, it is the only way of caring in an organised and accountable manner: caring for and about all. This may not mean, however, satisfying everyone's claims.

2. Innovation

2.1 It was the importance of promoting innovation throughout the NHS and the perception that NICE did not do so as effectively as it could, but rather serves as a check to innovation, that prompted the setting up of this study. The QALY/ICER analysis at the heart of NICE's approach was particularly singled out for criticism. QALY stands for quality-adjusted life years. ICER stands for incremental cost-effectiveness ratio.[9]

2.2 In the original Directions to NICE, the Secretary of State for Health specifically required NICE to take into account in its appraisals '… the potential for long term benefits to the NHS of innovation'.[10] Furthermore, NICE in its own Guidance enjoins its Appraisal Committees to take account of the 'innovative nature of the technology, specifically if the innovation adds demonstrable and distinctive benefits of a substantial nature which may not have been adequately captured in the QALY measure'.[11] Thus, it is clear that NICE formally recognises the need to consider innovation, and is under a duty to do so. The question is what happens in practice.

2.3 To be clear, what is claimed as regards innovation is that it brings a particular benefit or value which should qualify a product demonstrating innovation for some special treatment by NICE. In other words, it constitutes a social value, but of a different order from other social benefits, such as a benefit to a particular group of patients, or benefiting productivity by enabling people to return to work. The difference lies not only in the duty laid on NICE to take specific account of it, but also in its importance as

[9] See NICE's *Guide to the methods of technology appraisal* (2008). According to York University's Health Economics Consortium 'an incremental cost-effectiveness ratio [ICER] is a summary measure representing the economic value of an intervention, compared with an alternative (comparator). It is usually the main output or result of an economic evaluation. An ICER is calculated by dividing the difference in total costs (incremental cost) by the difference in the chosen measure of health outcome or effect (incremental effect) to provide a ratio of 'extra cost per extra unit of health effect' – for the more expensive therapy vs the alternative. In the UK the QALY is most frequently used as the measure of health effect, enabling ICERs to be compared across disease areas'.

[10] Hansard does not record any definition of 'innovation' being offered by the government in the debate on the Order establishing NICE, 3rd Standing Committee on Delegated Legislation, 10 March 1999.

[11] At note 35, para 6.2.23.

representing the constant pursuit of the frontiers of real excellence on behalf of patients and the NHS.

2.4 Before exploring in greater detail what we should mean when we talk of innovation, there is a prior question of great importance and some complexity. The answer to it calls for a grasp of both policy as applied to health and the economy, and a detailed understanding of the model used by health economists in the ICER/QALY analysis. The question at its most general is: to what extent should any special treatment given to innovation be achieved by changes in the supply side, in the demand side, or both. Changes in the supply side are not part of NICE's brief. They are a matter of government policy and action. Changes in the demand side are, in part, within NICE's powers to effect.

2.5 There is a view that the current ICER/QALY system should not be adjusted (more than it currently is in exceptional cases) to accommodate innovation. Indeed, the view goes further and holds that if a product does indeed constitute real innovation, it will be seen as bringing more benefits. It will therefore attract more QALYs and thereby be capable of commanding a higher price. In other words, the demand side already does enough to promote innovation, and any further promotion should rest with government. Furthermore, to make inroads into the ICER/QALY approach, which I have said previously is at the heart of NICE's approach, would be to put in jeopardy the system of predictable (within limits) and consistently applied resource allocation which works to the benefit of all, not some.

2.6 These are powerful arguments. But, I suspect that they are too purist. I have no doubt that changes to the supply side are required. I also have no doubt that, if carefully orchestrated, (to avoid such well-known problems in government plans as perverse incentives or gaming) such changes could provide Pharma[12] with significant incentives to aim for innovation. But, I am sure at the same time that, as regards the demand side, some adjustment to the approach adopted by NICE is possible, without undermining its fundamental purpose and rationale.

2.7 In what follows, therefore, I will make some proposals as to how NICE's system of appraisal might be adjusted to take account of innovation. In doing so, I will seek to identify the challenges that these proposals represent to NICE and how they may be met. I will then suggest changes in the supply side.

2.8 The claim is that innovation should attract some special treatment from NICE. That special treatment could, for example, take the form of approving the product at a price which would otherwise take it beyond NICE's threshold, even after taking account of the QALYs awarded, because of the increased benefits achieved. (If the price was such as to mean that the product fell within the threshold, there would be no need for any special concern for innovation, save for speedy approval.) Clearly, the view of Pharma is that innovation warrants special treatment of this kind and if it is not granted, deleterious consequences for the industry (in the UK) and for patients and the NHS will follow. This is the issue for the demand side.

[12] The term commonly used to describe the pharmaceutical industry.

The Meaning of Innovation

2.9 In addressing this question, my first challenge was to establish what was meant by innovation in the particular context of pharmaceutical products, (recognising again the somewhat different circumstances of devices, diagnostics and psychological therapies, which I will consider later). It will come as no surprise that, while everyone was content to use the word, and everyone agreed that innovation was a good thing,[13] it was not easy to identify what was being discussed. In fact, as is common in policy-making, the absence of any hard centre of meaning allows people from all quarters to appear to be in agreement, without the need to nail down what it is that they were agreed on.

2.10 There is no shortage of definitions of innovation.[14] Their very number suggests an amorphous concept. It is clear to me that the notion of innovation has a range of connotations which are, to a degree, context-specific. And, the world of pharmaceutical products is one such context. As a first step, it may help to know what Sir David Cooksey had in mind when he called for this study. When I spoke to him he referred to innovation as connoting 'different ways of doing things which bring improved outcomes'. This helps. There is the idea of difference, or newness, and the idea that it represents an improvement on what went before. But, before going further, I remind myself what is being considered. The case being put is that a claim that a product represents an innovation entitles it to special treatment in the form of a higher price, or put another way, that the ICER/QALY threshold should be raised to accommodate a calculation of cost-effectiveness that exceeds NICE's normal range.[15]

2.11 If this is what is being urged, then it should be clear that something more than newness (or difference) plus some degree of improvement in effectiveness may be necessary to qualify as innovation in this specific context. This is because, in essence, what is at stake here is the effective use of incentives. The question for us is: should any incentives relating to innovation be put in place to make Pharma successful in its own right and in meeting the needs of patients, and what will enable NICE to get the best out of Pharma by way of a constant pursuit of innovation for patients and the NHS? The response is: the NHS needs the best, most up-to-date and effective products. NICE's system of appraisal and approval should reflect this need. NICE's system should serve to encourage Pharma to meet the NHS' needs. It should be so designed as to give Pharma

[13] See, for example, Lord Darzi's endorsement of the key importance of innovation in *High Quality Care for All: NHS Next Stage Review Final Report* (Department of Health, 2008) and the very recent *Life Sciences Blueprint*, note 9.

[14] Examples include: 'the successful exploitation of ideas' (DTI, 2003); 'the adoption of new-to-the-organisation or new-to-the-NHS technology products and/or service delivery processes, comprising incremental or disruptive change, and resulting in a significant improvement in patient outcomes, experiences, safety and potentially cost effectiveness' NHS National Innovation Centre (long on words but short on comprehensibility); 'when new drugs provide medical breakthroughs or significantly improve on standards of care delivered by existing treatments' (Office of Fair Trading, 2007).

[15] It is worth noting that of the countries studied by NICE's Decision Support Unit, few gave any particular weight to 'innovation' per se. Exceptionally, in Belgium the distinction is specifically drawn between 'innovation' and 'adaptation' and 'alternative' compared with existing products, but there are no procedures set out to reflect and give effect to this distinction.

an incentive to concentrate on products that are truly innovative, highly effective, and, critically, are valuable to the NHS. There should be no incentive to innovate in products which, for whatever reason, are not of any, or only very limited value to the NHS in meeting its responsibilities. Products that offer a limited variation on already-existing products will, of course, still be developed, (and some incremental improvement in such products is desirable[16]). But, they will not warrant any special treatment. Only if they are priced in a way that meets NICE's established approach will they warrant approval. Such products may be described as innovative, but the claim alone will cut no ice, nor bring any special treatment.

2.12 Where innovation becomes important, therefore, is when Pharma states that a product meets three initial criteria, in that the product:

- is new;
- constitutes an improvement on existing products;
- offers something more: a step-change in terms of outcomes for patients.[17]

As I have said, I am conscious that some would argue that the ICER/QALY analysis, properly conducted, would capture all of these features and leave no justification for a price which would take the product over the threshold. What I argue for here challenges that view. It calls both for a recognition of the increased social value of innovation,[18] and of the need for properly articulated criteria to recognise this value.

2.13 As a consequence, NICE's system of appraisal could adopt a variation on its usual approach to recognise innovation (as defined) in a particular case and, thereby, give a more general signal of this recognition. I realise that the term 'step-change' in the third criterion I set out is question-begging to a degree. Pharma can rightly say that it needs some guidance. For my part, I would suggest that NICE consider the following as being possible indications of a 'step-change':[19]

- the product significantly and substantially improves the way that a current need (including supportive care) is met;[20]
- the need met is one which the NHS has identified as being important;

[16] I discuss the notion of incremental innovation in para 2.20.

[17] Arguing that neither newness nor effectiveness separately or together constitutes innovation, Morgan and others may set the bar too high when they state that 'Pharmaceutical innovation requires novelty of effectiveness. Pharmaceutical innovations create value for society by making it possible to generate improvements in patient [sic] health … that were previously unattainable. It is the uniqueness of such health improvements that defines … innovation' (Morgan, Lopert, Greyson (2008) 1 *Open Medicine* E4–7).

[18] Health economists might argue that the value is not to the NHS but to the manufacturer in being able to operate in a more favourable (for the manufacturer) economic environment. But this is the point here: that there is a value to the wider economy in having Pharma working in the UK's economy and contributing to it, and the trick is to ensure that a quid is gained for the quo.

[19] What is sometimes called 'disruptive' innovation, Morgan, 'Innovative Health Technologies' Presentation to NICE's Citizen's Council, May 2009.

[20] When asked to rank the innovations they regarded as most valuable, NICE's Citizen's Council at its meeting in May 2009 ranked most highly an innovation which increases the quality of life.

- where appropriate, research on stratification (as referred to in Sir David Cooksey's review) has identified the population(s) in which the product is effective.[21] This may be all of the population with the particular condition or just a subset;
- the product has been shown to have an appropriate level of effectiveness – for example, benefiting 70% of the intended target group; and
- the product has marketing authorisation for the particular indication.

Recommendation: NICE should formulate a definition of 'innovation' along the lines set out in para 2.12 and criteria along the lines set out in para 2.13 so that a judgement can be made that a product meets the NHS' needs. The Secretary of State for Health should from time to time make explicit the priorities of the NHS regarding intervention and treatment.

Process for Responding to Innovation

2.14 If NICE were to adopt a special approach to innovation as defined, how should it proceed? The following process could serve as a basis:

- Pharma would need to signal as early as possible in the process of development that its product could well amount to an innovation as defined
- NICE would then need to work much more effectively with manufacturers and patients' groups to align the data to be produced from research not only with the needs of the regulator, but also with NICE's requirement for information to appraise and approve the product, with particular regard to what makes the product an innovation. A welcome start has recently been made by NICE in its creation of its Scientific Advice Programme. This is a key development in improving links generally between Pharma and NICE and is crucial in the case of innovation. Given the importance laid on stratification, such alignment should ordinarily begin from at least the point at which Phase III trials are embarked upon.
- To encourage competition within Pharma, (the key defining feature after all of a market), NICE could seek to ensure that sufficient advice and support (for example regarding data collection, see para 2.23) were made available to newer companies, so as to enable them to compete on level ground.
- As an incentive to Pharma, in the case of innovation a higher price could be accepted for some patients or indications, or even across the board, taking the cost-effectiveness of the product beyond the normal threshold. There could be an agreed higher threshold, determined by NICE. The price could then be maintained for a set period of time, eg 3–5 years, after which it must be adjusted to bring the

[21] It is high time that agreement was reached on the pooling, with appropriate safeguards, of NHS data for the purposes of stratification and bio-marking. The data is unique in the world. Using it wisely and carefully can produce a sea-change in the treatments on offer to patients and the care that they receive, as well as enabling manufacturers to succeed.

product within the normal threshold. NICE could achieve this by establishing a special protocol for innovation. Or, NICE could undertake the appraisal using one of the new schemes established through the recent revision of the Pharmaceutical Prices Regulation Scheme (PPRS) (2009), the 'flexible pricing' scheme, or the 'patient access' scheme.[22] It would be inherent in this approach to innovation that health losses would exceed health gains in the particular case. The justification lies in the incentives it offers to Pharma to strive for innovation and the consequent long-term benefit to the NHS and patients. Putting it another way, the health gain for the NHS though less than the health loss has an enhanced and beneficial value in that it amounts to an innovation, as defined. Also, it can be justified by the fact that it is only for a short and fixed time.[23]

- The fact that the NHS would lose in the short term means that, in this context, the ICER/QALY system and the consistency of approach that it represents are, to an extent, undermined. It follows that the criteria would need to be applied with extreme rigour.
- Agreeing a higher threshold, or using one of the schemes under the PPRS, in the case of products which constitute an innovation (as defined), will inevitably lead to a reduction in the funding available to the NHS to purchase other products. Given that the total sum available is fixed, and is likely to fall as public expenditure is cut over the next several years, the consequence might be that the threshold for a product which is not an innovation will have to be reduced.

Recommendation: NICE should establish a mechanism whereby Pharma can signal as early as possible that a product may constitute an 'Innovation' as defined in paras 2.12–13.

NICE should work closely with Pharma, using for example its scientific advice programme, to ensure that the data required by NICE to make this judgement is generated.

NICE should offer advice and support to newer companies to facilitate competition in the sector.

NICE should consider, as incentives to Pharma, agreeing a higher threshold in the case of 'Innovation' (as defined) and maintaining it for a fixed period (eg from 3–5 years) or agreeing the use of a scheme under the revised PPRS ('flexible pricing' or 'patient access').

NICE should revisit the threshold to be used in the appraisal of products which do not meet the criteria of innovation if a higher threshold or one of the schemes under the PPRS is used as an incentive to promote innovation.

[22] These schemes are complex. I see it as my role here to offer the challenge that they be employed to best advantage. The operational details are for NICE and others.

[23] Moreover, there are already a number of precedents for NICE's approving a product despite its exceeding the cost-effectiveness threshold, Submission from NICE, 'Value of Innovation', para 2.12.

2.15 Clearly, if NICE's Board regards such inroads into the ICER/QALY approach as unjustified, then, if it wants to recognise the special case of innovation, as it is obliged to do, it must either demonstrate in the clearest possible way how innovation as I have defined it is already encouraged within the current approach, including within the threshold. Alternatively, it must press for changes in the supply side to achieve similar results. For my part, I am persuaded that, if operated vigilantly and with constant attention to the extent of any gain to the NHS when set against the loss of quality-of-life-years of others, an approach of the sort I have suggested warrants adoption.

2.16 There is always the danger that the product fails in time to live up to expectations, despite the best efforts of those who originally evaluated it. The concern is clear. The manufacturers will have enjoyed a higher price, and the NHS suffered a commensurate loss until this failure is discovered. Subject to its continued effectiveness (even though it has not proved to be an innovation) it would remain something that those commissioning healthcare would be obliged to purchase, but at a reduced price to bring it within the established threshold. But, how will the NHS' loss be recouped? The most pessimistic answer is that it could not be, such that this problem means that the approach that I am suggesting in para 2.14 is not viable and should not be contemplated. But, there are other responses. The first is that, if the scrutiny of the claim of innovation is sufficiently rigorous, the problem is unlikely to occur, such that it is a risk worth taking in pursuit of incentives for Pharma and the best therapies for patients. Secondly, whether by Regulation or by agreement, NICE could have the power to re-appraise the product at a lower cost, as being an effective but not innovative (as defined) product. This might, of course, persuade the manufacturer to cease to produce it if it is no longer profitable (and if the later price has knock-on effects globally). Thus, a third option could be a straightforward system of reimbursement of the NHS, in a manner to be established by agreement between NICE, the NHS and Pharma, once it has been agreed by relevant experts that the product has not met expectations.

Recommendation: NICE should establish a mechanism whereby the NHS is compensated for the financial loss which will have been incurred under para 2.14 if a product subsequently proves not to meet initial expectations.

2.17 Of course, to be able to come to a view about whether the product is actually continuing to deliver the effective therapy which caused it to be treated as a special case as an innovation depends on continued surveillance of the product's performance. I will set out below (in paras 2.22–2.24) ways in which this need could be addressed. They too raise fundamental questions about the relative burden of cost to be borne by Pharma and others, including the NHS.

2.18 If the approach set out in para 2.14 were adopted, the NHS would get products to meet needs identified as important priorities. NICE would be able to meet the Secretary of State's direction that it takes account of the value of innovation to the NHS, and provide incentives to Pharma to do so. Pharma would receive clear signals as to what areas of development would be most rewarded, would be able to collaborate effectively with NICE, and be rewarded for success. The aim would be to realise the vision of Sir David Cooksey in his report that NICE, working with manufacturers, could not only ensure that patients receive early access to the best possible products, but, also give the UK a competitive advantage, by providing early assessments of the economic impact of products, so that manufacturers could understand and predict the market for their products with greater certainty. Indeed, NICE, having already established the reputation as a world leader in appraising products, could acquire the further reputation of leading the world in developing a system of appraisal which relentlessly looks for and drives innovation in the treatment of patients. The UK could become the crucible for the early adoption of treatments which constitute a real step-change in treatment for patients.

Recommendation: NICE should build on its reputation as leading the world in the appraisal of products to establish itself also as a world leader in promoting innovation and the early adoption of treatments.

2.19 NICE cannot do this alone. It can affect the demand side. It can and should bring together the various elements of this side of the equation into a coherent whole, in which it plays the role of both agent and sponsor of change. Pharma, as has been said, need to be engaged and know what is expected of them on the demand side. But, the supply side, whether additionally or alternatively, must also be addressed. The Department of Health, through its various agencies must facilitate research and the collection of data[24] before and after licensing, including through some properly controlled form of co-funding. The recently created Academic Health Science Centres must be brought into the picture, given their links with Pharma and their obligation to translate research into treatment in the NHS locally and more widely, even globally. And Whitehall, from the Treasury to the Department of Business, Innovation and Skills,[25] must play its part in making necessary adjustments to the supply side in such areas as financial support, incentives and taxation. The 'Blueprint' for the Life Sciences, emanating from the Office of Life Sciences and endorsed by the Department of Health, is an indication of the government's intention to adopt a cross-government strategy. It brings together proposals to 'give patients faster access to cutting-edge medicines',[26] to build 'a more integrated life sciences industry', to facilitate access to finance and to improve incentives through the tax system. All must be mutually reinforcing.[27] All must be done in the name of innovation – real innovation as I have suggested that it be understood.[28]

[24] It is worth saying here that the data to be collected must be the best obtainable to give the most robust evidence. Thus, regardless of what might satisfy the regulator, products coming to NICE for approval against the background of seeking to maximise innovation should be compared in trials with the best existing therapy, rather than the least effective or with placebos.

[25] [As it was then – currently the Department for Business, Energy and Industrial Strategy].

[26] On which see para 2.27 onwards.

[27] Sometimes referred to as the 'innovation ecosystem', Sainsbury 'The race to the top. A review of government's science and innovation policies' (2007).

[28] As Lord Drayson put it to me 'we must be mercilessly clear that we mean real innovation'.

Recommendation: NICE should urge government to make appropriate adjustments to the supply side, as recommended by Sir David Cooksey and the Office of Life Sciences to encourage innovation on behalf of the NHS and patients.

The Promise of Innovation

2.20 So far, I have considered the situation in which the manufacturer claims that a product amounts, here and now, to an innovation. What of the claim that the product holds out the promise of being an innovation, although currently it barely differs from existing products? It was put to me strongly that innovation is often incremental, and examples were cited. I accept the point. But, of course, this still leaves open the question of what to do when there is only the promise of something. It was suggested to me that the mere promise[29] of something amounting to an innovation at some time in the future should be enough to warrant a higher price now, and thus a higher cost-effectiveness ratio, going beyond the threshold. I find the argument unconvincing.[30] It really is a question of risk: who bears the risk of failure in the future and who profits from success? It is not clear to me why Pharma should be insulated from the normal winds of commerce. The makers of Betamax held out the promise of their machine as the future for video-recording. They got it wrong and lost out. There was no question of being able to charge a higher price as insurance against failure. The makers of VHS took the risk. They got it right and profited accordingly. Given that the market for medicines is much more stable and predictable, it seems to me that Pharma should bear this particular risk.

Recommendation: NICE should only offer incentives for innovation when it is realised.

2.21 But, that said, in keeping with my aim of seeking some incentives for Pharma to maximise the benefits to the NHS through innovation, this should not be the end of the story. I propose the following way forward as regards products which, it is claimed, hold the promise of innovation. Provided that the product in its current state is cost-effective within the threshold, as judged by NICE, and that the promise is of innovation of the nature previously described, the process of appraisal and approval could be adjusted to take account of this promise. There are several options already available to NICE. They are:

- approval on the basis that further research is carried out, sometimes referred to as 'in the context of a well-designed programme of research' (ie 'only in research'), or as 'approval with evidence of development'. (I discuss in para 2.23 how to ensure that the work is done and how the cost should be borne);

[29] The ABPI's submission argues that 'the failure to recognise or reward innovation in one area ***may*** compromise an entire pathway of … follow-on developments' (my emphasis); AstraZeneca in its submission talks of '***possible*** innovations' being lost to patients (my emphasis).

[30] As did NICE's Citizen's Council at its meeting in May 2009. And see the report of the Office of Fair Trading, *The Pharmaceutical Prices Regulation Scheme: an OFT market study* (2007).

- approval for a particular sub-group of patients;
- approval through a 'patient access' or 'flexible pricing' scheme.

NICE may argue that it already acts, or is beginning to act in this way. My point here is that what is needed is a formal and transparent process, triggered by a claim of the promise of innovation.

2.22 Two comments by way of further explanation are needed. First, use of the 'patient access' or 'flexible pricing' schemes may be the most attractive both to NICE and Pharma. For example, the 'flexible pricing' scheme could be operated in such a way that the product would be approved at a price which brought it within the current threshold, since it currently offers little by way of change. If the contemplated promise materialises, (and even allowing for the fact that an adjustment of the assessment of QALYs could, in fact, result in its remaining within the threshold), Pharma could receive, from the time that the increased benefit accrued to the NHS and patients, a higher price for a period of time, on the same basis as that which I have already suggested in para 2.12–2.13 for immediate innovation. Again, this would constitute a departure from the ICER/ QALY approach. This, in turn, would again mean that the consistency in principle and practice which currently underpins NICE's appraisals, would, in this context, be at risk. And, it would represent a net health loss to the NHS. It is a matter for NICE's Board to weigh this risk. For my part, I am persuaded that it is a risk which could well be taken, provided NICE remains vigilant that the rules of engagement, as set out, are observed and that Pharma commit themselves to staying within them. As a precautionary measure, NICE could pilot the approach for a period of time, eg three years, with the clear message that it will not be continued if the gain (real and projected) to the NHS does not justify its continued use.

Recommendation: NICE should consider establishing a formal and transparent process, using such options available to it as are referred to in para 2.21 to offer incentives to Pharma when a product is said to have the promise of innovation.

NICE should pilot the process for a period of (eg 3 years) if it decides to establish it.

Evidence of Continuing Effectiveness – Sharing Costs

2.23 Secondly, in all cases, further research or surveillance of the product's effectiveness and performance is called for. This is expensive. Moreover, Pharma would have little interest in conducting research, if it carries the risk of proving in some cases that a product is not what it was thought to be. Thus, some kind of arrangement to share the costs of further research and collection of data between the Department of Health, on behalf of the NHS, and Pharma may be necessary. The arrangement would stipulate that the product would only be made available to that number of patients necessary to conduct the required research or data collection, and that continued approval of the product would be contingent on the necessary research being carried out within a specified time-frame.[31] Any arrangement must, of course, avoid the situation in which Pharma gains while the product is being purchased and again through a subsidy of its research, while the NHS loses in paying the higher price for the product and also paying in part for the research which establishes the product's effectiveness. Support for the costs of R&D, in the form, for example, of cost-sharing, is not, however, a matter for NICE. It requires an adjustment to the supply side. If a way can be found to ensure that the costs of research are shared in such a way as to avoid the problems just referred to, Pharma and the NHS will gain if a product is, indeed, an innovation. The NHS will gain, through saving resources, if the product proves disappointing in due course.

2.24 This idea of sharing the cost of further research is one of the ways in which, as I have indicated, modifications can be made to the supply side. A parallel can be drawn with the support by way of public funding given in the USA and the UK to research in the form of Phase III clinical trials. Such trials are a very large component of the cost of developing a new product. Publicly funded support for them has been advocated by the Nobel Laureate in economics, Joseph Stiglitz.[32] In the US over $4 billion is spent by the NIH, and thus the federal taxpayer, on supporting clinical trials. In the UK, by contrast, government spends very considerably less. The principle can also be applied to other research, the aim of which is to gain further evidence about a product's effectiveness and performance. A way needs to be found whereby funds, from government, from the Medical Research Council, from the major charities which support research, and from Pharma, can be applied to carry out both the research and collection of data contemplated here. Great care must be exercised so that, on the one hand, Pharma does not gain undue reward, while also enjoying the incentives entailed in what is being proposed, and, on the other, that the nation's strategic focus regarding research is not skewed by an overemphasis on research into pharmaceutical products, important as it is. The need for a system of joint funding was, of course, recognised by Sir David Cooksey in his review of publicly funded research in healthcare: 'funding [should] be identified and formal arrangements be established between the NHS HTA [Health Technology Assessment] Programme, NHS SDO [Service Delivery and Organisation] Programme and NICE'.[33] I am aware that NICE, through the Medical Research Council, has commissioned research to take full advantage of the 'only in research' option. But, funding through the Department of Health remains a sticking point.[34] If government is serious about supporting innovation, this state of affairs, with all its complexity regarding the relationship between private enterprise and the public purse, needs to be addressed as a matter of urgency. The Office of Life Sciences' 'Blueprint' recognises the need to 'provide[s] an excellent environment for clinical trials and investigations',[35] but the proof of the

[31] I recognise that it is difficult to withdraw approval of a product once patients are receiving it, albeit that the number of patients may be limited to those involved in the gaining of further evidence.

[32] A Jayadev and J Stiglitz, 'Two ideas to increase innovation and reduce pharmaceutical costs and prices' (2009) 28(1) *Health Affairs* 165–68.

[33] Cooksey, *Review of UK Health Research Funding* (2006). The Health Select Committee was somewhat lukewarm in its support of the idea.

[34] I am aware of tensions in the Department of Health over funding, whereby quasi-semantic distinctions between eg types of 'research' (experimental and observational) and 'post-market surveillance' or 'audit' (as a general term) to determine the real effectiveness of a product, are drawn to protect funds. While understandable, a way through has to be found.

[35] Note 9 para 2.1 and 2.10 onwards.

pudding will be the ability to make collaboration between government departments and between government and industry really work.

2.25 It might be thought that my references to the supply side take me beyond my brief which is to consider the role of NICE. But NICE operates in a larger context. The context is one in which NICE needs evidence and data so as to carry out the best possible evaluation of a product. It is crucial, therefore, for NICE that appropriate research is carried out. Currently, for reasons beyond NICE's control, research of the sort which would assist both NICE and Pharma is not always being carried out. This state of affairs operates against NICE's interests (and, therefore, those of patients, the NHS and Pharma). It should be addressed.

Recommendation: NICE should make urgent representations to government, particularly the Department of Health, that its ability effectively to evaluate the value of products depends on the existence of data and information from appropriate research and study.

NICE should urge government to examine the funding of research and further study, working with Pharma and all other relevant parties, particularly academic health science centres, so as to generate data thereby enabling NICE to evaluate products as effectively as possible.

NICE should urge the Department of Health to support, with others, the funding of post-marketing surveillance of products' efficacy as well as safety.

NICE should work with the Office of Life Sciences to ensure that the proposals of the Office relating to research and data collection are acted upon promptly.

2.26 The same arguments can be made concerning the development of products for rare diseases. Currently, based on NICE's aim of maximising the gain in health from limited resources, rare diseases affecting small populations have not attracted the same expenditure on R&D and, thus, on development. Incentives of the sort already discussed could, therefore, be offered to Pharma to promote development and innovation in this area. The R&D costs could be subsidised, through involvement of the public purse, the enjoyment of 'market exclusivity' could be pursued, or, for an agreed period of time, the ICER/QALY threshold could be raised.

Recommendation: NICE should consider whether the same or a similar package of measures as those set out in para 2.14 should be used to give incentives to innovation and development of products for rare diseases.

Fast Track 'Innovation Pass'

2.27 Before leaving this discussion of innovation, I offer some comments on the proposed creation of a 'fast track' for certain products. The idea, as set out in the Office of Life Sciences' 'Blueprint', is that in certain limited cases, a product would be made available through funding from public sources without undergoing appraisal by NICE. Primary Care Trusts (PCT) would not, therefore, be under a duty to purchase the product for patients, but it would be available for purchase. The proposal is that the 'innovation pass' should be piloted for one year (2010–2011).

2.28 This notion of an 'innovation pass' clearly has implications for what I have been asked to look at. I begin by suggesting that if what I have already proposed regarding innovation is accepted, the need for a 'fast track' will be less strong. If, however, the idea is to be adopted nonetheless, there are a number of matters to be addressed. First, what products is this procedure intended for? Arguably, it should be limited to a product:

- which currently may only have 'conditional marketing authorisation';
- which, in the view of a Committee of experts is very innovative,[36] such as constituting, for example, a new mechanism for action, or reaching a new target;
- which, where relevant, is accompanied by evidence relating to stratification;
- where the body of evidence is still relatively limited and immature, but, in the view of the Committee of experts, is strong enough to suggest a high degree of effectiveness;[37]
- which is intended for a relatively small population of patients;
- which will not cost a great amount of money.[38]

When I refer to a Committee of experts, I contemplate the establishment of an expert advisory group, preferably by NICE as guardian of the system for approving products, to receive proposals and to determine whether they qualify. The process of decision-making must, of course, be clear and transparent, although, as ever, the decision will constitute a judgement by the experts. The Committee's decision should take the form of a recommendation to NICE, which would, in turn, advise the Department of Health.

2.29 The second question is who will pay for products approved under the proposed innovation path? Even though not approved by NICE, Primary Care Trusts could well come under pressure to purchase a particular product as a result, for example, of some campaign. The moment that products begin to be purchased without being exposed to analysis by NICE as to their cost-effectiveness, the whole system of rational resource allocation within the NHS would be threatened. Thus, if there is to be any 'fast track', the money to support it and allow for the products to be purchased, which will not be a large amount (ie in the tens of millions of pounds), must not come from the NHS, and thus not be part of the accounts of PCTs. It must be provided through some central government mechanism. The Office of Life Sciences' 'Blueprint' talks of £25 million from a

[36] For the reasons already set out I do not think that it is enough to have the 'promise of innovation', because it takes us from the realm of incentive to the realm of subsidy.

[37] The Committee would need to be alert to the dangers that if new products are diffused too early and without a proper assessment of their cost-effectiveness, it will be difficult (eg for reasons of ethics) to generate the necessary evidence as to efficacy, and that once a product is available, it will be more difficult to remove it through non-approval. This condition, in other words, must not be used as a back-door to approval by NICE.

[38] These criteria are more detailed than the general statement of intent set out in para 2.5 of the 'Blueprint', note 9. They constitute my recommendations to NICE, given that the 'Blueprint' states that NICE 'will play a key role in developing and applying eligibility criteria for the Pass', para 2.5.

'new ring-fenced budget' for the one-year pilot. (This might be thought to be rather too modest a sum to have any real impact.)

2.30 Thirdly, there should be a fixed time for which the product enjoys freedom from appraisal by NICE, perhaps up to three years. During this time, the further research necessary to confirm its value should be carried out. There may be a case, in keeping with what I have said previously, that the research could be funded jointly by Pharma and government, through some appropriate mechanism. Arguably, such funding should not come from the NHS, given that until NICE carries out an appraisal, the ratio of health gain to loss will not be known and the resources of the NHS might be already inappropriately depleted given what it is getting in return, without also funding research to see whether this is so. Moreover, Pharma has an incentive to conduct the necessary research, given the reward of approval by NICE and consequent requirement on PCTs to purchase the product. Finally, to advance the interests of what may be called UK plc, it would be appropriate to require that the research be carried out in the UK.

2.31 At the end of the period of freedom from appraisal, the product must be subject to NICE's established system of appraisal. In that appraisal it must be shown to be cost-effective within NICE's threshold. If it is not, or put another way, the manufacturer seeks a price that takes it beyond the threshold, it will not be approved. The three years of grace is a significant incentive to concentrate on innovation. Should the product not be approved by NICE at the end of the period, patients already receiving it should continue to do so, if it is deemed clinically appropriate, at the manufacturer's expense.

Recommendation: NICE should work with the Office of Life Sciences such that, if an 'Innovation Pass' is thought necessary and appropriate, conditions such as those set out in para 2.28 apply.

NICE should establish a committee of experts to advise on whether the criteria for use of the 'Innovation Pass' are met.

NICE should seek to ensure that funding for the purchase of the products subject to the 'Innovation Pass' comes from a specially created fund and not from the NHS.

NICE should seek to ensure that the 'Innovation Pass' during which a product is not evaluated by NICE should last for a fixed period of time (eg a maximum of three years).

NICE should seek to ensure that at the expiry of the fixed period of time the product is appraised by NICE and falls within the threshold for approval.

3. Diagnostic Tools, Devices and Other Therapies

3.1 It was clear from various submissions and from other comments that those involved in the development of diagnostic tools, devices and other therapies, particularly psychological therapies, felt that they were 'poor relations' as regards NICE's system of appraisal. The view expressed was that the paradigm for appraisal was the submission of evidence generated from randomised clinical trials (RCT) typically by Pharma. This approach, it was said, was often not appropriate, whether because, as in the case of diagnostic tools and devices, change is often experiential and continuous, or because RCTs are difficult and expensive to organise and might even slow up development. In the case of psychological therapies, similar comments were made about the inappropriateness of RCTs as well as the expense of conducting them. NICE, it was urged, should rely on other, different forms of evidence.[39]

3.2 I am aware that NICE recognises the different circumstances of those who develop these other technologies and has embarked on an examination of how best it can appraise them. Manufacturers, patients' groups and healthcare professionals have much to offer in such an examination and I am confident that their views will be sought. Clearly, the key lies in what constitutes evidence on the basis of which NICE may confidently make a decision. I welcome NICE's decision to establish the Medical Technology Advisory Committee as a way forward in dealing with claims of innovation in the evaluation of diagnostic tools and devices. NICE will now be able to engage with manufacturers regarding the evidence required and how such evidence can be developed and synthesised so as to make it possible to undertake a proper cost-effectiveness analysis. It is envisaged, as I understand it, that the Committee will decide which products require evaluation, and then, either direct the evaluation to one of NICE's programmes of evaluation or itself appraise the product and advise the Board, or call for more research and encourage the research to be done, even through co-operation with the NHS. In doing so, NICE will be reflecting the agreement of the House of Lords' Committee on Science and Technology with Professor Sir John Bell's view that there is a 'need to identify a new agency that can handle the clinical utility evaluation of diagnostics'. The Committee recommended that NICE take on this role.[40]

Recommendation: NICE through its Medical Technology Advisory Committee should play an increasingly active role in encouraging research into medical technologies to be carried out in the UK.

Psychological Therapies

3.3 As regards psychological therapies, there are clearly differences, as against pharmacological therapies, in what might constitute evidence of clinical effectiveness and how such evidence might be generated. The RCT is most suited to establishing the effectiveness of drugs, not least because the trial can be properly 'blinded'. As a consequence, the role of the therapist in the effectiveness or otherwise of the therapy is less significant, as compared with psychological therapies. That said, NICE cannot issue guidance without having some sound basis on which to proceed. Moreover, it is unlikely that a real understanding of the comparable effectiveness of a psychological therapy can be

[39] I am grateful to the submission of Schering Plough for pointing out that reliance on RCTs also presents problems in the area of paediatric care.

[40] See www.publications.parliament.uk/pa/ld200809/ldselect/ldsctech/107/107i.pdf p 32.

established without some form of trial. CBT (Cognitive Behaviour Therapy) has led the way in this acceptance of the value of trials and other forms of psychological therapy need to follow suit. NICE is conscious of the need not to privilege one form of therapy, simply because it can produce evidence from RCTs. What is needed is a systematic approach to evidence which is appropriately flexible and combines 'observed practice' with valid trials, moving from the former to the latter and then back to observed practice as further validation. Critical to the success of such an approach is both the need to collect data from practice and bring it together with data from other centres in the NHS, and the need to organise trials. NICE needs to emphasise the development of evidence of effectiveness and work with others to ensure that a proper research infrastructure is put in place. NICE might well seek to work with the newly established Academic Health Science Centres (AHSCs) or Collaborations for Leadership in Applied Health Research and Care (CLAHRCs) to make psychological therapies one of their research priorities, given the AHSCs' mission both to conduct research and to take the fruits of that research into the NHS locally and beyond. I am aware also that NICE is working with the Medical Research Council on research into the use of different types of evidence in its appraisals, such as 'colloquial' evidence and non-experimental evidence from disease registers.

Recommendation: NICE should work with others, particularly academic health science centres, to ensure that a sound infrastructure for research into the effectiveness of psychological therapies is established.

NICE should work with others to develop a systematic approach to evidence regarding psychological therapies, including the place of RCTs and non-experimental evidence.

Postscript

Apart from accepting the need to work more closely with Pharma, the Review made little headway. The 'fast track' initiative was soon abandoned. Pharma welcomed the part of the Review which suggested support (in the form of higher prices) for innovation, but objected to the notion of a quid pro quo whereby products which do not constitute any real improvement over existing products (often called 'me too') should receive less favourable treatment from NICE.

20

Research at Porton Down: An Ethical Assessment[1]

Introduction

The question I am asked to address is whether the trials involving volunteers which are described in the Historical Survey were conducted in an ethical manner. I interpret this to mean: did those carrying out the trials behave in a way which right-minded others would think at the time was ethically appropriate and justified, taking due account of prevailing values and circumstance. Of course, this proviso only goes so far. While it is important to recognise that views may change over time, for example, as to the balance to be struck between paternalism and freedom of choice, it must be said that there are outer limits to what is ethically appropriate conduct. Conduct which exceeds these limits cannot be justified by appeals to the prevailing values or circumstances of the times. Examples of ethically impermissible conduct in the context of research on humans, which no amount of references to the context or circumstances of the day could justify, would include 'experiments' involving the intentional infliction of torture, or the intentional causing of a person's death. These were regarded as repugnant long before the modern development of notions of human rights following the horrors of the Second World War. And, necessarily, it follows that appeals to cultural diversity, or the subjective right of states to determine for themselves what is morally acceptable, in this context cut no ice. Some moral prescriptions are universal in nature, if the notion of a common humanity is to mean anything.

What I will be asking, therefore, is whether the trials at Porton, even if carried out with honourable intentions (that is, the belief that the interests and rights of the volunteers were not being put improperly at risk and that the ends pursued were good and justified), in some way either went beyond the ethical standards of the day, or even

[1] This is the final chapter, which I wrote in the summer of 2002, of what came to be called *A Historical Survey of the Porton Down Volunteer Programme 1939–89*, issued by the Ministry of Defence in June 2006. Porton Down is the Government Research Establishment concerned with biological and chemical warfare. In the years between my writing my chapter and final publication, some changes were made to the Survey which I was not able to comment on. Thus, my chapter addresses facts made known to me in 2002. The Survey other than my chapter was written by a civil servant in the Ministry of Defence. The terms of my engagement were that I would make an independent assessment of what the Survey described, free from any editorial control by the MoD and that my findings would be made public without changes. The Survey and my chapter featured in the inquest in 2003 of Ronald Maddison, a National Serviceman who died in 1954 after taking part in a research programme.

beyond what should ever be contemplated by a civilised society. In the context of the Survey, the latter question, of exceeding the limits of what may be permissible whatever the times or circumstances, is largely of academic interest only. But, it must not be ignored, particularly given the backdrop of war and the threat of war which may be offered to justify conduct. For, this is the context of the research at Porton. It must be borne in mind that the temptation always exists to invoke external threats and the national interest as a means of justifying what would otherwise be thought morally doubtful or impermissible. The temptation may be to stretch the limits, or even to go beyond them. It is important for me, therefore, always to keep in mind what, if any, influence war or the threat of war and the consequent invocation of the national interest should be allowed to have on the conduct of research into aspects of warfare.

The trials conducted at Porton are described in the Survey. The Survey was conducted with very great diligence. The amount of research and analysis was considerable. The expressed intention was to examine and report openly on all the various sources of documentary evidence. I did not review the sources themselves. My comments here, therefore, relate to what was produced as a consequence of the research undertaken. I have no reason, however, to doubt that the Survey reflects its stated intention. I did review some films (which I refer to). I did not see all of the very many films which are held in the archive of the Imperial War Museum, the quality of which, in terms of preservation, varied considerably, To that extent, I gained only a partial picture and do not, therefore, greatly rely on them as evidence (although I do refer to them briefly at one point ('Formality of Consent' below)). I was, however, involved in the conduct of the Survey in one regard: from time to time I requested that further information be gathered which would allow certain central ethical concerns to be addressed. My requests were always met, subject to one exception which it was beyond the Survey to meet and which I refer to later (the recording of the recollections of the research scientists working at Porton during the relevant time). Moreover, my independence was respected at all times. As agreed, there was no editorial control on the part of the MOD over what I might say.

Guiding Principles

In writing this assessment, I adopted certain guiding principles, or assumptions. I set them down here, so that my approach to the material contained in the Survey can be understood (and, if appropriate, challenged). They are, in effect, a series of first principles, rather than the product of a synthesis of various Codes or Guidelines, though in large part, they do reflect them.

1. The ethics of research on human volunteers is an area of systematic study and enquiry which was relatively neglected until as late as the 1980s. Codes and Guidelines had existed for some time, and appeared more frequently from the mid-1970s onwards, but the awareness of them varied, as did the understanding of what they might mean when applied to the reality of actual research. Moreover, it is in the nature of the subject that there have always existed differing views as to what conduct is appropriate. Indeed, a book could still be published in 2001 by the British Medical Journal with the title *Informed Consent in Medical Research*, in which what most would regard as the core notion of research ethics, that of consent, is the object of critical and, in some cases,

skeptical appraisal.[2] Thus, we are not dealing here with an area of clear, agreed rules akin to a statute (if ever even statutory language were clear!). We are dealing with general precepts, largely in the form of exhortations to good conduct. The translation of them into practice has been left until recently, (with the advent of the supervisory role of Ethics Committees), to the integrity, the good sense and the conscience of the researcher.

2. It is crucial to recognise that my assessment represents my judgement based on the facts as they appear in the Survey. Being a judgement, there always exists the possibility that others may disagree. Such disagreement, to be valid, however, must be reasoned and not merely based on prior unproven assumptions or bias.

3. Conduct may only fairly be judged in the context of the times (subject to what was said earlier about the existence of limits which do not change over time). This means that it would be wrong to use as a standard for assessment the developed concern for human rights which is part of current discourse about research, when considering conduct which happened 40 or 50 years ago. The ethical evaluation of research has been an evolving process. It is still going on.

4. Research on human volunteers was not only conducted at Porton Down over the relevant period. It has been an established feature of the development of medical science and of pharmaceutical products for decades. Indeed, one of the first formal attempts to prescribe how researchers should conduct themselves appeared at the end of the nineteenth century in the form of the Prussian Code of 1900. Any assessment of the conduct of research at Porton, therefore, must be informed by some understanding of how research was conducted and monitored elsewhere at the relevant times.

5. The context in which trials were conducted at Porton was one of war and the threat of war and of civil disorder. The Survey covers first the period before the Second World War, when the horrors of the use of gas by the enemy in the Great War were still etched in the folk memory of the nation. Secondly, it covers the period of the 1939–45 War, when the nation's survival hung by a thread and the perceived risk of the use of gas and other chemical agents was great, as was the perceived need to retain an offensive capability. Thirdly, it covers the period of the Cold War, interspersed as it was with localised conflicts, during which the Soviet Union and other countries were understood to be developing a range of deadly chemical agents for offensive use. And, during this third period, there were times of civil disorder, both in the United Kingdom and in its Colonies, which the governments of the day saw as calling for responses which included incapacitating chemical agents. In short, the aim of the research at Porton was the defence of the realm, the protection of its military and (to a lesser extent) police, and the protection of its civilian population. The nature of the threat and, therefore, the challenge to the researchers at Porton are set out in the Survey. The trials conducted at Porton reflect Porton's response to this challenge.

As has been said, the extent to which this context may justify that which in other circumstances may be judged impermissible must be examined. But, it is not hard to imagine that those pressing for results in government and those carrying out the research saw the work at Porton as of a different order from the conduct of research by, for example, pharmaceutical companies developing new medicines. This is not at all to say that they regarded themselves as free from constraints. The Survey demonstrates

[2] Doyal and Tobias (eds), *Informed Consent in Medical Research* (BMJ, 2001).

that there was constant reference to safety and risk. It is merely to say that in their eyes, and I venture to suggest, in the eyes of the population generally, the work might have been regarded as simply more important in the scheme of things. It would be wrong, therefore, to ignore this sense of the importance of the work being carried out.

6. Despite the best efforts of those conducting the Survey, the picture which appears is necessarily incomplete:

(a) Documentary evidence exists. It is what the Survey relies on to a very great extent. But, it cannot tell the whole story. For earlier decades it is sparse or non-existent. Later, it is more complete, but must be seen against the background of other information, instructions and exchanges which did not find their way into documents but which were undoubtedly part of the context in which volunteers were recruited and took part in trials. In the absence of this undocumented evidence, there is a tendency to treat the documents which do exist as if they told the whole story. They do not. Moreover, because it is written down, there may be a tendency to give more weight to a particular entry in a record than it should properly be asked to bear. Selected quotations may be useful as giving an impression of what went on. To that extent, I shall use them. But, they are incomplete evidence, at best. They do not tell the whole story. They can lend support to a view, but they cannot serve as definitive proof of what was going on.

(b) The Survey is assisted by the recollections of volunteers. But, many, indeed most, of the trials took place long ago. Memories, therefore, may not be reliable. This is not to impugn the integrity of those volunteers whose recollections are reported in the Survey. It is merely to acknowledge that what may be remembered is inevitably filtered through and affected by the experience and events of intervening years. Moreover, the volunteers were not, of course, a homogenous group, nor do they all tell the same story. Furthermore, those whose recollections are recorded do not constitute a scientifically designed sample, such that their recollections may be relied on as representative of all. They are, in fact, a tiny proportion of all the hundreds of thousands who took part in trials over the decades. At best, therefore, their recollections are anecdotal evidence. That said, however, the volunteers whose recollections are recorded all have one thing in common. They were all on the receiving end of the trials which were carried out at Porton. To ensure as complete a record as possible, therefore, their recollections ought to sit alongside the recollections of those who conducted the trials. This is not so as to set up some sort of opposition, which may not, in fact, exist. It is merely to enable the researchers' recollections to add to and thereby enrich the account which the Survey seeks to construct. Unfortunately, for contingent reasons, having to do with the involvement of the police, the Survey was not apparently able to take account of the researchers' recollections. This is a serious gap.

It is serious not only because we are denied their evidence. It is also serious in terms of fairness. To the extent that the evidence which *is* available may suggest that the conduct of a trial (or trials) was not proper, this, directly or indirectly, may constitute an adverse comment on those carrying out the trial(s). Without the opportunity to hear their response, it must follow that, for the sake of fairness, any conclusions which I reach which reflect adversely on researchers must be regarded as tentative only: amenable to being displaced should further evidence be made available.

(c) There are some questions which I have not asked, even though they are clearly of considerable (some might say crucial) importance. These relate to why certain trials, or categories of trial, were carried out at all. An example may be the lengthy and risk-prone research on liquid nerve agents, such as GB [known as *Sarin*]. The effect of GB *vapour* could be said to be far more important, in the scheme of things, than the effects of liquid GB, not least because, if delivered, for example in a bomb, relatively few would be affected by the liquid who would not also have been affected by the explosion of the bomb itself. The critical effect to be studied would be that caused by the vapour produced and spread by any bomb. Yet, trials related to *liquid* GB went on for years.

One reason why this question might properly be asked is that it is an accepted rule of thumb that bad science is bad ethics: if a trial is scientifically flawed, it should not be carried out. To carry it out, therefore, is unethical. (An example might be the testing of the substance in the captured German shells discussed later ('Prior Research' below)) I have chosen to leave unanswered this question why research on liquid GB went on for years but others may wish to pursue it further.

My reasons for doing so are as follows. First, I am not a scientist and thus do not know, nor does the evidence tell me, enough to reach a firm conclusion. Secondly, there may have been evidence from intelligence or other sources which justified the research, but which is not revealed in the Survey. Thirdly, the research at Porton was, as I shall explain later, carried out under the supervision of various committees. It might be thought that these committees would have satisfied themselves that any proposed research was necessary. On this view, it would be difficult, though not impossible, to second-guess the judgement made at the time. In fact, however, the committees seem to have been concerned either with wider strategic questions as to the direction of research, or with the particular, and critical, issue of safety. The Survey does not identify how the territory in between, in which the questions whether Porton should, in fact, be doing these particular trials at all, or whether the information sought was necessary, was covered, if at all. So, the question lingers.

My Approach

It is important to state at the outset that it is not the aim nor intention of this assessment to examine each and every trial carried out at Porton during the period covered by the Survey. The reasons are obvious. There were many thousands of trials. They varied greatly in nature. And, the quality of the evidence available as to how they were conducted also varies greatly. Instead, the approach I adopt is to identify:

1. the mechanisms for supervising the conduct of trials;
2. the general patterns or trends in the conduct of trials which emerge;
3. specific issues or cases which warrant particular attention.

In following this approach, I take account of the rather gradual recognition among researchers (and even more so among the general public) that research on healthy human volunteers ought in some way to be supervised (the word 'regulated' may be too strong). Scientists did not feel the need to be told how to behave, (and some still do not!): to a degree it would have been seen as insulting in the tenor of the times. The strong assumption was that scientists, especially if they were also doctors, could be relied on to act properly. This view prevailed for much of the period under review, and, albeit in an attenuated form, survives to this day. Paradoxically, the emergence of the Nuremberg Code in 1947 was thought by researchers here in the UK to have little to say about the research which *they* carried out, because it grew out of the atrocities committed in the name of science and research by the Nazis before and during the Second World War. As Professor Beeson put it in 1964, as recorded in the *Journal of the American Medical Association*, 'I think we must read the Nuremberg Code in reference to the conditions under which it is written. This is a wonderful document to say why war crimes were atrocities, but it is not a very good guide to clinical investigation which is done with high motives'.[3] This comment is not repeated here to endorse it, but merely to record what influential commentators at the time thought. Subsequent Codes and Guidelines were also seen as, to a degree, remote from what researchers actually did.

A major incentive towards developing a greater engagement with ethics came with the involvement of organisations which funded research, not least the Medical Research Council. Its first formal statement on research ethics appeared as early as 1953, but it, like many that followed, was directed at clinical, therapeutic research on patients and its special problems, rather than research on healthy volunteers. It was only later, in 1963, that reference was also made to the latter form of research. By making the observance of certain ethical standards a condition for receiving funds to conduct research, the attention of researchers was obtained. But, perhaps the single most important stimulus was the decision of the Royal College of Physicians to take a lead both in championing the cause of the ethics of research and in setting down Guidelines which were accessible, comprehensible and measured. It was not until 1973, however, that the Royal College formally addressed the question of research on healthy volunteers.

Government then became engaged and from then on the ethics of research have received increasing attention. Guidelines have been refined; sub-areas, such as for example, research on children or the mentally incapacitated, have been developed; a scholarly literature has grown up; and teaching and training in research ethics is widespread. But, this particular flurry of recent developments has only occurred over the past fifteen years or so.[4] Much of it post-dates, therefore, the period covered by the Survey. Moreover, there is inevitably a considerable gap in time between the promulgation of what is represented avowedly as advice and its translation into the practice of those actually carrying out research. This being so, it is of the first importance to avoid looking back through the perspective of hindsight. This leads us again to the proposition that the only way fairly to assess the conduct of the trials by the researchers at Porton is by reference to the standards of the time.

[3] Grimley Evans and Beck, 'Informed consent in medical research' (2002) 2(3) *Clinical Medicine*.
[4] [Writing in 2002].

The Commissioning and Supervision of Research at Porton

Porton conducted research at the behest of the Services, through the War Office, later the Ministry of Supply and still later the Ministry of Defence and its Chemical Defence Research Department. This does not, of course, mean that Porton was obliged to do everything that it was asked, particularly, from the point of view of my assessment. That said, if research was undertaken, those who directed Porton and worked there remained responsible for the conduct of it. If conduct was improper, it remained so whether or not it was done in compliance with requests from others, even the government of the day. This is not to say that governments asked for research to be carried out which was acknowledged to be improper. It is only to say that, from the standpoint of ethics, it is not open to Porton to plead some form of 'superior orders' to justify whatever was done.

There is clear evidence that Porton recognised this. On a number of occasions, the evidence shows that those at Porton indicated that certain research:

1. should not be carried out on ethical grounds, for example, research on agents whose primary mode of action was to induce hypo- or hyper-tension; or
2. would have to be carried out first on animals (for example, the Committee for the Safety of Human Experimentation (COHSE) insisted that dyes be tested first on animals); or
3. would perhaps take longer than envisioned (human studies of T4423 (a nerve agent) were only begun after 10 years of work on animals).

Equally, there is evidence of constraints moving in the opposite direction, placed by government and its Scientific Advisory Committee (SAC) on what Porton might be allowed to do in fulfilling what was asked of it, (for example, in the case of V agents (nerve agents), and in the conditions laid down by the Adrian Committee, noted later).

In carrying out their research, Porton was supervised by committees which went by different names at different times. The word 'supervised' is important, since it appears clear that the committees not only monitored the strategic direction of research into chemical warfare, but from time to time gave technical advice, particularly advice on safety. As the Survey makes clear: '… the work at Porton, since it was opened in 1916, has been directed according to the needs of the Armed Services. Approval for work done at Porton with volunteers was obtained for *types* [*my emphasis*] of human studies up to the mid-60s. Thereafter, it became usual to seek approval *for every human study* [*my emphasis*]. From the mid-60s this approval was sought from a committee with members from outside Porton'. Thus, there are numerous examples in the Survey both of the relevant committee approving a research project and of stipulating that research was not to be carried out, at all or until certain conditions were met. One such example is the refusal by COHSE in 1976, on grounds of safety, to allow the carrying out of a trial into exposure to high concentrations of CR (a form of tear gas) over a short period of time.

The importance of referring to this system of supervision is twofold. First, it meant that Porton was accountable to others who might properly be assumed by those working at Porton and those outside (ultimately the general public) to represent and reflect the values of the day and, thereby, offering not only scrutiny but also validity to what was done. Secondly, the various supervisory committees over time contained a proportion of members who were outside the communities of the armed forces and research into chemical warfare. About half of the members of the Chemical Defence Advisory Board (CDAB), from 1946 onwards, were independent 'outsiders'. Further, about half of the members of the CDAB's five Sub-Committees were equally independent, including the important Applied Biology Committee (ABC). The same was true of the subsequent Medical Committee (MC). The ABC was established in 1965, following internal disagreement in Porton about the safety of trials on incapacitating agents, specifically to be the 'Father Confessor' for Porton's staff and to 'damn the proposals [for research] of those who were trying to go too far too fast'. The Survey describes how, at least after the ABC had become the MC in 1973, these 'outsiders' had the right, which they exercised, to meet as a separate group in 'closed meetings' to discuss particular aspects of the research at Porton (for example, the closed meeting to discuss trials of drenching with CR gas in 1973). This reinforces the proposition that the research at Porton was subject to external scrutiny, supervision, and approval.

Perhaps the most crucial development, described in the Survey is that, from 1965 onwards, the ABC, with members from outside Porton and government, was given responsibility for advising on safety *and ethics* and for approving studies on human volunteers which Porton proposed. This superseded the supervision which had been exercised from 1963 by the internal committee, COHSE. An example of COHSE's supervision can be found in the decision not to conduct further trials of TL 2833 (an incapacitant) because of the risk of cerebral hypoxia. The more wide-ranging discussion of safety which this decision formed part of is considered later. Further, in 1972, both the MC and COHSE exercised close supervision of the trials involving drenching volunteers with CS gas and CR gas.

It follows that the researchers at Porton were not free, (even had they wished), to ignore the views and values of the wider community. (There is at least one example which seems to suggest otherwise: the use of GF in studies in 1963–64. The Adrian Committee had stipulated in 1953 that, of the G agents,[5] only GB should be used in trials. No explanation is given for why this condition was breached, but it is suggested in the Survey that the fact that the results were widely published suggests that Porton may have received authorisation to conduct them. There is no evidence offered to support this view, but it appears to be plausible.)

It is important, however, not to press this point concerning supervision so as to suggest that the research carried out at Porton necessarily always was in accordance with the general ethical principles of the day. This is because, as was said earlier, the supervision seemed only to go so far. In translating any general permission that they received, the researchers still had discretion as to how exactly to proceed. Thus, although constrained generally, for example, to ensure that research was conducted with due regard to the safety of the volunteers, it was still open to the researchers in principle to interpret this constraint in ways which went beyond the permissible. This is one of the questions which I will consider in greater detail later.

But, the important point here is that the existence and exercise of scrutiny and supervision from outside suggest that it is hard to argue that the researchers engaged

[5] All varieties of nerve gas.

in *egregious* departures from the principles of proper conduct of the sort which would be condemned by all civilised society, unless it is argued that the 'outsiders' were all committed to the conduct of research in an unethical manner and colluded with the researchers at Porton in this. The existence and exercise of scrutiny and supervision do not demonstrate, however, that the researchers never behaved unethically, in the exercise of their discretion in conducting a particular trial. This remains for me to examine.

In this examination, it will be necessary to bear in mind that the researchers at Porton did not always speak with one voice. The Survey refers to examples when researchers disagreed among themselves as to how properly to proceed, and when there was disagreement between researchers and senior staff. The Survey describes one such example: tests of incapacitating agents on human volunteers were suspended in 1965 because of concerns over the programme. The Head of the Medical Division at Porton doubted the evidence that the agents were safe and expressed the view that 'it would be unethical' to conduct trials in peacetime. He banned all further trials involving hallucinogenic agents. The medical staff at Porton were also concerned. One was described as 'very near breaking point'. Two resigned. The Director of Porton, however, perhaps reflecting the pressure he was under from the Services, challenged this 'issue of medical conscience'. He convened a meeting of outside experts at University College London specifically to determine what 'our medical colleagues outside Porton would consider justifiable', that is, to discover what were the prevailing standards of the day.

The Head of the Medical Division was ultimately reassured by the views expressed and trials on incapacitating agents began again. The significance of this expression of concern and subsequent discussion lies in the fact that there was clearly an awareness of the need to conduct research in an ethically proper way and a preparedness to discuss how this should be achieved. This is not to say that the appropriate course was always adopted. But, it does say that those at Porton were sensitive to ethical concerns, rather than proceeding in some kind of ethical vacuum.

The Conduct of Research

As I said at the outset, I intend to concentrate here on what may be called general trends or patterns in the research at Porton. I will refer to specific examples when they may illustrate the discussion, but in doing so, I am conscious of the need to prevent a particular example from becoming the basis for a general conclusion. Examples belong in a context and I will seek to see them in this way.

It may be helpful to consider what I call general trends by reference to the various central ethical concerns which are relevant to the conduct of research on healthy human volunteers.

Prior Research

Given that research on healthy human volunteers should not expose them to risks of harm, (something which I will explore in detail later), it was accepted during the period of the Survey that research should first be conducted on animals, where appropriate, and that the relevant literature should be searched and studied. One example of extensive prior research can be found in the considerable work on GA, GB and GD carried out on animals.

An unusual exception was when, in 1945, the substance in captured German shells was tested simultaneously on rabbits and human volunteers. When one of the rabbits promptly died, the trial was immediately ended, and the substance washed off. The reason why this approach was adopted may be that it was assumed that the substance was a vesicant [an agent that causes blistering], similar to mustard gas. It turned out, however, to be an otherwise unknown nerve gas, GA. The approach taken may be criticised as exposing the volunteers to unnecessary danger. Routine tests carried out to determine which of the known substances it was would have shown that, in fact, the substance was unknown. At that point, suitable precautions could have been taken. Instead, volunteers were put at risk of serious harm. The approach can be compared to the appropriately cautious approach described in the Survey which involved putting the particular concentration of CR gas in liquid form into the eye of a rabbit 30 minutes before putting it into a volunteer's eye.

The aims behind the extensive use of animals included the identification of responses to particular substances and the point at which those responses became dangerous and even fatal. Assuming that the information obtained was transferable across species, from non-human animal to human, (different animals were used for different tests), the tests allowed researchers, in principle, to control the risks to which the volunteers were exposed.

There is ample evidence that research on animals was seen as an essential first step before trials of the effects of a substance on humans were carried out. Indeed, on some occasions, the research on animals took place over a number of years before researchers deemed it safe to proceed to trials on humans, (the Survey describes tests on animals which took four years (1947–51), before the nerve agents were tested on the skin, although, as I shall describe later ('Trials at the Edges of Knowledge' below), volunteers were still exposed to danger. Equally, the work on V agents [another group of nerve agents] was pursued for five years (1953–58) before human studies were begun).

The exception to the prior use of animals was in the case of psychoactive agents. The view taken was that prior research on animals would be of no benefit when what was being explored was the effect of an agent on a human's motivation or powers of concentration. Instead, the researchers relied on prior studies carried out on humans and reported in the open literature. For those incapacitating agents about which little was known or reported in the literature, the medical staff at Porton carried out tests on themselves before exposing volunteers, setting the initial doses very low and gradually increasing them until an effect was observed. That said, animals were, in fact, still used in the initial stages of research into these agents in 1961–63.

Consent

Consent is undoubtedly the most important ethical pre-requisite of research on healthy human volunteers. The word 'volunteer' signals as much. The guiding principle is that people are being asked to come forward to participate in research, the results of which are not intended to be of any direct benefit to them, and, as such, they should not be taken advantage of, or exploited. They should only be involved in research if it is clear that they have agreed (consented) to do so. In this way, proper respect is shown to each person's right to choose.

While the general principle of the supremacy of consent is simple to state, the emergence of consent as being of crucial significance, its meaning and its application to concrete circumstances are less clear. As regards its emergence, it is important to note that the need, or even desirability, of consent has prompted debate over the period covered by the Survey. But, it is fair to say that this debate has focused on what is called 'therapeutic research', that is, research designed directly to assist the research subject while at the same time generating information of a generalisable nature, pursuant to recognised scientific principles. Such research may well be conducted on the very ill and there have been those who have argued, and still argue now, that to seek consent in all circumstances may, in some circumstances, be inappropriate and even cruel. The same argument has not, however, been employed in the case of 'non-therapeutic' research, that is, research on healthy volunteers. In my view, it has no place in the context of such research. Thus, it has no place in my assessment of the research conducted at Porton. Nor is there any evidence that the argument was reflected in the approach to research adopted at Porton. Although, as will be seen, there is room for discussion as to the quality of the consent obtained in some circumstances, there can be no doubt that, as a matter of principle, the need for consent was recognised throughout.

Turning now to the meaning and application of the notion of consent, in what follows I will use the term 'real consent' to describe consent which can be said to be ethically sound. To be real, it is now accepted that consent has to meet certain criteria, although these criteria were only effectively articulated over the last two decades. Previously, it was more a case of their being intuitively understood, rather than expressly articulated. Three criteria are ordinarily identified, each of which itself calls for closer analysis. In short, real consent is not straightforward. The three criteria are:

1. that the volunteer be competent to consent;
2. that the consent be based on sufficient information to allow a choice to be made;
3. that the volunteer truly is a volunteer.

The issue of competence need not detain us here. It is largely concerned with the mentally ill or the mentally disabled, children of tender years, and the elderly who may be confused. The assumption may properly be made that those who volunteered to attend Porton did not fall into these categories, nor were they otherwise mentally incompetent to consent.

So, I turn next to the issue of information. This is of central importance. The accepted view is that a researcher has a duty to give to each research subject that information which will allow the subject to make a considered choice whether or not to take part in the research. Such information operates at a number of levels. At the most *general* level, it means that the research subject must be aware of the purpose for which he is being recruited: that is, that he is involved in some form of research, (a test, or trial, or some such word). At its most *specific*, it means that the subject should be made aware of the particular features of the particular test or trial in which he is being invited to participate. (I add, by way of parenthesis, that the Survey at one point gives too specific a meaning to the word 'purpose', interpreting it as referring to what a specific trial would involve, rather than to the general idea of being involved in research.)

General Information

The distinction between general and specific information is of considerable assistance in understanding and assessing the material described in the Survey. In my view, the distinction is helpful in understanding the approach adopted towards recruiting volunteers for research at Porton.

Prior to 1964, general calls were made for volunteers in a series of stages. The calls went out from the War Office to Service Departments, which then wrote to Units. After 1964, the system changed. Notices calling for volunteers appeared in the official administrative instructions issued by the MOD and the Service Departments, to which all service personnel had access. Notices issued by the MOD were then translated into Notices issued by the various Services. Porton also began in the 1960s to recruit directly from Units in the form of 'special intakes'. While there is a wide range of evidence in the Survey of the formal Notices which appeared after 1964, there is no direct evidence, other than the recollections offered by some of those who volunteered, of what was said or done later in the process of recruitment.

As regards the earlier calls, before 1964, that went from the MOD and Service Departments, the available evidence suggests that the proposed forms of words to be used contained little or no specific information for potential volunteers concerning the nature of the trials which they would be exposed to. The calls were general in nature and, at the same time, couched in reassuring terms. According to the Survey, the Army's wording in 1961, for example, stated that 'the tests carried out at [Porton] are carefully planned and are arranged so as to eliminate foreseeable danger. They are carried out under medical supervision'. Reference was made in only one Notice to possible physical discomfort, which is described as 'usually very slight'. Taking account of the generality of trials, however, this is undoubtedly true, though not particularly revealing.

As regards the Notices which were issued after 1964, in the form of Defence Council Instructions (DCIs), it is clear from the Survey that the various Notices differed among themselves and over time. Some were more specific on some matters, others did not mention matters which could, as a matter of first impression, be regarded as important in affecting the choice made by the volunteer. One such matter is whether or not the volunteer would be exposed to danger, and, if so, to what degree of danger. In fact, long before 1964 and the change in the method of recruitment, references were made to danger and to risk. The words used, however, were clearly intended to play down risks (although, by and large, the risks of harm were indeed remote). In 1950, for example, a War Office recruitment notice stated that 'the tests are carefully planned to avoid the slightest chance of danger' and this expression was used in a letter to Royal Air Force Units, and by the Army and Royal Navy. But, the assertion that there was no danger or risk at all, particularly after the fatal incident in 1953 (which I shall discuss later), prompted a review of recruitment notices. The Survey refers to the advice of the Treasury Solicitor. His advice is clearly right, that the notices ran the risk of appearing to offer a guarantee of safety when 'there was always some possibility (even if it be exceedingly remote) of a danger being discovered'. This cautious advice, although accepted by the War Office, was not, in fact, translated into practice in Notices produced by the Royal Navy and the Royal Air Force between 1958–63 although it was by the Army.

That there was a tension between the desire of Porton to recruit volunteers and not discourage them, and the need to be careful (and, perhaps, honest) in the words used, is clear. A meeting was convened at Porton in 1962 at which the concerns of Porton's staff were expressed. New wording, adopted in 1962, did not mention danger or risk. It did, however, and this is of equal importance in assessing the openness of the process of recruitment, state that the research was concerned with 'chemical warfare agents'; identify a range of tests which were commonly undertaken; and state that each test would be explained to the individual volunteer, who could refuse to take part if he wished. That said, the Royal Air Force's Notices still made no reference to the right to withdraw in 1962, or 1963.

One view of these discussions and their outcome could be that volunteers were being misled. Another view is that words such as 'foreseeable danger' may be thought to be too question-begging and also could dissuade servicemen from volunteering, when, in fact, the very great majority of trials were routine, any dangers were, at best, remote, and the assumption was that the volunteers would be given detailed explanations before any trial, thereby allowing potential volunteers to withdraw. The fact that some Notices did not, in fact, mention this right to withdraw is arguably of less significance if, as is suggested in the Survey, this complied with the approach suggested by Porton. Those drafting the Notices could perhaps legitimately take the view that, after all, it was the researchers at Porton who administered the trials and who could be assumed to cover such matters.

In my view, the paucity of direct evidence precludes any firm conclusion. A number of grounds exist, however, which may explain and justify the approach adopted. First, it is entirely plausible and tenable for those engaged in the initial process of recruiting volunteers, at whatever level, to take the view that it was their job to encourage volunteers to go to Porton. The words chosen to accomplish this objective might well vary on this view. That they did vary, and vary considerably, is clear from the Survey. Equally clearly, the precise wording used, particularly after 1964, became a matter for individual Service Departments. From the point of view of those at Porton, the wording was not their responsibility, even though they might make suggestions. Thus, it could not be said to constitute an attempt on the part of Porton to mislead potential volunteers. From the point of view of the Services, once the initial recruitment had taken place, it could be said, that it was then the job of those at Porton to explain in detail what was contemplated in the particular research and to offer the volunteer the opportunity to take part or not, based on that detailed briefing.

Viewed from this perspective, the actions of those drafting and circulating the Notices is comparable to the actions of pharmaceutical companies which, to this day, post general notices calling for volunteers for trials of drugs in such places as Students' Notice Boards in Universities. The details of the specific trial and the method of obtaining consent are then left to those conducting the trials. It is important here, however, to enter one caveat. From 1964 until at least the 1980s, Notices not only made no reference to risks, but positively asserted that there was 'no danger' involved in taking part in trials. This clearly ignored the advice in 1953 of the Treasury Solicitor. On its face, such an assertion is misleading as regards those volunteers who saw the Notices and relied on them, even though, as regards the great generality of trials, it was true. The fact that a volunteer had died in 1953 demonstrated that there was some degree of danger, even if the death could be explained as an idiosyncratic response (an explanation which I will consider (and reject) later) and even if, as was the case, no further studies of that kind were again carried out during the period covered by the Survey.

In my view, these Notices, during this period of time, placed a greater priority on securing volunteers than on entirely preparing them for what they might be exposed to. But, the word 'entirely' is important. The view could still have been taken that, as has been said, the large majority of trials posed only the remotest risk of harm and that, in any event, Porton could be expected, indeed could properly be relied on, to give the volunteer the particular, specific information he needed to allow him to choose, once he was at Porton. The wording of the Notices at that time, therefore, could in my view be justified, as being in the larger public interest, even though not entirely accurate.

Secondly, Units were left in no doubt that Porton needed a steady flow of volunteers. Those who led the Service Departments saw it as desirable to encourage men to volunteer. In such circumstances, it is not surprising that the Notices were couched in reassuring terms. As was said earlier regarding the Notices issued before 1964, on one view, this could be seen as a deliberate attempt to deceive and trick volunteers into attending and taking part in research which was in fact likely to expose them to danger and harm. On another view, which on balance I prefer, if, in fact, there was any systematic, long-standing attempt to trick volunteers in this way, it is very likely that word would have quickly got round among the servicemen. Porton would have been avoided. Moreover, and perhaps more telling, I repeat again that many thousands of trials were carried out at Porton during the period of the Survey. They varied enormously in nature. Very many, indeed what appears to be the large majority, were routine variations of long-established trials, which posed no risk of foreseeable adverse consequences. In such circumstances, to stress the idea that volunteers would be exposed to danger would have been to distort what was, in fact, the case. It would also have undermined the legitimate campaign to recruit volunteers. Of course, this is not to ignore the fact that some trials did expose volunteers to the risk of harm and, on occasions, were intended to cause some harm, for instance, burns or blisters, as I discuss later. These raise questions not about the general calls for volunteers but about the adequacy of the information given to volunteers in particular cases and I will examine them in due course, when I consider the actual consent given by volunteers.

Thirdly, while the various Notices differed in their language, all of those identified in the Survey after 1964 and most beforehand refer to 'Volunteers' and to 'Chemical Defence' or 'Chemical Warfare'. While it is not clear whether servicemen who volunteered actually saw these Notices, if they did, they cannot have been left in doubt as to what, in general terms, they were volunteering for. Of course, if they did not see the Notices (such that the Notices played no part in their decision to volunteer, and the Survey suggests that not all volunteers were recruited through Notices), then the concerns highlighted in the Survey about the reference, or otherwise, to danger fall away, since the volunteers cannot, on this reasoning, have been misled by them.

Research on the Common Cold

Before leaving the issue of general information as a basis for initial consent, it is necessary to comment on the recollections of many that they were, in fact, volunteering to take part in research on the common cold, rather than chemical warfare. The Survey describes at length the trials that were conducted into the common cold at the Common Cold Research Unit (CCRU) and elsewhere. Assuming for the sake of argument that those who recall attending Porton for research on the common cold did not see any general Notice headed 'Chemical Defence', the extent of this recollection, both in terms of numbers and over time, demands attention, notwithstanding the material differences in the practices used to recruit volunteers as between Porton and the CCRU.

The evidence described in the Survey makes it clear that no research on the common cold was conducted at Porton. Equally, while research involving service personnel was conducted into the *influenza virus* in the 1950s, these trials were not conducted at Porton, but, rather, were carried out at servicemen's Units.

Thus, if the recollections of recruits – that they were volunteering for research on the common cold as recorded in the Survey – are accurate, the evidence set out in the Survey – that no research on the common cold took place at Porton – is wrong. Moreover, a picture would emerge of wholesale and discreditable deception of volunteers over a long period of time as to why they were being recruited by the Services and by those at Porton. It has to be said immediately that whether such a deception could be sustained is open to doubt. But, more problematic still is the existence of direct evidence, from 1960–61 and from 1964–77, which on its face appears to contradict the volunteers' recollections. The evidence takes two forms. First, there was a survey from 1960 to 1961. Secondly, there is a card index, created from 1964–77, which is still retained at Porton, containing about 2250 cards in all, one for each volunteer who came to Porton during that period. As for the survey, it shows that, of 334 volunteers interviewed, only two said that they had volunteered for research on the common cold. The card index indicates that, when asked why they had come to Porton, only five of the 2250 made any reference to research into the common cold. And, moreover, according to the Survey, the evidence relating to the five is 'less than direct'. Admittedly, the card index only covers a period of 13 years and may not be representative of volunteers' views over the whole period during which research into the common cold took place. That said, however, its significance lies in its consistency.

My conclusion on this matter is that recollections have become confused over time. I do not suppose that there was any deliberate distortion of the truth. I only suppose that this is merely another example in which the passage of time and events has produced a 'folk memory' which appears to have no basis in fact.

Specific Information

It was the duty of the researchers at Porton to ensure that those who volunteered to come to Porton, were given such specific information about the particular trial which they took part in to allow them to make a considered choice whether to take part or not. (I will consider later whether the fact that they had been brought to Porton by the

Services *as servicemen* meant that the option not to take part was more theoretical than real.)

Ordinarily, the specific information regarded as most important from an ethical standpoint is that which relates to:

- the risks which the volunteer will be exposed to and the likelihood of their eventuating;
- the consequences of taking part in the trial, including what may happen if the risks eventuate, and more generally any discomfort which may be suffered, its nature and duration.

It is good practice now to prepare an information sheet for would-be volunteers, which they can study before deciding whether or not to proceed. This sheet will contain a fairly detailed account of the research and will cover, among other things, the matters referred to above. The practice of preparing such sheets, however, only became routine or standard towards the end of the period of the Survey and is commonly associated with, although its development is independent of, the emergence of ethics committees. Beforehand, the information given to the volunteers was not necessarily recorded. This would have been common in trials generally and not just particular to Porton. (As will be noted later, information sheets, called 'Lay Statements' were formally introduced at Porton in 1987.)

Thus, the Survey contains little or no *direct* evidence of what transpired between the researchers and volunteers over the whole period which it covers. (There is some documentary evidence, but the Survey, quite rightly, in my view, describes it as presenting only a 'faint picture' of recruitment practices.) It must be added that there is on this issue, as on many others, evidence of the recollections of some of the many thousands of volunteers who attended Porton during the period of time covered by the Survey. While not, for a moment, doubting the genuineness of these recollections, it would be wrong to rely on them as settling any issue. As I have said, those offering these recollections are very few in number, they are a self-selecting group, they do not constitute a group which has been so designed that its evidence is representative of the views of all volunteers, and there is no evidence available from the researchers as to what *their* recollections are.

Thus, it follows that there is very little material on which to base any firm conclusion about the information passed on to the volunteers, prior to their embarking on a trial. The Survey describes occasions, recorded in documents, on which specific information about trials was given to volunteers. The list is not long. The Survey cautions, however, that where a report does not mention that information was given to volunteers, 'it is not safe to assume that none was given'. This must be right, not least because the tendency to record these matters may have been a development which grew only gradually, mirroring, perhaps, the slowly growing recognition generally of the importance of the ethics of research. Then, from 1979 onwards, the practice grew of stating in the record of a trial that it had been 'conducted in accordance with the provisions of the Declaration of Helsinki'. This assertion does not, of course, constitute proof that the trial was so conducted. But, given the central importance placed by the Declaration on consent and the provision of appropriate information, it may well constitute a form of shorthand statement that the volunteer had been appropriately informed before consenting.

In the absence of direct evidence, I have to rely largely on secondary evidence. First, since the trials required the cooperation of the volunteers, some explanation of what they were to do and what they could expect to happen was obviously called for. Secondly, in those trials in which the volunteers would be exposed to discomfort, it is fair to assume that this would have been explained, not least so that the volunteer would continue to participate, for example, in the case of being exposed to gas in a chamber, by remaining in the chamber.

Of course, being told what is going to happen is not the same as being advised of the risks and consequences associated with taking part in a trial. Mere information, without any explanation of its significance or meaning, is not sufficient to allow a considered choice and thus does not, of itself, make the consent an informed consent. One example, which I also mention later in the context of risk, perhaps goes to the very edges, if not beyond, the permissible as regards obtaining real (in this context, informed) consent, even allowing for the fact that it was conducted in 1942 when the fear of H (mustard gas) was great. It involved a trial to explore 'the full extent of the danger' of H vapour to the male volunteers' scrotal region. It is hard to believe that servicemen would have volunteered for such a trial had they been adequately informed what the aim was. If I am right, and servicemen were not informed of such an obviously painful experience (even if short-lived and even if treatment was available), this trial was an unjustified departure from proper ethical standards.

Overall, however, the only conclusion available to me is that there is not enough evidence to allow me to reach a considered view on the amount and quality of the information given to the volunteers throughout the period covered by the Survey. There are occasional references to the information given to volunteers but not enough to indicate how common the practice was. I am persuaded that the possibility that a trial might expose volunteers to risks, the likelihood of those risks eventuating, and the consequences for the volunteers if this should take place were all actively considered and discussed by the researchers at Porton, particularly in the case of certain trials. I am not, however, able to reach a view as to whether these considerations were consistently passed on to the volunteers. The Survey does contain one example of detailed information being passed on to volunteers (it relates to a trial in 1955 of various routes for administering atropine and is a good model of its kind even now). But, as I have said, it is not possible, on the available evidence, to determine whether it represents common practice, or was exceptional.

By way of comment at a very general level, I can say that the degree of information deemed necessary to obtain real consent is significantly greater now than at the beginning of the time covered by the Survey. Until at least the middle of the 1970s, paternalism tended to hold sway in the conduct of research. It was reflected in the propositions that the volunteer need not be concerned about details, which he might well not understand, and that his safety and welfare could safely be left in the hands of the researchers. This approach was thought to be justified, if challenged, by the argument that the duty of the researcher was to convey such information as was necessary to allow the volunteer to make a considered choice. The unstated assumption was that the best judge of what was necessary was the researcher. The recital of risks which were remote and of consequences which were hypothetical was regarded, on this view, as counterproductive and likely, unnecessarily, to put the volunteer off. Implicit in this approach, of course, was the assumption that if there were a conflict between pursuing research deemed important (by the researcher) and telling the volunteer about unlikely risks and consequences, the deemed imperative to carry out the research should prevail. This was the tenor of the times. If reflected in the approach adopted at Porton, it would have been in accordance with practice at the time. It would also have had the added perceived justification that the research being conducted was in the national interest. But, this is speculation.

There is one area of research which warrants special attention: the trials involving psychoactive agents. I shall need to come back to these trials when I discuss the notion of risk and the limits to what a volunteer should be exposed to. But, here I am concerned with consent and whether it was sufficiently informed. The approach adopted by Porton in their trials relating, for example, to LSD was that it would defeat the purpose of the trials if the volunteer knew what he was being exposed to, since what were being tested were psychological responses and attitudes. So, these trials were deliberately conducted without giving the volunteers certain information. They were told in general terms what they were expected to do and precautions were taken to respond to any untoward occurrences. But, they were not informed about what they were being asked to take and, it follows, what were the likely risks and consequences. Volunteers, the Survey reports, were given a 'general outline of the purpose of the trial and assured of their safety. For obvious reasons they could not be informed of the nature of the compound to be used'. (Another example of deception appears elsewhere in the Survey when men were caused to believe that they were to inhale a small amount of nerve gas, when in fact they were inhaling air. Given the importance of determining the effect of GB on pulse rate, and given that the volunteers were not, in fact, exposed to any agent, it would be hard to argue that this trial went beyond the accepted standards of the time.)

Two points arise. The first is that the fact that there was discussion at Porton about what information should be given to the volunteers lends further, albeit weak, support to the proposition that, *ordinarily*, volunteers would have been given more detailed information as to what they were being exposed to. The second point is that, in the case of the trials involving psychoactive agents, a deliberate decision was taken to keep information from, if not deceive, the volunteers. On the face of it, this may seem to constitute unethical conduct. But, as in all things to do with ethics, the picture is not as clear as appearances might suggest.

There has long been a debate over the existence and extent of exceptions to the researcher's duty to obtain the informed consent of volunteers. One particular area of debate has been the deliberate deception of the volunteer in, for example, research in the social sciences. Currently, the chances are remote that a research proposal in the area of the medical sciences, which did not include a requirement that volunteers be given appropriate information, would be approved by the relevant ethics committee. But, before the advent of ethics committees, and in the area of psychological research in particular, the insistence on informed consent was not always as strong. Indeed, the issue has been one of some controversy.

It has long been argued strongly that if the only way to discover what was thought to be of importance was to engage in some form of deception, then this was permissible. The provisos were that the research should be of sufficient importance and not trivial and that, on available evidence, the volunteer would not come to harm, (but see the notorious Stanford experiment which involved one group of students delivering what they believed were electric shocks of increasing strength to a group of actors who feigned being shocked).[6] These, I would suggest, were the standards which operated in the 1950s and 60s. They are the standards against which the researchers at Porton should be judged, whatever the Codes or Guidelines of the time may have said. For, as has been said, these Codes were not paid great attention, being thought to apply to others, rather than to *bona fide* researchers engaged in work of national importance.

Thus, I conclude that, judged by the standards of today, the trials involving psycho-active agents would be difficult to justify, but by the standards of the time they were not so at variance with accepted practice as to merit being described as unethical. (I leave out of account here any discussion of the legality of the trials involving, for example, LSD. Consideration of the law is not part of my task. I am aware that the trials involving the use of LSD have recently attracted the attention of the police and, therefore, make no further comment.)

Voluntariness

The last element in this consideration of consent is the issue of voluntariness. The question can be put simply: were the servicemen who took part in the trials truly volunteers? It is too simple to respond that they answered a call for volunteers and went of their own accord to Porton. What has to be established is that, both initially and once they were at Porton, they did what they did of their own free will and did not feel and were not placed under improper pressure.

At the stage of their initial recruitment, the point has already been made that there is very little direct evidence of the process of recruitment, save for the Notices which were posted but may not have been seen by all those who volunteered. The first question which needs to be asked is, given that they were serving members of the armed forces, were they, in fact, ordered or otherwise placed under pressure to come forward? The answer is that there is no direct evidence to suggest that they were. The available documentary evidence points in the opposite direction. Early Notices to Commanding Officers urged them to 'allow' or 'permit' men to volunteer. The picture is one in which Commanding Officers were reluctant to lose men and thereby deplete their Unit's strength, rather than ordering men to volunteer to meet Porton's, or the government's, targets.

The calls for volunteers made it clear that extra pay and a certain relaxation of the discipline of military life, such as wearing civilian clothes, were also available to those who volunteered. The question raised is whether these could be said to have constituted an improper inducement. An inducement is considered to be improper in the context of research when it causes someone to volunteer for something which he would not otherwise wish to do, merely to obtain that which is offered. It is not deemed improper if it constitutes reasonable recompense for the contribution made by the volunteer and for any inconvenience or discomfort experienced.

As regards the offer of a modest amount of extra pay, the payment of volunteers taking part in research has long been the subject of discussion. There are those who, for

[6] Milgram, *Obedience to Authority* (Harper and Row, 1974).

example, in the past have criticised the pharmaceutical industry for recruiting students and the unemployed for trials of drugs, through the offer of money. It is an area in which differing views have been and are held. The differences of view, however, tend to be about whether the money or other material inducement offered is too much. Few hold to the view that no money at all should be made available. Moreover, at the level of principle, there is no reason to suspect that an offer of money *ipso facto* undermines a person's capacity to choose what to do. It might provide a reason for choosing, but rarely will dictate the choice. The best that can be said, therefore, is that reasonable judgement is called for. And, on that basis, I would suggest that the offer of financial and other inducements to the volunteers at Porton did not prevent them from being volunteers. It may be worth adding that, as the Survey makes clear, the ethical issue of inducement was recognised and considered by Porton in the late 1970s. The Medical Committee noted in 1978 that the Medical Research Council was not in favour of paying volunteers, but, nonetheless, decided to continue its practice of offering payment.

The next question to ask is whether, once they were at Porton, the volunteers effectively lost the capacity to change their minds. At least two grounds can be advanced for holding this view. First, a volunteer might feel under what is called 'peer pressure' not to pull out. In the ethos of the armed forces pulling out could be seen as weakness. But the argument has to be pressed further. It is not simply that this pressure may have existed, but that the researchers at Porton should have been aware of it and made allowance for it in their procedures for obtaining consent. For my part, I take the view that this feeling is not limited to the armed forces, but is a commonplace in all walks of life. Of itself, it cannot, in my view, be said to have converted the servicemen into non-volunteers. Furthermore, the researchers at Porton, on the available evidence, seem to have emphasised that volunteers could leave if they wished. It is difficult to see what else they could have done, without treating the servicemen as if they were unable to decide for themselves. Had they done so, it would, of course, have constituted precisely the kind of paternalism which the notion of consent is supposed to displace.

The second ground which can be advanced to suggest that the servicemen were not really able to change their minds and leave, (were not truly volunteers), is more substantial. They were serving soldiers and therefore attuned to obeying orders and doing what they were told. In the language of the ethics of research, they were a vulnerable group. The idea behind the notion of vulnerability, as undermining voluntariness, is based on the existence of a relationship of power, in which the researcher is the more powerful.

As a factor to be considered when examining the ethics of research, the vulnerability of the research subject has been discussed for some time. The most obvious example was the use of convicted prisoners in research. It was said that they were easily induced to take part, (not least, out of the hope of some reward), and were rarely true volunteers. The more subtle application of the notion of vulnerability to research on employees, students, and members of the armed forces, is more recent. During the 1970s and 1980s, and even into the 1990s, the use of employees, for example, was still commonplace in some pharmaceutical research. (Porton abandoned the practice of recruiting members of its staff as volunteers in 1978, on ethical as well as scientific grounds.) Moreover, the use of those who might *prima facie* be vulnerable will still be defensible, provided extra care is taken to ensure that they are in fact making a free choice. Indeed, few would argue that in no circumstances should members of these groups, merely by virtue of the fact that they are employees, students or whatever, ever be allowed to volunteer to take part in research, if it is to be carried out by their employer or professor. Given that the issue of vulnerability is the object of continuing discussion in current reflections on research ethics, it would be wrong, in my view, to conclude that the use of servicemen in research at Porton was ethically improper, simply on the basis that they were servicemen and, by this fact alone, were unable truly to volunteer and give real consent.

I turn now to another and extremely important feature of voluntariness. Intrinsic in the notion of consent is the notion of refusal. Someone is only truly a volunteer if he feels that he may refuse to take part in a particular trial, having once been informed of what is involved, or, having embarked on the trial, he feels he may withdraw at any time during it, without attracting any sanction. As regards the evidence in the Survey, there are various Notices referred to, beginning with the wording suggested by Porton in 1962, which explicitly drew attention to the fact that a volunteer need not take part and could withdraw at any time. Even assuming that the volunteer saw these Notices, however, this does not tell us what happened in practice. There is also evidence of a Note in 1944 which refers to 'full freedom to refuse'; of discussions in the Biology Committee in 1958; and of a Briefing Note by Porton's staff in 1959. Moreover, the Survey refers to MOD documents which record that the right to withdraw was explained to volunteers. But, as has been said, these documents and Notes do not, of themselves, necessarily reflect what was done in practice. There is also some limited direct evidence, in various experiment logs, of volunteers refusing to take part. Again, it is not possible to say how comprehensive these logs are, nor how typical were the cases recorded. Further, it is not possible to say what their relative infrequency demonstrates: that, ordinarily, volunteers felt unable to refuse; that they were ordinarily content to proceed; or, simply, that refusals and withdrawals were not regularly recorded.

The most instructive evidence, perhaps, of what may have happened in practice can be found in the way in which many trials were designed and carried out. For example, those exposed in a chamber to gas were told that they could leave the chamber at any time and, indeed, many did. Also, in the design of some of the trials of riot control agents, considerable attention was given to allow a volunteer to withdraw; to facilitate the escape of a volunteer should he be unwilling to carry on with the trial, (for example, by making arrangements so that volunteers could escape from CS gas, either by getting through a gap left at the bottom of the hessian 'wall', or through escape panels cut into the walls at intervals, each of which was attended by staff from Porton ready to lend assistance); or to have access to assistance, (for example, COHSE insisted that the trials of drenching with CR be carried out close to the showers to minimise the delay in decontamination, should a volunteer wish to terminate a test). The Survey describes an example of a volunteer refusing to continue a trial involving drenching with CS gas. Another example, in 1942, during wartime, involved two volunteers refusing to take further part in a run over an assault course, while being exposed to harassing agents, despite the existence of financial inducements. Moreover, a trial in which participants were the offered financial inducements if they were prepared to tolerate being exposed to gas in the holding chamber for longer periods of time, carries the necessary implication that the volunteers had a choice as to whether to carry on, and did not have to do so, if they did not wish to. And, incidentally, I do not regard the offer of these additional sums of money, in the context, as an improper inducement. It seems to be a good example of reasonable compensation for undergoing additional discomfort.

My conclusion is that there is no direct evidence of volunteers being coerced to take part in trials or to carry on when they wished to stop. There is, on the other hand, evidence of general statements to the effect that volunteers could refuse or withdraw. And, there is evidence of practical arrangements to give effect to the exercise of this choice by the volunteer.

One postscript might be added to the discussion of voluntariness. On a number of occasions, the researchers at Porton subjected themselves to tests before conducting trials on volunteers. Currently, this is a practice which is not encouraged for a variety of reasons, not least that the resulting information may not be sufficiently objective, that some researchers, in their enthusiasm may exceed what is safe, that atypical tolerance of certain substances may be acquired, and that it is a process which bypasses the procedural arrangements now in place to monitor research. But, historically, it was not uncommon. Researchers, in accordance with what was a commonly held view, felt that they should not to expose others to the possibility of harm which they themselves would not be prepared to be exposed to. Further, initial tests allowed the researchers to calculate more accurately what volunteers could safely be exposed to. There is no evidence that the research staff at Porton were under pressure to submit themselves to such tests. Rather, it seems to be a case of selflessness, born perhaps of a sense of the importance, in their eyes, of the work that they were doing.

Formality of Consent

I turn now to what may be described as the formality of the process whereby consent was obtained from volunteers. By the 1960s, it was being argued that consent, particularly in the case of research on healthy volunteers, should be recorded in writing, signed by the volunteer. The practice was not always observed, but certainly by the time that ethics committees emerged, it was regarded as a standard requirement. It is important to notice immediately, however, that a written consent form is not a substitute for real consent. A person may, for example, sign a form without really understanding what it says, or the implications of signing it. A signed consent form provides evidence of consent, but is not conclusive. Equally, the absence of written consent is not proof, nor is it even evidence, that consent was not given. What is important, therefore, is not so much the formalities of consent as the process whereby consent is obtained: the imparting of necessary information and the testing of voluntariness. But, some record in writing might be said to be a useful start.

In general terms, the absence of consent in writing makes it that much more difficult, of course, to determine what in fact took place, and thus to decide whether the process for obtaining consent was appropriate. This is true of Porton during most of the period of time covered by the Survey. Written consent was not obtained from volunteers. Only in 1987 was a written consent form introduced, presumably at the insistence of the newly created Independent Ethics Committee. Of its kind, it seems brief but satisfactory. It appears that it was accompanied from 1987 onwards by a 'Lay Statement', the purpose of which was to give the volunteer more specific information (as discussed earlier). This combination of Consent Form and Lay Statement (or Information Sheet) brought Porton into line with standard practice. But, they were only introduced at the end of the period covered by the Survey.

Thus, for the time prior to 1987, I have had to rely on less direct evidence to form a view as to whether the volunteers at Porton really did consent to take part in trials. It is important from the point of view of establishing the context, however, to recognise why written consent did not form part of the formal arrangements at Porton. It seems that the desirability of recording consent in writing was already recognised in the late 1950s. The Survey describes the discussion prompted by the Admiralty in 1959 and the response of the War Office. Whether the initial intention of the Admiralty was to ensure that consent was recorded as a 'safeguard' (the word used in the original Admiralty document) against future complaint, or arose simply from the desire to allow a volunteer to record his exercise of choice is not clear. Officials at the War Office were initially opposed. The grounds given for the opposition are worth repeating: '… either the certificate [consent form] would become pure routine or it would make them suspect that they were about to be subjected to something very dangerous, the responsibility for which we are trying to pass on to them'.

Officials also raised two further objections: security; and the fact that volunteers had not been prepared to come forward on those occasions when they had been required to sign something. The principal objection, however, appears to revolve around the idea that the document to be signed would be seen as what is graphically called a 'blood chit': a certificate purporting to absolve the War Office of responsibility if a volunteer were harmed. Thus, Ministers were advised to encourage a procedure whereby volunteers 'clearly understood what they were being asked to undergo', but advised to reject the idea of a signed document, because of the connotation of its being a 'blood chit'. The Admiralty tried again in 1960 but without success. The Survey also describes an occasion in 1980 when a form of written consent was considered but was still 'deemed undesirable'. Finally, in 1985, the idea was accepted.

The initial discussions between the Admiralty and the War Office follow a pattern which anyone remotely aware of the workings of government departments will recognise: wires got crossed. What was canvassed by some as a formal demonstration of consent was seen by others as an agreement by the volunteer to waive liability. Such a waiver was thought, quite properly, to be inappropriate. Thus, forms were not to be used. That this inaction lasted nearly 50 years is a tribute to the longevity of decisions once taken, no matter that they be wrong-headed. It also suggests that 'political' considerations and concerns over security took precedence over considerations of what were seen as formalities. It does not suggest that the need for consent was to be ignored, or was unimportant. That forms were not used is unfortunate from a historical perspective. It says nothing, however, about the conduct of the trials at Porton and whether or not they were conducted with real consent.

A second postscript may be added. In 1964, a film was made about the process of recruiting volunteers (the Survey contains a transcript of the material parts of the film). On its face, the film could be said to provide evidence concerning the consent and voluntariness of volunteers. In the event, I do not place any reliance on the film, for two reasons. First, it is not of itself evidence of what actually took place at Porton. Secondly, it was made by the MOD as part of the process of encouraging recruits and so cannot be said to be an objective and impartial account. This is not to say that it was intended to, or did, misrepresent what went on at Porton. It is merely to say that it may be wiser not to rely on it.

By contrast, other films which are held by the Imperial War Museum and which I was able to see, are of some assistance at least tangentially, suggesting as they do cooperation from which could be implied consent. A few of the films I saw recorded trials being carried out. I have no reason to believe that they were selectively biased to present a particular picture of what went on. Two specific factors struck me as significant. One was the degree of supervision by staff during the conduct of trials, suggesting the availability of assistance if a volunteer suffered discomfort. This tends to reinforce the description of the approach adopted by Porton described in the Survey: 'during studies, measurements were taken continuously of physiological parameters which were thought might be affected by the substance being used, and the study stopped if limits were approached'. The second factor was the presence of what appeared to be medical care when a volunteer did, in fact, encounter distress or discomfort. These observations are relevant as I turn now to discuss risk and safety.

Risk and Safety

In the conduct of research on healthy volunteers, it was an accepted principle from the start of the period of time covered by the Survey that the safety of volunteers should not be put at risk. What is more problematical is what this principle was understood to mean. The first question is: risk of what? The answer is initially clear. The volunteer may not be exposed to the risk of death or significant injury, physical or mental. Significant is to be contrasted with trivial, but there is a large middle ground over which disagreement may exist. This is because the answer to this first question depends in part and is inextricably linked with the answer to a second question: what risk? A risk of some deleterious consequence may be very great or remote. Further, the consequence of a risk eventuating may be great or slight. In concrete terms, there may be a slight risk of something catastrophic, such as death, and there may be a real risk of something trivial, such as a temporary headache. Putting these parts of the principle together produces a sharper proposition: that the researcher should not expose a volunteer to any risk which involves even a remote chance of death or significant, serious harm, nor to any risk which involves anything other than a remote chance of more than trivial harm. This suggests that in the case of trivial harms, the risk may be run if it is unlikely to occur. In such a case, the researcher must have taken all reasonable steps to prevent the risk from occurring.

If this is not complex enough already, there is a further, distinct, strand which runs through the modern history of research on healthy volunteers: that the risk to which a volunteer may be exposed may be proportionate to the importance of the information which is sought. It can be found in the first (1964) Helsinki Declaration's reference to, and thus apparent endorsement of, a balance which can be struck between risks to a research subject and importance of the objective, and, thus, the benefits to others.

Although this notion of proportionality cannot be read to justify exposing a volunteer to a real risk of death or significant injury, it is clear that it can serve to tip the balance somewhat towards taking greater risks if the prize (of information) is great enough. It does not say that the interests of society *should* prevail over those of the research subject, but merely suggests that the balance may be struck more subtly. Moreover, it is an issue which remains to this day the object of debate, such that distinguished commentators were able to write in 2002: '… there was, and still is, uncertainty over the circumstances in which the potential benefits of research to many people might outweigh inconvenience and risk to a few'.[7] Thus, a remote risk of death may come into the equation, as may a somewhat more likely, though still unlikely, risk of more than trivial harm. This notion of proportionality, of course, takes on great significance in the context of research relating to defence against weapons of war and of appeals to the national interest. Indeed, the Survey refers specifically to the 'good of society', as justifying research being carried out which might otherwise be impermissibly dangerous, in reporting the meeting in 1965 convened by the Director of Porton, following the ban on trials of incapacitating agents.

It is necessary also to include in any account of safety and risk the observation that the mere fact that someone may be willing to expose himself to a risk, aware that it may cause him more than trivial harm, does not mean that it is thereafter proper to proceed. There is at some point a duty on researchers not to expose volunteers to such harm, despite their preparedness to be exposed. The reasons are complex. It may well be in the public interest to promote research. But, it is also in the public interest to protect people from themselves, at some point. Freedom of choice, at some point, is made to give way to benevolent paternalism. One obvious justification is that the cause of research would be damaged if a volunteer were to be exposed to something which was expected or likely to harm him significantly. But, this may not be the real reason. At bottom, the reason may have more to do with the researcher than the volunteer, or the cause of scientific research. It may be that there is a sense that to permit such activity would brutalise or desensitise the researcher and, by association, make society, by permitting or encouraging the activity, complicit in it.

How do these general reflections relate to Porton? They form the background to the enquiry whether the researchers exceeded the limits of what was ethically proper. Did the researchers expose the volunteers to trials which carried too great a risk of harm and thereby improperly endanger their safety?

Before addressing these questions, there is a prior point of some importance to be made. The researchers, before they conducted trials on human volunteers sought to establish from research on animals, study of the available literature, and, on occasions, tests on themselves, what might be the expected consequences of research on humans. They sought, in other words, to establish as best they could the nature of the risk, so as to avoid any reasonably foreseeable risk of serious harm to volunteers. It is worth noting, for example, the tests involving T3436 [an incapacitating agent]. Between 1969 and 1971 and 1971–72, COHSE and ABC closely monitored the dose used, starting with low doses and approving gradual increases, as evidence emerged about safety. The general approach adopted, therefore, was one of seeking to work in the realm of the known or the reasonably predictable, so as to be able to control the consequences and thereby protect the volunteer. This is in keeping with the researchers' ethical responsibility.

[7] See fn 2

There were occasions, as will be seen, when this approach was not followed, but these were exceptions which tend to prove the rule.

Secondly, as has been seen, on a number of occasions until the practice was stopped in 1978, researchers first tested compounds on themselves, particularly in the case of nerve agents and incapacitating agents, (the Survey describes a number of examples including the preparedness of an RAF ophthalmologist to expose his eyes to GB, so as to understand its effects and thereby to design appropriate trials). Although this approach is not approved of now for the reasons already set out, at the time it may have been said to demonstrate a commitment to doing what was ethically proper in the realm of risk in two ways. It gave the researchers further information about the agent being tested and thus allowed them to design better and safer trials. And it reflected, as has been said, a commitment to what, for a long time during the period under review, though not now, was thought of as the 'golden rule' of research ethics: that a researcher should not expose a volunteer to a test which he would not be prepared to undergo himself. Thus, in at least two ways, the researchers sought to respect and give effect to what they understood at the time to be the ethical standards underlying research.

Returning to the questions posed above, it may be helpful in answering them to proceed in stages, which reflect, in general terms, the degree of risk involved.

Routine Trials

First, a large majority of the volunteers were exposed to trials at Porton, which were almost humdrum or routine in nature. They involved no recognised risk. They often consisted of painstaking variations on established themes, such as the testing of different fabrics, or of protective clothing. They raise no issue as to ethical propriety.

Intention to Cause Discomfort and Distress

Next, there was a large number of trials which exposed volunteers to discomfort and distress. It was known or predicted that this would the case, indeed many of the trials were conducted to measure the extent of the distress, (not whether it would occur), and how long it could be withstood. Thus, distress and discomfort were intentionally caused. Did such trials exceed what was ethically permissible? In my view, they did not. The volunteers, as has been said, appeared to be aware of what was likely to happen and consented. The risks were not such that they should not have been asked or allowed to consent. The distress could be expected, *ordinarily*, to be of short duration, for example, a matter of minutes. The risk of any long-term effects was remote. The volunteers were accompanied and attended by medical staff who could intervene and render assistance if it was called for.

On occasions, the distressing effects of being exposed to a particular agent lasted longer than could have been expected, or a volunteer's distress was atypically more pronounced (the Survey gives the example of a trial in which miosis – excessive constriction of the pupil of the eye – which lasted for five days). Medical assistance was available and, where necessary, a volunteer remained at Porton until he had recovered (an example being an unexpectedly long depression of a volunteer's blood pressure which 'gave cause for concern' according to the ABC).

Such occurrences, even if unusual, could give rise to the suggestion that the researchers, at least on these occasions, exceeded the limits of the permissible. But, a distinction needs to be made between responses which could ordinarily be expected and those which were unpredictable, or out of the ordinary. If the researchers took measures to control the trial such that they could reasonably be said to be able to predict the range of responses and to be entitled to expect that the responses of the volunteers would be within the predicted range, then this may have been enough by the standards of the times to comply with their ethical responsibility.

It may be objected that the unexpected should be expected and, thus, provided for. Leaving aside the obvious logical paradox, it should be remembered, first, that, with a very few exceptions, the researchers were working with young fit men, who could be expected to respond in a predictable manner. Secondly, from at least the 1950s onwards, volunteers underwent a careful medical assessment before being involved in a trial. These examinations became more extensive over time, particularly as trials of different agents were carried out. Moreover, they covered not only what may be described as routine matters, such as blood samples, but susceptibility to certain agents, for example, mustard gas, and also psychological well-being. It seems clear from the Survey, therefore, that significant precautions were taken to assess volunteers and exclude those who might be predicted to be put at undue risk in any trial.

Thirdly, particular efforts were made in the trials involving psychoactive agents to eliminate unsuitable volunteers. This resulted in the fact that from 1961–65 80% and in 1967–68 66% of the volunteers reporting to Porton were excluded from these trials. The stringent application of the tests and their results, which resulted in volunteers being excluded, provoked tension between Porton and the ABC. It was felt that the need to conduct trials was being frustrated by Porton's concern for safety. Eventually, Porton gave ground by admitting into the trials those who were categorised as 'borderline'. In my view, this relaxation of their position does not warrant criticism since it was at the margins and was the result of legitimate differences of opinion as to where the balance was to be struck. Had Porton gone further, my view may well be different, particularly given the fact that the risk 'of inducing an irreversible effect in some men' had been discussed in 1959 at a meeting of CDAB concerned with the safety of trials involving psychoactive agents.

A further example of excluding potentially vulnerable volunteers can be found in the introduction of a new eye-testing regime in relation to work on miosis in 1982, because of the suspicion (which I consider later) of a relationship between myopia and detached retina, in addition to the introduction of SFEMG – a method of recording electrical activity in muscle fibre – at the behest of the Medical Committee in 1987 and EEG – for measuring brain activity – in 1979 at the behest of COHSE. In addition, the Survey records that some volunteers were barred from studies of CR because they were hypertensive

Fourthly, idiosyncratic reactions, not otherwise predictable, do happen, even despite efforts to make the trial as safe as current knowledge allowed. An example may be that described in the Survey in which a volunteer developed microcysts but 'no significant residual damage' after the trial of a CR squirt.

The conclusion I am drawn to, therefore, is that in this second category of trials, the researchers did not exceed what then or now would be thought to be ethical in terms of the risks to which volunteers were exposed to. Moreover, this view is reinforced if account is taken of the context, that of defence against chemical warfare, and the proportionate value of gaining information as compared with the extent of the risk to which the volunteers were exposed.

Intention to Cause Harm

A third category of trials is more problematic. These are the trials in which the purpose of the trial was to inflict harm on the volunteer. That is to say that the researchers intended that harm be caused, rather than sought to discover the effects of an agent in circumstances in which some might suffer some distress which would be temporary, or from which they could remove themselves if it occurred. This distinction is not, of course, clear-cut, as the trials of nerve agents illustrate. In one trial, the aim apparently was to estimate the 'threshold' dose of GB vapour. Such a trial clearly, by its nature, carries a risk of harm, though it may not be intended to cause it. In fact, all three men in the particular trial who were exposed to GB without protection did suffer what is described as 'early signs of systemic poisoning'.

A clear example of this third category of trials is the trial into the effect of CS gas on the eyes: according to the Survey, the concentration sought was that which would produce 'severe pain and sustained blepharospasm' (involuntary twitching of the eyelids), albeit for a brief period of time. Other examples of trials which were intended to produce harm were those involving vesicants and other agents in which the intention was to cause blistering and burning. Here there was more than a risk of harm. There was an inevitability of harm, and harm which was not trivial. It may, of course, be said that the volunteers may have consented knowing what was intended. But, this may be one of those cases in which the consent of the volunteers does not necessarily make the trial ethical, because of the degree of harm which they were exposed to.

It is very unlikely that the sort of trials which fall into this third category would be countenanced now by an ethics committee. But, this does not necessarily help us, since it imposes the standards of today on research conducted decades ago in very different circumstances, including during a World War. In my view, three arguments in particular can be advanced to suggest that the trials, in principle, can be justified as having been ethical at the time.

First, in most cases, particularly in the later years covered by the Survey, as more information became available, the trials were carefully controlled. Secondly, the outcome was predictable and, therefore amenable to being managed and controlled. (Certain trials of nerve agents, however, may be an exception and I will consider these separately.) Localised blistering or burning, for example, was the expected and intended outcome (although the severity was not always accurately predicted) and treatment was known, effective and available.

Thirdly, applying the notion of proportionality, it could be argued that the information sought was sufficiently important to warrant exposing volunteers to harm, if the harm was limited and the trial was conducted in a controlled environment. It may be one of those cases in which the concern for defence against chemical warfare agents and the tenor of the times may justify that which otherwise would be difficult to justify. Many of the trials falling into this third category were conducted during the Second World War and later in the 1940s. Furthermore, after the abandonment of the development of new offensive agents, the imperative for the Services and, hence, the main thrust of research, was to develop effective forms of treatment for service personnel who might be exposed to nerve agents and to H (mustard gas) and other vesicants, (it should be remembered that H was regarded as a threat throughout the whole of the period covered by the Survey). Indeed, decades of research were dedicated to developing protection against nerve agents.

To develop treatments, the researchers had to establish the point at which the agent became effective. Hence, there were the trials which involved causing some degree of harm, such as blistering and burning. There is little doubt that some of the trials produced and were intended to produce injuries of 'casualty severity', that is, sufficiently serious that the man would not be able to take part in military activities. The trials walked a tightrope between 'controlled harm' and significant injury. Sometimes, the line was crossed, safety was compromised and trials were stopped. Trials involving H (mustard gas) were particularly challenging – the effects of a trial in 1942, for example, were described as 'much more severe than expected' and all three volunteers required treatment in hospital.

These trials make for uncomfortable reading now, particularly those when, for example, two of four men 'required immediate admission to hospital' and one was admitted some days later with burns to his scrotal region. This sense of discomfort exists even though more than trivial harm may only have been suffered in a few of the thousands of trials which took place. While it may not be enough to say that the country was at war, the nature of the perceived threat from the enemy, in my view, justified the trials, notwithstanding the fact that, on occasions, the harm caused was considerable. It was not disproportionate in the context and against the background of efforts made to ensure that volunteers were not put to what would *then* have been viewed as disproportionate risks. For example, volunteers in 1943 were given a full ophthalmic examination before a study of the effect of HN-1 on the eyes. That said, while the trials, as trials, may have been justified *in principle*, as I have already made clear earlier ('Specific Information' above), I entertain the most serious reservations about the reality of the consent obtained in, and thus the ethical propriety of, some of the trials, particularly those involving H.

That volunteers came forward during the early years of the War from all sections of Porton's staff, not just the medical but also the administrative staff, (and some research was conducted exclusively on staff at Porton), serves as a further reminder of the standards of the times and that those working at Porton, who might be considered to be aware of trials and their implications, considered them to be proportionate.

I accept that views may differ. Indeed, the researchers themselves expressed concerns on occasions, as, for example, when, after initial trials of BZ – a response to poisoning with nerve gas – the researchers doubted that further tests could be justified in terms of the risks of psychological harm posed to volunteers. Equally, Porton opposed the use of agents the primary mode of action of which was to induce hypo- or hyper-tension, as being 'too dangerous', despite pressure from CDAB. But, the fact that views may differ suggests, in my view, that it would be wrong to conclude that the trials which fall within this third category were, for that reason alone, ethically improper.

Trials at the Edges of Knowledge

I identify from the Survey a fourth category of trials which is the most problematic. It relates to the trials of nerve agents. There seems little doubt that there was great concern in the late 1940s and the 1950s about the possible use by the Soviet Union of G agents which were not previously known. Much work was needed and it was painstakingly carried out. But, as the Survey indicates, on some occasions, researchers were operating at the edges of their knowledge when exposing human volunteers to various trials

Because of the importance to my assessment of this category of trials, it may be of assistance if I separate it into two sub-categories, so as to analyse as carefully as possible the trials to which it applies.

1. The first subdivision consists of those trials in which the outcome was not really predictable from the knowledge available to Porton. This meant that the trial and its outcome could not effectively be controlled. And, since the ability to control what might happen is a crucial ingredient in safeguarding those exposed to the trial, the inability to exercise this control meant that volunteers were put in danger. Moreover, the level of danger was equally unpredictable: it could include death or serious injury. A number of trials fall into this sub-category.

- In a trial described in the Survey, six volunteers were exposed in 1951 to a dose of GD vapour weaker than one fortieth of the dose estimated in 1949 to be lethal. Yet, 'the symptoms suffered were much more severe than expected'. On one view, therefore, the lethal dose was not known with sufficient precision and must have been underestimated, exposing volunteers to danger.
- The Survey suggests that the reliance on ChE inhibition measured in a particular way, as the means of calculating the lethal dose of G agents, and the maximum dose to which volunteers could be exposed, was less than sound.
- The maximum dose of GB to which volunteers could be exposed was reduced after the case of severe poisoning in April 1953, but this reduced dose used in a subsequent trial two weeks later still led to a fatality, as will be described later.
- In 1963, trials were conducted into the effects of the nerve agent GF (contrary to the conditions laid down by the Adrian Committee, as previously mentioned ('The Commissioning and Supervision of Research at Porton' above)). The results of the research (involving 30 men) were described as 'unduly variable', particularly as regards ChE depression, and further work was banned.
- As a sign of a growing sense of caution and concern, in the light of previous experience, Porton, in 1964, applied a 'local safety margin' by setting the level of ChE depression lower by some 20% than that approved by the Biology Committee.
- The trials in 1953 which resulted in a fatality, which I will now review in detail.

For the purposes of my assessment, the most significant trial which falls into this subcategory is that which resulted in the death of a volunteer in 1953. This is a matter which is currently under review by the courts and the Wiltshire Coroner. I have no more information than that which appears in the Survey and, therefore, confine my comments to this. Clearly, the death of a volunteer is an appalling tragedy. It does not follow, however, that its occurrence *ipso facto* points to improprieties in the conduct of research. The question which I must address is whether the volunteer was exposed to a trial which was so much at the edges of knowledge and so fraught with risk of serious harm or death that it should not have taken place. An initial answer would appear to be that a number of volunteers were exposed to the same or similar trials and did not suffer serious harm. But this answer, (which, in any event, is not entirely true, as will be seen) may not go far enough. Two further matters must be explored. First, were the risks involved in the trials of nerve agents, of which the one involving the death of the volunteer was part, sufficiently known and understood so as to allow the researchers to guard against or manage them? Or, were these trials so far at the edges of what was known that the researchers were exposing volunteers to risks which they could neither calculate nor guard against?

Clearly, in so important a matter, it is crucial that any view must be based on the particular details of the trial in 1953 as a consequence of which the volunteer died. That said, however, the trial must be seen in a context. And that context, I repeat, is one of researchers operating at the edges of knowledge and understanding. An example, not related to the trial in 1953, may illustrate this context. The review by Porton in 1982 of its past work on miosis in trials of GB is instructive: 'good fortune rather than wise decisions have [sic] been responsible for the safety record'. Of particular concern was the relationship (if any) between miosis and detachment of the retina after exposure to GB. While any such relationship was thought to be speculative, it is clear that the trials were conducted against a background of incomplete understanding of the dangers to which volunteers were exposed. While researchers should not be criticised from the vantage point of hindsight, it was agreed at the time of the review that the ophthalmic screening procedures were 'inadequate and inappropriate'. Certainly, reading the available evidence concerning the trials of nerve agents, there is, as has been said, a very real sense that the researchers were at the edges of danger and suspected it. (Another indication of the context at that time, not involving work on nerve agents, can be found in the discussion surrounding the suspension in 1965 of the trials of incapacitating agents, referred to earlier ('The Commissioning and Supervision of Research at Porton' above).) The ABC acknowledged in 1965 that some of the work on the newer incapacitating agents went 'very far into the realms of the unknown' in terms of assessing the safety of trials.

Returning to the fatal incident, the information base in relation to the effects of GB in 1953 was limited. Insights were being gained experientially and factored into the next set of trials. The agent which researchers were dealing with was lethal at an appropriate dose. Its effects, for example, on skin appear not to have been wholly understood, notwithstanding the several years of tests on animals. As the report on the fatal incident indicated: 'Comparatively small variations in absorption might … encompass the lethal dose'.

In the case of the volunteer who died, everything appeared to turn on the amount of skin fat in his arm, since his RBC (red blood cell) ChE activity (another critical indicator of the effect of GB) was found on post-mortem examination to have been within the normal range. The role of skin fat (both surface and sub-surface) in the penetration of the skin by GB had been demonstrated by earlier research in 1951 and 1952. Then, in April 1953, one of six volunteers suffered 'severe poisoning' when a dose of GB was administered to fabric fixed to his arm. The man recovered after being hospitalised and suffering convulsions and temporary cessation of breath.

After the incident, his surface skin fat was measured and found to be much lower than the average. While other factors were thought to have contributed to his reaction, the role of skin fat, particularly in the light of the findings in 1951–52, could be thought to be significant. The trial involving the volunteer who died took place in May, 1953, only two weeks later. His surface skin fat was found on post-mortem to be below, but not greatly below, the average. But, his sub-surface, or subcutaneous, skin fat was found to be 'practically absent'. Given the apparent importance of both types of skin fat, the first question which I must ask is whether a procedure for measuring surface and sub-surface skin fat existed at the time, or could have been developed. If such a procedure was available, or could have been developed, then failure to employ it in the case of the volunteer who died constitutes improper conduct. It also means that it was wrong to expose any of the volunteers to this trial, since they would all have been at risk.

If such a procedure for measuring both types of skin fat was not available nor could be developed, I must ask a second question. In the light of the serious incident two weeks previously, were the researchers at Porton justified in carrying out further trials, particularly the trial in which the volunteer died? (All nerve agent studies with humans were banned thereafter, until after the Report of the Adrian Committee.)

Skin fat affected the response to GB. Assuming, for the sake of argument, that a procedure did not exist to allow it to be adequately measured, then volunteers clearly ran the risk of being exposed to serious harm. Moreover, it appears to be the case that skin fat not only affected the response to GB, but affected it in such a way as to make a significant difference to the risk to which a volunteer was to be exposed. On the hypothesis that no procedure for measuring skin fat was or could have been developed, I am drawn to the conclusion that, knowing its importance and being unable (on this hypothesis) to measure it, meant that volunteers were exposed to an uncontrollable danger of serious harm, or death. That being so, on these assumptions, it was wrong to carry out the trial both on the volunteer who died, and on the others involved.

It could, of course, be objected that the volunteer's response was idiosyncratic, and thus, by its nature, could not be predicted nor guarded against. There have been occasions in which volunteers involved in trials of new drugs have suffered injury, or even died, as the consequence of an idiosyncratic response.[8] No blame attaches because the tragedy was both unforeseeable and unpreventable. But, this argument does not hold water here. The trials in 1951–52 had pointed to the role of skin fat and the trial in April 1953 had then raised questions about skin fat (admittedly surface skin fat), such as to implicate it as affecting the volunteer's response, even though RBC ChE activity was also implicated. If the idea of an idiosyncratic response were advanced here, it would amount to blaming the volunteer for having fat-free arms.

If the assumptions advanced above are valid, the volunteer died because the trial was not safe, not just for him, but for all, since none of the volunteers in the various

[8] Foster, *The Ethics of Medical Research on Humans* (Cambridge University Press, 2001) p 207.

trials appears to have undergone any procedure for measuring skin fat. And, if such procedures were not available, the trials became uncontrollably dangerous. This is not, I submit, the judgement of hindsight. The pressure to develop knowledge about G agents was great, above all to develop forms of treatment to protect service personnel and the wider society. This pressure, this imperative, must not be overlooked. But, in my view, there were trials carried out as a consequence which went too far.

2. The second sub-category of trials which I have described as being at the edges of knowledge relates to what I might call a conscious and deliberate flirtation with danger. It involves a trial not involving volunteering servicemen, but the medical staff at Porton. Again, perhaps they were seeking to follow the 'golden rule', but in this case going beyond courage to foolhardiness. The report of the trials talks of 'careful consideration' having been given to the trials. But, it involved trials in 1958 of the nerve agent VX, whereby volunteer medical officers were exposed to what was then accepted as the *lethal* dose, a dose which was only later revised. It cannot be doubted that despite any 'careful consideration', the trial could reasonably have been expected to flirt with the risk of serious injury and death. Any such trial cannot be justified and should not have taken place, nor have been condoned by others at Porton.

As regards this fourth category of trials, my conclusion, therefore, is that there were clearly occasions on which the safety of the volunteers (including the medical staff) was put at risk, and that this was acknowledged by Porton. By this I mean the risk to safety amounted to something more than a particular predicted harm, which, it could reasonably be assumed, could be controlled and managed. As has been said, it is clear that in the case of nerve agents, the imperative to know was, of course, deemed to be high. Good examples of this imperative are the work on miosis and on VX nerve agent. Equally, the pressure to find out was high. But, I am of the view that at least a *prima facie* case exists that there were trials involving nerve agents which posed such a risk of serious harm as to go beyond what was ethically permissible, notwithstanding the context of defence and the threat of war.

The crucial issue is the researchers' ability to vouch for the safety of the volunteer. When this was in question, there is a case for saying that the researchers crossed the line from the proper to the improper. It is not for me to speculate on their motives, which may have been of the best. I can only say that in these apparently rare cases the boundaries of what should be done were exceeded, even by reference to the standards of the time. I list the trials which I regard as having exceeded these boundaries in my Conclusion (below).

Long-term Effects

Before concluding this section on safety and risk, two further points warrant attention. First, it is clear that researchers were concerned about any long-term effects which could follow from volunteers being exposed to certain agents. There were follow-up studies, for example, of exposure to GB and a detailed examination over a long period of time into the possible carcinogenicity of CR, carried out in conjunction with experts at the Chester Beattie Cancer Research Institute.

Concern about long-term effects was particularly present in the case of psychoactive agents. The risk of short-term effects and their consequences were explored and, once identified, were monitored and managed. But, whether these agents produced long-term effects was not known. This might suggest that trials should not have been embarked on at all if, however remote, they were risks of really serious harm, such as permanent changes of personality. Indeed, as has been seen, the Survey describes how the safety of tests was discussed by the CDAB and 'in particular, the risk of inducing an irreversible effect in some men'.

Again, any judgement is not clear-cut. There was, for example, very real concern that psychoactive agents could be used against the armed forces or the civilian population, from which grew the perceived need to understand and, if possible, counteract their effects. This creates the ethical background against which the trials must be judged. Thus, notwithstanding the fact that the available literature did not provide a definitive picture of the extent of foreseeable reactions, the decision was taken to devise a test, so as to exclude from the trials those volunteers who might be more vulnerable to the agents. The intention was to remove, or at least reduce to a remote possibility, the risk of long-term harm. As was commonly the case when the researchers were uncertain, the test was designed by experts from outside Porton (from the Maudsley and other Hospitals). The advice from experts at the Maudsley Hospital was that 'as long as subjects for human studies were chosen carefully and small doses used, permanent damage was not likely'. This may invite the conclusion that, if the proposition that it was imperative to carry out the work is accepted, the researchers, by consulting outside experts, took such precautions as to suggest that they did not offend against the standards of the times.

This view may perhaps be reinforced by the decision to follow-up volunteers over time so as to monitor any long-term effects. The volunteers' Service medical records were routinely annotated to record the fact they had attended Porton, which would have put medical personnel elsewhere on notice, should something untoward and otherwise inexplicable arise at a later date. Monitoring long-term effects was the responsible thing to do. That it was not always, in fact, done effectively, by relying, for example only on Service medical records, speaks of administrative ineptness and, perhaps, cost-cutting, rather than any ethical impropriety on the part of the researchers.

The case of H (mustard gas) and the long-term effects on volunteers, and servicemen generally, of exposure during training or trials was different. This concern did not involve monitoring volunteers in the future, but having to decide whether to abandon the practice then current of exposing service personnel to H, because of the possibility of long-term risks of cancer, raised in 1978. COHSE took outside advice and concluded that, although the risk was low that a single exposure would result in adverse consequences in the long-term, the use of H for a 'confidence test', as part of every serviceman's training, should cease. Porton initially did not regard this as applying to their research work, since volunteers were only exposed to a single dose. Porton also did not regard it as necessary to warn of what it regarded as a 'non-existent risk'. COHSE, for its part, recognised the tension between the safety of volunteers, on the one hand, and the perceived needs of the Services for information about the effects of H which would help them to protect their service personnel, noting that if work on H were abandoned, the further development of protective clothing would be 'seriously affected'. But, the interests of safety prevailed and penetration studies of clothing using H were suspended. The MC subsequently discussed the issue. No further tests were carried out.

I turn finally to three matters which an assessment of the ethics of the research at Porton should mention. I can deal with them somewhat more briefly.

The Role of Ethics Committees

Ethics committees are, in effect, institutional mechanisms to superintend the conduct of biomedical research so as to ensure that scientific advances are made while protecting the interests of research subjects. Described in this way, it will be realised that from at least 1965, if not before, as was pointed out earlier ('The Commissioning and Supervision of Research at Porton' above), Porton had such a mechanism. Initially, it was the Applied Biology Committee, then the Medical Committee. A significant feature of these bodies was that from the outset they included independent members from outside Porton and the armed forces. Equally significant, as was referred to earlier, they exercised a supervisory role over the conduct of the research at Porton and, in particular, appear to have reflected on a number of ethical issues which arose.

To this extent, Porton might be thought to have been sensitive to the need for external supervision and, as important, advice on the ethics of proposed research, long before the general emergence of ethics committees took place. In 1987, an Independent Ethics Committee was created, characterised by its wholly independent status and membership. The requirement that all proposals for research should be submitted for approval was continued. In this respect, Porton brought itself into line with the practice of other institutions where research was carried out. But, a supervisory mechanism, with a significant degree of independence and authority, (which, on occasions were exercised, for example, through 'closed meetings'), had long existed.

Compensation

One of the more contentious issues surrounding the conduct of research on healthy volunteers is whether researchers have a duty to compensate (in terms of money) those harmed as a consequence of participating in the research. A duty exists in law, but only if the research subject can show that the researcher has been negligent and that he has suffered harm as a consequence, (leaving aside the (very rare) situation in which the volunteer's apparent consent was vitiated by fraud or duress). The existence of an ethical duty, regardless of the requirements of the law, is not, however, universally accepted.

Against this background, the Ministerial statement in 1930, referred to in the Survey, appears to stand in some contrast. By this Statement, the Secretary of State for War explained that volunteers at Porton would be covered by what was called the Injury Warrant, and could, therefore, receive 'compensation under the procedure as injury attributable to service'. There is virtually no evidence in the Survey of the extent to which this Statement reflected actual practice then or later. The two exceptions are when the widow of the serviceman who died after the trial in 1953 is described as having been paid a pension under the Injury Warrant and when COHSE is described as reaffirming the continued applicability of the Warrant in 1980. If the practice adopted did indeed mean that compensation was available without the need to bring any legal action, or even the need to show conduct which was actionable in law (for example, negligence), it suggests that, in this regard at least, the government of the day and later successors were alive to what many would regard as an ethical obligation, as being the counterpoise to the willingness of the volunteer to come forward for the good of research.

That said, the newly appointed Independent Ethics Committee reviewed arrangements for compensation at its first meeting in 1987. Crucially, the Committee indicated that the future approval of research would depend on an 'appropriate' system of compensation. A draft was prepared, drawing on the Guidelines issued by the Royal College of Physicians and on those proposed by the Association of the British Pharmaceutical Industry. The Medical Committee at Porton accepted the draft and formal arrangements were introduced to provide for compensation for anyone suffering 'injury, disability or death as a result of participating as a volunteer in research …'. These arrangements were set out in a document which, it appears, was intended to be given to all volunteers. It contemplates that compensation may be claimed without the need to demonstrate negligence or take legal action. It leaves open to the claimant the option to pursue legal action should he wish to do so. The claimant must, however, demonstrate that the harm complained of was 'as a result of participating …'. This approach is consonant with accepted practice and constitutes a recognition of the ethical responsibilities owed to the volunteer by the institution engaged in research.

Awareness of and Compliance with Codes and Guidelines

The Survey says little about the role which Codes and Guidelines on research ethics had on the conduct of research at Porton or on the minds of the researchers. There are occasional developments which, on one interpretation, can be said to reflect the emergence of a particular Code or Guideline, if only because they are roughly contemporaneous. But, it is not until 1979 that entries begin to appear in documents indicating that a particular trial was conducted in accordance with the Declaration of Helsinki. Given the importance that this Declaration gives to consent, these entries may be intended to demonstrate that volunteers' consent was obtained. But, as has already been said, bald assertions of this kind are no evidence of what in fact transpired. At best, they are evidence that there was an awareness of the existence of the Declaration and the need to comply with it. Why it became routine practice to record this is not revealed. It needs to be said, however, that while there is little formal acknowledgement of Codes and Guidelines, it must not be thought that they were necessarily ignored. The debate in 1965 over the ban on trials of incapacitating agents sees references being made both to the (then) recently published Guidelines of the Medical Research Council of 1963 and to the Nuremberg Code of 1947.

Conclusion

In this assessment I have concerned myself, as I indicated at the outset, with the general pattern of conduct at Porton in carrying out trials during the period of time covered by the Survey, and certain specific issues and cases. I have not examined each trial, not only because there were very many thousands, but also because of the wide variation in the evidence available.

I have come to the conclusion that research was carried out at Porton in a thorough, painstaking, careful and often ingenious manner. Examples include the trials relating to nerve agents. The elaborate and extensive trials of riot control agents (not least because the safety of the wider public was also at stake), provide a further example, as do the very large number of tests on the penetration of agents through a wide variety of fabrics described, and the trials relating to atropine. The results were obviously of great importance in assessing military effectiveness, (and see the laconic, but deadly serious observation reported in the Survey that a soldier suffering from miosis may discern a shape as a tank, but 'would be hard pressed to say if it was Russian or British').

Secondly, I have come to the view that there is no evidence to justify a conclusion that the conduct of the trials at any point went beyond the limits of what should ever be contemplated, far less tolerated, in a civilised society.

Thirdly, however, I am persuaded that there were trials, albeit a few out of the many thousands of trials conducted at Porton, (there were many hundreds of studies conducted just in the period 1939–45), when it may be said that the research may not have met the ethical standards required of the researchers and, where relevant, those who approved the trials. They are the following:

- the trials of liquid nerve agents on bare skin, carried out between 1951–55: they include, but are not limited to the trial which led to the fatality in 1953;
- the trials in 1951 of the nerve agent GD, in which the lethal dose was not known with sufficient certainty;
- the trial in 1958 of the nerve agent VX, which involved the use of what, at the time, was regarded as the lethal dose;
- the trials in 1942, involving the exposure of volunteers to H vapour in the scrotal region, if, as seems likely, there was no real consent;
- the trial in 1945 of the substance in the captured German shells, which exposed volunteers to danger without first seeking to determine the nature of the substance.

In addition, a question mark can also be raised in relation to the trials conducted from the 1950s to the 1970s to determine the extent to which GB induced miosis, in so far as a real danger that a volunteer might suffer a detached retina existed but was not controlled. The trials might be said by some to have constituted too great a step into the unknown.

These trials clearly amount to serious departures from what should have been done. But, on the evidence of the Survey, they are few in number and spread over several decades. Indeed, that they are few in number may be thought, perhaps, to be worthy of note and a tribute both to the volunteers and the researchers. The work was conducted at Porton in difficult times: during the 1930s with the memory of the Great War and the threat of more war to come; during the Second World War, when the survival of the nation was at stake; and during the acute tensions of the Cold War and, later, of civil disturbance. It involved research into agents which were deadly, or agents which had to be made safe. This must not be forgotten. Nor must the past be viewed with hindsight, or from a perspective which is far removed from the tenor of those times. As is clear from the Survey, a very great debt of gratitude is clearly owed to those who volunteered to take part in the research at Porton and to those who carried it out.

PART V

A Public Figure

I am by nature bookish and reserved, shy even. For those interested in personality I am at the far end of the spectrum of 'introvert' according to the Myers Briggs categorisation. An old story goes as follows. An extrovert and an introvert are told that they are invited to a party and may ask three, but only three questions. The extrovert begins. Who'll be there, what should I wear, will there be food? The questioner cuts her off as she fires off further questions – only three questions allowed. Then it's the introvert's turn. You have three questions he is told. I only have one he replies – do I have to go?! That's me!

How come, therefore, that much of my professional life has been played out in public? The cynic may say that the introvert stuff is just an act. But it isn't. In fact, there are two factors which, taken together, seem to have conspired to make me a public figure. The first is that, above all else, I see myself as a teacher. I really do believe that education is a fundamental right and also, for those with the necessary awareness and skill, a fundamental responsibility. So I've spent a lot of time trying to explain things to as wide an audience as possible – from the seminar to the lecture to the speech to the broadcast to the Public Inquiry.

The second factor is that I am seen as an outsider, belonging to no-one. As such, I can be trusted to chase things down and draw the necessary conclusions. It may not always bring me friends but that comes with the territory. It means that I've been asked to take on tasks in the public sphere which come with some controversy, whether it's rabies and pets, the deaths of children undergoing heart surgery, the regulation of the NHS, or the regulation of MPs. Such assignments are not for the faint-hearted, but someone has to do them.

In this section I let you see how the media dealt with me as I navigated my way through public life and how I dealt with them. In footballing terms, perhaps a score draw!

21

Meet the Press[1]

I was appointed as the Chair of IPSA [the Independent Parliamentary Standards Authority] in November 2009. Within two days, I realised that this was going to be a different job from all those I'd previously done. I'd had my fair share of difficult jobs, operating in the rough and tumble of Whitehall and Westminster with regular attention from the media and commentators. Over the previous 10 years I had chaired a Public Inquiry into the deaths of babies and children after paediatric cardiac surgery at Bristol Royal Infirmary and then established and chaired the Healthcare Commission, the first organisation to regulate the NHS. I thought I was used to the press.[2] I thought that my reputation was secure – someone who was his own man and told things as he saw them without fear or favour. That's probably why I was handed IPSA.

Well, within two days I felt the full force of the political press, an animal I was relatively unused to. In previous lives, I had found reasoned argument and honesty ensured, more or less, that the story came out with some semblance of the truth. Things were about to change.

IPSA barely existed. There was a Chairman, an acting Chief Executive, some eager young civil servants seconded from the Ministry of Justice, and some advisers. One adviser came up with the notion that I should meet the lobby journalists, a clique which move as a pack and are given privileged access on terms that no-one is quoted, not even through that much-loved device of 'a source'– in other words, they were given the inside story on a non-attributable basis.

I knew the media specialising in healthcare, science, and higher education. I didn't know the lobby. They filed into a tiny room in the temporary offices that IPSA shared with the Boundary Commission. There were about 9 or 10 of them on that Wednesday morning. My adviser, a long-term veteran of Whitehall media, welcomed them and explained that I was giving them an opportunity to put a name to a face and to ask some general questions. Nothing was to be on the record. One of them, Tim Shipman, then of the *Daily Mail*, pressed the point. Could something be attributed to a 'source'? No, this was to be a completely off-the-record conversation.

Several in the group did not look happy but appeared to acknowledge that these were the accepted rules of engagement.

Now, we need to back up for a moment.

[1] Extract from Chapter 2 of *Cleaning up the Mess: After the MPs' Expenses Scandal* (Biteback, 2019). Reprinted with permission.

[2] See my rather over-confident views in Working with the Media (Chapter 22).

IPSA had only recently been established by Parliament. The four other members of the Board (in addition to me as the Chairman) had not been appointed. Meanwhile, in another part of the Whitehall jungle, the Committee on Standards in Public Life, under the chairmanship of Sir Christopher Kelly, had been invited by the then Prime Minister, Gordon Brown, to offer its views in response to the scandal over MPs' expenses that had so shaken Westminster and Whitehall. The Committee chose to seize the moment and fill the vacuum of comment and recommendation on what should be done. Sir Christopher had decided that he was the person who should speak for an outraged nation. So, he called a press conference and spoke. His Committee had considered the matter and drawn up a Report. It included a lengthy list of things that should be done. And, Yes, he said in response to questions, they not only should be done, they *must* be done and done straightaway.[3]

Back to my meeting with the lobby journalists. Those most closely associated with the expenses story had liked what Kelly had said. It was suitably draconian. It seemed to be in sympathy with their anti-politician, anti-politics agenda. So, the first question put to me was, quite simply, not a question but, rather, a proposition – 'you are here to implement Kelly, aren't you?' This, after all had been what the media had been calling for – to 'Implement Kelly'. Many MPs, including political leaders, had echoed this call, recognising that there was no mileage in anything other than in breast-beating declarations of guilt and remorse. The charge was led by Rosa Prince of the *Daily Telegraph*, who was seeking to hold on to the notion that the expenses scandal was the *Telegraph*'s and her story, and by the *Daily Mail*'s Tim Shipman who saw himself as head boy.

My response was, I thought, measured. I remarked that legislation had been enacted, IPSA was being created, and IPSA's job would be to look at what might be needed so as to carry out its statutory mandate, not least to help to restore confidence in Parliament and Parliamentarians. This response was met by the journalists with an incredulous and vaguely frustrated repetition of the question, 'Yes, but you are here to implement Kelly'. When I explained in my, perhaps, professorial style, that IPSA was there to make up its own mind as an independent body (that was what the I in IPSA stood for), it was clear that I had lost the room. I wasn't on message. I was referring to another and quite unacceptable script. And who was I, anyway, to think that I might have a mind of my own, that I might for a moment imagine such a thing as independence existed? The meeting ground to a halt with an angry lobby not getting its way.

By the Friday and over that weekend, the convention that lobby briefings were confidential, non-reportable and non-attributable was in tatters. I was attacked for my views. Front pages and banner headlines in the *Daily Telegraph*[4] – and the *Daily Mail*[5] – were dedicated to the fact that I knew Alastair Campbell, until recently the press spokesman

[3] Anything other than a cursory reading would have revealed that much of what Sir Christopher was recommending would in fact have required primary legislation.

[4] *Daily Telegraph*, 6 November 2009.

[5] The creative Tim Shipman, under a headline reading, 'MPs' expenses report WON'T be torn up: Sir Ian Kennedy caves in over reform', talked of 'frantic 'phone calls between the two' [Kelly and me], 11 November 2009. In fact, no such telephone calls took place. Members of IPSA's staff merely agreed with Kelly's staff that we would keep Kelly's Report in mind as we did our work. In the event, much of what we came up with was similar to elements of Kelly's Report.

for Mr Blair. Indeed, I was so close to him that I had been his 'phone a friend' when he appeared on TV in 'Celebrity Who Wants to be a Millionaire'. Pages of Alastair's published diary were splashed across the papers describing how we holidayed together in the summer. The point was obvious. I was a patsy, in thrall to the political elite. My appointment had been fixed so that IPSA would not stand up to MPs.

Not true, but who cares? In fact, as regards the TV show, I had been asked by Alastair to help him raise money for Leukaemia Research, a worthy cause, save in the eyes of those who see the world according to their values. As regards summer holidays, our children went to the same school, and Alastair's partner drew our attention to a place she knew of in a village near where they spent their summer holidays. And, in any event, I had declared this friendship, and other connections to politicians whom I knew socially, to the chair of the interviewing panel when I was interviewed for the appointment as Chairman. But, why let facts get in the way of a smear?

These same newspapers also turned their fire on my family life. Journalists worked the houses on my street asking neighbours for whatever might be hurtful or damaging. Drawing a blank (my neighbours were decent folk), they pitched camp outside my house, such that on one occasion when I was due to take my younger son to watch Chelsea play his (then) beloved Manchester United, I had to climb over the back wall to avoid the photographers massed at the gate. My older son was harassed by a journalist as he came home and followed as far as the front door. When he (politely) closed the door, the journalist shouted through the letter box and left a note with her phone number on it urging him to call her. Having found that my wife and I had recently separated, the story in the *Mail* became that I was so bereft that I was not up for the job.[6] The journalist, one Simon Walters, resorted to the old device of citing a 'friend' so as to peddle his humbug. (Journalists don't reveal their sources, which is particularly convenient when the source is made up). The 'friend' was reported as referring to me as 'the poor chap'. Even in the very unlikely event that a friend would talk about me to a journalist in such circumstances, my friends don't speak like that. And, so as not to leave a stone unturned, a journalist was sent to 'doorstep' my mother-in-law and sister-in-law, who happen to live 100 miles north of Los Angeles (over 6000 miles away). And, my wife and her friends and colleagues were harassed.

What was my sin? I was someone who had dedicated his life to public service. There were no skeletons. Why, this attack, this attempt to suggest that I was unsuitable as Chairman on political or personal grounds?

Simple. I, who was to them a nobody, had had the temerity to indicate that I was my own man and would decide for myself and with my Board, once appointed, what IPSA would do. The collective had decided that I was to be undermined. I was to be shown what would happen if I didn't go where elements of the media wanted me to go. Welcome to the birth of IPSA!

Word got back, as it always does in Westminster, that I was being harassed by the media. I had taken one of my sons to the local pub for dinner. We ordered our food and my mobile 'phone rang. I stepped outside into a chilly November night. First, Harriet

[6] 8 November 2009.

Harman, then Leader of the House, and then Mr Speaker called me. Both were keen to show solidarity with me. Also, of course, having seen me appointed they didn't want to start all over again if I got cold feet and quit. It was good of them to call. I indicated that I had no illusions about the press, but that there was an important job to be done and that I would do it. I was on the 'phone and in the cold for over two hours. My dinner was also cold when I got back inside. My son had waited patiently but had had the good sense to eat his food while it was still warm.

Two Postscripts

First, two days after meeting the lobby journalists, I received a handwritten letter from Patrick Wintour, the *Guardian*'s lobby correspondent, apologising for the behaviour of his colleagues and saying that in all his time in the lobby he had never known such a flagrant disregard for the conventions. He went on to apologise that he had himself used the story, once it had appeared elsewhere, under pressure from his editor. It was good of him to write and I appreciated it.

The second postscript concerns the appointment of members of IPSA's Board. As the very newly nominated Chairman, I was to join the Panel that had recommended my appointment so as to take part in the process of appointing my future colleagues. The *Telegraph* had by then published its front page story about my knowing Alastair Campbell. As I joined the group, the member of the Panel who was an ex-judge (the Panel had to include an ex-judge), Sir Christopher Rose, immediately went into his best cross-examination mode and pompously demanded to know why I hadn't mentioned my involvement with 'Who Wants to be a Millionaire'. I was struck by the aggression of his questioning. Whatever it said about the individual, it also demonstrated the power of the media to distort reality and massage prejudices. I was somewhat reluctant to reply. I had declared my links with Alastair and others in politics whom I knew socially when I was interviewed. Moreover, my involvement in the particular TV programme could not have the slightest relevance to my fitness to chair IPSA.[7] So, I simply said that I was not going to let the *Telegraph* pick my friends. But, Sir Christopher was not appeased. He persuaded the chair of the Panel that though I might be involved in the interviewing, I should be barred (for some reason – perhaps my keeping bad company) from involvement in the decisions to be made, once the interviews were over, as to who should serve as my colleagues on the Board. No reason was given, perhaps because prejudice is hard to substantiate in reasoned terms. It was a shabby display by him. But, it was an important lesson about the world that I was entering: that it would be lonely and the knives could come from anywhere.

[7] As it happens, I gave the wrong answer and wrecked Alastair's fundraising!

22

Working with the Media: A View from the Frontline[1]

Introduction

I am honoured to have been invited to deliver the British Academy's Isaiah Berlin Lecture for 2010. Sir Isaiah was a man of the greatest distinction, numbering among his many honours the Presidency of the British Academy. He was described as

> ... a brilliant speaker who delivered rapidly and spontaneously, richly allusive and coherently structured material whether for a lecture series at Oxford, or as a broadcaster for the BBC 3rd programme, usually without a script.

I am conscious of the fact that my being invited to follow in such distinguished footsteps may be part of a cunning plan on the part of the Academy to demonstrate the urgent need for funding in these straightened times by showing how desperate things had become since the great man strutted his stuff!

This Lecture appears in the interstices of a Conference considering the impact of the media on developments in Bioethics (I shall use this term throughout as a synonym for health law, ethics and the development of policy in relation to them). I bring some long experience of dealing with both bioethics and the media. It will be for you to judge whether any wisdom has emerged as a consequence.

Some short introductory remarks. I am delighted beyond measure that bioethics has achieved the prominence it deserves. When I started, several centuries ago, there was no book, far less a course in medical law (as it was more narrowly described, including by me) in the universities. Applied ethics was principally concerned with the justice of warfare and was beginning to be interested in forms of unfair discrimination. Medical ethics was barely recognised as a subject in its own right, though consideration of topics such as what was loosely (and still is loosely!) called euthanasia, and abortion, was as old as literature. Now, bioethics in its various forms is a significant area of discourse attracting distinguished scholars and commentators. And, as it is Manchester which is sponsoring this Conference, it is right to pay proper tribute to the contribution that the University of Manchester has played in this process.

[1] The British Academy's Isaiah Berlin Annual Lecture, 2010.

Bioethics is also a very popular area of discourse with those who do not necessarily see it as bioethics – a discipline – but, rather, see it as an area of interest or concern which frequently touches their lives and the lives of those around them. The conversations in the street, in the pub, around the kitchen table frequently touch on bioethics. This couple is trying for a baby but they've had three goes at IVF and the clinic wants them to reconsider. So-and-so can't get that latest cancer drug and is on her last legs. Mrs X wasn't told that they were going to take her womb out when they operated on her. John is terrified that the school where he teaches will learn that he is HIV positive. And so on.

The conversations are motivated by concern and by interest in what are genuinely human and genuinely difficult real-life dilemmas. Bioethics is not unique among areas of law, ethics and policy in attracting popular attention. Criminology and sentencing policy are other such areas (though they may not be spoken of using these labels). Real property or trusts do not attract the same attention, save for the enthusiast, although not short of ethical dilemmas. The key lies in the way that bioethics connects with people's lives, its immediacy, and its intrinsic human interest.

And, of course, this is where the media appears.[2] Mention human interest and the collective ears of the media prick up. From its appearance on the stage of public awareness, bioethics has had for the media a heady and irresistible mix of the scientist/boffin/nutty professor, the caring doctor/angel/nurse, the battle/war against disease, the plucky/brave patient, the breakthrough/wonder drug, and the chance to express an opinion on the rights and wrongs of abortion, euthanasia, and all points in between.

This is the context of my Lecture. Before setting off, I ought to say that, in honour of Sir Isaiah, I have taken something of a liberty with the title. I need to make it clear from the outset that the Lecture is a personal account. In much that follows, I shall be drawing on my personal experiences. I do so because it is the 'frontline' that I know, it offers some understanding of the development of bioethics, and because it may be of interest to others at various stages of their careers. So, let's begin.

The Question

The question I've set myself to address is the impact of the media on the development of bioethics, having regard particularly to my experience. I shall try to do this in two ways. In the first part, I shall explore active engagement with the media, from the perspective of someone who has worked in the field for many years. Then, I'll look at things from the perspective of reactive responses to the media. The context in both cases will be the media's place in the discourse of bioethics and the effect that the media has had on developments. As I have said, I shall draw on my experience. I recognise that I must steer a careful course between self-indulgence and self-flagellation. You will be the judges.

So, first, active engagement and use of the media.

[2] I shall treat the word 'media' sometimes as if it were singular (depending on the context), putting to one side my seven years of Latin!

The Starting Point – The Educator

At a conference organised by a university and taking place in the British Academy, I will take it as given that the stance, the point of departure for discourse, is that of the educator. Of course, educators are not a homogenous group. Particularly in the area under discussion, they have perspectives. They have assumptions which are unstated but operate powerfully. They may all agree that there are important matters to be considered. They may all agree that these matters are worthy of consideration in their own right as intellectually challenging. But, some may stop there. To educators such as these, the abstract world of the thought experiment and the mental/linguistic puzzle is more than enough to wrestle with.

To educators of a different stripe, however, the challenge is different. Yes, the issues are intellectually challenging. Yes, there are problems of language to grapple with. But, while they can be dealt with abstractly, it is important to go further. The issues touch on the real world of real people and the choices that people have to make in going about the business of living, and dying. So, for this second group of educators, their discourse is rooted in the untidy mess of life. To them, the educator's stance calls for more than abstract reflection. It demands forensic rooting out of facts (leaving aside for the moment what facts are *the* facts). It calls for objective, dispassionate analysis, taking account of the facts and putting to one side prejudices (another word for pre-judgements). (Unlike the Red Queen, in *Alice in Wonderland*, it's important to avoid the approach which says: 'Sentence first, verdict afterwards'!) Their stance then calls for them to do something which some resile from as a matter of faith, while others, particularly those blessed with the gene of certainty, do with relish. This second group of educators have to *reach a view*.

I count myself among this second group. Their approach tends to be my preferred option, without, I should say, the gene of certainty. I am not sure whether it is because I have operated in the field of public policy for so long that I am drawn to this approach, or because the approach draws me to the world of public policy. I'll leave that to others.

Finally, the last step for the educator of whatever persuasion is communication. Two matters then arise, one, to a degree, dictated by the other. Who is the audience with whom the educator seeks to communicate and what medium should be used?

The Educator and the Media

The medium that I am concerned with here is the media. So, the media and whom they reach is the audience. They may not be the chosen audience or even the preferred audience. But, for the purposes of this Lecture, they are the audience. And, let me be clear, I have no problem with this, challenging as it may be. If the educator is wrestling with matters which touch on the lives of people and affect the choices that they make, the media are also interested. They are interested because some have a sense of their mission as being to discuss issues of the day. They are also interested because all of them need to turn a profit. They do so by ensuring that they maintain and, if possible, increase their revenue. This revenue, of course, derives from their holding onto and continuing to appeal to their readers/viewers/listeners so that advertisers will continue to invest in them, safe in the knowledge what they are selling is reaching the desired audience.

All of their audiences are interested in bioethics. So, the media's audience is not the small community of like-minded souls who together constitute the community of educators. Rather, the media's audience collectively is the heterogeneous mass that we call the public, albeit that different parts of the media seek to appeal to different elements of that public.

Control

To the educator, if the medium of communication is the media, something crucial needs to be recognised straightaway. We can call it 'control'. With most of the other audiences that they aim to reach, educators stay in control of what is said. There is the lecture or the seminar where the educator sets the rules, the subject matter, and the particular 'take' on the matter at hand. There is the paper, in which the editor of the journal may mess about with the words, but, if it is accepted for publication, educators get their messages across. Equally so if it's a book. And, now, equally so with a blog. But, the media is different. The educator must communicate through a medium, through someone else. Control is lost. What you want to say may not be said. The 'take' may be different. And, more fundamentally, the very reason for being of the educator, to engage in considered discourse, drawing on reasoned argument, may not mean anything to, or be the principal concern, of the media.

Purpose

The media exists to sell a product. They seek to entertain. The more lofty will also say to inform. Few would add the word educate. That's not their job, they might say, except tangentially.[3] But, if educating's what the educator lives for, there's a danger that things could end in tears.

[3] It would be wrong in any Lecture on the interaction between the media and bioethics, to ignore occasions on which the media, though, as I've suggested, not ordinarily concerned to educate, has, in fact, itself played the role of the educator. I have in mind circumstances in which the media has investigated activities and practices and exposed them as wrong and harmful to patients and the public. The areas of product liability and safe care come particularly to mind. If ever there was a watershed in thinking about the safety of drugs and the need to care properly for those harmed by them, it was the scrutiny of thalidomide by the Insight team of the *Sunday Times*. Through the paper's efforts, the whole structure for the regulation of pharmaceutical products, which we now take for granted, was born. Through its efforts a fund was created which still receives new applications for assistance, nearly five decades on. Other examples of the media's influence in the area of safety include the exposure of concerns about the Dalkon shield and the drug Opren. These were examples of the media initially going it alone and serving the interests of the wider public and are to be celebrated.

Democratisation of Knowledge

As if the lack of control over the discourse and the difference in purpose between the educator and the media were not challenges enough, there's something else to add to the mix. I refer to the media as it exists now; so different from just 20-odd years ago. The internet has appeared. From one perspective, it is, of course, a boon to the educator. The market place of ideas now straddles the world. Educators can send their messages to anywhere on earth and start a conversation. Those who would wish to censor what is discussed are fighting a losing battle. This is the good news.

But there is a downside. Only recently, Bob Woodward of Watergate fame lamented 'the torrent of internet and cable news driven "by speed and impatience and simplification and manufactured controversy"'.[4] And, I would add an obsession with personality, and trivialisation: 'sound-bite solutions to complex problems', as President Obama recently observed. One particular downside from our perspective can be characterised as the democratisation of knowledge. It takes as its defining premise that a fundamental feature of scholarly discourse, the notion of 'authority', is outdated, anti-democratic, oppressive. Something can be so if it is asserted sufficiently strongly or stridently and/or a sufficient number of people are prepared to assert that it is so. The need for argumentation, for the weighing of evidence, for the very notion of evidence, for reasoned discourse, is not so much rejected as ignored. This really is a new world for the educator. The MMR vaccine causes autism. Full stop. Anyone arguing otherwise is out to harm children, to perpetrate some awful experiment, to line their pockets, or all of these. And what has come to be called 'the mainstream media' pick this up and run with it. They do so claiming that they are merely reporting a social phenomenon. But, they also do so because there's nothing more attractive in terms of circulation than a good fight, particularly if it pitches 'the establishment' against the little guy and, particularly, if it can run and run.

The MMR vaccine is just one recent example. You can go into the bleaker reaches of the internet to find many more. They are the product of poor education, the growth of unbridled subjectivism, a rejection or suspicion of 'authority', and the embrace of causes, ranging from animal rights to GM crops, in which no argument is brooked and direct action is a valid option. Indeed, discussion of GM offers a perfect example of the coming together of the counter-culture of distrust and ignorance and the media, keen to stoke the fears of the less thoughtful and thereby appear to be on the side of traditional notions of wholesomeness. The encapsulation of the debate into two words by the TV programme *World in Action*, echoed in the *Daily Mail*, was an act of near genius: 'Frankenstein Foods' has shaped (and blighted) grown-up debate for the past decade.[5]

So, what have we identified so far as the challenges awaiting educators as they venture forth from the ivory tower? Loss of control over what's said and how it is said, a different, much more diverse audience, a different purpose in communication, and a

[4] Times, 16 October 2010.
[5] See B Dixon, 'What are science journalists for?' (1999) *Information Services and Use* 75–81.

challenge to the notion of authority and even, perhaps the notion of evidence. Put like that, the environment looks hostile. A rapid retreat to the tower may beckon: back to the community of scholars and educators who talk the same language and observe the same rules. The temptation is huge. Many find it irresistible, because they ventured out of the tower and found the experience sufficiently unpleasant as not to be worth repeating, or because they've seen what happened to others. And don't forget that subset of educators who reinforce this view. I refer to what used to be called caustically the 'telly don', the person always ready with a smile and leather patches at the elbows of his sports coat to offer a view, and thereby earn the contempt and envy of colleagues in about equal measure.

The Educator's Duty

What I am going to suggest here is that the temptation to retreat should be resisted. The educator should engage with the media as developments in bioethics are explored and views expressed. The hostile environment can be negotiated. I make this suggestion out of a strong conviction about the role of the educator in the world we live in: a role that Sir Isaiah Berlin himself embraced. I would go so far as to say it is a duty: we have a duty as educators to engage with the media. This, certainly, is how I have lived my life.[6]

The engagement can be on the educator's terms and on the media's terms. The former is more comfortable. Both must be taken on. Let me take them in turn. In doing so, I remind you again that I will draw on my own experiences, as the title of the Lecture invites me to do. I will do so with what I hope is a degree of objectivity. This will be an early test of my powers of communication! I may fall at the first fence!

As a young teacher, I was constantly aware that, in embarking on the study of bioethics, I was wrestling with big and, at the time, largely unanalysed, let alone unanswered, issues of morality arising from contemporary developments in healthcare. I was doing so in the presence of a few students and interested others. It was quite clear from the attention they attracted from time to time in the media that the issues were of great interest and concern to the wider population. It was also clear that there was nowhere for people to go to satisfy what I took to be an appetite for understanding.

I had this very real sense that it was the educator's and, therefore, my duty to reach out beyond the classroom and the lecture theatre. I saw myself as having a duty to bring my questions, my analysis, my insights, such as they were, to the community of interested fellow citizens: to set up my stall, if you will, in the market place of ideas and risk the brickbats. I believed and still do in the democratisation of education – an entirely different notion from the democratisation of knowledge that I referred to earlier.

[6] [Since I wrote this Lecture the change in the landscape of communication (or shouting) has completely changed. Social Media rules! More than half the population in the USA get their news from Facebook, which, defining itself as a 'platform' and being allowed to get away with this description through its all-powerful lobbying, washes its hands of responsibility for the stuff that graces its platform. How to respond was only just beginning to surface as a question. Now it demands a book in its own right let alone a Lecture!]

If it was my duty as an educator to reach as wide an audience as possible, the question became one of finding the right means. Enter the media. This meant the press, radio and television. It is important to remember that back in the 70s, when I began, university teachers did not trespass into the media very often. And, if they did, they ran the considerable risk of earning the disapproval of colleagues as having 'sold out'. There is that delicious story of the two elderly dons in Oxford discussing a young high-flyer's flirtation with the media, whereupon one remarks, after appropriate expressions of regret, that 'if he's not careful, they'll ask him to do the Reith Lectures'! But, I was happy to take the risk. Let me give you some illustrations.

Printed Media

Journals

As regards the printed media, the first stop for the educator is the journals and the specialist publications. As regards the law, the established organs took a long time to be persuaded to take offerings about medical law as serious contributions to scholarship, rather than oddities. What made it even harder was the difficulty faced by those who saw themselves as guarding the sacred flame of legal scholarship. Where did this stuff about death and surgery and consent fit in? Was it criminal law, family law, or torts. It had to be one of them! The assumption was that the subject matter had to fit into the existing legal taxonomy. Otherwise, it wasn't proper law. The taxonomy itself was not to be messed about with.

I wrote a piece on the case of *Corbett v Corbett*.[7] To me, the case involved very deep issues about the nature of self and identity, as well as the nature of marriage, all arising in the context of what were, in the 1960s and 70s, rather exotic surgical practices (the one party to the 'marriage' was a transsexual who had undergone surgery). The article was rejected by all the established journals. You may conclude that it was the writer and his writing, not the subject, which condemned it. But, in this case, at least, that may not be right. For, in my concern to see it published, I sent it to the great man himself, someone who had written brilliantly for years on matters we now describe as medical law, but which he largely saw as aspects of criminal law – Professor Glanville Williams. He held the principal chair in law in Cambridge and had achieved near God-like status. He had encouraged me as I was starting out. I explained that I couldn't get it published.

On receipt of the paper he wrote that he thought it was an important contribution and that I should leave it to him: he would get it published. Well, even his imprimatur did not do the trick. It was still refused. Finally, I was advised of a new journal that was starting out and was keen for copy. So, the article found a home: in the *Anglo-American Law Review* of 1973.[8] What was the problem? I think that it was a combination of conservatism as to what constituted proper legal discourse, coupled with a degree of

[7] [1970] 2 All ER 33.
[8] (1973) 2 *Anglo-American Law Review* 112.

concern that the details of surgery on transsexuals was not proper fare for the denizens of law schools. But, in broader terms, it indicated the reticence in that part of the media controlled by other educators to give a platform for a discourse which they were unfamiliar with. All developments in scholarly discourse confront this challenge. Bioethics was no exception. But, in my view, this conservatism on the part of law journals did, for a while, hamper the development of bioethics.

My experience with medical journals in the US, by contrast, had been different. Bioethics as a discipline was somewhat more established there.[9] I was interested in the concept of death. In the United States, the State of Kansas had passed a remarkable law in which it set out effectively two sets of circumstances in which someone could be said to be dead. I thought that this was a bad idea. I argued, not very contentiously, that it might be wise to stick with one notion of death, since that's what we'd lived (and died) with since the beginning of time. The appearance of machines capable of keeping the heart going had to be factored into how we managed the treatment of the dying. But, it should not serve as a basis for the notion that whether you were dead or not depended on what was happening to you: whether you were on a machine or not. Death must be an unambiguous state and its presence or absence could not be contingent on circumstances. Well, I sent the article to the leading US medical journal, the *New England Journal of Medicine* and they readily took it.[10] And I'm happy to say it had some effect on the future shape of legislative attempts to define death in those States which chose the route of legislation.

Of course, the world of journals of whatever stripe has changed beyond recognition since those early days. The medical journals are packed with papers on ethics and have regular sections on law. The traditional law journals are less sniffy. And, in true entrepreneurial spirit, once a gap in the market was identified, journals were simply set up from scratch to meet the unmet need for an outlet in which to discuss bioethics. *The Journal of Medical Ethics* and the *Medical Law Review*, the birth of both of which I had a hand in, are two of the best recognised of the many now in existence. For example, I began my lonely (and still so far unsuccessful) campaign for 'opting out' or 'presumed consent' in the context of organ donation in the *Journal of Medical Ethics* (*JME*) over three decades ago.[11] And, as early as 1975, Bob Edwards, the recent recipient of the Nobel Prize for Medicine, co-authored a paper with me criticising a Report by the Law Commission on the proposed Bill on Civil Liability for Congenital Disability and its potential impact on developments in new reproductive technology.[12] Here, the media, in the form of the *JME*, was putting down an early marker of its preparedness to take on important issues of the day and, thereby, take forward in a positive way the discourse of bioethics.

[9] The President's Commission for the study of Ethical and Legal Problems in Medicine and Biomedical and Behavioural Research was created by President Carter in 1978.

[10] 'The Kansas statute on death – an appraisal' (1971) 285 *New England Journal of Medicine* 946–51.

[11] 'The donation and transplantation of kidneys – should the law be changed?' (1979) 5 *Journal of Medical Ethics* 13. I repeated the call in my recent Hoffenberg Lecture in March 2010 (see Chapter 10 above). [See now, at last (!), the Organ Donation (Deemed Consent) Act 2019.]

[12] (1975) 8 *Journal of Medical Ethics* 116.

The Press

Let me turn now to the press. To remind you, what I am exploring is how educators can so manage their interactions with the media that they can, through their active engagement, influence discourse about and developments in bioethics. I am exploring how, in doing so, they can fulfil their duty to reach an audience beyond the classroom and the textbook in a way which is intellectually respectable and at the same time accessible to those who have the interest and appetite to read without always a background of experience or expertise in the subject. The simple and obvious answer to the question that I pose is to write something for a newspaper or periodical and submit it.

Simple and obvious? Sadly, not as simple as it sounds. You have to pick the topic and the moment. And you have to use the language of everyday speech, challenging as that may be when talking about brain-stem death, pre-implantation diagnosis, or the difference between contraception and contra-gestation. These are bread and butter, as it were, to us, but, to extend the metaphor, not everyone's cup of tea. If you can, you should seek to ground what you want to explore and think aloud about in the world of everyman. A story, like a photograph, is worth a thousand words. Of course, there is an ever-present concern that stories by their nature do not constitute evidence. They are anecdotes and may not be generalisable. This is undoubtedly true. But, it is something for the purist to worry about. You need to engage the reader. Stories about real people and real occurrences do so. You can explain in your piece, if you want (though the sub-editor will strike it out), that the story is merely a peg on which to hang the discussion. But, such explanations are not really necessary. The reader will work that out. Indeed, if ever there is one rule in communicating interesting but complex ideas to a wide audience it is that you should trust your audience. Do not confuse or bamboozle them. But, equally, never talk down to them.

I mentioned the sub-editor a moment ago. As I have already made clear, when you get beyond the classroom, you begin to lose control of what is said. Writing a piece for a newspaper is a low risk activity. If changes are made, they will usually take the form of cutting sentences or paragraphs, because at some point the challenge becomes available space and column inches rather than the detailed steps in the logic of the point being explored. There is no way to circumvent this, particularly when you are starting out and have no bargaining power – it is an empty threat to say that you will take the piece elsewhere or never write for them again: that only works when they come to you! I interject that one newspaper did once come to me in those early days. I was asked by the *Sun*, at the dawn of interest in bioethics, to be their correspondent on the subject (I can't remember how it was described). Sadly, I was never called upon to express an opinion and I must presume that after all this time the arrangement has lapsed.

The best advice as you start out is to stick to the number of words prescribed and draft the piece with an eye to including something that could be cut. Perhaps the greatest risk is the headline or title. This is what will catch the readers' eye and draw them in. I well remember writing a piece with my then colleague, Simon Lee, about the legality and ethical propriety of sterilising a young girl who lacked capacity to consent. The article's publication was timed to appear on the day that the case came before the House of Lords.[13] It was a suitably punchy piece for *The Times*.[14] The headline (nothing to do with us) on the centre page read 'This rush to judgement'. Well, Lord Hailsham, the Lord Chancellor, frothed with indignation that we might suggest justice might be dispensed too quickly. He was encouraged by counsel,[15] who was able to say that I had been his pupil at the Bar but had clearly learned nothing. Lord Hailsham concurred! In fact, Simon Lee and I had said nothing about any rush. We had remarked that the case was being decided with unusual expedition, perhaps because the young girl was about to have her 18th birthday and thus become an adult in the eyes of the law, which would make sterilising her more problematic. The headline was the sub-editor's device to attract attention. And, of course, the judges and lawyers knew that. They knew that authors are not responsible for headlines. But, it provided a cheap laugh and more important, gave counsel and the House of Lords a reason to dismiss the article without having to address what it said. Clever tactics: lousy lawyering. What made the case even more remarkable was that, given its huge importance in terms of human rights, there were no cases nor papers before the court, except for the judgment of the court below, and our article – the first and perhaps the only time that a single sheet of newsprint was the only 'authority' before the court.

This is not the place to debate the merits of the case. The point that I wish to make is that seeking to use the media, as Lee and I were trying to do, to argue a case outside the courtroom, in the court of public opinion, is a legitimate activity for educators. It was particularly so in that case, where so little by way of legal argument was otherwise available. The media was there to be engaged actively and used in a way which could have had a significant effect in one of the most troubled and troubling areas of bioethics. That it was stymied by the intervention of the sub-editor illustrated the limits intrinsic in what I referred to earlier as a loss of control.

Radio

Let me turn now to the broadcast media, beginning with radio. Radio was, and to a certain extent remains, a significant medium for discussing serious issues.[16] The audiences are not huge, but certainly more than you'd get in a Lecture Theatre! There is only one imperative in using the radio to discuss serious matters. It applies to bioethics as to everything else: remember that, at the press of a button, the listener can switch you off. The link between your voice and the listener's ears is like a fragile thread – easily broken. This makes the radio an exciting but challenging medium. In the areas that we are interested in, two figures stand out as representing the best that radio can do by way of informing and stimulating, of engaging with the medium to advance understanding in a wide audience: Geoff Watts and Lord Bragg. The latter almost single-handedly has

[13] *Re B (a minor) (Wardship: Sterilisation)* [1987] 2 All ER 206 and see further my 'Patients, Doctors and Human Rights' in Kennedy, *Treat me Right* (Oxford University Press, 1988) pp 392–98.
[14] 1 April 1987.
[15] Alan Ward, later Lord Justice Ward.
[16] [Though increasingly giving way to the podcast.]

kept the discussion of things scientific and philosophical alive against the dumbing-down of both the BBC and New Labour, more interested in filling Number 10 with role models such as Noel Gallagher than with scientists, doctors, nurses and teachers. The former has commented intelligently on developments in health and healthcare for three decades or more.

In my case, recognising both what I have identified as the educator's duty and, as a consequence, the need actively to engage with the media, I started by writing and broadcasting ten to fifteen minute talks, on such issues as the development of healthcare policy, or mental illness. They were on the BBC's Third Programme, (one thing I do have in common with Sir Isaiah), tucked into the interval between Acts in operas, or between two pieces of music. That's where you learn the trade. How to write with an immediacy that captures and holds attention; how to write as we speak – no 'howevers' and 'notwithstandings'; how to modulate your voice. I then moved on, first to documentaries and then the Reith Lectures.

Documentaries on the radio were an early example of taking bioethical issues to a wide audience. There was a real opportunity to address important issues of the day and seek to affect how they might develop. You had 45 minutes or more which allowed you to consider a subject in some depth. You could interview the leading players and leave the audience with questions to ponder: no different, in essence, from the tutorial or the seminar. Two programmes stand out in my memory.

The first involved bringing together the two arch rivals in what was literally a life and death struggle. A major issue of the day, the early 70s, was termed 'selective non-treatment of the new-born'. It revolved around, though it was not limited to, the care of those born with spina bifida. A surgeon, John Lorber, provoked some considerable controversy when he wrote that, after intervening surgically for a number of years in all cases in which a child was born with spina bifida, and having followed the subsequent outcome for each child, he had come to the view that surgery was only justified in certain cases.[17] In others, where the child was very severely disabled, it was better not to operate and to let the child die. Something of a storm broke out, led by Robert Zachary. He was also a distinguished surgeon. His view was that surgery should be offered in all cases. The arguments were ventilated in a leading medical journal.

I became interested because, to me, and this was to be a theme that I explored for years, the issue was not one for doctors to debate among themselves. There were questions for all of us. Is there such a thing as a life which is not worth living? Who should make such a decision? On what criteria? At the time, there were those who thought me presumptuous to raise these questions, and even worse to talk about them in public. But, I did not agree. There could be no doubt in my view that this issue was something for all of us to wrestle with, rather than the preserve of a particular professional group. So too, I thought, was the wider question of how to enable all who might wish to do so to engage with the discourse of bioethics and the real-life decisions which flow from it. Actively using the media, in the form of BBC Radio, allowed the discourse to reach this wider audience. It gave another incremental element of validation to the notion that there was a subject here worth exploring which, while it wrestled with lots of disparate

[17] (1972) 47 *Archives of Disease in Childhood* 854–73.

problems, had certain underlying principles which made it a discrete subject, especially in its concern for human rights and the interests of patients.

The second programme I'll mention explored a notion which is now at centre stage of bioethics but was not something often addressed in polite company in 1978, when I made the programme: physician-assisted death. While I was teaching in San Diego, California, I had happened upon a case which I thought would be an excellent vehicle for exploring the subject, both abstractly and in the real exchanges between doctor and patient. Once back in England, I spoke to my long-time colleague, David Paterson who was the science editor for the BBC. We went to California (you could in those days!) and interviewed those involved. Then we made the programme. Because of what it described, we changed the names. Fundamentally, it described the killing of a patient by his doctor. But that is far too crude a description of what was a moving and complex interaction.[18]

This programme represented my attempt to draw a subject long regarded as taboo into the light. My aim was to encourage (licence would be too hubristic a term) debate and thereby ensure that this awfully difficult issue would be aired and addressed. I'm not sure that the programme made the inroad into popular consciousness that I was hoping for. The subject remained largely undiscussed for another two decades. But, at least it showed that it was possible to talk in public about previously taboo subjects. To that extent, it succeeded.

I have two particularly vivid memories of making that programme. The first is of sitting in the front room of the doctor's house looking out on the Pacific Ocean, talking to him, with David crouching on the floor holding a microphone. We sat/crouched there as the sun slowly sank into the Pacific and as I gradually eased the doctor to the point when he felt able to describe what had happened. The patient had asked that his respirator be turned off. But the doctor said no, for two reasons: the patient would be distressed as he died and he, the doctor, would be distressed at watching him die in this way. Instead, the doctor said that he would inject him with morphine and 'turn down' the respirator. It took nearly four hours to get to this point in the doctor's story. It was almost dark. David had barely moved.

Then, the second memory. There was a long gap between my question about whether he had committed homicide and the doctor's answer. It was over 20 seconds. We were genuinely torn when making the programme over whether we should leave the gap on the tape, and the agonising it represented. Our fear was that with a gap that long, listeners might think that their radio had gone on the blink and start fiddling with it, so missing the denouement. We left it in. In my view it is powerful in its own right and as a statement of how questions such as this give us pause.

I said a while ago that, in the context of using the radio as a means of actively engaging with the media and reaching a wider audience so as to affect the development of the discourse of bioethics, I would talk about the Reith Lectures, which I gave in 1980. I will do so shortly. Before I do, let me just say a word about television: using it as a medium for developing the discourse.

[18] See Chapter 14, p 190 and my 'The Check-out: A Humane Death' in *Treat me Right* (Oxford University Press, 1992), pp 308–10.

Television

In terms of the audiences to be reached, given the potential size of the audience, this is where the educator/communicator wants to be.[19] There are two ways of seeking actively to engage with and use television: your way and their way. Their way first, and what I say here applies equally to radio. This is when you are invited to appear: it may be a talk show, a news programme, or some such. Have no illusions. You are there to take forward the story (not your story, but theirs), or to demonstrate that they have captured for display the big cheese (or as big a cheese as they can get). The likelihood that you will be able to advance understanding about the issue under discussion varies from limited to remote. The best you can hope for is something sensible, in which the syntax holds up, and you do not look furtive or deranged, by, for example, glancing around. This, admittedly, is a somewhat jaundiced view. You may entertain more positive ambitions. I merely draw on my experience!

That's their way: what about your way? Again, the key is the first break. It comes from having a good idea, knowing how to package it for TV (I'll tell you a brief story on that theme in a minute), knowing whom to approach, and having some sort of track record. The Reith Lectures gave me a way in. And, my radio producer had moved to TV. I'd had an idea. It was simple. It was to transfer the technique of the seminar to the TV screen. (In fact, I wanted to use the device of making a programme as if I was teaching a class but my producer was not sure that it would work. He later used the technique in a brilliant programme he made with the philosopher Jonathan Glover, in which the students in the virtual class were in fact Jonathan's two sons).

We sold the idea to BBC 2 as a series of six programmes. Modelled on the seminar, the programmes were built around vignettes based on real cases. We found trained actors to play the part of patients, and real, practising doctors and nurses who were prepared to take on the case. Each case was so organised that it raised difficult ethical issues. The doctors and nurses watched the vignettes and then there was a consultation between them and the actors who stayed in their roles. The actors were briefed and rehearsed to ensure that it was the ethical issues that were at the forefront of the consultation. The clinicians were required by the actors to address these issues. It made for sometimes tense and gripping television. Once the case and the consultation were over, I led a studio-based discussion. The programmes did sufficiently well, getting audiences of 2.5 to 3.5 million, that we made a second series of six.

What the programmes showed was that there was a very considerable appetite for thought-provoking presentations of real dilemmas. It was possible to deal intelligently with ideas. The programmes offered no answers. The audience was left to talk about what they had seen, just as students leave the seminar with questions bouncing around in their head. And, people did respond. Indeed, much to my gratification (if not my enrichment!), pirated videos of the programmes served as teaching materials for nursing studies for some years.

The programmes showed that you could do it your way: you could actively engage with television as a medium and use it to raise the visibility of the discourse of

[19] [Written before the days of You Tube!]

bioethics. Quite whether the new generation of bioethicists have the same opportunities, or wish for them, is another story. But the opportunity, not only to communicate but also, perhaps educate, plus the chance to influence the direction and shape of policy about healthcare,[20] was there for the taking and should surely be part of every bioethicist's raison d'etre.

There was one further feature of the series which was very important to me as the educator/communicator. Healthcare as represented on television was (and sadly remains) synonymous with acute care in hospitals, preferably surgery, and with life or death emergencies, coupled with the esoteric: conjoined twins, or 'test-tube' babies. Bioethical discussion, such as there was, was drawn into focusing on this particular corner of healthcare, even though the experience of people and the reality of healthcare was that it was much more associated with the GP, the midwife, the Community Nurse, and the occupational health practitioner, than with acute care (after all, over 90% of contacts between doctors and patients are in general practice). Moreover, and I saw this as an extremely important point to make for the development of bioethics, ethical problems are not confined to the hospital and the dramatic. They are just as pressing and difficult in the GP's surgery, or the school health team's work. I purposely chose for my programmes cases from these settings and the ethical dilemmas that they gave rise to: telling the truth; respecting confidences; obtaining valid consent; the nature of mental illness and responses to it; and allocating scarce resources. In this way, I was able to make an overarching point about the real nature of healthcare and the ethical issues which it gives rise to.

I did a variety of other TV programmes. The most interesting, however, was the one that I didn't do! It involves the story I promised you a moment ago. It offers an insight into the direction TV was beginning to take: as dumbing-down met the cult of personality. It indicates the increasing difficulty that I and others began to encounter in keeping alive the notion of serious discourse about serious issues in which a wide audience could take part. I had developed an idea for a series of programmes which would look at health and healthcare around the world and compare the relative roles of high-tech interventionist medicine, preventative care, health promotion, education, and social welfare in achieving good health for all – the ambition of the World Health Organisation's Declaration of Alma Ata in 1978.

I was intending to look at the experience of a number of countries, including the UK, other parts of Europe, Cuba, South-West India, South Africa and the USA. The working title was 'The Health of Nations'. The BBC needed co-funding for such a project. Australian and Canadian participation was quickly obtained. But, a major funder from US TV was needed. An executive from one of the big three networks flew over. He liked the idea, although he thought it a bit 'commie'! Things were going well till he asked who would be presenting the series. My producer replied that I would. The US executive demurred. He opined that no-one had heard of me. Instead, he said that he had in mind Paul Newman. My producer conceded that he was much better known and infinitely

[20] As for example in the case concerned with the allocation of scarce resources, specifically access to kidney dialysis and transplants, when the then Secretary of State for Health, Kenneth Clarke, having appeared on the programme, announced the following week a significant increase in funding.

more good-looking than I, but pointed out that he didn't know anything about health policy. 'That's OK', came the reply. 'Ian can write his script'. 'What about the interviews', which would be the heart of the programmes, the producer asked. 'Paul can wear an earpiece' came the answer. As I said, the series wasn't made!

The Reith Lectures 1980

Let me now get to the Reith Lectures.[21] Here was an incredible opportunity to work with the media to develop the discourse of bioethics. I would be able to reach a wide audience, in this case through a prestigious set of six Lectures broadcast at peak time weekly and published contemporaneously in the *Listener*. In those days, you had to talk for 28 minutes and 40 seconds and hold your audience. And my producer was a purist. The recording had to be done all in one 'take'. Doing a part and then taking a break wasn't on. Your voice might be slightly changed. As you can imagine, this also meant that there could be no 'Mmm …', or noises as you slid a page away to read the next. 'Start again, from the top' came the voice through my earphones. The fourth Lecture involved seven takes over two days!

The Lectures offered a chance to put the discourse of health policy, and to a degree, ethics (only one Lecture, in fact, was wholly devoted to ethics), on the map. They provided the perfect opportunity to take my notion of the educator's duty to inform and educate and put it into practice on a big stage. In what follows, I will describe my active use of the media and the responses which were evoked. Only when they are taken together, both my use of the media and the use of the media by others to respond, can some understanding be formed of the effect that the Lectures had on the development of bioethics.

As some will remember, I pursued a range of themes: the language or rhetoric of health, illness and disease; the transformation of the vision of a national health service into a national illness service; the lack of priority given to the welfare of children (a subject I returned to at the request of the Department of Health only a few months ago to report that little had changed[22]); the nature of and response to mental illness; and, with the ringing title of 'First, let's kill all the lawyers', a plea to develop ways of holding health care professionals to account which were better than relying on the hopeless system of suing them. But, the theme which attracted most attention was that addressed in the fourth Lecture. From the distance of 30 years it looks unremarkable, anodyne in the extreme. At the time, it caused feathers to fly.

In Lecture 4, I observed that many decisions taken by doctors were not technical-medical in nature, but moral. As such, I argued, they called for a broader approach and more developed conceptual vocabulary than that which formed the basis of medical education at the time. I called for exposure to ethical reasoning to be incorporated into the curriculum of Medical Schools. Bread and butter to the first year student of today. But, then!

[21] Published as *Unmasking Medicine* (revised paperback edition, Paladin, 1983).
[22] *Getting it Right for Children* (Department of Health, 2010) and see Chapter 2.

In the first Lecture I had talked of the imbalance of power intrinsic in the relationship between any professional and a client and how this imbalance was particularly important to recognise and address in the case of the doctor-patient relationship. I argued that it placed special responsibilities on the professional, who as a professional, existed to serve the needs of the patient. This proposition formed to some extent the context for the discussion of medical ethics later. Well, references to power and the need to be educated as to how to use and manage it seriously got up the noses of many of those who claimed to speak for doctors. Nurses welcomed what I was saying, as did a number of clinicians who saw me as saying no more than that which they had been saying for some time. I was giving their views a wider airing. But, to the majority of medical commentators, I was to be attacked and dismissed.

The Lectures are seen by some as constituting something of a watershed in the development of bioethics.[23] They challenged the conventional discourse. They were intended to provoke. They provoked! They used the media to argue for a different discourse. What was so challenging?

The Challenge – Whose is the Discourse of Bioethics?

The first challenge lay in the simple fact that I was not a clinician, yet I had commented on matters medical. This was seen, within the traditional discourse, as presumption, made even less tolerable by virtue of the fact that I belonged to that class of sub-humans known collectively as lawyers. (The fact that I had had a go at the law in the sixth Lecture seemed to go unnoticed!). The significance for the audience of today is that I had taken a step on the road to making it acceptable to comment on things clinical without being a clinician, a road now very well trodden and needing no satnav to guide you. At the time, however, this was not so. (Of course, there had been non-clinical commentators before me but they tended to be benign supporters of the *status quo*).

Secondly, and following on from this first point, the Lectures ensured that the discourse of health and healthcare had been made accessible to a wide audience. It had been demystified. People could look behind the mask. It was recognised through many gritted teeth that the genie was out of the bottle. The discourse would be forever changed. Some accommodation to a new world would be needed. And, as we all know, change is never welcome or easy.

Thirdly, I brought to the discourse a concern for the interests and rights of patients. This was seen by some as fighting talk, inevitably destined to harm patients. The principle that 'doctor knows best' still stalked the wards and surgeries. I remember one doctor dismissing my concern for the interests of patients with the remark that if I had my way, 'patients would die with their rights on'! I still remember the anger with which I read and incorporated into Lecture 4 the story of the doctor who, when faced with the young woman seeking an abortion, said that if he could make her cry, he knew that he'd won, that he'd stopped her from going ahead. To him, abortions were wrong and to be prevented. Female patients were there to be manoeuvred into 'keeping the baby'.

[23] See, eg, Reynolds and Tansey (eds), *Medical Ethics Education in Britain 1963–93* (Wellcome Trust, 2007).

They were not people to be talked to as equals, wrestling with a huge moral and practical challenge. It was this theme, that the parties to the medical transaction, the doctor and the patient, are equals, each with their areas of expertise, that I was seeking to expose and explore. It led some to level the charge that I was advocating 'patient power'. Not so. I specifically rejected it as a false God. Partnership, for me, was the way forward.

I've already touched on a fourth reason why the Lectures challenged the conventional discourse of bioethics and, thereby, provoked discomfort and anger. In pointing to the moral dimension of the transaction between patient and doctor, I disempowered doctors, as they saw it, and empowered others. Patients were given licence to challenge. Doctors were reminded of the limits of their expertise, of their responsibility and of their privilege. (From the vantage point of hindsight, most clinicians welcome the ability to step down from Olympus and be just mortals, although some doctors currently have similar difficulties with patients using the internet!) At the time, this notion of challenge was new and, to many, unwelcome. They were used to unconditional approval. Now, here was someone suggesting that they had to be more respectful of the interests of others.

These are just a few of the hotspots created by the Reith Lectures. Commentators of today will recognise that there is still quite a bit of heat in all of them. It is, of course, for others to gauge the impact that they had in affecting developments in bioethics.

The Media's Response

So far, I've discussed the Lectures from the perspective of the use that could and can be made of the media to develop the discourse of bioethics. But this is only part of the story of this particular example of the relationship between bioethics and the media. What did the media make of the Lectures? This is equally an important question to ask in assessing the effect that the media may have on developments in bioethics.

There were, perhaps, three forms of response. The first was one of surprise, coupled with enthusiasm that the BBC had spotted this growing area of interest just at a time when a number of issues were being ventilated in public. I have mentioned already the care of severely handicapped new-born babies, and the definition of death (and its association with transplantation). The media recognised that in terms of the development of bioethics and the media's engagement with it, the Lectures constituted a watershed. Previously, the media addressed issues, all of which we might recognise as having to do with bioethics, in an ad hoc manner. There was no particular understanding that uniting all the specific examples and cases were certain underlying and unifying themes. In the reporting of the Lectures, the media began to see the dots and that they might be joined. As commentators will know, the precise picture created by the dots is still a matter of debate: is it a story of human rights; the collapse of trust and rise of consumerism; an assault on professionalism; a struggle between autonomy and paternalism; the relationship between medicine and health; or all of the above?

A second response was an interest in particular themes. The lectures attracted two Editorials in *The Times* and, again from the perspective of the development of bioethics, the themes chosen by *The Times* are worth noticing. They did not dwell on what became the cause celebre, the ethical content of clinical decisions. They focused on the politics and the policies of the NHS, and, surprisingly, given the limited attention received elsewhere (unfortunately) then and thereafter, on the proposals to replace the hopeless system of litigation for medical negligence with a system more likely to achieve the accountability of professionals which the tenor of the times demanded. (I proposed the creation of an inspectorate on the model of education and the police, something which took nearly 25 years to come to pass).[24]

A third response was from the medical profession, as filtered through the media; the profession was not admittedly a homogenous group, but was not far off in this case. Some, whom we might call the modernists or even reformers rallied to the cause of health promotion, and disease prevention, the better care of children, and the like. They even saw, since they had been arguing it themselves for some time, the value in addressing the ethical dimension of caring for patients.[25] They, however, were in a minority. For the most part, the media, both general and specialist, echoed with cries of foul.

The first thing of interest to note was that, by and large, the general media looked to doctors for comments. This reflected the prevailing view, which those interested in bioethics need to understand, that commentary on things having to do with medicine and health was thought to be, if not exclusively, then largely, for doctors. This was a significant feature of the interaction between bioethics and the media: that, if there was to be a discourse, it was to be among like-minded professionals. The message of the Lectures, of course, was that bioethics was for all. But, this was not initially understood by those whose first reflex was that medicine equals doctors. There were exceptions, but this was the general rule. So, this largely meant that the response to the Lectures in the general media was not greatly different from that in the specialist journals.

The responses ranged from near apoplexy to a sense of hurt feelings – how can we be criticised when we have only good intentions? There were also those who dismissed what was said as irrelevant, ill-informed and, at the same time, old hat. It's quite difficult to pull off an argument that says that what I was saying was nonsense but that, anyway, doctors had been saying these things for years, but Dr Anthony Clare, a well-known broadcaster himself, pulled it off.[26] The tone of hurt feelings rested, of course, on a sense that the Lectures constituted an attack on doctors. As I've made clear, they did not. They were concerned with medicine and healthcare and decision-making. But, to repeat myself, medicine was for doctors: 'outsiders' should keep out.[27]

[24] Clearly, even after 28 years the message had still failed to reach some. Dingwall, a sociologist, in reviewing a book by Miola called *Medical Ethics and Medical Law* wrote (remarkably) that Kennedy 'had been advocating … legal intervention to compel ethical practice … since the 1970s exemplified by his Reith Lectures'. He comments that my appointment to chair the Bristol Public Inquiry suggests 'an arguable case that those who appointed Kennedy … had a particular outcome in mind [what Dingwall calls the 'legalization of society'] and that the process was a vehicle for their interests'. It beats me where he gets all this from!!

[25] See the assessment some years later by Professor Larry Gostin in (1997–98) 14 *Journal of Contemporary Health Law and Policy* xi.

[26] (1981) 7 *Journal of Medical Ethics* 194–96.

[27] In the recent book by the Wellcome Trust's Centre for the History of Medicine, Stephen Lock, a distinguished ex-editor of the *British Medical Journal* and a supporter of the Lectures (!), remarked that, while Baroness Warnock was the Pavlova of the group of bioethicists around at the time, I was the Stravinsky. The lectures, he said, 'had very much the same effect on the doctors as The Rite of Spring had on the audience at the Theatre des Champs-Elysees just before the First World War'. A footnote points out that the 'shocking music and primitive movements outraged the audience whose shouts and fights stopped the performance': see fn 23 above, n 14.

The sense of being attacked led to responses which were personal.[28] As one wag put it, 'Kennedy is a difficult man to ignore, but it's well worth the effort'! Personal attacks are something that increasingly educators have had to face if they want to explore ideas rigorously through the media. Not everyone will agree with the positions that you take. The media frequently turn such disagreements into *ad hominem* assaults. You may not like it but you have to take it in your stride and get past it. The trade magazines such as *Pulse* and *Hospital Doctor* took the party line on the Lectures: 'he's not a doctor, so what does he know'. I was to be exposed as a charlatan. The relatively recently established *Journal of Medical Ethics* was torn. Bioethics, as a discipline in its own right, was in its infancy. Its Editor was a doctor who was also a leading figure in the then small world of bioethics. His response was appropriately scholarly. He decided to dedicate a whole edition to the Lectures, commission articles from various commentators, and invite me to respond to them.[29] But, many of the articles were commissioned from doctors. The consequence was that a goodly number of them had the hurt tone of the misunderstood about them, even if it was they who were misunderstanding the emergence of bioethics. One piece by Wilkes gloried in the title 'I'm still proud to be a doctor' – both missing the point, and making the point, of the Lectures![30]

Not all comment on the Lectures was negative, as I have said. Indeed, it is refreshing to read what Dr Campbell wrote in his address to the new intake of medical students in Belfast in 2006. He refers to the Lectures and writes 'Reading through the Lectures 25 years on, they seem to have a prophetic air. Many of his questions, comments and criticisms have been acted on and become part of standard medical practice'.

Perhaps the last word should rest with Sir Isaiah Berlin. It was he who once wrote, 'Few new truths have ever won their way against the resistance of established ideas save by being overstated'.

Having set out these responses, what do they tell us about the interaction between the media and bioethics and the impact of this interaction on developments in the field? They suggest that the media was beginning to see a discrete area of thought and activity (which we now call bioethics): that the media was beginning to discern, to a greater or lesser extent, the interconnectedness of issues. They indicate those areas that the media initially identified as important themes – the state of the NHS and the role of litigation – and what they did not regard as important – the discussion of mental illness and the care of children (which still remains the case). The exploration of the moral dimension of medical decision-making did not, of itself, attract great attention. What attracted the attention was the suggested limits to the clinician's areas of competence and responsibility. This illustrated the nose that the media has for a punch-up. Medical professionals

[28] Friedson, for instance, writing in 1982, called the overall tone of the Lectures 'doctor-bashing, science-baiting and machine-smashing': 'Review Essay' (1982) 4 *Sociology of Health and Illness* 95–97.

[29] (1981) 7 *Journal of Medical Ethics*.

[30] Lest any think that all the wounds have healed, I refer them to one Dr Ward, Chairman of the Society of Clinical Psychiatrists. His annual address to his Society as recently as November 2009 graces the ether of the internet. I am singled out as, above all others, the 'one figure that [sic] has damaged the profession (and with that, inevitably, patient care)'. Ward goes on to pile on me obloquy which is not even original, having first appeared on the web through the good efforts of the author of *Spiked* (see, eg, 19 January 2001 and passim). Remarkably, I am, at the same time, part of a conspiracy to do down medicine and the medical profession, while at the same time being part of the medical elite!

were lining up for the attack and they were given the opportunity. We were all treated to what Gostin called 'the intimidating authority'[31] of the medical profession.

Reacting to the Media and the Development of Bioethics

References to how the media responded to the Reith Lectures allow me now to turn to the other perspective that I promised to offer when I began this discussion of the interaction between the media and bioethics. The media intends to say or has said something which is of importance to the development of bioethics. How should you react?

I have already pointed out that the aims of the educator and the media are different: the one to inform and stimulate discussion, with a view to advancing understanding; the other to sell a product and inform in a way compatible with the sale of that product – in truth, a particular take on life and values. In pursuing these different goals, there may be some overlap between the educator and the media in what is communicated, and how. But, you have to accept that it is not necessarily the case. The media are in a different game. There is no point in bemoaning this state of affairs or, for example, lambasting the press for trivialising this, or emphasising the 'wrong' thing. All that educators can do is to develop strategies. And, fundamentally, there are three situations which you need a strategy for. Let's take them in order and consider some examples.

The first is where you want to take an issue to the public and you seek to enlist the media in the task. I have in mind the publication of research results, or of a review, or a study. You want to engage the media in the development of some aspect of bioethics, but, more importantly, you want to manage that engagement. The media is interested. There will be some sort of story in any event. What you have to do is to react to that interest in a way which contributes beneficially to the discourse of bioethics.

Briefing

It is common sense for the educator who wishes to engage with the media to have developed, or to develop, some sort of relationship with relevant reporters, whatever the medium. From this will emerge an understanding on both sides of whether the reaction that you want to make public is appropriate for/will suit this or that newspaper, or outlet, or whatever. If it is, by working with them you will also gain an understanding of what 'line' the reporters will take, a combination of the overall editorial policy of the paper or outlet and the reporters' personal take on things. This latter element will be a combination of their interests/prejudices and their desire to get something published/broadcast rather 'spiked' as being, for example, too boring, too dry, or too lacking in human interest.

The next step is to prepare something for the reporters which will meet your ambitions and, at the same time, serve their needs. This is the crux of the symbiotic relationship which you would seek to have. It may be a press release, an executive summary

[31] Above, n 25.

of a Report, or a briefing note. Whatever it is, it must achieve at least two aims. It should tell the story as you wish it to be told. This may not succeed in completely dominating what is reported, but, at the very least, it will shape the discourse: it will provide the reference points around which any reporting and discussion will revolve. The second aim must be to ensure that what you provide has some quotable quotes. This is where knowing a reporter's agenda comes in. They need something to catch the reader's and, first, the editor's eye.

Remember that the issue is how you react to and manage a story which is of interest to the media; how the media can be recruited in the development of intelligent discourse about developments in bioethics. An example from the Bristol Inquiry comes to mind. As Chairman of a Public Inquiry I was not, of course, principally playing the role of educator as I've referred to it so far. But, there is clearly something by way of an intention to educate in issuing reasoned recommendations. A major concern of the Inquiry and consequently of the Report was the neglect of the care of children in, and by, the NHS. The media's interest in the Report was somewhat narrower: the number of children who had died when with appropriate care they could have lived, and who/what was to blame. There was a danger that broader messages might get drowned, but, if anything was to change, it was the broader messages that needed to be heard. Thus, I decided to insert into my statement to the press a comment that the chapter on children 'had been written in anger'. I remarked that children's services had been described as a Cinderella service, but that 'this Cinderella had not been to the Ball'. The quotes were picked up and the wider point was recognised. (Sadly, little by way of action was taken by government, such that, as I have said, I was asked a decade later to carry out a review of children's services in the NHS and found myself repeating the same analysis and views).

The second situation for which you need a strategy is when the media is commenting on some issue in which you are involved and comes to you.

Responding

If it is on friendly terms, then you can seek to manage the discourse in the way that I've suggested a moment ago. But it may not be friendly. Here you are on your mettle. As an educator, you may be unused to needing to justify yourself. Well, when the media come calling, get used to it! Get the facts straight, get your take on the facts straight, and measure every word. And, reconcile yourself to the fact that, in football parlance, a draw may be a result!

Let me offer an example from the world of regulation. I am extremely interested in the role that regulation can play in developments in health and healthcare, and in the role that the media can play in shaping the discourse within which regulation is addressed. Regulation is a much-misunderstood creature. It is misrepresented as a form of policing: telling people what to do and punishing them if they fail. It is seen as a burden, requiring those with better things to do to 'tick boxes'. It is supposed to stultify initiative and embed a conservative aversion to risk. Properly understood and operated, regulation is none of these. It has enormous potential for good. It can promote improvement, encourage self-reflection and facilitate appropriate accountability, both in terms of performance and cost-effectiveness. But, regulation had and has its opponents, not least those who are held to account. And opponents are not limited to what might be called the managerial class. They include the more conservative professionals, opposed to change and unwelcoming of scrutiny. And, if they have an outlet in the media, the discourse about regulation can be derailed, with lasting effects.

I cite in evidence the editorial written by Richard Horton in *The Lancet* which had the gloriously tendentious headline: 'Why is Ian Kennedy's Healthcare Commission damaging NHS care?'[32] As an opening gambit, not a bad start! Well, where do you begin in responding? For a start, the Healthcare Commission was not Ian Kennedy's: there was a Board of 15 and around 750 staff. But, *ad hominem* attacks work better in getting the juices flowing. It helps the cause to create a bogeyman. Secondly, at the time of the Editorial the Healthcare Commission had been in existence for only three and a bit months; a bit early, you might say, for judgement to be passed on its effects or effectiveness. But, damage was done and unfairly so. War on regulation, through the creation of a false picture of it and of a bogeyman running it, was declared. Myths were perpetuated and the discourse of bioethics was prejudiced. Of course, I wrote a letter by way of response, which was eventually published, but, if not the lie then the misrepresentation was by then half way round the world. In due course, in the margins of some meeting, Horton thanked me for a 'marvellous letter'. But, it was not a jousting match for me. It was a deadly serious concern about how to improve the care of patients.

The third situation is where your duty as the educator draws you into getting involved when you think that the discourse has gone off the rails (if it was ever on them).

Getting Involved

I have in mind the situation in which the media has picked up on a subject and either got the wrong end of the stick or simply misrepresented the issue for whatever reasons (usually, the perceived prejudices of the audience). You may wish, wearing your educator's hat and zeal, to put the record straight or get the argument on the right track. First, you've got to get the media's attention, something we've already discussed. Then you've got to craft some intervention which does not make you look like some sad, otherworldly boffin, nor some pompous know-it-all. The former will tend to confirm the media's point of view, the latter will certainly do so.

Obviously, the best recent example, which I was not involved in, relates to the MMR vaccine. It has been clearly one of the major issues of bioethics in the past decade. It brought together a heady brew; research, the analysis of data, publication ethics, and the nature of scientific discourse. The background was one of declining trust in the authority of science, an aversion to risk, both of which had been given impetus by the BSE debacle, and a 'do-it-yourself' approach to evidence and proof, whereby if you believed something and there was something on the internet which agreed, then it was right. For bioethics, it was a nightmare. The considered view from the outset was that the claims made relating to autism were unsustainable. But, there was a significant lobby, courted

[32] (2004) 364(9432) *Lancet*.

by the media, which simply asserted otherwise. And what was at stake was not some scientific abstraction, but the welfare of children at risk, particularly of contracting measles and being harmed as a consequence. It was not a glorious hour in the relations between the media and bioethics. Indeed, it was one of the darkest hours. Undoubtedly, damage was done, not just to the nature of discourse, but to real people. And that's the reminder we all need to heed. Bioethics is about arguments and principles and cases. But, ultimately, it's also about people.

An example where I did get involved is the occasion of what to those involved in the early days of bioethics was a notorious television programme: the BBC's Panorama programme in 1981 on the nature and diagnosis of death. The definition of death, the interplay with transplantation, and the notion that someone might be defined as dead while his/her heart was still beating, were 'hot topics'. The clinical, legal and ethical challenges were considerable as attempts were made to map out responses to developments in intensive care and in transplantation surgery. There was a real danger that beneficial developments in care and treatment could be slowed or even halted if the various challenges were not met carefully. It was important to acknowledge misgivings and address them with scrupulous care and honesty. Enter Panorama! The programme made the remarkable claim that a number of patients who had all been diagnosed as dead, had, through further care, been brought back to life. The message was loud and clear: the current approach to determining death was flawed and dangerous; patients were being consigned to the morgue or worse when they were still alive. It is difficult to think of anything better calculated to frighten the horses and have a major effect on the development of this area of bioethics.

The difficulty with the programme was that it was nonsense. None of the patients referred to met the criteria of death in use in the UK. Putting it as clearly as possible, in the reverse of the Monty Python sketch, they were not dead patients. They had not been brought back from the dead. Such a process was/is impossible: once dead, you remain dead.

What to do? The community of experts who had been so diligently engaged in the area in a measured way was outraged. I approached the *Sunday Times*. I had only recently done the Reith Lectures so I had what is now called 'name recognition'. I proposed that I write a piece for the centre page, condemning the programme, calling for an appropriately measured second programme and arguing that the second programme not be chaired by David Dimbleby, the chief presenter of Panorama, since he had so clearly identified with the Panorama programme at the time, and defended it subsequently. In the light of my article, the BBC accepted their responsibility (not without a struggle). There was a second programme, not chaired by Dimbleby. Fears were addressed and, I think, allayed. But it was an awkward moment in the development of bioethics. Interestingly, I was due to attend a formal dinner as the BBC's guest only a few days after my attack on Panorama had appeared. Unsurprisingly, it was not the liveliest of evenings. I was regarded as something of a traitor: I had betrayed the BBC. It was a strange assumption: that because I'd done some programmes for the BBC I was 'one of them', duty-bound to defend the indefensible. The Managing Director of BBC Radio, Aubrey Singer, cornered me as I came in and demanded, 'Did you see the original programme?' I responded, I hope politely, with a 'Good evening, Aubrey', followed by, 'I can't see how you could possibly ask me that question', with the unstated observation

'How could I write about it if I didn't see it'. My response was perhaps too subtle. A finger was poked into my chest and the question repeated 'Well. Did you see it?' Before I could answer, the wonderful Alastair Milne who was the Controller of Radio 4 at the time intervened. He turned to his colleague and said, 'Aubrey, you shouldn't judge everyone by your own standards'.

The then Director-General, Ian Trethowan, my host, did not exchange one word with me all evening. Dealing with the media is never easy!

Conclusion

In this paper, I've drawn on my experiences in dealing with the media to seek to illustrate how interactions with the media can and do affect developments in bioethics. I've also suggested that, despite the occasions on which the media gets things wrong as in the Panorama programme, the educator should, indeed has a duty to engage. Not only would the media get more things wrong than is currently the case, but, and this is by far the more important point, the wider public would be deprived of the insights that the educator can bring to the discussion of any issue relating to bioethics. And, since bioethics will continue to challenge, unnerve, inspire, raise and dash hopes, and intrigue the public around us for the foreseeable future, the educator needs to be out there in the media, shaping the discourse.

PART VI

Tributes

I have been fortunate to sit and learn at the feet of a number of distinguished and wonderful people. The tributes that follow celebrate three particularly special people in my life whom I admired greatly. All three were doctors. They taught me so much, not merely in the realm of knowledge and experience but also, and perhaps more importantly, how to keep faith with values such as service, duty and integrity.

23

Professor Aidan Halligan

This is my tribute to Professor Aidan Halligan[1] who died on 29 April 2015 aged 57, delivered on 7 May at his Memorial Service held at Holy Cross Dominican RC Church and Priory, Leicester. Perhaps his two greatest achievements were to establish the NHS Staff College, in conjunction with colleagues from the armed forces, to teach leadership, and Pathway, to address the healthcare needs of the homeless. I was a Trustee of both and worked under Aidan's inspiring leadership. Previously, he had been a Consultant and Professor in Leicester and then Deputy Chief Medical Officer for England.

Aidan and I met regularly for dinner, arranged with her customary care by Mandy, at St Pancras Station in London, at the unfashionably early time of 6.30pm. He could then catch the 20.26 to Leicester and I could go to Marks and Spencers at the station to buy something for dinner, having put on the abstemious act while with Aidan so that he wouldn't eat quite all of his chips.

We would routinely claim that it was the other's turn to pay. With his rightly celebrated skills of persuasion, I was usually brought round to the idea that, yes, he was right, it *was* my turn!

We would gossip – wonderful, scurrilous gossip. We would talk shop. We would discuss his next plans to change things for the better. We would offer each other counsel on what was happening in our lives – he talking so proudly of his girls, me talking of my sons, who knew and loved him.

These dinners captured some of the essence of Aidan: the kind, caring man; the man in a hurry to achieve things; the man who refused to take no as anything more than an invitation to press on; the man with a vision (or several), tilting not at windmills but at the multiple forms of man's inhumanity to man; the man always there with a ready ear, a kind word, and wise counsel.

Over time, I saw Aidan in many contexts. My first encounter made a lasting impression, which I'm sure is equally true of you all here today. He had been designated the senior officer in the Department of Health, responsible for relations with the independent Healthcare Commission, which I chaired. My previous experience of such dealings had not been easy. Independence was not a notion well understood by the Department.

[1] MA, MD, FRCOG, FFPHM, MRCPI, FRCC.

Aidan's first words to me were: 'This is your meeting. How can I help?' Of course, the reality of the harsh world of money and politics didn't change. But what changed profoundly was the chemistry. Nothing had changed, yet everything had changed. Here was a man who saw the point of what it was to be a leader – to reach out and help, to empower others, to make you want to stay the course.

Aidan would not forgive me if I didn't illustrate this point with some famous person's words, even if I can't summon up the perfect aphorism as could Aidan from his mental library, whether it be the words of Mahatma Gandhi, Martin Luther King, Marlene Dietrich, or Madonna. I will settle on the words of Ralph Nader, the consumer activist of the 70s and 80s: 'It is the job of leaders to create leaders, not followers'.

Aidan lived this injunction to the full. He empowered. He made you believe you could. He even sometimes made you believe it was your idea!

Aidan kept a pocket full of fairy dust which he sprinkled on people whom he met – ones and twos, or hundreds; in private meetings with clinicians and patients, or in lecture halls.

He was a kind of benevolent Pied Piper. We would follow him. If he 'phoned me and said he was putting together this idea and was convinced that I was just the person to get involved, all my usual defences fell away – too busy, not my area, too out of touch. No. I was suddenly the enthusiastic adventurer, called again to sign up for whatever voyage into the unknown Aidan was pitching for that day. And, of course, all the voyages were launched and taken forward, and, while Aidan was already working on the next one, all those who surrounded Aidan and worked so passionately on his behalf, made sure that the various voyages remained set fair to reach their destination.

Aidan was a remarkable man. He was much, much more than the sum of his parts. He was remarkable in so many ways, with so many achievements. He was also my friend, someone whose values I shared and whom I respected and loved.

Aidan, another quotation: these are the words, slightly adjusted, which were spoken at the funeral of another leader who died too young. They are apt here.

> Aidan need not be idealised or enlarged in death beyond what he was in life. He should be remembered simply as a good and decent man, who saw wrong and tried to right it, saw visions and tried to achieve them, saw suffering and tried to heal it. Those of us who loved him and who see him to his rest today, pray that what he was to us and what he wished for others will someday come to pass for all.

24

Sir Donald Irvine

This is the tribute that I delivered in honour of Sir Donald Irvine[1] at the Royal College of General Practitioners on 19 June 2019. He was a pioneering President of the Royal College of General Practitioners and, later, of the General Medical Council at a time when the medical profession was confronting the need to change to accommodate the interests of patients and be more accountable to the wider society. Donald died on 19 November 2018, aged 85.

Donald Irvine was a man whom I greatly admired and was honoured to call a friend. That admiration and friendship grew out of my membership of the General Medical Council (GMC) in the 1980s. It was a strange body when I was appointed to it – about 110 members of whom just 11 of us were non-doctors and of whom, by the relevant statute, the majority had to consist of elected members – code for the British Medical Association, the doctors' union. As an outsider, it was not clear to me whether the GMC was a regulatory body, concerned with the conduct of doctors, or a trade union, yes, concerned with the conduct of doctors but in a way designed to protect them from external forces such as patients and governments. For the most part, it seemed to be the latter – concerned with disciplining those who fell foul of one of the three As – adultery, alcohol, and advertising.

Donald was in the vanguard of those who thought that change – radical change – was needed. He held to the quaint idea that patients were important in the business of being a doctor. He was already suspected as being unreliable but he was also increasingly someone to be reckoned with. It was agreed, therefore, that, once a member of the GMC, he could safely be allowed to be the Chair of the Committee on Standards in the certain knowledge that this was a Committee with no power (and power was everything), a Committee which uttered platitudes from time to time to which the collective could nod in approval. It was, as one power-broker put it to me, a backwater. Donald could be shunted there. He would pose no threat.

Well, they got that wrong! Donald saw the Committee as the standard-bearer of what was central to the GMC's mission – the standards that doctors should observe: and, crucially, the standards to be observed in their dealings with patients. From the perspective of where we are now, this is at best a statement of the bleeding obvious. But, make no mistake, it was not bleeding obvious then. Indeed, it was almost treasonous to some.

[1] OBE, CBE, Kt, DObst, MD, PRCGP.

Donald saw that the key would be to lead his Committee in a wholesale revisiting of the standards. The crucial first step, the break-through, was so simple that it had the mark of genius. Don't let's talk about what the doctor shouldn't do, he argued. That way lay the approach of the clever lawyer finding her way through a pesky tax statute. Let's talk about what the doctor *should* do. And let's talk in terms of the good doctor, inviting all doctors to strive for that description.

So was born at the end of the 1990s *Good Medical Practice.* This guide to ethical practice spoke of the doctor's *duties* and echoed Hippocrates in urging that a doctor should 'make the care of your patient your first concern'. It stands as a magnificent achievement and fitting memorial to this wise doctor.

But, far from being lionised, Donald became a marked man for some who saw him as the enemy of their preferred status quo. Why? Because he saw Good Medical Practice as just the beginning. The GMC must be more open, more responsive to the world beyond medicine, more prepared to accept that passing exams in your early 20s should not endow you with a lifetime's guarantee of professional practice, free from scrutiny, until you retired or something went wrong. And during Donald's tenure as President of the GMC a number of things had gone disastrously wrong – not least the Bristol Inquiry, Alder Hey, and the Shipman murders.

Having to render an account, having to justify continued practice, having to submit to a process of 'revalidation' was a declaration of war to some. The GMC was divided on itself. Tribal warfare broke out – after all, Donald was only a General Practitioner! Some recalled the famous remark of Lord Moran, Churchill's doctor, that a GP was someone 'who had fallen off the specialist ladder'. As ever, when the message was unwelcome – that change was needed and was coming, like it or not – the messenger became the target. An unprecedented challenge was mounted against his continuing as President. Unsurprisingly, the BMA passed a motion of no confidence in the GMC – always a sign that you are doing the right thing.

Richard Smith, then the Editor of the British Medical Journal, described how, when Donald appeared before the BMA's Council, those whom Richard called the BMA's 'stegasauruses' viscerally opposed as they were to revalidation, 'tore into him with gusto … questioning every statement and doubting his motivation and morals'. 'It was,' Richard wrote, 'like the crudest of badger hunting'. Donald was accused of 'leading a crusade without ensuring that others were with him'. He was denounced as an 'autocrat', ever the fate of leaders who seek to break the mould. Bruised and disconsolate, he stood down a year early.

But Donald was on the right side of history. Patients were brought in from the cold, the GMC was reformed, and the profession learned to live with regulation and accountability. Donald's place as a hero of modern medicine is secure. His time at the GMC may not have been easy but we have all benefited hugely from what he achieved.

25

Sir Eric Scowen

This is my tribute to Sir Eric Scowen on the occasion of the first Scowen Lecture delivered in his presence on 13 November 2001 at King's College London. He died only 10 days later. He was a giant in the history of medicine in the mid-twentieth century, most notably in relation to the development and safety of medicines. He was the Chairman of the British Pharmacopoeia Commission and of the Committee on Safety of Drugs before being appointed Chair of the newly created Committee on the Safety of Medicines in 1969 after the Thalidomide scandal of the early 1960s.

This evening I am to give the inaugural 'Sir Eric Scowen Lecture'. It is named in Eric's honour. Thus, it is appropriate to begin by honouring him, made even more so by the fact that he's able to be here. But, since the whole evening must not last more than an hour, including what I have to say in the Lecture and a few questions, I must be brief, without appearing perfunctory, in paying due reverence to Sir Eric.

In so doing, I will take for granted that you already know much about him. He was one of the great doctors of his day and one of the great teachers. That he has reached such a venerable age (91) is one proof of his powers as a teacher, since most of those who have cared and looked after him so well over the past few years have been his ex-students. This gives a whole new meaning to the idea of a pension plan!

I will take for granted also that you are aware of the honours that have rained down on him.[1] I will take for granted that you know of his extraordinary public service, from the doctor who worked at his beloved Barts, day and night, as the bombs of the Second World War fell about his ears, to the extraordinary challenge of chairing the Committee on the Safety of Drugs after thalidomide. I will take it for granted that you know of his erudition, his grasp of languages, his matter-of-fact preparedness to converse in Latin with a Professor of Theology recently arrived at King's from Rome, his casual reference over tea to the distinguished philosopher Bernard Williams that he might find the works of a particular German philosopher interesting and what a pity that there were no translations. In the argot of the day, we are talking Renaissance man here.

You all know all that. What I want to dwell on here for just a moment is the time Eric came into our lives here at Kings. He became an MA student in the new course in Medical Ethics and Law that I had set up in 1986. If you do the arithmetic, he was 76. He had decided to do the course rather than go to the Bar!! He was an extraordinary student, not because he taught me lots of things: all students do that.

[1] Kt, FRCP, FRCS, FRCPE, FRCPath, FRPharmS, FRCGP.

Why he was extraordinary was his rapport with the other students, (an eclectic assortment), and his passion to learn. Not for him the leaning back and the challenge to the teacher to tell him something he didn't know. Rather, there was this urgent thirst to be guided and to understand, coupled with a genuine humility. He knew that he was in *terra incognita* and thus wanted to be offered a map. At the same time, out of earshot of the others he would occasionally take me aside and indicate that my grasp of anatomy or genetics was a touch wonky, but he did it to help, never to gain an upper hand. There was none of the formidable Professor I had heard rumours of. He was the student, whatever his distinction in other fields, and he wanted us to feel at ease and accept this. The students loved him, as did we all. He was the wise one. He was the source of advice, not only on a recent article, but who was the best dentist, or the person to see about your back.

It was clear to me that medical ethics in particular had opened a new chapter for him. He strove to acquire that rigorous analytical quality associated with law and moral philosophy which, curiously, is not always present in the study and practice of medicine. He wanted to grasp a new way of thinking, in which intuition and hunch gave way to exegesis. This has been his challenge and joy for the past decade or so. For, once he graduated, I made it clear that he had been classified by the Centre of Medical Law and Ethics as a national treasure and was to be bound to the Centre in perpetuity, through the device of registering for a PhD. He gladly accepted this bondage, as did my successors in holding the reins or chains.

I must not finish this all too brief encomium without mentioning that one quality in Eric which is ever-present and all-pervasive. I refer to his kindness. Eric is just the kindest man you could wish to meet. I don't just refer to the parties and sumptuous dinners at the Savoy Grill. Many here will remember how Tony, the Maitre d' would guide him to his table and enquire whether he wanted 'the usual?' My wife Andrea once asked him when he had first eaten at the Grill. Eric reflected for a moment and then said that it was when he was 11 (ie 1921). So, clearly, we should all try to get the recipe of Tony's 'usual'. No; when I refer to Eric's kindness, I have more in mind the quiet 'phone calls when he'd ask how you are and, with his old fox wisdom, suggest this or that. Many here will recognise this and have benefited from it. Truly, Eric is a giant among men and among friends. A lecture in his honour is but a small token of the esteem in which he is held here at the Centre of Medical Law and Ethics. For my part, I consider myself honoured to be invited to give the Lecture named for someone whom I have learned to revere and cherish.

PROFESSOR SIR IAN KENNEDY BIOGRAPHY

As an academic lawyer, he was a pioneer in the establishment of medical law and ethics as a discipline in its own right. He was invited to deliver the BBC 1980 Reith Lectures on the subject. Alone and with others, he has written leading works in the field, founded an internationally recognised centre for research and graduate teaching, and built up in the centre a major collection of scholarly materials. The contribution of the centre was recognised by its being awarded the Queen's Award for Excellence in Higher Education in 1996.

While at King's College London, he was Dean and Head of the Law School for ten years, Chairman of the College's Research Committee for five years and a member of the College Committee, the College's Executive Committee, for eight years. He was also Director of the Centre of Medical Law and Ethics for over 20 years. At the end of his tenure as Dean, the Law School was ranked first equal in the UK.

His contribution to scholarship and public policy has been recognised by his knighthood, election as a Fellow of the British Academy, election as an Honorary Bencher of the Inner Temple, appointment as an Honorary QC, Fellowships at two London Colleges (UCL and King's), Honorary Doctorates in Science (Glasgow), Medicine (Birmingham), and Public Policy (York), and Honorary Fellowships in six Medical Royal Colleges.

For more than 30 years, both while a University Professor and in the years since leaving academic life, he has chaired, or been a member of, public authorities and bodies at a national level. The areas involved include law, health, ethics, public policy, regulation, science and technology, education, and defence.

Over the past 25 years, he has chaired the Public Inquiry into Paediatric Cardiac Surgery at the Bristol Royal Infirmary, an Inquiry into Xenotransplantation for the Department of Health, an Inquiry into Rabies and Quarantine for the then Ministry of Agriculture which led to the introduction of 'Pets' Passports', the Healthcare Commission (the original NHS regulator), the International Panel on Academic Health Science Centres, and the Independent Parliamentary Standards Authority (IPSA).

He has also produced reports on 'Innovation' for the National Institute of Clinical Excellence (NICE), on 'NHS services for children' for the Department of Health, on the 'Quality and Sustainability of Centres carrying out paediatric cardiac surgery in England' (as Chair of the Expert Panel) for the National Commissioning Group of the Department of Health in England, (and subsequently for the relevant health bodies in Scotland and Northern Ireland), on the 'Quality of general practice in the NHS' for the King's Fund (as Chairman of the Working Group), and on the 'Response of Heart of England NHS Foundation Trust to concerns about breast surgery carried out by Mr Paterson – the Kennedy Review', all of which have been published. In 2013, he was a member of the group which advised the Department of Health on PIP breast implants and subsequently on the regulation of cosmetic surgery. He was also a member of the National Mortality Group advising the Department of Health concerning the issue of higher than expected mortality in NHS hospitals.

In 2013–14, he carried out a Review for Birmingham Children's Hospital to advise them concerning their collection of children's hearts in which he set out the basis for a national policy, and subsequently advised Alder Hey Children's Hospital on the same issue. He was commissioned by NHS England in 2015 to serve as consultant in a further review of children's heart surgery at Bristol Children's Hospital (chaired by Eleanor Grey QC). The Review was completed and published in July 2016.

He has a particular interest in regulation and governance, having chaired regulatory bodies for a dozen years. Appointed in the wake of the scandals relating to expenses in 2009, he established an entirely new, independent regulatory body, IPSA, and created a new system for handling MPs' business costs and expenses, and subsequently, a new scheme for MPs' pay and pensions. Having been reappointed in 2014, he served as Chairman until the end of May 2016.

He has worked with a range of government departments and Ministers, including the Department of Health, the Ministry of Defence, Defra, the Home Office, the Ministry of Justice, the Department for Children, Schools and Families, the Department for Education, the Cabinet Office and the Department of Business Innovation and Skills, and with regulators such as the Audit Commission, the National Audit Office, the Commission for Social Care Inspection, the Care Quality Commission, Monitor, NICE, the General Medical Council, and the Nursing and Midwifery Council.

He was a founder member and subsequently Chair of the Nuffield Council on Bioethics, which is the national body that advises on law and ethics in biomedicine and biomedical sciences.

In the voluntary sector, with others, he set up and chaired for 10 years the UK Research Integrity Office (UKRIO Ltd), a registered charity, concerned with establishing best practice in research ethics, which publishes and keeps up to date a Code of Good Practice and a Code for investigating allegations of misconduct, and for advising whistleblowers and others. He is a Trustee and Director of a charity (Pathway) concerned with providing healthcare for the homeless, originally in London and now across England. He was also involved in the establishment of the Staff College: Leadership in Healthcare, and of Well North, a project aimed at integrating healthcare, social care and other public services in the North-West.

He has extensive experience in broadcasting; writing and presenting both radio and television programmes for the BBC and hosting a late-night discussion programme for Channel 4.

He has spoken and lectured all over the world (USA, Canada, India, Australia, New Zealand and most countries in Europe) and advised governments (Spain, New Zealand, Singapore) and international agencies, (WHO, OECD). In the past several years, he met senior members of the legislatures and governments of Canada, Australia, New Zealand and France to advise on the experience of IPSA concerning the law and practice relating to the regulation of funding for Members of Parliament. In the Spring of 2016, he was invited to advise on reform of the regulation and governance of international sport. More recently he was keynote speaker at the Congress of the

Australasian College of Healthcare Management in Brisbane. Currently, he is a member of the Assurance Group supporting the Chair of the Review into Gender Identity Services for children and young people.

During the past three years he has written a short book on Leadership (in draft) and an account of his time as Chairman of IPSA (*Cleaning up the Mess: After the MPs' Expenses Scandal* (Biteback, 2019)).

Professor Sir Ian Kennedy, QC (Hon), FBA, LLB (1st Class), LLM, LLD, DSci (Hon), DMed (Hon), DUniv (Hon), FRCS England (Hon), FRCS Edinburgh (Hon), FRCP (Hon), FRCPCH (Hon), FRCA (Hon), FRCGP (Hon)

info@iankennedyconsulting.com

INDEX

www.ingramcontent.com/pod-product-compliance
Lightning Source LLC
Chambersburg PA
CBHW071305180926
51613CB00001B/126